EUROBAROMETER

Jacques-René Rabier
(Photograph by J-L Debaize, Brussels)

EUROBAROMETER

The Dynamics of European Public Opinion
Essays in Honour of Jacques-René Rabier

Edited by

Karlheinz Reif
*Head of the 'Surveys, Research, Analyses' Unit,
Commission of the European Community and Privatdozent,
University of Mannheim*

and

Ronald Inglehart
*Professor of Political Science
University of Michigan*

MACMILLAN

First published 1991

Published by
MACMILLAN ACADEMIC AND PROFESSIONAL LTD
Houndmills, Basingstoke, Hampshire RG21 2XS
and London
Companies and representatives
throughout the world

Printed in Great Britain by
Billing & Sons Ltd, Worcester

British Library Cataloguing in Publication Data

Eurobarometer: the dynamics of European public opinion:
    essays in honour of Jacques-René Rabier.
    1. Western Europe. Public opinion
    I. Reif, Karlheinz 1943–   II. Inglehart, Ronald   III. Rabier, Jacques-René
    303.38094

ISBN 0–333–52754–2

Contents

List of Tables

List of Figures

Preface

This volume of essays has been written in honour of Jacques-René Rabier. The essays, by authors from seven countries on both sides of the Atlantic, were presented to Rabier on his seventieth birthday (16 September 1989) in recognition of his unique contributions to the integration of Europe, and to the evolution of social science research.

Rabier has pursued distinguished careers both in the civil service and as a social scientist. Apparently born with a perspective that transcended national boundaries, he took part in constructing Europe already as a young man. After graduating from the Law Faculty of the Sorbonne, he did graduate work at the l'Ecole Libre des Sciences Politiques in Paris. He then joined the editorial staff of the review *Esprit* and joined the Commissariat General du Plan in 1946, serving as Directeur de Cabinet to Jean Monnet, the founder and first chief of this institution which initiated France's innovative system of economic planning. When Jean Monnet moved to Luxembourg in 1953 as the President of the High Authority of the European Coal and Steel Community, Rabier went with him as his Directeur de Cabinet (1953–1954) and Chef de service des rapports généraux (1954–1957).

With the founding of the European Economic Community in 1958, Rabier moved to Brussels, serving as head of the Commission's Directorate general for Press and Information. On the occasion of the Commission's reorganization, after Britain, Denmark and Ireland joined the Common Market, in 1973, he officially retired from this post, but he continued contributing energetically to European integration. As a Special Advisor to the Commission of the European Communities, he launched and directed the Eurobarometer surveys -- a unique program of cross-national and cross-temporal social science research. This effort began in early 1970, when the Commission carried out simultaneous surveys of public attitudes toward the Common Market and other European Community institutions, in the six original member-countries. These surveys also examined the goals given top priority for one's nation, and a number of important political issues. These concerns have remained a central part of the European Community's research efforts, which were carried forward with another six-nation survey in the summer of 1971; and again in a survey of the publics of the European Community countries – now nine in number – carried out in September, 1973. At this point the surveys took on a broader scope in content as well as in geographical coverage, with measures of subjective well-being and the perceived quality of life becoming a standard feature of the European Community public opinion surveys.

In 1974, Rabier launched the Eurobarometer surveys, a survey research program designed to provide regular monitoring of the social and political attitudes of representative national samples of the publics of the nine member-nations, France, West Germany, Great Britain, Italy, The Netherlands, Belgium, Denmark, Ireland and Luxembourg. The number of countries surveyed increased to ten in October 1980, on the eve of the entry of Greece, which became a member of the Community in 1981; and the number increased to twelve, with the addition of Spain and Portugal in October, 1985. Carried out in the spring and fall of each year, a total of 32 Eurobarometer surveys had been completed by the end of 1989. In addition to obtaining regular readings on support for European integration, national goals and political issues, political party preferences, ideological orientations and subjective well-being, given Eurobarometers have explored a variety of special topics such as attitudes toward poverty and unemployment, gender roles, interpersonal trust, energy and environmental problems, attitudes toward work, attitudes toward science and technology, and attitudes toward immigration and foreign workers.

The Eurobarometer surveys have grown larger in recent years, partly because the Commission of the European Community has increased their functions and scope, but also because other institutions, governmental agencies as well as academic research centers in Western Europe, and also in the United States, have independently participated in the surveys. The additional items enrich the dataset that is made available to the social science community.

The Eurobarometer surveys were carried out under the direction of Jacques-René Rabier, Special Advisor to the Commission of the European Communities, until the end of 1986. The Eurobarometer series alone now contains 313 national surveys coordinated across both time and space. Key questions in this data collection have been asked in comparable form across twelve nations at numerous time points, and across a period of nearly twenty years in given countries.

One indicator of the value these data have for the social science community is the widespread demand for the surveys that have been released to date. The European Community surveys have become one of the most widely-requested datasets handled by the survey data archives; in the field of comparative politics, nothing approaches their level of use. These datasets have been furnished to hundreds of research institutions and the data are utilized in scores of publications each year, in the fields of political science, social psychology, sociology and economics.

The Eurobarometer surveys have made a unique and immensely important contribution to social science research. By asking standardized questions over a long time sequence, these surveys make it possible to carry out longitudinal analysis of social and political change – something about which survey researchers often speculate but are rarely able to analyze empirically. By gathering data in twelve countries simultaneously, these surveys make it possible to analyze sociopolitical change in a comparative perspective – in which the culture and institutions of given countries become variables, rather than constants that cannot be analyzed. Finally, by providing data from all twelve member countries of the European Community in each survey, the Eurobarometer surveys have done a great deal to integrate West European social science. For, increasingly, social scientists have grown accustomed to comparing results across all twelve countries, rather than focusing exclusively on their own nation. As the possibilities for carrying out meaningful cross-national analyses have improved, cross-national collaboration has increased.

Each of the contributors to this volume has drawn on the results of the Eurobarometer surveys in his or her research – in most cases, on many occasions. Their existence is due to the dedicated and generous efforts of Jacques-René Rabier. The Eurobarometer surveys, in turn, have contributed both inspiration and standardized survey items to several other major cross-national survey research efforts, such as the Political Action surveys and the World Values surveys, carried out on all six inhabited continents. Through his encouragement, advice and enthusiastic support, Rabier has helped nourish these and numerous other research projects. He may well have done more to advance the cause of cross-national survey research than any other individual. Together with many other social scientists, from many countries, we wish to express our heartfelt thanks.

Ronald Inglehart
Karlheinz Reif

Notes on the Contributors

Samuel H. Barnes is Professor of Political Science at the University of Michigan and Program Director at CPS-ISR. His major publications include *Party Democracy, Representation in Italy, Political Action* (with M. Kaase et al.), *Politics and Culture.*

Klaus von Beyme is Professor of Political Science at the University of Heidelberg. Major publications include *America as a Model. The Impact of American Democracy in the World, The Soviet Union in World Politics, Political Parties in Western Democracies* and *The Political System of the Federal Republic of Germany.*

Russell J. Dalton is Professor of Political Science at the University of California, Irvine. Major publications: *Challenging the Political Order* (with M. Kuechler), *Politics in West Germany, Citizen Politics in Western Democracies.*

Jan W. van Deth is Professor of Political Science at the University of Nijmegen. He is the author of *Continuity in Political Action* (with K. Jennings et al).

Cees van der Eijk is Professor of Political Science at the University of Amsterdam. His major publications include *Electoral Change in the Netherlands* (with B. Niemoeller), *Longitudinal Survey Research* (editor).

Werner J. Feld is Professor Adjunct of Political Science at the University of Colorado, Colorado Springs. Major publications: *Arms Control and the Atlantic Community, American Foreign Policy: Aspiration and Reality, West Germany and the European Community, International Relations – A Transnational Approach, The European Community in World Affairs.*

Mark N. Franklin is Professor of Political Science at the University of Houston and Visiting Professor of Government at the University of Strathclyde. Major publications: *Electoral Change* (co-author), *The Community of Science in Europe, The Decline of Class-Voting in Britain, A User's Guide to SCSS Conversational Statistical System* (co-author).

Miles Hewstone is Reader in Social Psychology at the University of Bristol. Major publications: *Causal Attribution: From Cognitive Processes to Collective Beliefs, Understanding Attitudes to the European Community: A Social-psychological Study in Four Member States.*

Marita Rosch Inglehart is Senior Research Associate and Adjunct Assistant Professor of Psychology, University of Michigan. Major publications: *Reactions to Critical Life Events – A Social Psychological Analysis*, several books and numerous articles.

Ronald Inglehart is Professor of Political Science and Program Director in the Institute for Social Research, University of Michigan. Major publications: *The Silent Revolution, Culture Shift in Advanced Industrial Society*, author of nearly 100 publications.

Ghiţa Ionescu is Professor Emeritus at the University of Manchester, Editor *Government and Opposition*, Chairman of the IPSA Research Committee on European Unification. Major publications: *The Political Thought of Saint-Simon, Centripetal Politics, The European Alternative* (ed), *Between Sovereignty and Integration* (ed), *Politics and the Pursuit of Happiness*.

Richard S. Katz is Professor of Political Science at the Johns Hopkins University. Major publications: *Party Governments: European and American Experiences* (ed), *The Patron State* (ed), *A Theory of Parties and Electoral Systems*.

Jan Kerkhofs, S. J., is Professor Emeritus at the Katholieke Universiteit Leuven. Major publications: *L'Univers des Belges, De smalle weg, Progress and Hope*.

Manfred Kuechler is Professor of Sociology at Hunter College, City University of New York. Numerous articles and book chapters on voting behaviour; co-editor (with R. Dalton) of *Challenging the Political Order*.

Thomas T. Mackie is Senior Lecturer in Politics at the University of Strathclyde. Major publications: *International Almanach of Electoral History* (3rd ed.) (with R. Rose), *Europe Votes III, Unlocking the Cabinet* (with B. Hogwood).

Anna Melich is Principal Administrator at the Service 'Surveys, Research, Analyses', Directorate General 'Information, Communication, Culture', Commission of the European Communities. Major publications: *Identité nationale et media contemporains, Comment devient-on Suisse? Enfants et apprentissage politique*.

Oskar Niedermayer is Associate Professor of Political Science at the University of Mannheim and Executive Director of ZEUS (Zentrum für Europäische Umfrageanalysen und Studien). Major publications: *Inner-*

parteiliche Partizipation, Europäische Parteien?, Multinationale Konzerne und Entwicklungsländer, numerous articles.

Emile Noël is Principal of the European University Institute, Florence, former Secretary General of the Commission of the European Communities. Major publications: *Les rouages de l'Europe, Les institutions de la Communauté européenne.*

John Pinder is President of the Union of European Federalists, Visiting Professor at the College of Europe (Brugge), Chairman of the Federal Trust. Major publications: *National Industrial Strategies and the World Economy, Europe after de Gaulle* (with Roy Price), *Britain and the Common Market.*

Karlheinz Reif is Head of the Service *'Surveys, Research, Analyses'*, Directorate General 'Information, Communication, Culture', Commission of the European Communities, Privatdozent at the University of Mannheim. Numerous publications on political sociology, European elections, and public opinion.

Hélène Riffault is Managing Director of *Faits et Opinions*, Paris and President EOS, Bruxelles; President Gallup International. Numerous reports such as *European women in paid employment, Europeans and the ECU, Europeans and their holidays, Europeans and their environment, Europe against cancer.*

Hermann Schmitt is Director of ZEUS (Zentrum fúr Europäische Umfrageanalysen und Studien), University of Mannheim. Major publications: *Neue Politik in alten Parteien, Neumitglieder in der SPD* (co-ed), *Das Parteiensystem in der Bundesrepublik.*

Dusan Sidjanski is Professor of Political Science and Social Sciences at the Graduate Institute of European Studies, University of Geneva, Switzerland. Major publications: *Dimension européenne de la science politique, L'Europe des affaires* (with Jean Meynaud), *Les groupes de pression dans la Communauté européenne, Les Suisses et la politique* (co-author), *Europe élections, De la démocratie européenne*; author of over 100 publications.

Jean-François Tchernia is Managing Director of *Faits et Opinions*, Paris. Numerous reports on public opinion in the European Community.

1 Analyzing Trends in West European Opinion: the Role of the Eurobarometer Surveys

Ronald Inglehart, University of Michigan, and Karlheinz Reif, Commission of the European Communities and University of Mannheim

SUMMARY

The Eurobarometer surveys have played an important role in facilitating the analysis of political and social change. By providing a relatively long time series of cross-nationally consistent measures of mass orientations toward key subjects, this research program has made it possible to gain new insight into the evolution of a sense of European identity, the quality of life in Western societies, and cultural change. To illustrate this point, some recent findings are presented.

INTRODUCTION

Probably the most important achievement of the European Community institutions has been to help develop an environment in which war between the nations of Western Europe seems out of the question. Another more modest, but nevertheless impressive achievement of these institutions, has been their contribution to integrating social science research in Western Europe by developing a long-term series of cross-nationally comparable surveys that make it possible to analyze ongoing processes of political and social change among the publics of the twelve European Community countries. No other region of the world has produced a social research program that is comparable in cross-national scope or in the regularity with which these measures are conducted.

The regular monitoring of the orientations of Western publics has made it possible to analyze processes of social change that could not have been measured in any other way. For example, repeated measurement of the value priorities of mass publics, from 1970 to 1988, has demonstrated the presence of an intergenerational value shift. This process is subject to short-term fluctuations in response to changes in the socioeconomic environment, but it also displays a strong long-term tendency, based on population replacement. By 1988, a substantial net shift toward Postmaterialism was manifest. The implications of this shift seem far-reaching, and have only begun to be explored. Without a long-term research program such as the Eurobarometer surveys, which repeats standardized measures consistently over a number of years, it would have been impossible to measure this shift – and impossible to distinguish between its long-term and short-term components (and thereby move toward reliable social forecasting).

Another finding from these surveys has been the presence of large and relatively stable cross-national differences in levels of subjective well-being. Despite this overall stability, a drastic shift in the subjective well-being of the Belgian public began in 1979 and has not yet reversed itself. Throughout the early surveys, from 1973 to 1978, the Belgians were consistently one of the happiest and most satisfied publics in the Western world, but this outlook deteriorated dramatically and by 1982–8 they ranked among the least satisfied. Interestingly, a similar decline did not take place in most neighboring countries. This phenomenon is one of several intriguing puzzles that remain to be explained in the realm of subjective well-being. It could only have been detected through longitudinal cross-national empirical research.

This paper will present some recent findings concerning value change among West European publics. First, however, let us briefly review the evidence concerning public support for European integration.

The Evolution of Support for European Unification

Public support for European integration has stabilized at a high level during the past two decades. It is stronger among the publics of the original six member nations and among the publics of the two new members, Spain and Portugal, than among the publics of the countries that first entered the Community during the economic distress of the mid 1970s and early 1980s; but overall, solid majorities favor membership in the European Community and support further efforts to unify Western Europe.

At the close of World War II, Western Europe was prostrate and divided by deep antagonisms. World War II had been the third round of a seemingly endless conflict between Germany and France. The European movement was launched, in large part, to avoid yet another round of West European civil war.

Public support for European integration has grown gradually since that time, with major advances and setbacks. The best available indicator of these long-term changes is a question that was first asked in a series of US

Information Agency surveys in the 1950s and 1960s, and has been included in the European Community Eurobarometer surveys in modified form from 1970 on. The question asks: 'Would you say that you are very favorable, rather favorable, indifferent, unfavorable or very unfavorable to the efforts beings made to unify Western Europe?'

This question is designed to tap one's general feeling of support or opposition to European unification. It is virtually the only relevant item that has been asked repeatedly over a period of many years: it is precious by virtue of its rarity. But clearly, it cannot be viewed as an absolute measure of support levels. It has a floating referant: the 'efforts toward uniting Europe' that the question evoked in 1952 may have been the comparatively modest Coal and Steel Community; in 1957, one probably would have thought of the Common Market. In the 1980s, far more ambitious plans were being discussed, including a plan for political integration into a European Union.

Bearing this in mind, let us turn to Figure 1.1, which charts the rise and fall of responses to this question over a thirty-five year period in Britain, France, Germany, and Italy (the USIA generally carried out European surveys only in these four countries). The pattern reveals several important points. First, let us note that in the period prior to 1958 – the year the Common Market began to function – responses in all four countries fluctuated *together*, apparently in reaction to current events. We cannot demonstrate the causal linkages, of course, but it seems likely that the Korean War, together with the founding of the Coal and Steel Community in 1952, gave an early impetus to support for European integration: North Korea's invasion of the South gave rise to fears that Western Europe might be next on the agenda; while the achievement of integration in the steel industry may have encouraged the feeling that further integration was feasible. Conversely, the failure of the European Defense Community in 1954 apparently depressed European morale and led to a withdrawal of support; while renewed fears of war, stimulated by the Soviet invasion of Hungary and the Suez crisis late in 1956, may have rekindled a sense of urgency for European unification.

In any case, we find a series of pronounced upward and downward shifts in the 1950s, in which all four countries move together. But starting from about 1958, the pattern changes. The British – who had ranked second only to the Germans in support for unification – start to move out of phase with the other three publics. *Within* the three Common Market countries, fluctuations taper off and support levels gradually converge upward toward the German level; by the mid-1970s, the Italians and the French were virtually indistinguishable from the Germans. Previously, the Germans had consistently been the most pro-European public, but in the 1970s and 1980s, the Germans, French, and Italians all showed strong pro-integration consensuses, and in a given year any one of the three might rank highest.

SOURCE: USIA surveys from 1952 to 1964 and European Community surveys from 1970 through 1987.

FIGURE 1.1: *Percentage 'for' efforts to unify Western Europe, 1952–87.*

Missing data is included in percentage base (thus in 1952, 70% of German public were 'for', 10% were 'against' and 20% were undecided).

The British level, by contrast, fell drastically after creation of the Common Market, dropping below the 50 per cent mark at the time of the first veto of British entry to the European Community and far below it after the second veto. Britain finally was admitted in 1973; two years later, British support for integration again rose above the 50 per cent line, and continued moving upward for the next few years; nevertheless, a decade later there was still a large gap between the British and the three original European Community publics, although the British were gradually moving toward convergence. This does not mean that the British were *less* European in 1975 than in 1952; on the contrary, in 1952 they were unwilling to join even the Coal and Steel Community by a decisive margin. What the pattern does indicate is that a large *relative* gap opened up between the British, on one hand, and the publics of the original six Common Market countries on the other.

Until 1973, the British remained outside the European Community framework, while the publics of the Six shared common experiences, and gradually developed an increasingly European outlook.

Aside from the divergence between the British and the other three publics, Figure 1.1 shows another almost equally striking phenomenon: the French and Italian publics – who originally were far less European than the Germans – progressively narrowed the gap, to the point where it had virtually disappeared by 1975. By 1987, the French and Italian publics were slightly *more* European than the Germans. This reflects the development of a pro-European consensus among the French and Italian publics; and the most important element in the process was winning over the large Communist electorates in these countries.

For the French and Italian Communists initially perceived the European integration movement as an alliance directed against the Soviet Union. And, indeed, in the Cold War era when the threat of Soviet invasion sometimes seemed imminent, the idea of uniting for the common defense contributed to the movement's appeal. But with the defeat of the European Defence Community in 1954, defense against the Soviet Union no longer seemed a salient part of the Community's functions. Moreover, West European prosperity rose to unprecedented levels during the 1950s and 1960s, and to some extent this was attributed to the effects of the European institutions: Britain, which remained outside them, did not experience similar economic growth. Accordingly, the Communist electorates of the Six were gradually won over from suspicion to overwhelming support. In October 1950, a representative sample of the French public was asked: 'Are you for or against the efforts being made to unify Europe?' Among the French public as a whole, 65 per cent were favorable; among supporters of the Communist Party, the figure was 19 per cent.

A heavy majority of the French public at large favored integration, but a heavy majority of the French Communists opposed it. This tremendous gap between Communists and non-Communists persisted through the early years of European integration; in 1957, 53 per cent of the general public favored unification – compared with only 13 per cent of the Communists. The birth of the Common Market in 1958 helped transform this pattern. Its early years were a period of rapidly-growing trade among the Six, and remarkable prosperity. By 1962, Communist voters among the French public were predominantly favorable to European integration and supported it almost as strongly as the public at large: 72 per cent of the total electorate favored unification – and so did 60 per cent of the Communists. This newer pattern remained fairly stable in subsequent years. The rest of the French electorate remains somewhat more favorable to integration than the Communists, but even among the Communists support is vastly more widespread than opposition.

A similar process of conversion took place in Italy, but it has gone even farther than in France. In 1973, 70 per cent of the total Italian public were favorable to integration – as were 65 per cent of the Italian Communists. By 1975, the gap had disappeared almost totally: 77 per cent of the general public favored integration, along with 75 per cent of the Communists. In response to some questions (for example, a proposal for political union of the European Community countries), the Communists were actually a trifle more European than the electorate as a whole.

This remarkable change of heart among the Communist electorates of France and Italy was followed by a parallel movement at the elite level. By the mid-1960s, it had become politically costly to oppose European Community membership in these countries. Partly for this reason, the Communist Party leadership of both countries abandoned overt opposition. But there were important differences between the positions of the French and Italian party elites, which reflected their contrasting relationships with the Soviet Union.

On one hand, the Italian Communist Party began to display a large measure of independence from the Soviets, developing a flexible and distinctively Italian approach to European politics. Since the early 1970s, Italian Communist deputies have participated in the European Parliament, and have played a constructive and increasingly active role. The French Communist Party, on the other hand, has remained one of the most Moscow-oriented parties in the West, defending the invasion of Afghanistan and the repression of the independent worker's movement in Poland, while the Italian Communists were condemning them forcefully. Still acutely sensitive to cues from Moscow, the French Communist Party tends to reflect Soviet antipathy to the European Community, but does so in muted tones. To advocate French withdrawal seems out of the question – it would be overwhelmingly unpopular with both the Communist and non-Communist public. But the party leadership has remained hostile to any proposal that might strengthen the European Community. Increasingly out of touch with its mass base, the party has gone into decline, receiving less than 10 per cent of the vote in the 1986 elections, and again in the 1988 elections to the National Assembly, and the 1989 elections to the European Parliament.

During the first fifteen years following the founding of the EEC, the publics of the six original member countries developed a consensus supporting membership in the European Community and ongoing efforts to unify Europe. But the British public developed a very divergent perspective: in 1973, only 37 per cent were favorable to the efforts to unify Europe – only half the level of support that existed in France, West Germany, and Italy.

The expanded nine-nation European Community came into being in 1973, on the eve of the most serious economic recession since the 1930s. In sharp contrast to the prosperity of the Community's early years, the publics of the expanded Community experienced periods of extraordinarily high inflation, economic stagnation and the highest levels of unemployment since the immediate postwar era, during the late 1970s and the early 1980s.

Though they differ in detail, almost all of the major theorists who have worked in this area concur that favorable economic payoffs are conducive to – and perhaps even essential to – the processes of national and supranational integration. Similarly, Easton views mass support for a political system as the result of positive governmental outputs. In time, a series of beneficial outputs may build up a reservoir of 'diffuse support' that is not contingent on immediate payoffs, but diffuse support can be traced back to favorable outputs at an earlier time with economic outputs being the most obvious type and perhaps the most widely appreciated one. Has mass support for the European Community institutions continued to develop in the uncertain economic climate that has prevailed since 1973, or has there been a growing sense of disenchantment?

It seems that both things have occurred in connection with different aspects of mass attitudes. In order to grasp what has been happening, it is important to distinguish between diffuse or 'affective' support, and 'utilitarian' support – a calculated appraisal of the immediate costs and benefits of membership in the Community. The latter declined somewhat from 1973 to 1981 followed by a partial recovery in 1982 and 1983. But along with this development, a sense of solidarity among the nine nations of the European Community has emerged among all ten publics.

The question concerning support for efforts to unify Western Europe seems to tap a general affective orientation, rather than a cost-benefit analysis; and it indicates that some rather impressive gains were made in the development of a pro-European consensus during the decade following 1973, despite the severe economic problems that were experienced. In Germany, Italy, and France, from 68 to 78 per cent of the respective publics were in favor of efforts to unify Western Europe in 1973; a decade later, these figures had moved up to range from 77 to 81 per cent. But the changes that took place among the British public were far more striking: in 1973, only 37 per cent were in favor of the efforts being made to unify Western Europe; a decade later, the figure had risen to 65 per cent – a decisive positive shift.

Nevertheless, a large gap still existed between the attitudes of the original six publics and those of the six newer member nations admitted in 1973, 1981, and 1986. This gap was particularly wide in regard to utilitarian support, as Table 1.1 demonstrates. In all six of the original member countries, those who view membership in the Communities as 'a good thing' outnumber those who view it as 'a bad thing' by ratios of at least seven to one and in some countries by as much as twenty to one. The positive assessment of the early years left a lasting imprint. Among the publics of the six newer member nations, however, the picture was rather

TABLE 1.1: *Attitudes towards European Community membership and European unification, by nation: 1982–85*

		Utilitarian Support: Percentage saying that their country's membership in E.C. is:			Affective Support: Percentage 'favorable' or 'very favorable' to efforts being made to unify Western Europe
		'a good thing'	'neither'	'a bad thing'	
Original Members	Netherlands	82%	14%	4%	86%
	Luxembourg	80	17	4	88
	Italy	76	20	4	93
	Belgium	67	27	6	89
	France	64	29	7	91
	Germany	62	30	8	87
Newer Members	Spain	67	23	10	90
	Portugal	53	30	17	85
	Ireland	50	28	22	80
	Greece	47	35	18	79
	Denmark	37	32	31	48
	United Kingdom	35	30	35	77

SOURCE: Combined data from Eurobarometer 17–24 (1982–85) (combined N=100, 245)

different in the early 1980s. Among the Irish and the Greeks, positive assessments of membership in the European Community outweighed negative assessments by better than two to one. The Danes were almost evenly divided throughout the first eleven years of their membership, with positive assessments prevailing only narrowly over negative ones. And among the British public, negative assessments of the effects of membership were actually sometimes more widespread than positive ones from 1973 through 1985 (though in given years the balance has shifted from one side to the other).

This relatively negative utilitarian assessment by the British public is understandable. For despite the fact that Britain is now one of the poorer members of the Community, she is (with West Germany) one of only two nations that contribute most to the Community's finances. This quirk of the European Community financial system, by which the British public helps subsidize some of their wealthier neighbors, has been a bone of contention throughout Britain's membership in the Communities, and contributes to a perception that their membership in the Community is disadvantageous and inequitable.

For the British public's support for integration is far higher than their utilitarian assessment. Though only 35 per cent viewed their country's membership as a 'good thing', fully 60 per cent supported the efforts being made to unify Western Europe, during 1973–83; in their hearts, the British are as European as the Irish or the Greeks – but there is a widespread perception that British economic interests are not well served by membership in the Community. The decade after 1973, when they finally joined, was one of severe economic difficulties; and the tendency to place some of the blame on the European institutions was reinforced by the perception that the British contribute more than their fair share to the European Community budget.

The Danes provide an interesting contrast to the British. By sheer economic criteria, Community membership is almost certainly beneficial to the Danes, and they tend to acknowledge the fact; but their hearts were not in it; Danes were the only one of the twelve publics that did not have a strong majority in favor of efforts to unify Western Europe. Less than half the Danish public supported West European unification, which was conflicting with Denmark's long-standing ties to the other Nordic countries.

Interestingly, the attitudes of the two newest member publics – the Spanish and Portuguese – were more favorable than those of the publics who entered on the eve of the disastrous economic recessions of the mid 1970s and the early 1980s. Their perceptions that membership is 'a good thing' were almost as one-sided as is the case among the publics of the original six members.

How has this situation evolved since the early 1980s? Table 1.2 shows affective orientations among these twelve publics in 1989. The results reflect both the improved economic outlook of recent years, and the stimulus to European morale that was provided by the current plans to create a single European market by 1992.

Today, the prospect of a European Community that is united not only economically, but also politically, is no idle dream. To a surprising extent, the publics of the member nations are already ready to accept it, and the publics of some of the newer member nations, such as Spain, Greece, and Portugal, now rank among the most enthusiastic proponents of integration. The overwhelming majority are favorable to the general idea of unifying Western Europe: as Table 1.3 shows, across the twelve nations, supporters of unification outnumber opponents by almost eight to one. Moreover, support for unification outweighs opposition by an overwhelming margin in eleven of the twelve countries. The sole exception is Denmark, and even there 56 per cent of the public are now favorable.

When we move from the general idea of unification to the specific proposal to form a European government, responsible to the European parliament, we are dealing with a much more demanding test of one's commitment to European integration. But here, too, pro-European sentiment is remarkably widespread, with those favoring the formation of a

TABLE 1.2: *Support for European unification in twelve European Community Nations, 1989*

Question: 'In general, are you for or against efforts being made to unify Western Europe?'

	Percentage For	Percentage Against
Italy	89	3
Belgium	86	4
France	86	8
Spain	83	2
Netherlands	80	14
Greece	78	10
Portugal	76	2
Germany	75	17
Ireland	74	8
Luxembourg	73	15
Britain	70	18
Denmark	56	35
European Community	80	11

SOURCE: Eurobarometer 31 (April, 1989). The difference between the totals shown above and 100% reflects the percentage giving no opinion. Thus, in Italy, 8% of the public gave no answer.

TABLE 1.3: *Support for formation of a European government, 1987*

Q: 'Are you for or against the formation of a European government, responsible to the European Parliament?'

	Percentage For	Percentage Against
Italy	70	11
France	60	19
Belgium	55	12
Luxembourg	52	21
Spain	49	10
Netherlands	45	21
Portugal	42	14
Germany	41	28
Ireland	39	23
Greece	39	21
Britain	31	45
Denmark	13	64
European Community	49	24

SOURCE: Eurobarometer 28 (November, 1987).

European government outweighing its opponents by two to one. Solid majorities favor this proposal in ten of the twelve nations; a plurality oppose it in Britain and an overwhelming majority oppose it in Denmark.

The parochial nationalism that seemed so pronounced in France under DeGaulle has vanished. Today, the French are among the most solidly pro-European publics in Europe. Only in Denmark is opposition to the construction of a politically united Europe overwhelming. But Denmark, with less than 2 per cent of the European Community's population, is not crucial to the enterprise; a United Europe could flourish with or without her. British membership, on the other hand, probably *is* crucial. For the time being, British opposition constitutes a major obstacle to political unification. But in Britain, unlike Denmark, opinion is fairly evenly divided. Moreover, the British have come a long way, from refusing to join the Common Market at all when it was founded, and being divided about whether to remain in the Community until recently, to a current consensus in favor of membership and a very favorable attitude toward the broad idea of European unification. If British attitudes continue to evolve as they have during the past two decades, European political unity may come about early in the coming century.

Intergenerational Value Change and the Rise of the New Politics

In 1968 a wave of student protest manifested itself throughout the Western world. In the 1980s, a phenomenon described as the 'Yuppies' began to be noted in the United States; a new environmentalist party entered the West German Bundestag for the first time; by the time of the 1989 elections to the European Parliament, Environmentalist parties had surged past long-established parties, to win seats in the delegations from most of the twelve European Community countries.

These seemingly dissimilar phenomena have something in common: they reflect a process of intergenerational value chage that is gradually trans-forming the politics of Western societies. This process – a shift from Materialist to Postmaterialist value priorities – has brought new political issues to the center of the stage, and provided much of the impetus for new political movements. It has split existing political parties and given rise to new ones. It has a significant impact on support for European integration. And it seems to be linked with the rise of a new pattern of political conflict in advanced industrial society.

The possibility of intergenerational value change was first explored in the European Community surveys conducted in 1970 (Inglehart, 1971). We hypothesized that the basic value priorities of Western publics had been shifting from a Materialist emphasis toward a Postmaterialist one – from giving top priority to physical sustenance and safety, toward heavier empha-sis on belonging, self-expression and the quality of life. Our investigation was guided by two key hypotheses: (1) *A Scarcity Hypothesis*: An individual's priorities reflect the socioeconomic environment: one places the greatest subjective value on those things that are in relatively short supply; and (2) *A Socialization Hypothesis*: The relationship between socioeconomic environment and value priorities is not one of immediate adjustment: a substantial time lag is involved for, to a large extent, one's basic values reflect the conditions that prevailed during one's preadult years. The scarcity hypothesis is similar to the principle of diminishing marginal utility in economy theory. The recent economic history of advanced industrial societies has significant implications in the light of this hypothesis. For these societies are a remarkable exception to the prevailing historical pattern: the bulk of their population does *not* live under conditions of hunger and economic insecurity. This fact seems to have led to a gradual shift in which needs for belonging, esteem and intellectual and aesthetic satisfaction became more prominent. We would expect prolonged periods of high prosperity to encourage the spread of Postmaterialist values; economic decline would have the opposite effect.

But it is not quite that simple: there is no one-to-one relationship between economic level and the prevalence of Postmaterialist values, for these values reflect one's *subjective* sense of security, not one's economic level *per se*. While rich individuals and nationalities tend to feel more secure than poor ones, these feelings are also influenced by the cultural setting and social welfare institutions in which one is raised. Thus, the scarcity hypothesis alone does not generate adequate predictions about the process of value change. It must be interpreted in connection with the socialization hypothesis.

One of the most pervasive concepts in social science is the notion of a basic human personality structure that tends to crystallize by the time an individual reaches adulthood, with relatively little change thereafter. This, of course, doesn't imply that no change occurs during adult years. In some individual cases, dramatic behavior shifts occur, and the process of human development never comes to a complete stop (Brim, 1966; Mortimer and Simmons, 1978; Levinson, 1979; Brim and Kagan, eds, 1980; Riley and Bond, 1983). Nevertheless, human development seems to be more rapid during preadult years than afterward, and the bulk of the evidence points to the conclusion that the likelihood of basic personality change declines after one reaches adulthood (Glenn, 1974, 1980; Block, 1981; Costa and McCrae, 1980; Sears, 1981, 1983; Jennings and Niemi, 1981; Jennings and Markus, 1984).

Taken together, these two hypotheses generate a set of predictions concerning value change. First, while the scarcity hypothesis implies that prosperity is conducive to the spread of Postmaterialist values, the socialization hypothesis implies that neither an individual's values nor those of a society as a whole are likely to change overnight. Instead, fundamental value change takes place gradually; in large part, it occurs as younger birth cohorts replace older ones in the adult population of a society. Consequently, after a period of sharply rising economic and physical security, one would expect to find substantial differences between the value priorities of older and younger groups: they would have been shaped by different experiences in their formative years. Furthermore, if Postmaterialist value priorities emerge among those groups that have experienced relatively high levels of economic and physical security during their pre-adult years, then we would expect these values to be most widespread among the more prosperous strata of any given birth cohort.

These hypotheses were tested in a cross-national survey carried out in 1970 with representative national cross-sections of the populations in Great Britain, France, West Germany, Italy, the Netherlands, and Belgium. Our respondents indicated which goals they considered most important among a series of goals designed to tap economic and physical security, on one hand; or belonging, self-expression and the non-material quality of life, on the other hand (Inglehart, 1971). Those whose top two priorities were given to the former type of goals were classified as a pure Materialist type; those whose top priorities were given exclusively to the latter type of goals were classified as a pure Postmaterialist type. Those who chose some combination of these goals were classified as mixed types.

As predicted, we found that those raised in relatively prosperous families were most likely to emphasize Postmaterialist items. The predicted skew by age group is equally manifest. Figure 1.2 depicts this pattern in the pooled sample of six West European publics interviewed in our initial survey. Significant cross-national differences exist, but the basic pattern is similar from nation to nation: among the older groups, Materialists outnumber Postmaterialists enormously; as we move toward younger groups, the proportion of Materialists declines and that of Postmaterialists increases. Thus, among the oldest cohort, Materialists outnumber Postmaterialists by a ratio of more than twelve to one; among the youngest cohort, the balance has shifted dramatically: Postmaterialists are about as numerous as Materialists.

The Materialist and Postmaterialist types have strikingly different opinions on a wide variety of issues, ranging from women's rights, to attitudes toward poverty, ideas of what is important in a job, and positions on foreign policy. Within each age group, about half the sample falls into the Mixed value types. On virtually every issue, their position is about halfway between the Materialists and Postmaterialists: they seem to be a cross-pressured group that could swing either way.

The age-related differences shown in Figure 1.2 are truly striking. But one immediately wonders whether this pattern reflects life cycle effects, birth cohort effects, or some combination of the two. Though our theory predicts the emergence of birth cohort differences, it is conceivable that

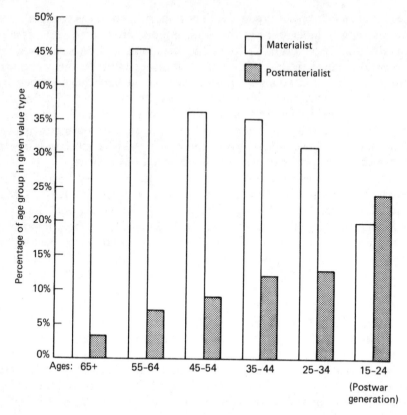

FIGURE 1.2: *Value type by age group, among the publics of Britain, France, West Germany, Italy, Belgium, and the Netherlands in 1970.*

these remarkable differences between the priorities of young and old might reflect some inherent tendency for people to become more materialistic as they age. Is it possible that aging makes one place ever-increasing emphasis on economic and physical security, perhaps through some immutable physiological process?

Since Materialist/Postmaterialist values were first measured in 1970, the battery used to measure them has become a standard feature of the Eurobarometer surveys carried out each spring and autumn in each of the European Community countries from 1973 to the present. These values have also been measured in surveys carried out in the United States from 1972 through 1988, and in surveys in many other countries, including the 1981 World Values Survey. Our longest time series, with the most frequent measures, comes from the six nations first surveyed in 1970. Let us examine these results.

Figure 1.3 traces the balance between Materialists and Postmaterialists

15

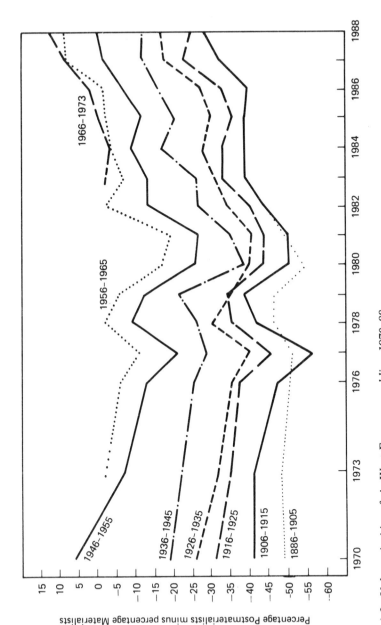

FIGURE 1.3: *Value priorities of six West European publics, 1970–88.*
Based on data from representative national samples of publics of France, Great Britain, West Germany, Italy, Belgium and the Netherlands, interviewed in European Community surveys of 1970, 1973 and Eurobarometer surveys 6 through 29 (total N=190, 129). Principal investigators were Jacques-René Rabier, Karlheinz Reif and Ronald Inglehart. Data available from ICPSR survey data archive.

within given birth cohorts from 1970 to 1988. This analysis is based on the pooled data from all six nations, totaling more than 190 000 interviews. Each cohort's position at a given time is calculated by subtracting the percentage of Materialists in that cohort from the percentage of Post-materialists. Thus, the zero point on the vertical axis reflects a situation in which the two groups are equally numerous (which is about where the cohort born in 1946–55 was located in 1970).

There is no sign whatever of the overall downward movement that would be found if the age-differences reflected life-cycle effects. Each cohort retains its relative position with striking consistency throughout the eighteen-year period. There are also significant short-term fluctuations; each cohort shows a brief downward swing in 1977 and again in 1980–81. These fluctuations seem to reflect period effects linked with the economic recessions of the mid-1970s and early 1980s, with inflation rates being a particularly important factor. But by 1986, inflation had subsided approximately to the 1970 level. With period effects held constant, there is no indication of the gradual conversion to Materialism that would be present if a life-cycle interpretation were applicable.

The fact that we find a much narrower gap between the 1966–75 cohort and its predecessors, than the gap between the two other postwar cohorts and their predecessors, is another indication that these value differences reflect historical change rather than some permanent life-cycle tendency for the young to be less Materialist than the old. For the recent narrowing of this gap reflects the impact of the relatively uncertain economic conditions of the past fifteen years of the youngest cohort – but to explain it in terms of life-cycle effects, one would need to invent some reason why the human life cycle had made a sudden change in the 1980s. Overall, we find large and enduring inter-cohort differences, which cannot be attributed to life-cycle effects. The pattern seems to reflect value change based on cohort effects.

A great deal of population replacement has taken place since 1970. Are these demographic shifts reflected in the distribution of Materialists and Postmaterialists in Western Europe? Very much so. In 1970–71, within the six nations as a whole, Materialists outnumbered Postmaterialists by a ratio of almost four to one. By 1988, this ratio had fallen to four to three. The Postmaterialists were much closer to an even balance with the Materialists. Even in the United States, the change has been substantial: in 1972, Materialists outnumbered Postmaterialists by 3.5 to one. In 1987, this ratio had fallen to only 1.5 to one (Inglehart, 1990).

Cultural Change and Environmentalist Action

The Materialist/Postmaterialist dimension has become the basis of a major new axis of political polarization in Western countries, leading to the rise of environmentalist parties, and to a realignment of party systems in many Western countries (Inglehart, 1977, 1987, 1990; Barnes, Kaase et al., 1979; Dalton, Flanagan, and Beck (eds), 1984).

Public attitudes toward environmental problems have been studied in Eurobarometer surveys carried out in 1982, 1984, and 1986. The results indicate that public concern over environmental problems is widespread and growing over time. In all twelve European Community countries, strong majorities express general approval of the environmentalist movement. But a more crucial question is whether they are ready to *do* anything to protect the environment. Postmaterialists are likelier than Materialists to approve of the environmentalist cause and *much* likelier to act on its behalf. For example, in 1986 across the twelve countries, 37 per cent of the Materialists strongly approved of the environmentalist movement, as compared with 53 per cent of the Postmaterialists – a ratio of 1.4 to one. But when it comes to actual participation, less than one-half of one per cent of the Materialists said they were active members of some environmentalist group, as compared with 3.5 per cent of the Postmaterialists – a ratio of seven to one.

A similar pattern applies to other types of pro-environmental behavior: Postmaterialists are likelier than Materialists to report having actually *done* something to protect the environment; and they are far more apt to report having some relatively 'difficult' action (such as taking part in demonstrations or contributing money) as compared with 'easy' actions (such as recycling things or avoiding littering). When we move to the societal level, we find that those nations with relatively large proportions of Postmaterialists report considerably higher levels of pro-environmental activity than those with lower proportions of Postmaterialists, as Figure 1.4 illustrates. The process of value change seems to bring changing patterns of behavior.

The shift from Materialist to Postmaterialist priorities appears to be only one component of a broader process of cultural change that is pervading industrial society. For example, Postmaterialist values are linked with a shift in emphasis from maximizing economic gains, toward maximizing the quality of life. This cultural shift may account for an interesting finding from the 1981–2 World Values survey: those nations with relatively high proportions of Postmaterialists showed substantially lower rates of economic growth from 1965 to 1984 than did those with predominately Materialist publics ($r = -.51$); but the former societies show significantly higher levels of overall life satisfaction (Inglehart, 1988).

Another shift that seems to be taking place in advanced industrial society is a decline in feelings of nationalism. Table 1.4 presents evidence from the 1981–2 World Values survey, plus relevant Eurobarometer surveys.

In all six countries for which we have data from 1970, there are indications of a decline in national pride from 1970 to 1985, as Table 1.4 demonstrates. In some cases – that of Belgium in particular – this decline is

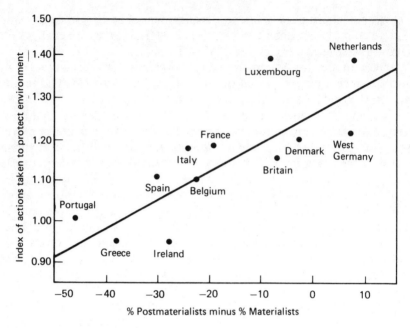

SOURCE: Eurobarometer 25 (April, 1986)
FIGURE 1.4: *Action taken to protect the environment, by prevailing values in twelve nations.*

astonishingly large: in 1970, fully 70 per cent of the Belgian public described themselves as 'very proud' to be Belgians; in 1985, only 26 per cent did so. The Belgian case is exceptional: cataclysmic changes have been occurring in the political culture of that country. But a similar trend is also visible in each of the other five countries for which we have data from 1970: the publics of Luxembourg, Italy, France, The Netherlands, and West Germany all show declines from 1970 to 1985, ranging from 17 to 24 points in the percentage who were 'very proud' of their nationality. No consistent pattern appears in the two years from 1983 to 1985; if anything, national pride seemed to have risen in that period. But the long-term decline is mirrored in the response patterns of the respective age groups and value types. As Table 1.5 reveals, Postmaterialists are only about half as likely as Materialists are to describe themselves as 'very proud' of their nationality; and the youngest age cohort is far less likely to be 'very proud' of their nationality than is the oldest cohort. Here too, we have indications of an intergenerational shift which the available longitudinal evidence tends to confirm.

Moreover, the shift from Materialist to Postmaterialist values seems to be part of a still broader process of cultural change. For example, data from the 1981 World Values Survey demonstrate that throughout ad-

TABLE 1.4: *Feeling of national pride in twenty-two nations, 1970–85*

*Question: 'Would you say you are very proud, quite proud, not very proud, or
not at all proud to be (Nationality)?'*
(Percentage saying 'very proud')

Nation	1970	1981	1983	1985
Greece	–	–	76%	72%
US	–	76%	–	–
Australia	–	70	–	–
Hungary	–	67	–	–
Mexico	–	65	–	–
Spain	–	51	–	64
Canada	–	62	–	–
Luxembourg	81%	–	51	62
Iceland	–	58	–	–
Britain	–	53	57	54
Ireland	–	67	52	53
Argentina	–	49	–	–
Italy	62	40	40	45
Norway	–	41	–	–
France	66	31	36	42
Denmark	–	30	39	40
Sweden	–	30	–	–
Netherlands	54	20	34	34
Portugal	–	–	–	33
Belgium	70	29	24	26
Japan	–	30	–	–
West Germany	38	21	17	20

SOURCES: European Community survey carried out in February–March 1970; World Values survey, 1981–2; Eurobarometer 19 (April 1983), and Eurobarometer 24 (October–November 1985).

vanced industrial society, the young attach far less importance to religion than do older groups. Table 1.6 shows one piece of data from a far broader array of similar evidence.

Although there is a great deal of cross-cultural variation in the proportion who view themselves as religious, in every country the young are much less likely to do so than the old. Overall, the vast majority of those over 65 years of age described themselves as religious, while only about half of those aged 15–24 in 1981 did so.

By itself, this does not necessarily prove anything about cultural change. It is possible that the pattern in Table 1.6 simply reflects a tendency for people to get more religious as they age. On the other hand, it could reflect a major historical change, in which the old continue to reflect the traditional pattern more faithfully than the young. A substantial body of time series data will be required in order to decide this question conclusively.

TABLE 1.5: *National pride among West European publics by value type and age group, 1983*

Question: 'Would you say you are very proud, quite proud, not very proud, or not at all proud to be (nationality)?'
(Percentage saying 'very proud')

	%	N
1. By value type		
Materialist	47%	(3,380)
Mixed	40	(4,655)
Postmaterialist	24	(1,127)
2. By age group		
15–24	29	(1,834)
25–34	35	(1,632)
35–44	37	(1,637)
45–54	39	(1,433)
55–64	52	(1,385)
65+	54	(1,439)

SOURCE: Based on data from Eurobarometer survey 19 (April 1983).
Note: Percentages weighted according to population of each nation.

But it seems significant that we find a surprisingly strong correlation between religiosity and Materialist/Postmaterialist values: while the over-whelming majority of Materialists view themselves as religious, less than half of the Postmaterialists do so. This pattern holds true of a number of other indicators of religious/secular views. Moreover, as we will see below, Postmaterialists show strikingly different attitudes from those of Material-ists toward divorce, homosexuality, child rearing, the importance of the family and numerous other aspects of life. All of this suggests that Figure 1.3 may only reveal the tip of the iceberg: the shift from Materialist to Postmaterialist values may be only one symptom of a much broader shift away from an entire syndrome of traditional cultural values that have been central to Western societies for centuries.

In virtually every society included in the 1981 World Values Survey, the young are markedly more tolerant of homosexuality than the old. On the average across these nations, the oldest group is about twice as likely to say that homosexuality can never be justified, as is the youngest group. And in virtually every country, Postmaterialists are much less likely to say that homosexuality can never be justified than are other value types, even though the items used to measure Postmaterialism have nothing whatever to do with sexual preferences. This is part of a pervasive pattern. As Figure 1.5 demonstrates, Postmaterialists are far more permissive than Material-ists in their attitudes toward abortion, divorce, extramarital affairs, prosti-tution, and euthanasia. They also emphasize very distinctive values among the qualities that are considered important to teach children when they are

TABLE 1.6: *Religiosity by age group and country*
(Percentage describing self as 'a religious person')

Age Group	Japan	Sweden	Norway	France	Britain	Australia
15–24	31	15	36	42	34	40
25–34	24	21	42	40	47	55
35–44	22	37	45	56	64	58
45–54	21	33	46	62	64	67
55–64	29	40	54	64	72	76
65+	49	55	63	70	77	71
(Total)	(28)	(34)	(46)	(53)	(55)	(58)

Age Group	North. Ireland	Spain	West Germany	Ireland	Hungary	Iceland
15–24	32	48	44	56	59	55
25–34	44	52	53	66	61	65
35–44	62	67	72	60	67	73
45–54	75	72	77	70	72	79
55–64	87	76	77	69	76	78
65+	83	80	84	86	80	80
(Total)	(61)	(64)	(65)	(66)	(67)	(68)

Age Group	Denmark	Nether-lands	South Africa	Canada	Mexico	Belgium
15–24	42	59	61	67	77	73
25–34	56	61	68	74	76	80
35–44	76	72	75	76	82	80
45–54	84	74	77	77	86	90
55–64	89	85	79	90	90	84
65+	90	84	89	86	–	88
(Total)	(69)	(69)	(71)	(76)	(79)	(81)

Age Group	USA	Italy	MEAN
15–24	75	78	50
25–34	79	77	56
35–44	85	86	65
45–54	89	91	70
55–64	92	89	74
65+	92	90	79
(Total)	(83)	(84)	(63)

SOURCE: World Values Survey, 1981–2.

growing up. As a broad generalization, Materialists are much more likely
to adhere to traditional societal norms than are Postmaterialists. Although
Materialist values are not a core element of traditional religious value
systems, in the contemporary historical context they show strong empirical
linkages with traditional norms.

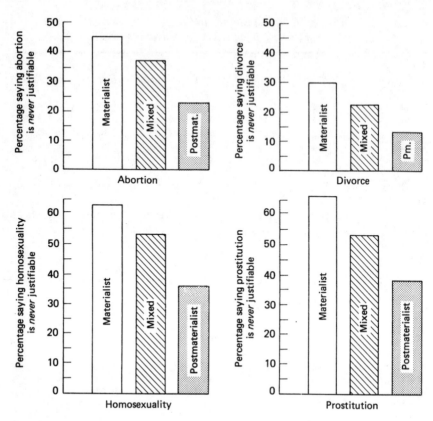

FIGURE 1.5: *Moral and social attitudes, by value type*

Each of these norms also shows striking differences across age groups. In virtually every country, the young are far less likely to feel that divorce can never be justified than are the old. Similarly, the young are more tolerant of extramarital affairs than the old; overall, the old are almost twice as apt to see them as never justifiable.

Postmaterialism and Changing Attitudes Toward War

The development of nuclear power has been virtually halted in certain countries by determined public opposition; quite disproportionately, it comes from Postmaterialists. Similarly, the rise of environmentalist movements, and environmentalist political parties reflects the political expression of Postmaterialist values. Finally, the peace movement that emerged in Western Europe and the United States in the early 1980s was in large part a Postmaterialist phenomenon. This is indicated by the fact that Postmaterialists are much likelier to approve of the movement than are Materialists or mixed types, as Table 1.7 demonstrates. This tendency is present throughout the European Community nations.

Nevertheless, Table 1.7 underestimates the importance of Postmaterialism in the rise of the peace movement. For Postmaterialists are about half again as likely to approve of the peace movement as are Materialists; but they are fully *ten* times as likely to be actual members. Table 1.8 shows the evidence on this score. Active membership is, of course, relatively rare: only 1.2 per cent of the European Community publics claim membership in the movement. And though the pure Postmaterialist type comprised only 12 per cent of the sample, they account for *half* of the movement's total membership; most of the rest are mixed types; only a handful are Materialists.

The recent Peace Movement, of course, reflected a number of factors, and can be analysed on a number of levels. It can be traced to specific political decisions made by specific political leaders, in a specific strategic context. The presence of Postmaterialists would not automatically have generated the movement, in the absence of these other factors. But it *does* seem clear that the emergence of Postmaterialism was one of the key conditions that facilitated the development of the peace movement, and that enabled it to mobilize larger number of supporters than any of its various forerunners, from the early days of the Cold War, through the Vietnam era.

Why were Postmaterialists so much likelier to be active in the peace movement than those with other values? Is it because they are more afraid of war? The answer to the latter question is no: Postmaterialists are concerned with war, but they are no likelier to feel that World War III is imminent than the rest of the public. Instead, the linkage between Postmaterialism and the Peace Movement seems to reflect two main elements, one of which is a relative sense of *security*. For Postmaterialist values develop from a sense of economic and physical security, and the latter part of the syndrome includes a sense of national security, as well as domestic security. Postmaterialists are likelier than Materialists to take national security for granted. Accordingly, they are more apt to feel that the American presence in Europe is unnecessary, and that additional arms are superfluous.

The other side of the coin is that Postmaterialism has emerged in a setting in which war seems absurd. Since the end of World War II, it has seemed that the only war likely to take place in Western Europe, would be a total war involving both of the superpowers. In the thermonuclear age, the costs of such a war would almost certainly outweigh the gains by a vast margin. Indeed, if the nuclear winter hypothesis is correct, it would wipe out human life in the entire northern hemisphere, and possibly the southern one as well. By any cost/benefit analysis, this is not a paying proposition.

This has not always been the case. Throughout most of history, it has

TABLE 1.7: *Support for peace movements, by value type*

	France			The Netherlands			West Germany			Italy			United Kingdom			Western Europe*		
	1982	1984	1986	1982	1984	1986	1982	1984	1986	1982	1984	1986	1982	1984	1986	1982	1984	1986
Strongly Approve																		
Materialist	31	28	26	35	27	21	20	10	10	72	39	52	25	14	26	43	26	28
Mixed	38	32	31	36	33	27	26	23	21	72	58	62	28	23	28	47	33	35
Postmaterialist	53	44	53	61	59	52	66	57	52	79	70	67	44	40	50	63	52	55
Member of Peace Group																		
Materialist	0	<1	0	1	0	0	1	0	1	1	<1	1	1	1	1	1	<1	<1
Mixed	<1	<1	0	1	1	1	4	2	1	3	1	1	1	2	1	1	1	1
Postmaterialist	3	1	6	6	7	3	10	7	4	6	10	7	6	6	11	5	6	5

SOURCE: Eurobarometer 17 (April, 1982), Eurobarometer 22 (November, 1984) and Eurobarometer 25 (April, 1986). Figures for Western Europe are weighted according to population of each country. Data are available at all three time points only for these five countries.

TABLE 1.8: *Membership in peace movements, by value type (Percentage saying they 'are a member')*

Question: *'Can you tell me whether you are a member, or are likely to join, or would certainly not join . . . the anti-war and anti-nuclear weapons movements, such as CND?'*

	France			The Netherlands			West Germany			Italy			United Kingdom			Western Europe*		
Value type	1982	1984	1986	1982	1984	1986	1982	1984	1986	1982	1984	1986	1982	1984	1986	1982	1984	1986
Materialist	0.0	0.3	0.0	1.0	0.0	0.0	0.5	0.0	0.9	0.8	0.3	0.7	0.6	1.3	0.5	0.5	0.4	0.5
Mixed	0.4	0.2	0.0	1.1	1.1	0.6	4.1	1.7	1.4	2.7	1.0	1.2	1.1	1.6	1.4	1.4	1.2	1.0
Postmaterialist	3.3	1.0	0.6	5.5	7.4	3.0	10.4	6.8	3.5	5.6	10.1	6.7	5.6	5.7	10.8	5.6	5.9	5.3

been at least conceivable that the material gains of a given war might exceed the material costs. In an economy of scarcity, it was even possible that under extreme conditions, a given tribe or nation's only hope for survival might lie in a successful war to seize a neighbour's land or food or water supply. In advanced industrial society, the cost/benefit ratio has swung far in the opposite direction. On one hand, the costs of war have become very high; and on the other hand, the benefits are relatively low: with a high level of technology, there are easier and safer ways to get rich than by plundering one's neighbours (as the recent history of Germany and Japan, in particular, illustrates). From a Postmaterialist perspective, war seems absurd.

The declining economics of imperialism seem to be reinforced by an accompanying cultural shift: with economic development and the rise of Postmaterialist values, people not only have less need to plunder their neighbors, but seem to become less willing to do so. At the close of World War II, the United States may have become the first victorious power in history to extend economic aid to her defeated foes instead of plundering them. But subsequently, former colonial powers such as Britain, France, and The Netherlands have extended economic aid to their former empires. And the Soviet Union has now joined them. Though in the immediate postwar era, capital equipment taken from Eastern Europe was an important source of Soviet reconstruction, for most of the past fifteen years, the Soviet Union has been subsidizing her client states, with the costs of the Soviet empire clearly outweighing the economic gains.

The impact of technological modernization is reinforced by parallel cultural developments in advanced industrial society. Economic development and the emergence of social welfare institutions give rise to a sense of economic security that leads to a gradual shift from Materialist to Postmaterialist values among both elites and the general public. Though the Soviet Union still lags behind the West in absolute levels of income, we would expect her relatively high standards of job security and other forms of social security to give rise to an increasingly Postmaterialist outlook, as seems to have occurred in Poland (Inglehart and Siemienska, 1988). A recent study of Soviet emigres suggests the presence of similar intergenerational differences in the political orientations of the Soviet public (Zimmerman and Yarsike, forthcoming).

By themselves, such cultural preferences are not necessarily decisive. They are only one component of a complex system of causal factors. But the long-term outlook seems more conducive to convergence than to polarization between Soviet and Western societies. It seems possible that growing concerns over common problems in the global environment may reorient them toward cooperative behavior.

REFERENCES

Barnes, Samuel H., Max Kaase *et al.* (1979) *Political Action: Mass Participation in Five Western Democracies* (Beverly Hills, Cal.: Sage).
Block, J. (1981) 'Some enduring and consequential structures of personality', in Albert Rabin *et al.* (eds), *Further Explorations in Personality* (New York: Wiley) pp. 27–43.
Brim, Orville G., Jr. (1966) 'Socialization through the life cycle', in Orville G. Brim, Jr. and Stanton Wheeler (eds), *Socialization After Childhood* (New York: Wiley) pp. 368–88.
Brim, Orville G. and Jerome Kagan (eds) (1980) *Constancy and Change in Human Development* (Cambridge, Mass.: Harvard University Press).
Costa, Paul T., Jr and Robert McCrae. (1980) 'Still stable after all these years: Personality as a key to some issues in adulthood and old age', in Paul B. Baites and Orville G. Brim (eds), *Life-Span Development and Behavior*, vol. 3 (New York: Academic Press) pp. 65–102.
Dalton, Russell E., Scott Flanagan, and Paul A. Beck (eds) (1984) *Electoral Change: Alignment and Dealignment in Advanced Industrial Democracies* (Princeton: Princeton University Press).
Glenn, Norval D. (1974) 'Aging and conservatism'. *Annals of the American Academy of Political and Social Science* 415: 176–86.
Glenn, Norval D. (1980) 'Values, attitudes and beliefs', in Orville G. Brim, Jr. and Jerome Kagan (eds), *Constancy and Change in Human Development* (Cambridge, Mass.: Harvard University Press) pp. 596–640.
Inglehart, Ronald (1971) 'The silent revolution in Europe: Intergenerational change in post-industrial societies', *American Political Science Review* 65, 4: 991–1017.
Inglehart, Ronald (1977) *The Silent Revolution: Changing Values and Political Styles Among Western Publics* (Princeton, NJ: Princeton University Press).
Inglehart, Ronald (1988) 'The Renaissance of political culture', *American Political Science Review* 82, 4 (December): 1203–30.
Inglehart, Ronald (1990) *Culture Shift in Advanced Industrial Society* (Princeton, NJ: Princeton University Press).
Inglehart, Ronald and Renata Siemienska (1988) 'Changing values and political satisfaction in Poland and the West', *Government and Opposition* 23, 4: 440–57.
Jennings, M. Kent and Richard Niemi (1981) *Generations and Politics* (Princeton, NJ: Princeton University Press).
Jennings, M. Kent and Gregory B. Markus (1984) 'Partisan orientations over the long haul' *American Political Science Review* 78: 1000–18.
Levinson, Daniel J. (1978) *The Seasons of a Man's Life* (New York: Knopf).
Mortimer, Jeylan T. and Roberta G. Simmons (1978) 'Adult socialization', in *Annual Review of Sociology* 4: 421–54.
Riley, Matilda and Kathleen Bond (1983) 'Beyond ageism: Postponing the onset of disability', pp. 243–52 in Matilda Riley, Beth B. Hess and Kathleen Bond (eds), *Aging in Society: Selected Reviews of Recent Research* (Hillsdale, NJ: Lawrence Erlbaum).
Sears, David O. (1981) 'Life-stage effects on attitude change, especially among the elderly', in S. B. Diesler *et al.* (eds), *Aging: Social Change* (New York: Academic Press).
Sears, David O. (1983) 'On the persistence of early political predispositions: The roles of attitude object and life stage', in L. Wheeler (ed.), *Review of Personality and Social Psychology* (vol. 4) (Beverly Hills, Ca.: Sage).
Zimmerman, William and Deborah Yarsike (forthcoming) 'Intergenerational Change and the Future of Soviet Foreign Policy', unpublished paper.

2 Public Opinion about the European Parliament

Oskar Niedermayer, University of Mannheim

From the outset, the Eurobarometer surveys have followed up public opinion not only with respect to the European Community (EC) at large but also in regard to one of its major institutions, the European Parliament (EP). The following dimensions of public opinion about the European Parliament have been examined systematically: awareness, knowledge, evaluation and support.[1] Because the same operationalizations have been used over a long period of time, most of these dimensions can be analysed longitudinally. This will be done in the first part of this chapter, i.e. we will give a cross-nationally comparative overview about the development of public opinion about the EP in the course of time. The second part deals with the question whether the various attitudes about the EP and its political objectives are systematically interrelated.

AWARENESS

Awareness of the EP can be followed up over a rather long period of time. It must be taken into account, however, that the indicator used to operationalize public awareness comprises only the subjectively remembered imparting of information about the EP through the mass media and reacts in time to changes in the intensity of the information supply by the mass media as well as to changes in the degree of sensitization of the respondents towards this supply.[2] Although the data base is incomplete till the beginning of the eighties, the development of this indicator, both for the EC-average and for each member state[3], clearly shows the sudden rises of mobilization on the occasion of both previous direct elections. The respective increase of awareness before the elections, however, was followed by a decrease thereafter, i.e. the short-term increase of information supply and of the citizen's sensitization with respect to this supply still has to be transformed into a long-term stable awareness of the EP at a higher level (see Figure 2.1).

In spring of 1988, about a year before the third direct elections, on the European average less than half of the citizens claimed to have heard or read anything about the EP recently. Not surprisingly, the share of those who are aware of the EP is highest in Luxembourg with two-thirds of the

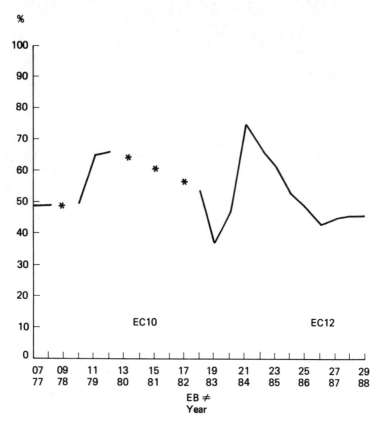

FIGURE 2.1: *Public awareness of the European Parliament*

respondents, whereas in most of the other countries this share is about 50 per cent and in the United Kingdom, Ireland and the Netherlands it even drops to little more than one-third of the respondents (see Figure 2.2).

KNOWLEDGE

Given the rather low level of awareness between the respective direct elections, it is small wonder that many citizens do not have sufficient knowledge about the EP. Unfortunately, the knowledge dimension can be analyzed for only one point in time. In spring 1983, little more than one year before the second direct elections, the respondents were asked about the composition of the EP and about how its members are chosen. Given three possible answers to the question about the countries represented in the European Parliament, only little more than half of the citizens chose the right answer (all the member states of the EC). The replies to the

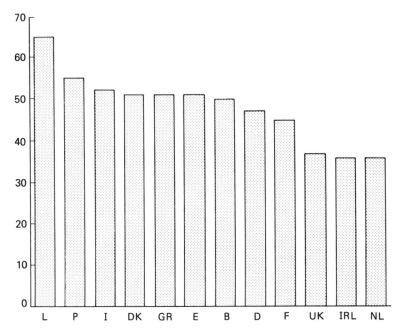

FIGURE 2.2: *Awareness of the European Parliament by country (Spring 1988)*

question as to how the Members of the European Parliament were chosen even showed a slightly lower level of knowledge. Here, in most countries less than half of the respondents replied that the MEPs were directly elected by the people rather than appointed by the respective national governments. With respect to both questions, about one-fourth of the citizens don't answer.

A nation-by-nation comparison shows that with respect to the composition question, there are relatively little differences between the respective member states, the highest level of knowledge being found in the Netherlands and Germany, the lowest level in Greece and the United Kingdom. With respect to the question about the way the MEPs are chosen, we in general find about the same amount of differences. Exceptions are France, where only about one-third of the respondents gave the right answer, and Greece, where more than two-thirds did this. The extremely high level of knowledge about the way the MEPs are chosen in Greece is probably due to the fact that the Greek members of the EP were not directly elected until the end of 1981 (see Table 2.1).

TABLE 2.1: *Knowledge about the composition of the EP and the way in which its members are chosen*

A: *'Representatives from various countries sit in the European Parliament. Which of the following statements is correct? (a) Representatives from some, but not all, member states of the European Community sit there; (b) Representatives from all the member states of the European Community sit there; (c) Representatives from all the Western European countries sit there.'*
B: *'How are the Members of the European Parliament chosen? Are they appointed by the government or directly elected by the people?'*

	B	DK	D	GR	F	IRL	I	L	NL	UK
A:										
some EC states	9	5	7	5	10	10	10	10	8	11
all EC states	53	54	63	52	55	55	52	58	65	51
Western Europe	10	9	9	10	9	8	11	10	9	9
d.k./n.a.	28	33	21	33	26	27	27	23	18	30
B:										
appointed	21	33	25	11	37	33	24	35	39	26
elected	55	42	51	69	36	45	45	50	47	48
d.k./n.a.	24	25	24	21	26	22	30	15	13	26

SOURCE: Eurobarometer 19; Spring 1983; percentages

EVALUATION

An indicator which combines aspects of knowledge and evaluation is the perceived importance of the present role of the EP in the life of the European Community. On the European average, the perceived importance of the EP's present role has slightly increased in the course of time (see Figure 2.3).[4]

Possible explanations for this development could be: (1) the discussion about the Single European Act, which has found a quite acceptable echo in the media, (2) the intensification of the public relations efforts of the EP itself, (3) the strategy of the EP to reach more attention in the media by the invitation of popular politicians to speak before the EP.

However, within the framework of a deeper analysis of this development, additional nation-specific explanation factors would have to be considered, because the improvements found on the European average are caused by a positive development in only about half of the member states. A positive development is most evident in Ireland and Greece, a slightly better evaluation of the importance of the present role can be found in France, Great Britain and Denmark. In the other countries, this indicator has been stable over the examined period of time. Concentrating on the

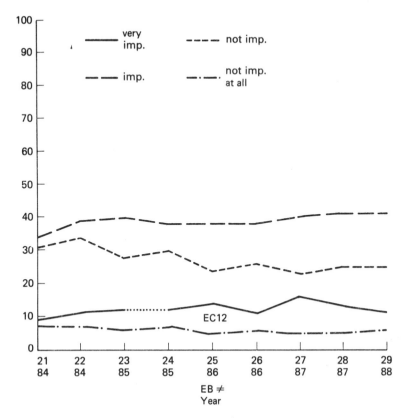

FIGURE 2.3: *Present role of the European Parliament*

newest data (spring 1988) with respect to the individual member states, two results are worth stating: (1) only relatively few people perceive the EP as playing a role within the political system of the European Community which is either very or not at all important; (2) the results in the individual member states do not differ extremely, as Figure 2.4 shows, using the mean scores of the four-point-importance-scale ranging from 1 (=not important at all) to 4 (=very important).

Another indicator which can be used if it comes to the evaluation of the European Parliament is the follow-up question to the question concerning the awareness of the EP asking the respondents whether what they read or heard about the EP has given them a generally favorable or unfavorable impression. In the same way as the awareness question, however, this indicator mixes the positive or negative tendency of the media coverage about the EP with the respondent's possible selective reception and evaluation of the applied information.

Of those who claimed to have heard or read anything about the EP

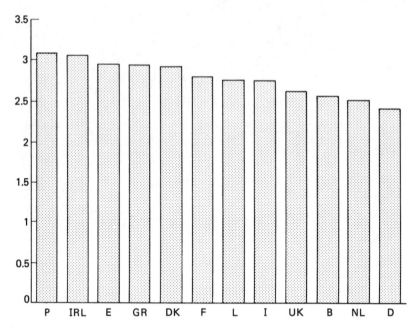

FIGURE 2.4: *Present role of the European Parliament by country (Spring 1988)*

recently, on the European average only about two-thirds gave an explicitly positive or negative evaluation of the EP in answering the follow-up question. Almost one-third were indifferent, an attitude that was neither suggested in the given question wording nor in the response-categories. The Commission of the EC therefore considers this attitude as a form of polite non-response to veil ignorance, indifference and lack of information of the respondent. However, it cannot be ruled out that at least partly an interview effect is present. Including those that really denied answering, this group adds up to a good third, a share that in the course of time has not changed systematically on the European average (see Figure 2.5).

In other words: only for about two-thirds of those who perceive information about the EP at all does that information rank high enough to at least rudimentarily process it and use it for opinion formation. Those who do this, however, in the course of time, increasingly report a positive impression gained from that information (see Figure 2.5), this being true, more or less intensively, for all countries.

With respect to the level of favorable evaluations, Figure 2.6 shows that there are remarkable differences between the individual member states, ranging from two-thirds of those who are aware of the EP in Ireland and Italy to one-fifth in Denmark.

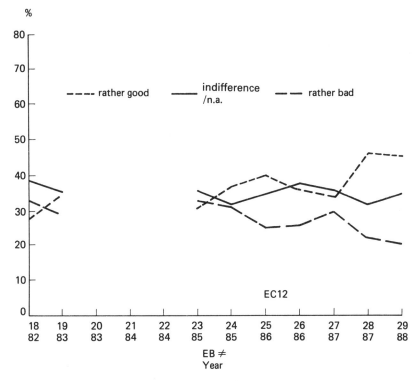

FIGURE 2.5: *Impression of the European Parliament*

SUPPORT

Regarding this dimension, the data allow an analysis of two aspects: the public support for a general strengthening of the European Parliament and the support for specific political objectives of the EP within the framework of its strategy of parliamentarization of the European Community's political system.

The extent of support by the European citizens for a general upgrading of the EP within the political system of the EC can be estimated using the answers to the question, whether one personally would prefer that the EP played a more or less important part than it does now. In spring of 1988 on the European average, almost half of the respondents favored a more important role for the EP, one-fifth was indifferent (same role) and one-tenth was in favour of a less important role for the EP. In all member states, with the exception of Denmark, those in favor of a more important role of the EP formed at least the relative majority of those questioned.

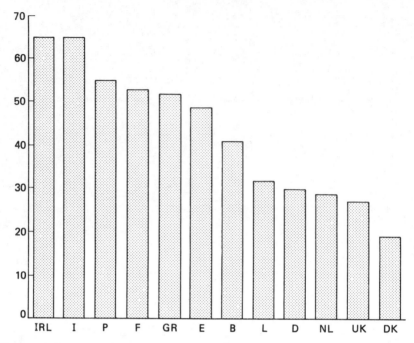

FIGURE 2.6: *Favourable impression of the European Parliament by country (Spring 1988)*

The objective of a general strengthening of the EP within the political system of the EC is thus considerably supported by the European population and explicitly rejected by only a few. On the other hand, the fact that about one-fifth of the respondents (a share that has not changed much since 1983) did not answer the question concerning the desired role of the EP shows widespread indifference towards the EP that is not to be underestimated. In addition, if one follows the previously used pattern of argumentation and classifies the answer 'same role', which was neither suggested in the question nor in the response-categories, as a polite form of refusal, one can assume a certain lack of interest in the EP in this category of respondents, too.

Following the chronological development of this indicator, it becomes clear that since the second direct elections in 1984, on the European average the number of those who support a strengthening of the role of the EP has significantly decreased and the number of those who do not want any change or who do not answer the question at all has increased, while those who would prefer a less important role for the European Parliament have stayed the same (see Figure 2.7).

The decrease in public support of a more important role of the EP can be found in almost all member states, most clearly in Luxembourg, France,

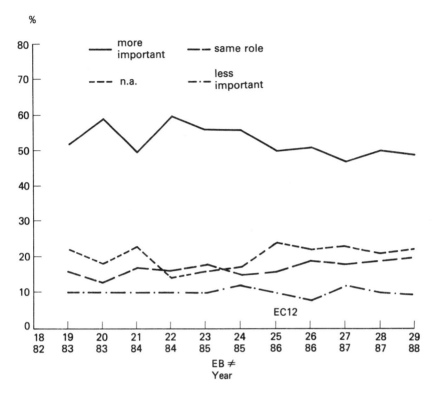

FIGURE 2.7: *Future role of the European Parliament*

the Netherlands, Germany and Ireland (see Figure 2.8). Denmark and Greece do not show a negative trend since the second direct elections in 1984 but before. In Germany, Denmark and, to a lesser degree, also in the Netherlands and Luxembourg this development is enhanced by the fact that the share of those who would explicitly favour a less important role for the EP is increasing. It is only in the two new member states, Spain and Portugal, that support for a more important role of the EP is increasing with the course of time (see Figure 2.9). In Spain, however, the number of those who prefer a less important role for the EP has also increased.

A possible explanation for the decrease in public support for a strengthening of the future role of the EP could be the fact that the evaluation of its present importance has slightly improved. One could argue that with the perception of an increased importance of the EP nowadays, fewer and fewer people see a necessity in further strengthening its role in the future. However, this argument can neither be supported on the aggregate data nor on the individual data level: the decrease in support can not only be found in countries in which the present role of the EP was rated increasingly important. There is also no systematically negative correlation on the

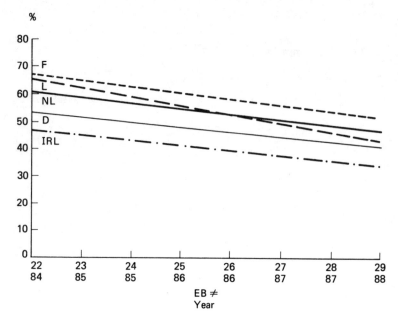

FIGURE 2.8: *Future role of the European Parliament: national trends 1*

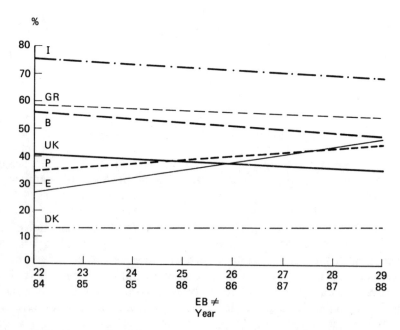

FIGURE 2.9: *Future role of the European Parliament: national trends 2*

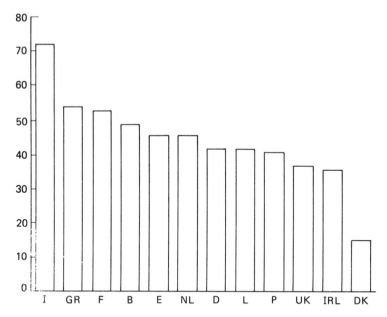

FIGURE 2.10: *Future role of the European Parliament by country (Spring 1988)*

individual level between the evaluation of the present and the desired future role of the EP.

Looking at the individual countries, we find considerable differences in the level of diffuse support ranging from nearly three-quarters of the Italian respondents favoring a more important role of the EP to only one-seventh doing this in Denmark (see Figure 2.10).

Contrary to the diffuse support for a strengthening of the role of the EP, the development of the willingness to support concrete objectives of the EP cannot be followed continuously over a long period of time based on unchanging indicators. However, a comparison of the results obtained by questions regarding the extension of competences of the EP that were asked in 1976, 1983 and 1987/88 ends in the same impressions as described regarding the diffuse support: (1) the parliamentarization of the EC-system through concrete extensions of the EP's competences is on the European average supported by about half of the citizens nowadays; (2) the large share of those not answering the questions reveals the lack of interest or at least the uncertainty of a large part of the public; and (3) there also seems to be a decrease in the extent of support in the course of time (the latter statement has to be taken with care since there were only a few measuring points and the questions were formulated differently). A comparison of the extent of support in the respective member states does not reveal astonishing results: all indicators show by far the lowest support rates in Denmark, followed by the United Kingdom, whereas in Italy the highest rates of support could be found over the whole period of time (see Table 2.2).

THE STRUCTURE OF ATTITUDES ABOUT THE EUROPEAN PARLIAMENT

The last three items of Table 2.2 can be seen as touching upon various dimensions of a parliamentarization of the EC's political system. If the answers to these questions reflect a structured set of attitudes, we would expect relatively high positive correlations between these items. Table 2.3 shows that this hypothesis is clearly confirmed in each of the individual member states.

Given these high correlations between the three items, we can calculate an additive index combining the answers to the three questions into a single parliamentarization-scale. Figure 2.11 shows the frequency distribution of this scale for the individual member states, the figures meaning the following: 1=all three questions were not answered ('indifferents'); 2=one or two of the questions were not answered; 3=negative answer to all three questions; 4=negative answer to two questions; 5=negative answer to one question; 6=positive answer to all three questions ('supporters of parliamentarization'). Figure 2.11 shows that in the 'old' member states, except Ireland, about one-tenth of the respondents are so indifferent, uninformed or uninterested in the question of a parliamentarization of the EC that they do not answer any of the questions related to this topic. In the

TABLE 2.2: *Public support for a parliamentarization of the European Community (percentages)*

	B	DK	D	GR	E	F	IRL	I	L	NL	P	UK	EC

'In a European Parliament, the Members of Parliament for (country) would not have the majority, even if they were all in agreement. Would you, or would you not, accept that the European Parliament passes laws in the fields that I am going to list, which would be applicable to all countries of the European Community, including (own country)?' As far as A) taxation matters are concerned (e.g. create a European tax); B) employment legislation is concerned (e.g. European regulations about professional training); C) public works are concerned (e.g. a European programme on motorways, rivers and canals); D) foreign relations are concerned (e.g. signing of a commercial treaty with a foreign country). (Eurobarometer 5, spring 1976)

would accept	%	%	%			%	%	%	%	%		%	%
A	41	18	47	–	–	42	43	48	59	56	–	37	44
B	64	46	63	–	–	73	67	68	76	70	–	48	63
C	62	48	73	–	–	80	60	70	76	80	–	48	68
D	56	40	58	–	–	62	45	62	56	60	–	43	56

'The European Parliament should have more power to control both the way the Common Market functions and also the budget of the European Community.' (Eurobarometer 20, autumn 1983)
tend to
agree   60 38 65 71 – 70 58 80 74 65 – 59 67

'The members of the European Parliament who will be elected in 1984 should, as a main aim, work towards a political union of the member countries of the Community with a European Government responsible to the European Parliament.' (Eurobarometer 20, autumn 1983)
tend to
agree   56 17 53 69 – 50 56 66 68 62 – 60 57

'Are you for or against the formation of a European government responsible to the European Parliament?' (Eurobarometer 28 (autumn 1987) and 29 (spring 1988))
for:
autumn 1987   55 13 41 39 49 60 39 70 52 45 42 31 49
spring 1988   56 11 43 42 52 62 44 68 46 45 42 31 49

'Are you for or against the European Parliament having power to pass laws that will apply directly in all member countries of the European Community, that is in (own country) as well as elsewhere?' (Eurobarometer 28 (autumn 1987) and 29 (spring 1988))
for:
autumn 1987   57 17 41 35 48 58 36 69 45 50 45 35 49
spring 1988   58 18 39 43 53 61 44 69 39 48 40 29 49

'Do you agree or disagree that the Parliament to be elected in 1989 should receive a mandate, that is given the power to prepare a draft constitution for a European union?' (Eurobarometer 28 (autumn 1987) and 29 (spring 1988))
agree
autumn 1987   61 20 58 38 51 69 42 76 67 56 50 45 58
spring 1988   63 21 51 49 52 68 48 76 54 57 47 43 57

TABLE 2.3: *Relationship between the three parliamentarization items (Pearson product-moment correlations)*

	EP laws/ resp. gov.	EP laws/ const. EU	resp. gov./ const. EU
B	.52	.51	.47
DK	.45	.47	.52
D	.73	.71	.78
GR	.66	.62	.65
E	.62	.53	.51
F	.47	.40	.44
IRL	.64	.53	.56
I	.56	.37	.45
L	.65	.44	.51
NL	.56	.49	.55
P	.62	.49	.65
UK	.56	.38	.48

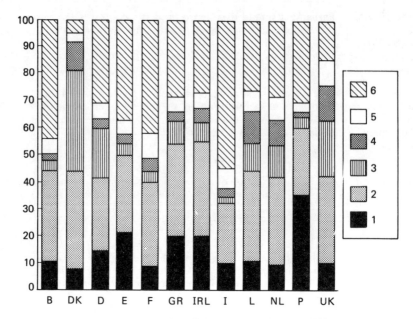

FIGURE 2.11: *Parliamentarization-scale by country (Spring 1988)*

new member states Greece and Spain, about one-fifth of the respondents belongs to this group, in Portugal even one-third. If one adds those who do not answer one or two of the items, the share increases to an amount between two- and three-fifths of the respondents. Those who clearly reject any notion of a parliamentarization are a small minority in all member states except Denmark and, to a much lesser degree, the United Kingdom and Germany. Of those who answer all questions, the supporters of parliamentarization, i.e. those who answer all three questions positively, form the absolute majority in eight and the relative majority in two member states, the exceptions being Denmark and the United Kingdom.

From the point of view of a strategy to win public support for the EP and its aims, not the clear opponents but those indifferent or uninterested are the most important target group. In the following, we therefore will describe this group in more detail by contrasting it with the supporters of parliamentarization.

Table 2.4 shows the results of the comparison of the two groups with respect to sociostructural variables. Given the fact that the gender gap with respect to the general political interest and participation still exists, we would assume that in regard to the attitudes or non-attitudes about a parliamentarization of the EC this gap can be found, too. Indeed, as Table 2.4 shows, among those indifferent, women form the overwhelming majority in each of the individual member states. With respect to age we do not find a clear relationship which applies to all countries. Regarding

TABLE 2.4: *Comparison of indifferents and supporters of parliamentarization with respect to sociostructural variables (percentages)*

| | Sex | | | | Age | | Education | | | | | |
| | male | | female | | average | | low | | middle | | high | |
	IN	SP	IN	SP	IN	SP	IN	SP	IN	SP	IN	SP
B	43	56	57	44	45	41	48	23	41	41	11	36
DK	30	73	70	27	41	51	52	31	35	26	13	43
D	27	54	73	46	49	43	60	31	27	40	13	29
GR	27	61	73	39	51	43	71	38	26	41	3	21
E	31	61	69	39	51	39	84	50	10	26	6	24
F	26	55	74	45	47	44	63	29	34	47	3	24
IRL	37	58	63	42	43	42	53	28	46	59	1	13
I	28	56	72	44	51	42	76	52	18	27	6	21
L	26	65	74	35	41	43	61	19	39	41	0	40
NL	24	60	76	40	48	43	51	22	35	36	14	42
P	38	50	62	50	47	40	87	70	10	20	4	10
UK	26	58	74	42	40	43	36	34	61	46	3	20
EC	29	57	71	43	48	42	66	39	27	36	7	25

TABLE 2.5: *Comparison of indifferents and supporters of parliamentarization with respect to Postmaterialism and opinion leadership*

| | Postmaterialists (percentages) | | Opinion leadership index (means) | |
	IN	SP	IN	SP
B	6	19	3,6	2,7
DK	7	14	2,9	2,4
D	19	27	3,0	2,3
GR	3	5	2,8	2,0
E	5	18	3,4	2,6
F	7	18	3,2	2,6
IRL	3	10	3,2	2,7
I	6	17	3,1	2,5
L	3	22	3,4	2,4
NL	19	31	2,8	2,2
P	3	6	3,4	3,0
UK	16	25	3,1	2,4
EC	10	20	3,1	2,5

education, however, we do find remarkable evidence that those with higher education are clearly overrepresented within the supporters of a parliamentarization of the EC, this result being in line with the relationship between education and favourable attitudes about the European integration in general.[5]

Table 2.5 compares both groups with respect to two other variables which are of great relevance in explaining general European attitudes: the

TABLE 2.6: *Relationship between the parliamentarization-scale and other indicators of public opinion about the European Parliament (Kendall rank-order correlation coefficients)*

	awareness	present role	desired role
B	.18	.17	.21
DK	.13	.12	.50
D	.13	.20	.59
GR	.05	.28	.21
E	.13	.30	.38
F	.14	.12	.24
IRL	.22	.33	.26
I	.01	.09	.14
L	.02	.04	.39
NL	.03	.15	.46
P	.04	.14	.25
UK	.08	.33	.53

Materialist-Postmaterialist index and the opinion leadership index.[6] Postmaterialists are defined as giving, among other things, participatory values a high priority. One therefore can expect that they will actively support a parliamentarization, i.e. a specific form of democratization, of the European Community rather than being indifferent. As Table 2.5 shows, this indeed is true for all individual member states. With respect to the second variable, we already know from previous analyses that there exists a positive relationship between opinion leadership and favourable attitudes about the European integration in general. The data shown in Table 2.5 confirm these results with respect to the parliamentarization of the EC's political system.

At last we will examine the relationship of our parliamentarization-scale with the other dimensions of public opinion about the European Parliament we have analyzed in this article. With respect to the awareness of the EP, to develop a clear hypothesis about the relationship with our scale is rather difficult. On the one hand, the indicator used to operationalize the awareness dimension comprises the intensity of the media coverage and this should not be systematically related to the attitudes of the respondents about the parliamentarization of the EC. On the other hand, the indicator measures the subjectively remembered imparting of information, i.e. the degree of sensitization of the respondent towards the information supply about the EP and its performance, and this could be positively related to a favorable attitude towards this institution. We therefore do expect a non-existent or slightly positive relationship between the awareness variable and our parliamentarization-scale. The correlation coefficients shown in Table 2.6 confirm this hypothesis.

Concerning the evaluation of the EP's present role, a possible argument could be that the more important one considers its present role, the less one sees the necessity to further strengthen the EP by a parliamentarization of the EC. On the other hand, one can assume that these two variables should be positively related to each other within a generally positive opinion about the EP. This could lead to a relatively high subjective importance of the EP, even if the objective importance, measured by its competences, is relatively low, and at the same time a desire to further strengthen the EP by giving it real competences. The results presented in Table 2.6 confirm the latter argumentation. Since the question about the desired future role of the EP operationalizes the diffuse support for a general upgrading of the EP and the parliamentarization-scale operationalizes the specific support for the EP's concrete political aims in this area, we expect a clear positive relationship between these variables, this being confirmed by the results shown in Table 2.6.

Our analysis has shown that the various dimensions of public opinion about the European Parliament are systematically interrelated. The attitudes of those respondents being interested enough in the EP to answer questions related to it form a consistent set, the theoretical hypotheses about the nature of the relationships between the individual variables being confirmed in each of the member states. However, the analysis has also revealed that a considerable part of the European citizenry is not interested in the European Parliament and its performance.

With respect to the individual member states we have, not surprisingly, consistently found a considerable amount of sceptical and negative attitudes about the EP in Denmark and, to a lesser degree, in the United Kingdom. However, other countries, i.e. Germany, show a certain scepticism, too. In addition, the longitudinal analysis has shown that the public support for both a general upgrading of the European Parliament within the framework of the EC's political system and the specific objectives of the EP is decreasing. These results should give rise to innovative considerations about the ways in which the public perception of the European Parliament could be improved.

NOTES

1. In addition, some questions related to the direct elections of the EP have been included.
2. The question wording is: 'Have you recently seen or heard in the papers, or in the radio or TV, anything about the European Parliament? That is, the Parliamentary Assembly of the European Community or Common Market.'
3. In order not to overload this chapter with tables or figures, we will not give a detailed documentation of the development of all analysed indicators in every

single member country of the EC, but only refer to country-specific differences in the text. The figures for the Community are based on the weighted average of the figures of the individual member states.

4. Figure 2.3 shows the results of the following question: 'How important would you say is the European Parliament in the life of the European Community nowadays?' (answer-categories: very important, important, not very important, not important at all).

5. Education is operationalized as: 'How old were you when you finished your full-time education?'; low = up to 15 years; middle = 16–19 years; high = 20 years and more.

6. The Materialist-Postmaterialist index is computed on the basis of a question dealing with different value priorities; opinion leadership is the new label for the cognitive mobilization concept. Concerning the exact question wordings and index calculations, see the Eurobarometer-reports of the Commission of the EC.

3 European Political Cooperation and Public Opinion

Werner J. Feld, University of Colorado at Colorado Springs

West European leaders have repeatedly stressed that the European Community 'must speak with a single voice' in order to gain increasing strength. This cry for a single voice was especially likely to be raised during struggles with outside powers, as in 1971 and 1973 when devaluations of the US dollar were damaging EC trade with the United States; and during the recurring economic and political frictions between the EC member states and the United States during the 1980s. Similarly, interaction between the Community members eventually requires a common EC foreign policy.[1]

It has been argued that when faced with external pressures, the solidarity of the Community increases, and the potential for unification rises.[2] The theory of 'externalization', developed by Philippe Schmitter, also suggests that in regional organizations such as the European Community, member governments, when pursuing joint policies pertaining to intermember or intraregional relations, 'will find themselves compelled – regardless of their original intentions – to adopt common policies vis-a-vis nonparticipant third parties.'[3] Although a minimal foreign policy base for the Community was already granted mainly in the EEC Treaty, it was a mechanism *outside* the Community system which produced a gradual approach to common external policies and this mechanism was *European Political Cooperation* (EPC).

EPC EVOLUTION

The EPC foreign policy coordination system dates back to an initiative at the Summit Meeting of the Heads of State of Government of the six member states in December 1969, and to the Luxembourg Report of the Foreign Ministers in October 1970 laying down the ideas and methods of pragmatic cooperation in the sphere of foreign policy. In the meantime. EPC has developed into a sophisticated method of foreign policy coordination now encompassing twelve member states and their foreign ministries. Through the Single European Act (SEA), which entered into force in

45

1987, EPC has received a legal foundation relating it to the EC. It has been strengthened in institutional terms by setting up a secretariat in Brussels which assists the EC Presidency in the discharge of its duties. While the SEA connection with the Community is a far cry from the European Parliament's ambition as reflected in the 1984 proposals for European Union, the overall progress of EPC in managerial terms during the last eighteen years has been remarkable. However, in terms of common decisional EC policy output, the results have been quite modest, because on many issues differing national interests of the member states tend to predominate. While a good number of joint declarations and statements have been issued during the 1980s, common policy *action* has been rare.[4] Hence, although it seems that the 'externalization' process, using Schmitter's term, has moved forward, the underlying theory cannot be fully confirmed so far. The question arises as to whether public opinion in the EC countries can have an impact on externalization and on the EPC mechanism and, if public opinion support for 'speaking with one voice' were favorable *and* effective, could one expect EPC to become a truly 'European' policy apparatus and thereby an instrument for European unification?

PUBLIC OPINION AND FOREIGN AFFAIRS

When examining the possible impact of public opinion in the EC countries on foreign policy or on the mechanism through which foreign policies may be formulated and implemented, it is important to distinguish between the mass public and leadership groups. Generally, the mass public (making up about 90 per cent of the entire public) is not much concerned with foreign policy issues unless they engender strong emotional responses. In the United States, the prime example of such an issue was the Vietnam War. With most other foreign policy issues, the leadership groups are the part of the public which usually show continued high interest and may exercise varying degrees of influence on policy making. William R. Caspary contends that overall, American public opinion is characterized by a strong and stable 'permissive mood' toward the international involvement of the United States.[5] This may be an overly positive view of the effect of public opinion; it may be more appropriate to say that public opinion sets broad limits for foreign policy makers.

Whether these general patterns also apply in Western Europe is uncertain. International relations and foreign policy issues may be of more direct concern to Europeans, since their countries are relatively small, transnational travel is frequent, and frequent exposure to foreign language increases their awareness to events beyond their national borders. In addition, the direct election of the European Parliament (EP) that began in

1979 may well have heightened Europeans' perception of personal involvement and influence in the European arena. Hence, European integration may no longer be a leadership preserve, and foreign policy issues, not infrequently an agenda item in the EP, may arouse greater interests and concerns of the public because, at least indirectly, they could be perceived as affecting the citizens' pocket books.

RECENT DATA

External relations, security and defense and cooperation with the Third World are topics which have been raised in the European Parliament repeatedly and 'security' has been enshrined in the Single European Act, which states that 'close cooperation on questions of European security would contribute in an essential way to the development of a European identity in external policy matters'.[6] Questions on security/defense and Third World cooperation were included in both the December 1987 and June 1988 Eurobarometer surveys, which covered nearly 12 000 respondents in the twelve member states.[7] One basic question concerns 'going even further than the single common European market toward the unification of Europe' and which directions this development should take. The second basic question was whether respondents supported the 'formation of a European government responsible to the European Parliament' and which powers such a government should have.

It is noteworthy that one respondent in four did *not* reply to the first question. Among those approving of going further (44 per cent of all interviewees), fully 84 per cent favored common action in external relations, 85 per cent in cooperation with the Third World, and 74 per cent in the domain of security and defense. Heavy majorities of those responding support a 'common' foreign policy in most countries, with somewhat lower figures coming from Belgium, Denmark, Portugal and Netherlands. Somewhat lower support is given to common defense and security policy. It must also be kept in mind, however, that the total of positive answers to the basic question is less than 50 per cent. For details, see Tables 3.1 and 3.2.

The second major issue surveyed is the formation of a European government responsible to the European Parliament. In both 1987 and 1988, slightly more than one-fourth of those interviewed did not respond. Among those responding, 50 per cent supported a 'common' foreign policy in 1988, six per cent more than in 1987. Similarly, cooperation with the Third World by this prospective government was supported by 51 per cent of interviewees in 1988 vs. only 42 per cent in 1987. Only with respect to security/defense was there a slight decline in 1988 from 1987: 57 per cent compared to 60 per cent. This strong support for security and defense policies is noteworthy and perhaps surprising.

TABLE 3.1: *Going further than a single common market (percentages)*

	Belgium 1988	1987	Denmark 1988	1987	Germany 1988	1987	Greece 1988	1987	Spain 1988	1987	France 1988	1987	Ireland 1988	1987
yes	55	56	13	16	41	48	47	50	40	38	47	47	35	27
no	16	21	70	61	29	27	19	15	26	20	30	35	27	30
no answer	28	23	17	23	31	25	34	35	33	42	23	18	38	43

	Italy 1988	1987	Luxembourg 1988	1987	Netherlands 1988	1987	Portugal 1988	1987	UK 1988	1987	EC 1988	1987
yes	71	79	35	44	40	48	43	46	24	28	44	48
no	12	10	36	36	43	32	15	21	57	49	31	29
no answer	17	12	29	20	17	20	42	43	19	22	25	23

SOURCE: Eurobarometer 29, June 1988, which includes December 1987 data, Table A-15.

49

TABLE 3.2: *Going further than a single common market: in which directions?*

	Belgium	Denmark	Germany	Greece	Spain	France	Ireland
External Relations	75	77	86	81	85	88	85
Cooperation with Third World	67	72	82	86	89	86	95
Security/Defense	69	65	68	81	71	84	69

	Italy	Luxembourg	Netherlands	Portugal	United Kingdom
External Relations	85	86	77	74	83
Cooperation with Third World	87	85	80	85	84
Security/Defense	72	66	75	80	77

SOURCE: Percentages of those who provided answer to first question. Data based on Eurobarometer 29 (June 1988), Table 10.

A breakdown by member states regarding the responses to this question reveals that in 1988 interviewees in Belgium, Spain, France, and Italy were the strongest supporters of a prospective European government with a slight increase from the 1987 data in Spain and a small decline in Luxembourg. Only British and Danish respondents are against a European government, the British moderately and the Danish quite strongly. See Table 3.3 for details.

A breakdown by member states shows generally higher support levels in 1988 than in 1987 on the common foreign policy and Third World issues, but lower support on security/defense (see Table 3.4).

It is interesting to note the socio-political profiles of those expressing in 1987 their support for the prospective powers of a European government. Clearly, as Table 3.4 suggests, opinion leaders favored common foreign policies and Third World cooperation more than the general public, but as far as the security/defense issues were concerned, both groups were equally in favor (59 per cent). With respect to the possible changes in EPC, the views of the opinion leaders may be significant; we will return to this point later. As Table 3.5 indicates, men and women supported external relations and security/defense equally, but men were more in favor of Third World cooperation. The higher the educational level, the greater the support for common external relations and Third World cooperation, but regarding security/defense, the least educated respondents ranked security and defense highest. As for value orientations, it is the Postmaterialists who are most in favor of common external relations and Third World cooperation, while the Materialists are more strongly for a European defense and security system. It may not be surprising that those who consider themselves politically on the right are more in favor of a 'European' defense and security policy than those on the left. But with respect to the other policy areas, political persuasion seems to make little difference.

EVALUATION

What will be the impact of public opinion on the fate of EPC, EC Third World policy, and on Security/Defense policy formations? Might member governments abandon EPC and transfer national authority in this issue area to the Commission? Would it be possible that 'European' Defense and Security policies would be established within the EC framework and what institutional facilities would be required for such a task?

Examining the problem of influence which public opinion as detailed by the Eurobarometer could exert on the issue areas requires first a determination of useful targets. Undoubtedly most members of the EP would be willing to promote the objectives reflected in the opinion data, but their ability to carry out the tasks necessary to bring about the policy-making

51

TABLE 3.3: *For or against a European government responsible to the European Parliament (percentages)*

	Belgium 1987	Belgium 1988	Denmark 1987	Denmark 1988	Germany 1987	Germany 1988	Greece 1987	Greece 1988	Spain 1987	Spain 1988	France 1987	France 1988	Ireland 1987	Ireland 1988
For	55	56	13	11	41	43	39	42	49	52	60	62	39	44
Against	12	25	64	67	28	30	21	18	10	14	19	16	23	18
No answer	33	19	23	22	31	28	41	39	40	34	21	22	38	38

	Italy 1987	Italy 1988	Luxembourg 1987	Luxembourg 1988	Netherlands 1987	Netherlands 1988	Portugal 1987	Portugal 1988	UK 1987	UK 1988	EC 1987	EC 1988
For	70	68	52	46	45	45	42	42	31	31	49	49
Against	11	10	21	32	25	30	14	9	45	44	24	24
No answer	19	22	28	22	29	25	44	49	24	26	28	27

SOURCE: Eurobarometer 29, June 1988, Table A-16.

TABLE 3.4: *Policy areas which should become the responsibility of a European government* (1987)*

	Belgium	Denmark	Germany	Greece	Spain	France	Ireland
External Relations	49	50	58	33	39	42	36
Cooperation with Third World	40	48	51	37	52	37	43
Security/Defense	60	69	57	49	58	72	50

	Italy	Luxembourg	Netherlands	Portugal	United Kingdom
External Relations	37	51	48	24	53
Cooperation with Third World	34	45	48	39	50
Security/Defense	53	60	54	40	64

* Percentages of those who provided answer to first question.
SOURCE: Eurobarometer 28 (December 1987) Table 12.

TABLE 3.5: *A responsible European government: socio-political profile by those in favour.*

	Sex		Age			Education			Incomes			
	Men	Women	-24	25-55	56+	-15	16-19	20+	++	+	-	--
In favor												
Generally	52	45	49	51	45	45	48	53	43	49	51	55
External Relations	44	44	47	44	43	38	46	53	41	43	42	49
Cooperation with Third World	44	41	41	44	41	39	42	51	44	38	42	40
Security/Defense	59	60	53	58	67	60	61	56	62	59	61	59

	Opinion Leadership				Value Orientation			Political Self-Placement			EC
	++	+	-	--	Materialists	Mixed	Post-materialists	Left	Centre	Right	
In favor generally	58	53	50	37	47	50	53	56	49	45	49
External Relations	48	48	44	35	38	44	59	46	43	46	44
Cooperation with Third World	46	47	40	35	37	41	55	46	39	42	42
Security/Defense	59	59	61	59	61	63	45	55	60	59	60

SOURCE: Eurobarometer 28 (December 1987) Table A-11.

changes is quite limited. This has been demonstrated by the rejection of the EP draft treaty for European Union on the part of most member governments. This treaty, if accepted, would have produced most of the external relations powers to which most of those who voice an opinion among the West European public opinion seem to aspire. The Commission as likely beneficiary of these changes would also be eager to be accommodative, but again lacks the political power to bring about a full Community foreign policy. But as an ally of the EP, it may be able to promote these EPC changes whenever favorable international opportunities may arise in the external relations competencies which the Commission exercises now.

An important part in moving the EPC and other policy-making initiatives forward will be played by the reaction of the national foreign policy bureaucracies to such a development. Research conducted during the late 1960s and 1970s seemed to indicate that national foreign ministry officials were more sympathetic to European Union efforts than other national bureaucracies because many of the former were intimately involved in the process of European integration.[8] What the attitudes of the national EPC officials are at present is difficult to ascertain without intensive field research. But basically one must assume that there is continuing competition between Eurocrats and national civil services, and the latter are not very eager to give up the prerogatives, power, and perks which they have acquired over the years by transfering EPC competences to the Commission. Nevertheless, national EPC officials could be profitable targets for the exertion of public opinion influence to bring EPC activities under complete EC control.

The final and potentially most rewarding target for public opinion influence must be the EC member governments and legislatures and through them the EC Council of Ministers. Acceptance of the EP draft treaty of 1984 would of course solve the problem at least as far as external relations and a common foreign policy are concerned, but defense and security are so intermeshed with current international, especially East-West, issues that the complexity of the latter problem area makes any purely European solution highly questionable for the time being.[9] On the other hand, it may just be the swirl of outside pressures which could convince the national governments that a 'European' government could offer vistas for the future which individual governments would be unable to pursue. Hence, while I think that public influence and pressure will be insufficient under the current constellation of both domestic and international politics to produce the desired results, some forward movement in the transfer of EPC to greater EC control cannot be completely dismissed and the Schmitter theory of 'externalization' may see further confirmation.

CONCLUSION

Public opinion survey data indicate that substantial numbers of Europeans would like to go beyond the proposals for 1992 and have a European government. They would also like to acquire a common foreign policy and move toward a common defense and security policy, although with a somewhat lower plurality. But how *deeply* these attitudes are held and how *eagerly* these goals are pursued, is uncertain. For years, opinion polls have shown strong support for European unification, but real progress has been quite limited. Nevertheless, the fact that leadership groups show decidedly stronger support for a common EC foreign policy than the general public, is reassuring.

It is also uncertain whether a possible socialization process among foreign policy officials in the member states has been operative during the last years and if a gradual adoption of 'European' values has taken place within the foreign policy bureaucracies that might make the future transfer of national policy control to EC control more acceptable. Full success in reaching the 1992 objectives may have a spillover effect on EC control over all external relations, and the continuation of the externalization process may also contribute to attaining what many Europeans see a desirable goal: a common foreign policy, further cooperation with the Third World, and perhaps eventually a European defense and security policy.

NOTES

1. For details see Luard, Evan (1986) 'A European Foreign Policy?' *International Affairs* (London), 62 (4): 1573–83.
2. See, for example, Mally, Gerhard (1973) *The European Community in Perspective: The New Europe, The United States and the World* (Lexington, Mass. Heath), pp. 51–68.
3. Schmitter, Philippe C. 'Three Neo-Functional Hypotheses about Regional Integration', *International Organization* 23 (Winter 1969): 165. See also his 'A Revised Theory of Regional Integration' in *International Organization* 24 (Autumn 1970): 848.
4. See the extensive information in *European Political Cooperation (EPC)* 5th ed. (published by the Press and Information Office of the FRG, Bonn, 1988).
5. 'The Mood Theory: A Study of Public Opinion and Foreign Policy' *American Political Science Review* 64 (1970): 536–46. See also William L. Lunch, 'American Public Opinion and the War in Vietnam', *Western Political Quarterly* 32 (March 1979), 21–44.
6. *European Political Cooperation (EPC)* op. cit., p. 84.
7. About 1 000 persons constituted the sample in each country. See *Eurobarometer* 29 June 1988, p. A–3.
8. Cf. Feld, Werner J. (1970) *Transnational Business Collaboration Among Common Market Countries* (New York: Praeger Publishers), pp. 87–96.
9. See Kirchner, Emil J. (1988) 'Has The Single European Act Opened the Door For a European Security Policy?' Paper delivered at IPSA (August).

4 The Political Prospects for Europe in the Wake of the Single European Act: a Response to Public Expectations

Emile Noël, Principal of the European
University Institute, Florence

The emergence of the Eurobarometer surveys made it clear that there was a gradually growing current of support for the idea of European integration in most Community countries. But at the same time, there was some scepticism as to whether rapid development was possible and whether the institutions were up to the task of bringing about changes of any substance. The number of voters who stayed away from the polls at the second European elections in 1984 was confirmation of that disenchantment.

The snail's pace of Community progress, especially during the last major crisis between 1979 and 1984, offered ample grounds for such scepticism. 'Europessimism' was the 'in' thing. Following the entry into force of the Single European Act in July 1987, and the success of the Brussels and Hanover European Councils in February and June 1988, however, Europe is now on the move again. There is widespread support for the single European market, not only in the world of business and finance but among the general public as well. What is more, the idea has become a 'hit' with the media, a topic of party political propaganda, and has even caught on with the advertisers. In short, it is the galvanizing force which Europe has so sorely lacked over the past twenty years.

The special Eurobarometer survey at the end of 1987 duly showed a renewed interest in the Community and its political and economic implications.

This new upsurge of popular enthusiasm for Europe is not just an artificially created phenomenon. And although it is the single market that has most caught the public imagination, that is only the beginning. Implementing the Single European Act in full should take us a great deal further than that, whether in terms of the economic and social dimensions of Europe or in the monetary sphere, not to mention other foreseeable or potential political developments. Will the Europe of everyday reality be

57

anything like the Europe of our dreams which the Eurobarometer surveys have so often identified? I should like to explore a few of the prospects for such a Europe.

THE ROLE OF THE SINGLE ACT

Let me begin by stressing the importance, in terms of the Community's future, of the new purpose which the Single Act has injected into the Treaties – the aim of establishing economic and social cohesion in the Community, in other words bringing the less prosperous countries or regions up towards the level of economic prosperity and social progress enjoyed by the central regions. There was some provision for this in the Treaty of Rome, but it was couched in very loose terms and nothing was done to give it any real substance until very late in the day. The Single Act has created an entirely different situation.

All through the period when the Act was being negotiated, the Commission and the Member States were confronted with a twofold imperative: the need to create the right conditions for vigorous action to establish the large internal market by the given deadline, and the need to make sure that certain less prosperous regions or countries in the Community would not be relegated to the sidelines as a result. Here the answer was to make more effective economic and social cohesion one of the Community's goals so that the countries concerned, the other Member States, and the Community as a whole could work together to make the aim a reality.

The Commission and the Member States resisted the temptation to set prior conditions. It was agreed to include two new chapters (on the internal market and cohesion) in the Single Act, both on an equal footing and equally binding, without one being subordinate to the other, so that action on them has to be planned jointly but independently.

This sets the stage for achieving a final interplay – synergy – which will have to be sustained throughout the period while the internal market is being set up and probably long beyond that. I would stress that new keyword – synergy – which I think will be the main feature of the Community's new strategy for the years ahead.

During the seventies and early eighties, abuse of the unanimity rule and the resulting near-standstill led to the routine use of package deals as a way of achieving fitful progress and settling what were sometimes very mixed bags of outstanding problems. The danger was that all-round agreement would simply come down to the lowest common denominator – and indeed this is what often happened. But with the Community now on the move again, a bolder approach can be pursued. Unlike the package deal, which is a static operation, synergy generates a forward momentum and acts as a spur to further progress. Fostering this interplay between two or more otherwise independent issues will mean that progression of one will help produce progress on the other, which in turn will contribute politically to the success of the first. The package deal is a levelling process, whereas synergy gives rise to a cumulative process building up towards maximum results in all the sectors concerned.

This new strategy has to be properly understood if we are to appreciate clearly what developments are possible or likely over the next few years. At first sight, the requirement for simultaneous progress on completing the single market and strengthening economic and social cohesion might seem to pose some difficulty, not to say a further obstacle, on the already stony road to a Community free of internal frontiers. But this view overlooks the fact that no country is prepared to let itself be relegated to the sidelines by an uncontrolled opening-up of the markets. And the lessons of the past have not been forgotten. Holding back progress in one field (whether it was the single market or cohesion) would inevitably trigger off a North-South conflict, halting all movement and bringing the Community to a standstill; whereas a determined effort to achieve the maximum in both spheres – swifter progress on the internal market and stronger cohesion – will mean transcending the stresses and strains, sustaining the Community's momentum and securing agreement while maximizing results.

A strategy such as this is something of a gamble. It needed to be put to the test, which is one of the reasons why the Commission moved so swiftly in presenting its communication on 'The Single Act: A new frontier for Europe' in February 1987. The Council's conclusions of the following February, which took up and in some respects even went beyond the Commission's proposals, confirmed the soundness of the new strategy. With vigorous progress on the internal market in prospect, agreement was reached on reforming the common agricultural policy (bringing production and expenditure under control), doubling the sums allocated to the Community's structural Funds, and giving the Community the new own resources needed to guarantee the continued development of the main common policies over the next five years, especially those intended under the Single Act to help boost economic and social cohesion.

More recently, the Council's adoption in June 1988 of a Directive providing for the complete liberalization of capital movements by the middle of 1990 is a further instance of the same strategy in operation. To prevent abuse of this new freedom, measures to harmonize tax law and certain prudential rules and to strengthen the European monetary system are essential. These were to be adopted by 1990, but they were not made a prior condition; instead the Community is relying on the momentum and the incentive for progress generated by the adoption of the Directive. Looking back to the Community's origins, we can see some resemblance between the present strategy and Jean Monnet's recipe of contriving a 'dynamic imbalance', in other words taking on commitments which, when fully implemented, necessarily entail further subsequent progress. At the time the ECSC Treaty, with a common market confined to coal and steel, was a fine example of this approach.

My first conclusion, then, is that this strategy of achieving progress through synergy, inherent in the Single Act, will shape the course of the Community's development over the years to come. The end in view is to combine completion of the internal market with greater economic and social cohesion so as to create not just a single market but a single European economic and social area.

A EUROPEAN ECONOMIC STRATEGY

These, then, are the bases on which Community policy for the near future will have to build, starting from the Single European Act. However, the Act should not be seen as the end of the road but merely as a stage in a continuing process, as stated in the preamble. In particular, the establishment of the single market and the economic and social area will soon make it necessary to strengthen the powers and responsibilities of the institutions so as to enable them to consolidate that market, ensure its internal consistency and keep an eye on the way it is run.

Studies on the Community's economic strategy (such as the report by Sr. Padoa-Schioppa in 1987) show that for the internal market to be viable it must:

– involve a certain degree of monetary union, with common bodies to regulate and manage the system;

– involve close coordination of the Member States' economic policies, with due regard for the demands of economic and social development in the Community as a whole;

– act and react as a single entity at international level.

The recent European Council in Hanover (June 1988) confirmed these guidelines when it embarked on the political road towards economic and monetary union by asking a high-level committee (consisting of the governors of the central banks and several leading independent figures) chaired by the President of the Commission, M. Delors, to submit to it 'proposals for concrete stages leading towards this union'. It is not for me to speculate on what conclusions the Committee will reach, but it can be expected to recommend the establishment of a European monetary authority with real powers (without this necessarily being, from the very outset, a 'European central bank'). Something will also have to be done to rectify the manifest inadequacy of the instruments provided by the Treaty of Rome for economic policy coordination and harmonization. For this is an area where unanimous Council decisions are required on a proposal from the Commission, and long experience has shown how weak this procedure is.

Lastly, the Community will have to be given commensurate external powers, in other words, very wide (perhaps even exclusive) powers over external economic and monetary policy. In all probability, such exclusive powers (far wider than any derived from the extension of the Community's internal powers sanctioned by the Court of Justice) would be essential to guarantee the cohesion of the European economic and social area *vis-à-vis* the outside world in the face of the tensions we can expect to see over the next few years.

This is the prospect which prompted M. Delors, speaking to Parliament in Strasbourg, to envisage the establishment of an embryonic 'European government'. The Single Act has already pointed the way with the new rule that executive powers should be the exclusive province of the Commission. This will gradually free the Council of Ministers of its residual executive functions so that it can devote itself to its role as legislator (working with the European Parliament). If the Commission's powers are to be reinforced in this way, not only in existing fields but above all in new areas connected with economic and monetary union, fresh thought will have to be given to its structure and the way its members are appointed so as to make it more efficient and bring in a more democratic system of appointment.

If the government in Europe is strengthened, democracy in Europe will have to advance at the same speed. It will not do merely to colour in the economic, monetary and social aspects of the Single Act in line with the requirements of economic and monetary union; the institutional aspect will have to be fleshed out as well, so as to give real legislative power to the European Parliament. Within the 'legislative authority' (Council, Parliament and Commission), an elected Parliament will need to have at least the same weight as the Council.

In putting forward all this, I am not simply giving a rehash of the spill-over theory of the early sixties, which was that political and institutional progress were the inevitable consequence of economic integration – an over-optimistic theory which took a heavy battering when it came to practical reality. The likelihood is that some form of interaction – or synergy – will develop between completion of the internal market and economic and monetary union on the one hand, and institutional progress (as regards Parliament and the Commission) on the other, as demands for enhanced economic instruments combine with demands for progress on the institutional front to bring about maximum reforms.

COOPERATION IN POLITICAL AND DEFENCE MATTERS

These are the likely developments in the Community of Twelve if it presses ahead with the Single Act with as much determination as it showed at the

European Councils in Brussels and Hanover. Throughout this chapter, I have been thinking only of the Community of Twelve – the Twelve who negotiated the Single Act and have embarked on the venture of the single market. But it has to be admitted that what may appear extremely ambitious to the Twelve (in view of the stand taken by some Member States) must seem extremely modest to the federalists, especially those – whether governments (such as the Italian or Spanish) or parliaments (such as the Italian or Belgian) – who have come out openly in favour of European political union.

Might progress in political cooperation (on foreign policy) be a way of moving in this direction? The Single Act confined itself to codifying the arrangements that had grown up from 1979 onwards on the basis of the Davignon report and subsequent reports. Procedures have been refined over the years, but political cooperation is generally agreed to have gone as far as it can towards the ultimate goal of a common external policy. There is no denying the fact that some of the Twelve (Ireland – because of its policy of neutrality – together with Denmark and Greece) have adopted a restrictive interpretation of the provisions of the London report and the Single Act by which the political and economic aspects of European security may be dealt with under political cooperation. And more generally, reservations on the part of some members and lack of commitment on the part of others has meant that the European view is not being put forward as such in any of the negotiations under way between the United States and the Soviet Union on the dismantling of medium-range missiles, even though those negotiations are of vital concern to Europe.

Maintaining security in Europe means responding to the imperatives of a continent which aims to retain control over its own destiny, and this calls for common consideration of the issues involved followed by a common stance. A European initiative in the field of security would be an opportunity for a genuine political revival of the European ideal, a revival which could be launched by those of the Twelve prepared to commit themselves right away. This was the goal which Altiero Spinelli and the European Parliament saw on the horizon in February 1984, when they proposed that their draft Treaty establishing the European Union should come into force in those countries which approved it, provided they represented a large enough proportion of the Community's population.

Is there any prospect of such a European initiative? By reason of geography and political realities, much depends on the position adopted in the short term by Germany and France. Statements by their leaders suggest that neither country has ruled out the possibility of moving in this direction; but nor has either of them taken any decision yet. Such an initiative would certainly find favour with a large section of public opinion in the Community. As in the early 1950s, there is a broad consensus (broader even than it was then) that the countries of Europe, or at least some of them, should act in unison on matters of security, defence and foreign policy.

This is as far as I will go as regards the possibilities, since there are major obstacles in the way in other areas (the structure of the Atlantic alliance, for example, or the status of national nuclear forces).

For a long time now, the Eurobarometer surveys have helped the Community institutions and activists working for the cause of European integration to sustain confidence despite the setbacks, to stay on course through fair weather and foul, and to safeguard existing gains come what may, so as to provide a foundation for revival. There were solid grounds for that confidence, and there is no doubt that underlying support from a great (though rather silent) majority of people in the Community helped both governments and the Community institutions – when the time came – to take the difficult decisions needed which have made a revival credible. On the economic plane, the interplay between the internal market, economic and monetary union, and institutional advances offers grounds for great expectations, while a quantum leap towards political union is once again on the agenda.

October 1988

5 Switzerland: To Be or Not To Be – in Europe?

Anna Melich, Commission of the
European Communities

'To be or not to be in Europe' – that is the (burning) question which a steadily growing number of Swiss have been asking themselves following the announcement of the date set by the European Community for the completion of the Single Market. As 1992 draws nearer, the Swiss need a satisfactory answer. But which individuals, which institutions have the right and the authority to decide one way or the other? What several centuries of history failed to do, the target set by the Single European Act has already achieved. Switzerland has started wondering about its place in the cultural, political and economic dimensions common to the European area. No one can deny that geographically it is part of the European continent. So what prevents the Swiss from feeling 'European' in every other way?

The scientific community, learned societies, the media, the political leadership and political parties, trade associations and the general public are all thinking harder and harder about 1992 and what it would mean for Switzerland to be left sitting on the sidelines of the European Community.

THE SCIENTIFIC COMMUNITY

Swiss academics, appropriately, were among the first to become involved in the debate. Scientific and philosophic Switzerland is and has long been closely identified with the European venture. In 1946, just after World War II, Winston Churchill delivered his main 'European' speech in Zurich. European federalists met several times in Montreux between 1946 and 1948. Thinkers such as Denis de Rougemont were pondering European identity and bringing together other figures keen to propose solutions of integration, federation or regionalization.

After the Congress of the Hague, in May 1948, Denis de Rougemont, under the auspices of the European Movement, founded the European Cultural Centre in Geneva. Since then, the ECC has had a hand in the creation of several institutions devoted to the study and development of the European venture with friends sharing the same ideals. Among them, the Institut Universitaire d'Etudes Europeennes (IUEE) in 1963 and the

Foundation Archives Europeennes in 1984. After Denis de Rougemont, in 1977 management of the IUEE was entrusted to Professor Henri Schwamm. The IUEE in Geneva is the force behind studies on manifold facets of European integration: the history of ideas and thought, political science, law, economics and regional policy. Professor Henri Rieben of the University of Lausanne chairs the Jean Monnet Foundation for Europe and is in charge of the European Research Centre in Lausanne.

It is in that same scientific community, where interest in the European idea is found mainly among those in the French-speaking universities and study centres in Switzerland, that the research and the reports compiled in the European Community (EC) institutions are carefully studied and analyzed.

In this connection, it can be said that the results of surveys made regularly by the EC Commission among Community Europeans, i.e. the Eurobarometers, are read and consulted with keen interest. The Eurobarometer is and has always been an unrivalled working tool no less for Swiss research scientists than for their Community counterparts. Could this be because the Swiss universities, especially the French-speaking ones, employ a body of professors and teaching staff consisting in large part of foreigners (mostly Europeans) and therefore naturally more concerned by non-Swiss affairs? This may have been so up to the late eighties. But the proportion of foreigners is now far lower than it was, for various reasons, only one of them being the Swiss Confederation's restrictive policy on foreign residents.

This then cannot entirely explain the increasing use of Community surveys in the world of research. It is simply that these data are invaluable for giving an insight into the attitudes of the people of Europe towards the European Community and its policies, towards the European Parliament or towards certain issues of immediate concern in Europe. There is no need to underline the value of fully comparable time series going back to 1973. Other results deriving from psycho-sociological and psycho-political measurements are the delight of political scientists, psychologists and sociologists.

One reproach, and not a minor one, made by readers of Eurobarometer outside the Community: it gives data only from samples taken in the twelve member countries of the present community (and previously, only ten or nine)! How often would non-Community readers have liked to be able to compare a particular attitude of the French, the Germans or the Italians with that of their own compatriots in Switzerland, Austria or Sweden! Greeks, Spaniards and Portuguese felt the same way during years of labour and research; but their wishes were granted before they actually joined the Community. As early as 1980 for Greece and 1985 for Spain and Portugal, Jacques René Rabier provided this information in his Eurobarometer.

But the same Jacques René Rabier, the man who lovingly watched over that splendid instrument of analysis that is Eurobarometer, from conception through early development to full maturity, did not overlook the universities of non-Community countries. He visited several of them on a number of occasions. He succeeded in identifying the people who could appreciate what he had to offer and help him with his undertaking. He made the researchers aware of the problems of European union and encouraged the young ones to pursue to greater depths analyses that would then figure in articles and papers at scientific meetings. He enlisted the aid of mathematicians who could help him in devising indexes, scales and typologies since incorporated into Eurobarometer's standard tabulations. The frustration felt in the non-Community countries left out of Eurobarometer was thus more than offset by the satisfaction of sharing in its compilation and use.

We are requesters, so let us by all means request, but at the same time offer resources through the projects that Switzerland could implement with the assistance of the EFTA countries so as to obtain an adequate critical mass. Which means? That we must forge links between the existing EEC projects and projects to be devised on the Swiss side involving EFTA. In particular, I have in mind all the research projects, university or other. It will cost money, but as the saying goes, you get what you pay for.[1]

This quotation taken from an article by the Professor of Political Geography at the University of Geneva rather epitomizes the spirit currently prevailing in the Swiss universities and particularly in the French-speaking universities. There is a great deal of disgruntlement about not being part of the ERASMUS programme. The feeling of being left out, especially among the students, is spurring the trend towards support for membership.

THE MASS MEDIA

It was when the Single European Act was making news at the end of 1987 that the more discerning circles began to take serious notice of the Europe of Twelve now in full swing. The press, especially the French-language press, was the beacon constantly flashing out warning to the neighbours of France, Italy and Germany. With the weekly magazine *L'Hebdo* in the front rank, in January 1988, a special study entitled '1992, Europe and us' was followed by a string of other articles and symposia organized by the magazine. There have since been other similar initiatives. In October 1988 there was a broadcast by the Radio Television Suisse Romande – 'Temps Present' showed '320 million Europeans, and us, and us . . .' Three days later, the same company put out an open debate on the subject 'If Switzerland went European?'

The point at issue is always the same: 'do we join and lose our identity and our own political features, or do we stay out and be left behind by the progress and wellbeing of the year 2000?' But the questions are warped by the political ideology and leanings of the questioner. Opinion has always been divided in Switzerland as to whether the country should be outward-looking or inward-looking. The marked divide corresponds to the language areas, with the press in each region echoing local feeling.

At the beginning of 1987 the French-language press took up the issue, while its German counterpart held off, reluctant to become involved in the debate. In 1988, at the general assembly of the French-speaking Union of Newspapers, Otto Stich, Head (Minister) of the Department of Economy and Finance, who had just recently been elected President of the Confederation for 1988, said he was astonished at being grilled on relations between Switzerland and the Community. 'It wouldn't have happened in the German-speaking area!' he exclaimed. He had been caught off guard. But it wouldn't happen again.

Towards the end of 1988 the debate was in full swing in the French-speaking part of the country and was becoming all-invading! There was scarcely a meeting, seminar, symposium or conference which did not in one way or another refer to 1992 and Switzerland's position. The press gave it wide coverage, and even took the initiative of commissioning its own surveys which faithfully reported the French-speakers' demands to be members of the 'European club'.

The substance of this debate even entered the realm of fantasy. 1992 stood for paradise, a magic date on which all European problems would be solved and when, Switzerland, left on the sideline, would begin its inexorable decline. If only the Community's own citizens felt the same way, President Delors would be in seventh heaven!

The German-language radio and television began to take notice shortly before, but especially after, the Federal Council published the 'Report on the position of Switzerland in the European integration process' in August 1982.[2] 'When the authorities become involved, there must be a reason': companies and occupational groupings which before that had been worried about the implications of the single market for Switzerland, had found their concern echoed only in the financial pages of the specialist press. The general public was still missing from the debate.

POLITICAL LEADERSHIP

The Federal Council's report on 'The position of Switzerland in the European Integration Process'[3] was compiled by the Integration Bureau of the Department of Public Economy and the Department of Foreign Affairs. It was already an innovation for the administration of the Swiss

Confederation to have created a Bureau straddling two Departments.

Published in the mid-summer of 1988, the Report says in short: for the time being Switzerland does not wish to join the European Community; it prefers to take a pragmatic and sectoral approach. But anything is still possible; the future is wide open and Switzerland might one day decide to enter the EC.

The way proposed by the Federal Council, which has been dubbed the 'third way,' 'parallel way,' or 'pragmatic way,' is officially called a 'policy of active integration'. It is based on two major principles: compatibility and reciprocity. It consists of continuing the current policy within EFTA, and reaching agreements within GATT to step up cooperation as far as possible with the European Community.

It needed two French-speaking members of the Federal Council at the head of two key departments to start 'talking European' and so speed up the thinking on relations between Switzerland and the European Community. The Vaudois radical Jean-Pascal Delamuraz, former mayor of Lausanne, Head of the Department of Public Economy, launched the movement with the motto 'have the European reflex!', which means adapt any new economic measure taken in Switzerland to Community standards. Should Switzerland then one day apply for membership, it would be more swiftly accepted by the other members. The legal framework would be compatible with the Community's. The Neuchatel socialist, Rene Felber, who took charge of the Department of Foreign Affairs in December 1987, set up, in his first days in office, the Comite de reflexion, or 'think-tank,' on Switzerland and the Community, consisting for the most part of diplomats. The Committee promptly buckled down to the task of identifying the effects and implications of non-membership. Was it quite by chance that these moves were made by the only two French-speakers among the seven members of the Federal Council?

'Accession is not possible today, for the political price that Switzerland would pay is too high', said the report on integration: neutrality compromised, direct democracy and federalism at risk. But the Federal Council was well aware 'that rejecting accession to the EC will undoubtedly have more serious repercussions today than in 1972,[4] for Switzerland will be formally excluded from the Community decision-making process whilst Community decisions will increasingly affect it.'[5]

In the cantons, many members of the Council of States and administrative councillors support closer ties between Switzerland and the European Community. Guy-Olivier Segond, the dynamic administrative councillor of the city of Geneva, attacked the Federal Council's report:

it is far too concerned with the economic approach. The question is not so much: does Switzerland want to join or not? For the popular answer, today at any rate, would probably be 'No.' The real question is whether

Switzerland can avoid accession. Personally, I don't think so. So we must begin preparing now. But whether we join or whether we stay out, there will be a price to pay, and it will be a political one. (*L'Hebdo*, 15 September 1988)

Segond lays the emphasis on the human and scientific problem and all that is connected with a people's Europe. MEDIA, ERASMUS, EUREKA, COMETT, and so on, are attractive projects which Switzerland is largely having to do without. The free movement of persons and workers within the Community is one of the most exciting objectives of the plans for 1992. But if the Swiss want to join in, they will have to revise all their immigration laws. What a thought!

POLITICAL PARTIES AND OCCUPATIONAL GROUPS

It is hard to rank the Swiss political parties according to their pro- or anti-European leanings. Nearly all the main parties appear to some degree attracted by the European Community. Perhaps the radical left and the extreme right are more openly antagonistic to the European idea. We can quote Francois Saint-Ouen[6] in saying that 'what is probably one of the main factors of the originality of the Swiss approach: the conceptual divides are "liberal" vs "bureaucratic," "supranational" vs "federal"'.

The Community is seen as belonging to the unattractive 'bureaucratic-supranational' category, the exact opposite of the 'liberal-federal', much closer to the Swiss tradition. But for all that, the Liberals, close to international trade and banking, stress the advantages of the free market; the Socialists try not to forget the international nature of socialism; the Christian Democrats, knowing the role of Christian Democrats in the making of Europe, are bound to support the initiatives in connection with the Europe of Twelve. Perhaps the most reluctant among the big parties are the Radicals, linked to the cottage industries, small business and the French-speaking farmers, and the Swiss People's Party, which represents the German-speaking farming community.[7]

Table 5.1 illustrates the reluctance on the part of Swiss firms to plunge into the Community pool of trade and industry. On the other hand, it highlights the enthusiasm of the politicians (notably the French- and Italian-speakers) for Switzerland to embark on the Community course. However, the European Union of Switzerland's survey can be qualified by other results. Researchers in the University of Geneva have questioned all the middle-ranking officers and leading figures of the four big Swiss political parties, asking them what were the most frequent talking points in the party, and produced an index[8] of importance according to frequency of discussion.

TABLE 5.1: *Surveys of socio-political groupings/companies*

Date published	Commissioned by	Sample	Accession (%) For	Against	*FS	For GS (%)	T
1987	European Union of Switzerland	414 candidates for National Council elections	70	30	84	63	84
Oct. 1988	GESO (European Synergy and Engineering Group)	Company heads	30	70			
Nov. 1988		347 companies	10	90			
May 1988	Vaud Chamber of Industry and Commerce	Exporting and non-exporting firms	75% of exporting firms and 60% of non-exporting firms say they are concerned about the problems of the Single European Market				

* FS = French-speakers; GS = German-speakers; T = Ticino (Italian-speakers)

TABLE 5.2: *Index of frequency of discussion of subjects in the
Swiss political parties*

	*RDP	*CDP	*SDP	*SPP
Local politics	4.87	4.61	4.81	4.59
Cantonal politics	3.92	2.48	3.79	4.59
Federal politics	3.03	2.85	3.28	3.00
European politics	1.39	1.23	1.75	1.53
International politics	1.31	1.14	1.92	1.31
Relations with the other parties	3.08	2.81	1.96	2.43
Internal party matters	2.35	2.30	3.44	3.30

*RDP = Radical Democratic Party (Parti Radical Democratique – Freisinnig Demokratische Partei)
CDP = Christian Democratic Party (Parti Democrate Chretien – Christlichdemokratische Volkspartei)
SDP = Social-Democratic Party (Parti Socialiste Suisse – Sozialdemokratische Partei)
SPP = Swiss People's Party (Union Democratique du Centre – Schweizerische Volkspartei)
SOURCE: Ural Ayberk: *Les leaders d'opinion suisses et les questions europeennes*, academic seminar on the 'European Dimension in Switzerland's Future', Forum Helveticum, Chateau de Lenzbourg, 7–10 March 1989.

The figures in Table 5.2 are hardly encouraging as to the frequency with which European and international issues are discussed by the leaders and officers of the Swiss parties. The Social-Democratic Party is slightly ahead of the others on the subject of Europe, but Europe figures less on its agendas than does international politics in general. The other three parties give an edge to European as opposed to international politics. These are subjective assessments but they do clearly reflect the attitudes of the big Swiss parties to the problem.

PUBLIC OPINION

Swiss opinion polls on European integration vary widely in content and quality (Table 5.3). The first one was conducted in October 1986 and published in *L'Hebdo* magazine of 13 November 1986. It showed almost level pegging between supporters (42.8 per cent) and opponents (42.5 per cent) of 'possible future accession'. A year and a half later, in February–March 1988, feeling was still as equally divided throughout the country: 43.8 per cent for accession and 44.4 per cent against. In May 1988, only 34 per cent wanted accession against 38 per cent who didn't.

Appreciable differences are nevertheless discernible between language areas. In these polls and those that followed, the gap between French-

TABLE 5.3: *Public opinion polls*

Date of interview Commission by (Conducted by)	Sample	Accession* (%)		Yes (%)			No (%)		
		Yes	No	FS+	GS+	IS+	FS+	GS+	IS+
November 1986 L'Hebdo (MIS)	1.006	42.8	42.5	54.6	36.4				
February–March 1988 Coop. Zeitung	600	43.8	44.4	68.4	31.5	60	18.6	53.7	23.6
February–March 1988 Institute of Political Science University of Lausanne (AES)	1.500	39.7	27.1‡	26.1	12.1		12.3	27.6	
May 1988 Sch. Handelszeitung (ISOPUBLIC)	969	34	38	45	30		20	44	
June 1988 Tribune de GE (MIS)	617	46.7	37	68.8	39.3		16	43.8	
July 1988 Swiss Society for Political and Economic Research (IMR)	500	54	30						
Dec. 1988/Jan. 1989 Department of Political Science, University of Geneva (ISOPUBLIC)	1.400	45	32	49	42	49	23	38	29

* The 'Don't knows' and 'No reply's', even when known, have been omitted.
+ FS = French-speakers; GS = German-speakers; IS = Italian-speakers.
‡ 'Switzerland must not stay out (. . .) it must go in . . . agree or disagree?'

speakers – far more receptive to the European Community – and that of German-speakers – distinctly averse – is very wide. Between November 1986 and December 1988, the average difference between the favourable opinions of the two populations was 9.17 per cent. Italian-speaking Switzerland, i.e. Ticino, is closer to the French-speaking part, but the samples rarely cover that remote and less populated part of the country.

From a study of various surveys, Roland Ruffieux concludes that the German-speakers are more consistent in their attitudes than the French-speakers:

> Although the German-speakers tend rather systematically to reject accession and its implications as well as any alterations to domestic policy that would bring Switzerland closer to the Community, they would appear to do so knowingly. The French-speakers, altogether more undecided, while knowing little about the various forms of European cooperation, desire accession, would even go so far as to vote 'yes,' but reject the main implications.[9]

Apart from language area, the supporters of 'Community Europe' are to be found among the young, the town-dwellers and the left of the political spectrum.

Among the reasons given against accession, we find the stock arguments paraded by political leaders and by the media: federalism, lack of compatibility of Community rules with Switzerland's status of neutrality and lack of compatibility with the political institutions rooted in semi-direct democracy, such as 'initiatives' and referendums. On the economic side, the existence of a cosseted farming industry and the special features of the banking and insurance systems rule out any possibility of alignment on Community standards. The arguments of those who want closer ties with the Community are inspired by fear of isolation, the danger of intellectual sclerosis, the feeling of being as European as the 'Twelve' and the need to defend the economic interests of their homeland.

The Lausanne University survey of February–March 1988 proposed a number of issues (Table 5.4) justifying cooperation between Switzerland and the European Community. The answers from those who accepted the conditions were half-hearted, to say the least, as soon as it came to measures at odds with the traditional political and economic system.

In the May 1988 survey, for the *Schweizerische Handelszeitung*, conducted by ISOPUBLIC, Zurich,[10] respondents were asked to instance the advantages and drawbacks of joining or not joining the Community, by means of an open question (Table 5.5).

From mid-1988 onwards (Table 5.3), the polls published in the media showed a slight swing in general public opinion. Opinions in favour of accession began to move slightly ahead of those against. In June 1988 the

TABLE 5.4: *Areas which would justify cooperation between Switzerland and the Community*

	%
Scientific and technological research	72.9
Free movement of goods	50.1
Same passport for all European nationals	40.3
Free movement of workers	40.1
Integration into a common monetary system (EMS) and a common currency	31.4
Cuts in protectionist measures (subsidies) for our agriculture	29.0
Introduction of VAT	19.4
Transfer to the EEC of certain powers of the Confederation and the cantons	13.4
Limitation of neutrality	12.1
Curtailment of popular rights (e.g. no more referendums)	8.0

TABLE 5.5: *Advantages and drawbacks of joining or not joining the Community*

JOINING	NOT JOINING
Advantages	*Advantages*
– advantage for the economy = 7% – less isolation = 7% (all the other answers less than 4%)	Preserving neutrality, sovereignty, autonomy and liberty = 4% (the other answers no more than 1%)
Drawbacks	*Drawbacks*
Loss of neutrality, autonomy, sovereignty and liberty = 22% (The other answers no more than 8%)	Isolation: 19% (26% in French-speaking area, 17% in German-speaking area) No change = 17% Problems with exports = 7% (The other answers no more than 6%)
Don't know/ No reply = 29%	Don't know/ No reply = 36%

weight of the opinion of the French-speaking area (68.8 per cent) pushed up the national average of those in favour to 46.7 per cent compared with 37 per cent against.

In January 1989, a survey by the Political Science Department of the University of Geneva based on a sample of 1 400 Swiss from all regions yielded even more positive results in favour of accession (Table 5.6).

The percentages are distinctly positive in the French- and Italian-speaking regions. However, should a referendum put the question of accession at the present time, the weight of the peripheral regions would

TABLE 5.6: *Swiss attitudes toward membership in the Community*

Question: There is a great deal of talk these days about Switzerland's relations with all the other European countries. As regards the European Community, that is the Common Market, do you think that Switzerland should belong to it?

	Total	FS*	GS*	IS*
Yes	45	49	42	49
No	32	23	38	29
Don't know/No reply	23	28	30	22
	(1 400)	(393)	(807)	(200)

If yes: Do you believe that Switzerland should apply for membership as soon as possible, that it should still wait to ascertain the situation after 1992 (Single European Market), or that it should wait longer than that?

	Total	FS	GS	IS
Apply quickly	41	49	39	33
Wait for 1992	42	35	44	47
Wait longer	11	9	10	18
Don't know/No reply	6	7	7	2
	(633)	(191)	(343)	(99)

If no: For what main reason do you think that Switzerland should not join the European Community: (a) because it does not need the EC to continue to play a world role; (b) because membership of the Community is incompatible with its status of neutrality; (c) because Community membership impedes the process of direct democracy?

	Total	FS	GS	IS
No need of EC	24	23	23	29
Incompatibility with neutrality	36	31	35	46
Incompatibility with direct democracy	25	34	24	19
Don't know/No reply	15	12	18	6
	(458)	(90)	(309)	(59)

* FS = French speakers; GS = German speakers; IS = Italian speakers
SOURCE: Anna Melich, *Swiss Value Study* (1989)

not be enough to secure acceptance. The dual majority of the population and the cantons would be essential on an issue such as this, and it could not be achieved without the support of the German-speaking population and cantons. Other similar issues with a large measure of support in a section of the population – accession to the UN for example – have already suffered repeated setbacks.

Many of the surveys are thus conducted for the press, while others are commissioned by trade and business associations. Not all of them offer the necessary scientific guarantees that would allow the results to be considered comparable. A survey covering 600 or 500 people throughout the country cannot represent the whole spectrum of Swiss opinion. Ticino, as already noted, is frequently left out. A fair distribution of 500 respondents throughout the country would work out at only some 125 for the French-speaking area and 375 for the German-speaking area. How can any conclusions possibly be drawn from those numbers?

If the question of accession was really put to the population, controversy would rage, but as often happens, not always with arguments relevant to the issues. The issues would be too close to history and traditional Swiss values for the referendum campaign to remain impartial. The current surveys do not, unfortunately, allow us to predict the outcome of such a consultation should it one day happen. Patriotic reactions 'peculiar' to Swiss national character have so often proved to be unfathomable!

SWISS ACCESSION SEEN BY THE 'EUROPEANS'

In 1970, 1976, 1980 and 1986, a Eurobarometer question concerned the degree of trust that nations show towards one another. On each occasion Switzerland led the field from the standpoint of the trust it inspired in the people of the Community. Commenting on Switzerland's score in 1986, J.-R. Rabier wrote: 'The Swiss enjoy the great degree of trust. Switzerland could probably be said to be the archetypal "trustworthy" country. Geographically small and militarily neutral, it poses no threat; its international image is probably one of peacefulness, sheltered from the dangers which threaten the rest of the world.'[11]

In Eurobarometer 30 of December 1988, another question asked on behalf of an American research institute invited respondents to express an opinion about which of a number of countries should be admitted in the more or less foreseeable future (Table 5.7). It was found that 32 per cent of Community respondents would be willing to accept the accession of Switzerland and that 36 per cent would accept 'all' of them.

But does Switzerland deserve the trust it inspires in its geographical and cultural neighbours? Is real trust as blind as shown by the 1980, 1986, and 1988 Eurobarometers? Many rather murky financial affairs involving Switzerland have come to light in recent years. They have taken some of the shine off the rather idyllic image that Switzerland enjoys in the eyes of certain Europeans. All the same, the way these affairs have been handed – out in the open as befits a democracy – is enough to reassure the public mind.

In the end, it is Switzerland itself that is being difficult. There are political scientists and lawyers who are asking whether the European Community's institutions are sufficiently democratic for Switzerland to do it the honour of joining.

The political and economic objectives of the Community and of Switzerland largely overlap. In the long term, it is even likely that our objectives

TABLE 5.7: *Europeans' support for admission of new countries*

Question: It has been suggested that the Community be enlarged to include Austria, Finland, Norway, Sweden, Switzerland, Turkey. In your opinion, which of those countries should be allowed to join the Community?

Average of the Twelve in %*
(except for Luxembourg and Northern Ireland)

None	10
All	36
Switzerland	32
Austria	26
Sweden	25
Norway	24
Finland	19
Turkey	3
Don't know	15

* As more than one answer was possible, the percentages total more than 100.

TABLE 5.8: *Confidence in the Community among Swiss ethnic groups*

Question: Will you please tell me to what degree you have a great deal of confidence, some confidence, not much confidence or no confidence at all in the European Community.

	Total	FS	GS	IS
A great deal of confidence	10	9	9	20
Some confidence	42	47	38	42
Not much confidence	21	15	26	12
No confidence at all	9	7	11	4
Don't know	18	22	16	22
	(1 400)	(393)	(807)	(200)

SOURCE: Anna Melich, *Swiss Value Study*, 1989.

will have a better change of being attained within Europe than outside it. The time will then have come for total commitment to membership with no strings attached. But this cannot happen until the European institutions have been made democratic, until the Community has more strongly asserted its independence in foreign policy and defence and until there exists a clearer federalist structure and political and economic stability.[12]

The survey by Geneva University mentioned earlier quite clearly reveals what Swiss public opinion is actually saying. Like any other international organization the European Community merits, for the time being, no more than 'some confidence' or even 'not much confidence' (Table 5.8). From all the surveys and public opinion polls so far, the same conclusion can be drawn: 'yes, maybe, to accession' but only when the effects of the 1992 single market are known and if it can be achieved without having to give up any of the 'things uniquely Swiss'.

NOTES

1. Raffestin, Claude, *Domaine Public*, No. 912, April 1988.
2. 24 August 1988, Bern, Office of Federal Publications, Doc. 88.045.
3. Op. cit.
4. Date of the industrial free trade agreement with the European Community.
5. *L'Hebdo*, 15 September 1988.
6. 'Facing European Integration. The Case of Switzerland', *Journal of Common Market Studies*, 36 (3), March 1988, 273–85.
7. Saint-Ouen, Francois, op. cit., 279–80.
8. The index assigns a weighting of five to 'frequently', three to 'sometimes' and one to 'never'. The index thus varies between one and five.
9. Ruffieux, Roland (1989), *L'opinion publique face à l'intégration européenne: que disent et que ne disent pas les sondages?* Academic seminar on the 'European Dimension in Switzerland's Future', Forum Helveticum, Chateau de Lenzburg, 7–10 March.
10. *EG 1992 und die Schweiz*, April 1988, Zurich, 6 May 1988.
11. Eurobarometer 25, Commission of the European Communities.
12. Delley, Jean-Daniel (1989), 'La Suisse et l'Europe, Pour une approche globbale', *Domaine Public*, 936, 26 January.

6 Public Opinion and Public Information Campaigns: the Value of the Eurobarometer

Miles Hewstone, University of Bristol

Since April–May 1974 the European Commission has collected, analysed and published public opinion data throughout the European Community. These twice-yearly surveys were carried out from the beginning 'in order to follow the trends in European public opinion with regard to Community activities, particularly the areas of most interest to the public'. (Eurobarometer, no. 1, 1974, p. 1) The name 'Eurobarometer' was chosen deliberately because:

> Just as a barometer can be used to measure the atmospheric pressure and thus give a short-range weather forecast, this EUROBAROME-TER can be used to observe, and to some extent forecast, public attitudes towards the most important current events connected directly or indirectly with the development of the European Community and the unification of Europe. (ibid.)

The Eurobarometer data set is of great value for three main reasons. First, because the same (carefully translated) questions are posed simultaneously to representative samples in all member countries of the Community. This strategy yields rich comparative data. Second, key questions are repeated on several occasions, some in every single survey, which means that short- and long-term trends in public opinion can be charted. Third, results are broken down by various demographic criteria – age, sex, socioeconomic status and so on – and include many cross-tabulations between replies to different questions (as well as, occasionally, multivariate analyses). This chapter illustrates how this vast set of fascinating data can be used to target a public information campaign.

At the outset it should be noted that many scholars have expressed misgivings about the impact of public information campaigns. The problems with such campaigns are numerous: those people who do not wish to be influenced by information will avoid it (Cooper and Jahoda, 1947); and, if they are exposed to such information, they will distort it (Berelson and

Steiner, 1964). Thus public information campaigns often fail (Hyman and
Sheatsley, 1947), or succeed only in 'preaching to the converted' (Titchenor, Donohue and Olien, 1970). Notwithstanding these doubts, the present chapter demonstrates how the Eurobarometer could be used to plan a
public information campaign in Britain.

BRITISH ATTITUDES IN COMPARISON WITH OTHER NATIONAL PUBLICS

This chapter is not the place for a detailed comparison of British attitudes
to the European Community with those of other national publics. It is,
however, well-known that British attitudes are considerably less positive
than those in the three other largest Member States – the Federal Republic
of Germany, Italy and France.

For a simple comparison, one can examine 'net' support for Community
membership. This index is calculated by subtracting the proportion saying
that Community membership is a 'bad thing' from the proportion saying it
is a 'good thing' ('neither good nor bad' and 'don't know' responses are
ignored here). Membership has consistently been favored by the French,
Germans and, especially, the Italians. Public opinion in the UK is, and
always has been, less positive than in these three other countries. Net
support for the Community reached its maximum in Britain in 1975, when
for the first time 50 per cent of respondents thought Community membership was a 'good thing'. This was, of course, the year of the referendum.
Since that time, net support in the UK has fallen quite steadily until early
1982, when it climbed again. But opinion in Britain is obviously much more
capricious than in these three other Member States. Every little dissatisfaction with the way the Community works can be transformed into a major
fluctuation in support.

The same difference between the UK and the other three countries is
clear from an analysis of 'net' support for European unification. There is
net support, but there is also a huge gap between the UK and these three
other countries. The lack of a reliable reservoir of support for the Community in the UK is readily corroborated by other data. In a 1985 poll, a
majority of British people interviewed (53 per cent) felt that their country
had not benefited from the Community; this response was given by far
fewer people in each of the other three countries (West Germany: 31 per
cent; France: 26 per cent; Italy: 16 per cent). Asked how they would
respond, were the Community to be 'scrapped', 46 per cent of those
questioned in the UK said they would be 'relieved' (compared with only 8
per cent in West Germany and France, and 4 per cent in Italy).

It is with such national comparisons in mind that a focus on British
attitudes can be sharpened. Clearly, one needs to examine the structure of
attitudes, trends in their regional variation, and their major social and

political contours in order to understand better what can be done to change British attitudes in a more positive direction.[1]

The Structure of British Attitudes to the European Community

This first analysis is based on British attitudes to the European Community (EC) as reported in Eurobarometer 24 (Autumn, 1985: British sample size = 1347). The following eight attitudinal questions were used as input to a principal components factor-analysis: variables were dichotomized, so that all 'pro-European' responses were coded '1', and all other answers (including 'don't know's) were coded 'O'.

(1) 'Taking everything into consideration, would you say that [Britain] has on balance benefited or not from being a member of the European Community (Common Market)?'
    Answer categories: benefited; not benefited; don't know.
(2) 'Generally speaking, do you think that [Britain's] membership of the European Community (Common Market) is . . .'
    Answer categories: good thing; neither good nor bad; bad thing; don't know.
(3) 'If you were told tomorrow that the European Community (Common Market) had been scrapped, would you be very sorry about it, indifferent or relieved?'
    Answer categories: very sorry; indifferent; relieved; don't know.
(4) 'If one of the countries of the European Community other than your own finds itself in major economic difficulties, do you feel that the other countries including [Britain] should help it or not?'
    Answer categories: yes; no; don't know.
(5) 'Are you, personally, prepared or not to make some personal sacrifice, for example paying a little more taxes [sic], to help another country in the European community experiencing economic difficulties?'
    Answer categories: yes, prepared to; no, not prepared; don't know.
(6) 'In general, are you for or against efforts being made to unify Western Europe?'
    Answer categories: For, very much; for, to some extent; against, to some extent; against, very much; don't know.
(7) 'Some people talk of the idea of forming a United States of Europe putting together the member countries of the European Community. This means a kind of political union like there is between the fifty states of the USA, the ten provinces that form Canada. Does the idea of forming a United States of Europe some day, including [Britain], seem a good or bad idea to you?'
    Answer categories: a good idea; a bad idea; it depends (volunteered); don't know.
(8) 'There has been talk of possible standardization of notices at frontier

posts, airports, and sea ports, of the countries belonging to the European Community. The new notices would carry the name of the country you were entering and also the words "Member Country of the European Community". For instance, travellers arriving in [Britain] would see [read out]: "Britain: Member Country of the European Community". Are you for or against this idea?'

Answer categories: for; against; don't know.

Two clear, negatively correlated factors emerged. The first dimension is one of 'affective support', an emotional sentiment in response to the idea of European integration. The highest loading is for the measure of affective support used by Inglehart and Rabier (1978) – helping out another Member State in economic difficulty – and the other high loadings (items 5, 6, 7 and 8) converge on the underlying theme of European solidarity.

The second, weaker dimension is defined by three high, but negative loadings (items 1, 2 and 3). It is named 'evaluative support', because evaluative or utilitarian support relates to perceptions of concrete gains and losses through the Community. Viewing EC-membership as a good/ bad thing, and perceived benefits of EC-membership have been used as measures of utilitarian support in previous research (Handley, 1981; Inglehart and Rabier, 1978; Mathew, 1980; but see Hewstone, 1986a). These two dimensions are labelled 'affective' and 'evaluative', respectively. For further, longitudinal analyses one item has been selected as representative of each dimension: *affective dimension*: 'In favour of Western European unification?'; *evaluative dimension*: 'Is EC-membership a good thing?'

BRITISH SUPPORT FOR COMMUNITY MEMBERSHIP AND WESTERN EUROPEAN UNIFICATION: THE PASSAGE OF TIME

As Inglehart and Rabier (1978) noted, 'the sheer passage of time under common supranational institutions may tend to instill the habit of viewing things from a broader perspective than that of the nation-state' (p. 78). It is therefore of considerable interest to examine trends, over time, in British evaluative and affective orientations to the Community, as measured in the Eurobarometer series. To examine trends over time, re-coding of the two main variables was necessary:

(a) 'Is EC-membership a "good thing"?' (evaluative dimension). The response categories 'good thing' and 'bad thing' are self-explanatory; 'no opinion' corresponds to the responses, 'neither good nor bad' and 'don't know'.
(b) 'In favour of European unification?' (affective dimension). 'For' corresponds to the responses 'for, very much' and 'for, to some extent'; 'neither for nor against' corresponds to the response categories 'no opinion' and

'don't know'; 'against' corresponds to the responses, 'against, very much' and 'against, to some extent'.

Before pointing to, and discussing, trends in the relevant data, it should be noted that such trends refer here to the statistical technique of regression analysis (least-squares solution); the trends shown in the Figures are regression lines.

BRITISH TRENDS

These analyses begin with Eurobarometer 4, because standardized collection of regional data (necessary for comparisons reported below) dates from this survey only.

Evaluative Support

As noted above, 'good thing' responses only reached 50 per cent in 1975 (Eurobarometer 10) and have not climbed that high since (see Figure 6.1). These responses slumped in the period 1979–82, but have recovered. Due to the slump, however, the overall trend is downwards. 'Bad thing' responses follow the same pattern over time, but the trend is stable. 'Neither nor' (undecided) responses, like the other answers, have fluctuated a great deal, but the overall trend is upwards. This last finding arguably reflects the indecision of the British public, and underlines the need for an information campaign.

Affective Support

These analyses begin with Eurobarometer 10, from which point this variable has always been included in the survey. These findings scotch the claim that the British are non- or anti-European (see Figure 6.2). The percentage of responses 'for' is, and always has been, above 50 per cent, and the trend is upwards. Responses 'against' European unification have, during the same period, declined, with the trend downwards. Finally, in sharp contrast to the data for evaluative support, 'neither/nor' responses are low, with a stable trend.

Comparison of Trends for British Evaluative and Affective Support

Trends in evaluative and affective support can be compared for Eurobarometers 10–24 (1978–85), and for 'positive' (pro-European), 'negative' and 'indifferent' responses, separately. When one starts at this point, the trend for positive responses is upwards for both dimensions, although the chasm

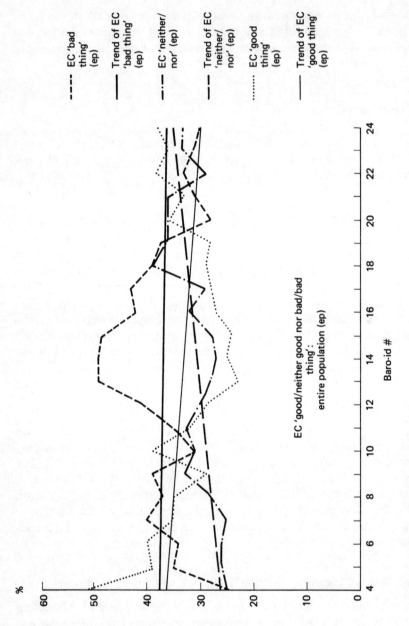

Legend:

- - - - EC 'bad thing' (ep)

——— Trend of EC 'bad thing' (ep)

–·–·– EC 'neither/nor' (ep)

— — — Trend of EC 'neither/ nor' (ep)

·········· EC 'good thing' (ep)

——— Trend of EC 'good thing' (ep)

EC 'good/neither good nor bad/bad thing': entire population (ep)

Baro-id #

SOURCE: Eurobarometer 4–24, 1975–85
FIGURE 6.1: *Evaluative support for the European Community in Britain*

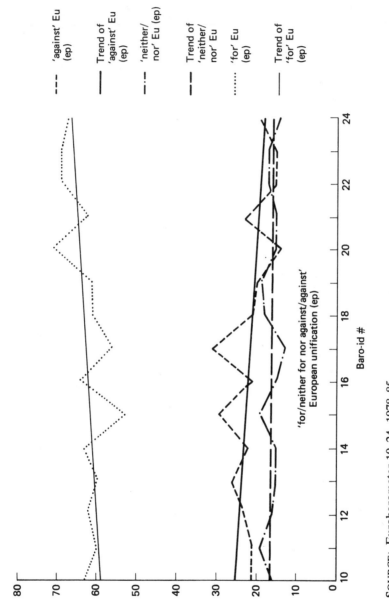

SOURCE: Eurobarometer 10–24, 1978–85
FIGURE 6.2: *Affective support for European unification in Britain*

between affective and evaluative support is deep. The trend for negative responses during this time is downwards for both items, although the trend is steeper for evaluative support. Only for 'indifferent' answers are the trends different for the two dimensions. The trend is downward for affective, and upwards for evaluative, support.

To summarize, the present state of British public opinion about Europe is far less drastic than is often claimed. The fact is that (since 1978) evaluative and affective support are rising, while opposition on both dimensions is falling. However, the rising trend in 'indifferent' responses on the evaluative dimension (i.e., saying that EC-membership is 'neither good nor bad' or answering 'don't know') suggests the need for a public information campaign now.

SUGGESTED REGION(S) FOR A PUBLIC INFORMATION CAMPAIGN

For purposes of regional contrasts, Eurobarometer divides Britain into twelve regions: North; Yorkshire-Humberside; Northwest; East Midlands; West Midlands; East Anglia; Southeast I; Southeast II; South-West; Wales; Scotland; and Greater London. To select a region (or regions) suitable for an information campaign, one should examine trends in both evaluative and affective support in each region, with the caveat that sampling methods, sample sizes and missing data make conclusions about public opinion at a regional level somewhat tentative. This chapter is not, however, the place for such exhaustive analysis. Instead, four criteria are used to identify regions that might be suitable for a public information campaign. First, support (whether evaluative, 'good thing', or affective, 'for') should be lower than in the population as a whole; i.e., an information campaign should be necessary. The measure of evaluative support will be given priority, as it is more specifically a measure of attitude towards the European Community. Second, opposition or lack of support ('bad thing' or 'against' responses) should be higher than the national level. Third, indifferent responses ('undecided') should also be higher than the national level, giving an information campaign something at which to aim. Fourth, choice of a region might be based on trends in the different responses; in particular, a downward trend for support and an upward trend for both opposition and indecision would suggest a region requiring a campaign. Finally, the choice of a region now might be guided by the percentage of respondents who gave each type of response in the last poll shown (Eurobarometer 24).

One immediate impression from comparing the twelve regions is that support tends to be higher in the 'south' (Southeast I, Southeast II and Greater London) than the 'north' (North, Yorkshire-Humberside, North-

TABLE 6.1: *Comparison of three potential regions for a public information campaign*

	Region		
Support	*North*	*E. Anglia*	*Scotland*
Evaluative			
'Good thing'	*	*	*
Trend	*	*	–
%	30%	29%	40%
'Bad thing'	*	*	*
Trend	–	*	–
%	30%	38%	25%
'Undecided'	–	*	–
Trend	*	–	*
%	42%	35%	34%
Affective			
'For'	*	–	*
Trend	–	–	–
%	68%	69%	72%
'Against'	*	–	*
Trend	–	*	–
%	18%	15%	19%
'Undecided'	*	*	*
Trend	–	–	–
%	18%	17%	9%
'Points'	7	7	6

NB: *denotes 'good thing' response *less* than national level, 'bad thing' and 'undecided' *more* than national level; *downward* trend for 'good thing', *upward* trend for 'bad thing' and 'undecided'.

west and Scotland). However, the three regions with lowest support are the North, East Anglia and Scotland. These three regions are contrasted, in terms of the above criteria, in Table 6.1. From Table 6.1 it should be clear that each of those regions could serve as the location for an information campaign. If 'points' were awarded for the extent to which each region was characterized by negative indicators (admittedly, a gross measure), then the North and East Anglia would be preferred as targets over Scotland. Forced to make a choice, the North appears the most suitable region. Evaluative support is low, and has been consistently so (see Figure 6.3); its trend is downward, with only 30 per cent of respondents giving 'good thing' responses in Eurobarometer 24. 'Bad thing' responses have been consistently high, but with a stable trend; 30 per cent of responses fall into the category (see Figure 6.4). 'Undecided' responses show an upward trend, accounting for 42 per cent of responses in Eurobarometer 24 (see Figure 6.5). This last fact should, perhaps, be accorded most importance, because studies on the effects of mass communication indicate that attitude

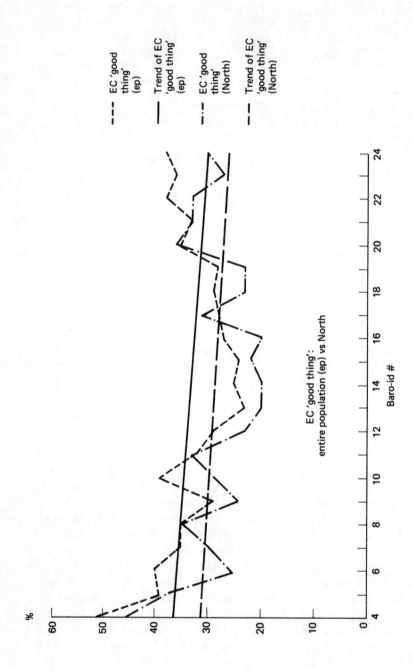

SOURCE: Eurobarometer 4–24, 1975–85
FIGURE 6.3: *Evaluative support for the European Community: entire population vs North of Britain ('good thing' responses)*

91

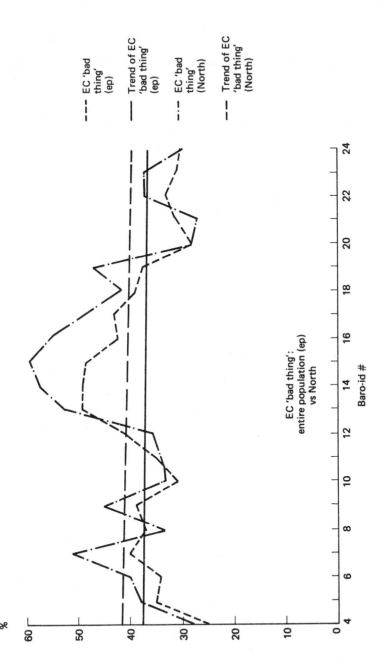

EC 'bad thing' (ep)

Trend of EC 'bad thing' (ep)

EC 'bad thing' (North)

Trend of EC 'bad thing' (North)

EC 'bad thing':
entire population (ep)
vs North

SOURCE: Eurobarometer 4–24, 1975–85
FIGURE 6.4: *Evaluative support for the European Community: entire population vs North of Britain ('bad thing' responses)*

92

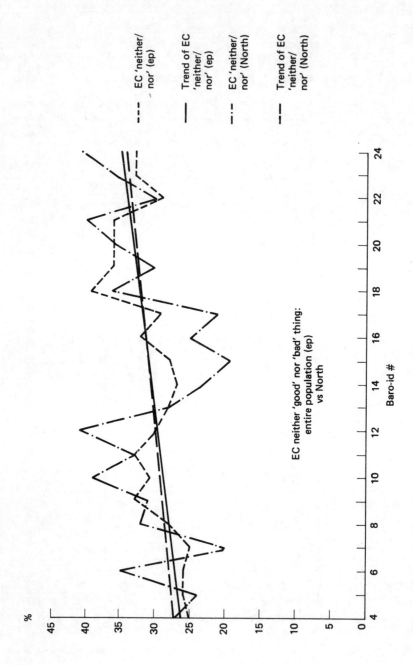

Legend:
- EC 'neither/nor' (ep)
- Trend of EC 'neither/nor' (ep)
- EC 'neither/nor' (North)
- Trend of EC 'neither/nor' (North)

EC neither 'good' nor 'bad' thing:
entire population (ep)
vs North

Baro-id #

SOURCE: Eurobarometer 4–24, 1975–85
FIGURE 6.5: *Evaluative support for the European Community: entire population vs North of Britain ('undecided' responses)*

change produced is commonly a small change in the extremity of intensity of the attitude, rather than a 'conversion' from 'good thing' to 'bad thing' responses (or vice versa; see Klapper, 1960, 1963). Thus the high numbers of undecided respondents can be seen as both a resource and a rationale for any public information campaign.

THE CONTOURS OF BRITISH PUBLIC OPINION

While the Eurobarometer can be used to identify a region for a public information campaign, it can also be used to pinpoint the types of citizens any campaign should attempt to target. Public opinion can be dissected according to various 'social-structural' and 'ideological-cultural' contrasts, in terms of which the Eurobarometer data have been coded. The five social-structural variables investigated were as follows: age respondent left school; respondent's exact age in years; family income quartiles; occupation of head of household; sex of respondent. The three ideological-cultural variables were as follows: party respondent would vote for ('political affiliation'); respondent's self-placement on a Left-Right continuum; respondent's classification according to Inglehart's Materialist/Post-Materialist index (see Inglehart and Rabier, 1978).

With the exception of the Materialist/Post-Materialist index, the following contrasts are all based on the cumulative Eurobarometer data-base (survey nos. 2–23). Due to a coding error, the Materialist/Post-Materialist data reported here can only be based on Eurobarometer 24. To increase the accuracy of inferences based on these contrasts, data for both evaluative and affective support dimensions ('EC-membership good/bad thing' and 'for/against European unification', respectively) are reported in each case, although trend analyses are limited to evaluative support. Following the recommendations made in each Eurobarometer report, it is assumed that a percentage difference of less than 5 per cent is below the acceptable level of confidence. Due to space limitations, only a summary of these data is provided (for detailed tabular and graphical presentation of the data, see Hewstone, 1986b).

Social-structural Contrasts

Age Respondent Left School

Evaluative Support
There is a clear trend for support to increase with school-leaving age, from fourteen to twenty-two or more years; 'bad thing' responses show almost the same pattern, in reverse; 'undecided' responses show less variation. Those still studying show a different pattern, with lower support than those

having left school at eighteen or more years, and a high percentage of 'undecided' responses.

Trends in Evaluative Support   For trend analyses, the ten categories were collapsed into 'low' (up to fourteen years, fifteen years, sixteen years), 'middle (seventeen to twenty years) and 'high' (twenty-one years – still studying) educational levels. These analyses show very clearly that the real effect, and a large one, is that those respondents with either a 'high' or 'middle' level of education, give more 'good thing' and fewer 'bad thing' responses, than do those with a 'low' education level. 'Neither nor' responses for the three groups are closer together. The trend for support is actually upward for the 'low' and 'high' education groups, but stable for the 'middle'. 'Bad thing' trends are all downward. The trend for 'undecided' responses is slightly upward, steeply so for the 'middle' group.

Affective Support

The upward trend of support and downward trend of opposition, with age, is again clear, although for affective support the 'undecided' responses fall with school-leaving age too. However, those still studying are again less positive than might be expected.

Respondent's Exact Age in Years

Evaluative Support

The youngest group in the sample (up to twenty years) and the oldest group (sixty-one to ninety-eight) give slightly fewer 'good thing' responses, but the differences are not very large in any case. The youngest group do, however, give rather more 'undecided' responses and rather fewer 'bad thing' responses than those aged forty-one to ninety-eight.

Trends in Evaluative Support   For trend analyses, these data were grouped into three categories: 'young' (up to thirty years), 'medium' (thirty-one to fifty years) and 'old' (fifty-one years and more). The 'good thing' responses show no large differences between the groups. There is, however, a difference in trends: upward for 'medium' and 'old' aged, only slightly upward for the 'young'. 'Bad thing' responses are also quite similar across age groups, with the 'young' lowest, and a downward trend in all cases. The real difference is in 'undecided' responses, where the 'young' are over-represented and the trend is upwards, but stable for 'medium' and 'old' aged groups.

Affective Support

Again, there is lower support in the youngest and oldest groups, with the youngest again most 'undecided'.

Conclusion
These findings suggest that the young in Britain (some of whom have, presumably, not yet voted in national or direct-European elections), whose attitudes are probably more malleable than those of the 'old', should be especially targeted in any campaign.

Family Income Quartiles

Evaluative Support
The major difference is that the poorest quartile are far less positive than the richest quartile. There is little difference in 'undecided' responses, but the 'poor' give more 'bad thing' responses than the 'rich'.

Trends in Evaluative Support For trend analyses, three categories of respondent were formed: 'poor' (category 1), 'middle' (2 and 3) and 'rich' (4). The 'rich' gave far more 'good thing' and far fewer 'bad thing' responses than did the 'poor'. The trend is upward in each case for support, and downward for opposition, but opposition is falling more steeply for the 'poor'. Differences between these two groups are less pronounced when one looks at 'undecided' responses. The trend is stable for 'poor' respondents, but rising for the 'rich'.

Affective Support
The same pattern was found for these responses, with the 'richest' especially positive, and hardly at all 'undecided'. In this case, however, responses 'against' are closer together, but with the same rich-poor division as for evaluative support.

Conclusion
These findings indicate that the Community must make a concerted effort to win the support of its 'poor' income citizens. The difference between 'rich'-'poor' support is around 20 per cent and the gap between the 'poor' and the entire population seems to be widening.

Occupation of Head of Household

It should first be noted that for these comparisons the cell sizes for some occupations were very small (e.g., 'farmers' and 'student/military'). It may also be added that the latter category is itself rather incongruous.

Evaluative Support
Given sample sizes, any differences noted must be tentative. However, only 'professional' and 'executive' groups have support over the 50 per cent level, and support is lowest in the 'housewife', 'manual work' and 'unemployed'

categories. In the case of housewives, it may be suggested that this group has rather close 'contact' with the Community, in terms of the effects of its policies on food prices. Another group that may have close contact with the community in their working life are those in 'business'; they are much less positive, and more negative, than those in the 'professional', 'white collar' and 'executive' groups. 'Undecided' responses do not differentiate much between groups, but 'bad thing' responses again point to the housewives, manual workers, the unemployed (especially) and the retired as dissatisfied with the Community. Given the ease with which the Community is, and can be, made a scapegoat, it may be that the unemployed blame their situation on the Community. It is indeed unfortunate for the Community, that politicians, newspapers and the public in Britain have displayed a marked propensity to ascribe all manner of economic ills to membership of the EEC (see Hewstone, 1986a).

Trends in Evaluative Support   For trend analyses these response categories were grouped into two classifications: occupations with 'low' status (farmer, manual worker, retired, housewife and unemployed) and occupations with 'high' status (professional, business, white collar, executive and student/military). There is, and always has been, a large gap between the support and opposition of these two groups. Support is, however, rising steeply for those with 'lower' occupational status, and gradually for those with 'higher' status. Equally encouraging for the Community, opposition is falling steeply for those with 'lower' status and gradually for those with 'higher' status. No clear pattern of difference emerges for 'undecided' responses. The trend is slightly upward for both groups.

Affective Support
A similar pattern of responses to those for evaluative support was found. Only the 'professional', 'white collar' and 'executive' groups are genuinely in favour of European unification ('students/military' are excluded), while the housewives especially are lacking in support. High numbers (over 20 per cent) of the housewives, manual workers and the unemployed are 'undecided', while these groups (and the retired) give more responses 'against'. Once again, those in business are less positive, and more negative, than the Commission might hope.

Sex of Respondent

Evaluative Support
Support for Community membership is higher among men than women; the women are not, however, more negative, only more 'undecided'.

Trends in Evaluative Support   Trend analyses reinforced the view that the main differences are that men give more 'good thing' and women more 'undecided' responses. 'Bad thing' responses for the two categories are much closer together. The trend in support is upward for both groups, especially for women. The trend, in both cases, is downward for opposition, and slightly upward for indifference.

Affective Support
Exactly the same pattern of results holds for affective support, although here very few male respondents are 'undecided'.

Summary of Social-structural Contrasts

The main contours of British public opinion regarding the European Community appear to include all five social-structural variables. Those Britons who are more positive about Community-membership and the goal of European unification are better-educated; middle-aged vs young (up to twenty years) or old (sixty-one to ninety-eight years); rich vs poor; professional and executive vs in business, housewives, manual workers and unemployed; and male vs female. Perhaps the housewives and those in business should be particular targets for any information campaign, as they (arguably) experience the workings of the Community more directly than do others polled (with the exception of the farmers, for whom the sample is very small).

Ideological-cultural Contrasts

Party Respondent would Vote for

Evaluative Support
The major cleavage due to political affiliation is, as expected, between Labour and Conservative voters. The former are both less positive and more negative (negative responses approaching 50 per cent).

Trends in Evaluative Support Trend analyses focused on the major division between Labour and Conservative party voters. Conservative voters show more support for the Community. The upward trend for both parties means that the gap, although apparently closing, is still very large. 'Bad thing' responses moved closer together in Eurobarometer 24, but traditionally Labour voters have shown much more opposition. The trend is downward in each case. 'Undecided' responses are very similar, with an upward trend.

Affective Support
Again, Labour voters offer least support; but now the Social Democrats

are as supportive as the Conservatives. The Social Democrats are also less 'undecided' than those with all other party affiliations. 'Bad' responses, as before, are given most by Labour voters and least by Conservative voters. These analyses suggest that Labour voters must be specifically targeted in any information campaign.

Respondent's Left-Right Placement

Evaluative Support
Support for European Community membership is lowest in the extreme left group; but there is also a marked division between those who place themselves 1–3 on the scale, and the rest. The extreme right (i.e., those scoring 10) show a slight drop in support, compared with those scoring 8–9. 'Undecided' responses differentiate little between the categories, but 'bad thing' responses again show that opposition is especially due to those respondents placing themselves at the left-most extreme, but also to those who place themselves at points 2–3.

Trends in Evaluative Support   For trend analyses respondents were classi-fied as 'left' (categories 1, 2, 3 and 4), 'centre' (5, 6, 7) and 'right' (8, 9, 10). Respondents on the 'left' have traditionally shown less support, but in Eurobarometer 24 they actually overtook the right; the trend is upward for both groups. 'Bad thing' responses of the two groups have now converged to the same point, and the trend is downward in each case. 'Undecided' responses have generally been higher for the 'right' than the 'left', with an upward trend for both.

Affective Support
The same pattern emerges for affective support, with respondents who place themselves at the extreme left giving less 'for' and more 'against' and 'undecided' responses.

Materialist/Postmaterialist Values Index

This variable is derived from two questions measuring first and second preference among four objectives. '1. If you had to choose among the following things, which are the two that seem most desirable to you: maintaining order in the nation; give the people more say in important government decisions; fighting rising prices; protecting freedom of speech? 2. And what would be your second choice?'
   The index is composed of a three-point scale of Postmaterialists (those who chose the second and fourth items together in both questions), Materialists (those who chose the first and third items together in both questions) and the mixed types (those choosing any of the remaining combinations).

Evaluative Support
Postmaterialists are, as expected, more positive towards the European Community than are either Materialists or 'Mixed' respondents. They are also less 'undecided'. There is little difference between the groups with respect to 'bad thing' responses.

Trends in Evaluative Support Trend analyses show that support has been rising for both Materialists and Postmaterialists but, over time, the latter are only slightly ahead. Opposition has been falling for both groups, but more steeply for the Materialists. 'Undecided' responses have varied considerably, but the level has generally been higher for Materialists; the trend is stable for both groups on this dimension, with the Materialists again showing least support, but not significantly less than the Postmaterialists.

Summary of Ideological-cultural Contrasts

The major ideological-cultural variable is that of political grouping. Those who give more support to the European Community, and favor European unification (although these differences are less marked) are Conservative vs Labour voters (with Social Democrats and Liberals in between), and place themselves on the political right vs (extreme) political left. The percentage difference in evaluative support for Labour and Conservative voters is 25 per cent, and for the political Left (scored 1–4) vs political Right (8–10) it is 20 per cent. Compared with these contrasts, the differential between respondents with Postmaterialist and Materialist values (admittedly, only on a three-point scale) is 12 per cent.

CONCLUSION

Mr Roy (now Lord) Jenkins, while President of the European Commission in 1977, warned that the Community 'must never forget to carry the people of Europe with them'. It is because the Community has been less than successful in gaining the support of the British public that a public information campaign would seem politically useful, if not necessary. This chapter has demonstrated the value of the Eurobarometer series for anyone planning such a campaign. In the space available, I have focused on how to *target* any such campaign, rather than on what issues it ought to address. Three possible regions of Britain have been identified as suitable for a campaign (with a preference for the North) and target citizens have been suggested by the main social and political divisions of public opinion (e.g., age, education, income and political ideology).

No researcher would be foolish enough to make strong predictions about the success of any such public information campaign. This positive step *towards* the citizens of Britain would, however, surely be better than merely waiting. As detailed, longitudinal analysis of British attitudes to the European community shows, there has been no simple increase in support over time (see Hewstone, 1986a). A public information campaign planned on the basis of Eurobarometer data would, at least, be a reasoned attack on what Jacques-René Rabier himself called *'ce formidable obstacle au changement qu'est l'apathie des citoyens'* (1966, p. 37).

NOTES

1. The term 'British' is accurate, and is used hereafter, because data from Northern Ireland have not been included.

REFERENCES

Berelson, B. R. and Steiner, G. A. (1964) *Human Behavior: an inventory of scientific findings* (New York: Harcourt, Brace and World).

Cooper, E. and Jahoda, M. (1947) 'The evasion of propaganda: how prejudiced people respond to anti-prejudice propaganda', *Journal of Psychology*, 23, 15–25.

Handley, D. H. (1981) 'Public opinion and European integration: the crisis of the 1970s', *European Journal of Political Research*, 9, 335–64.

Hewstone, M. (1986a) *Understanding attitudes to the European Community: A social-psychological study in four member states* (Cambridge: Cambridge University Press).

Hewstone, M. (1986b) *British public opinion towards the European Community* (Report prepared for the planning of a public information campaign by the Commission of the European Communities, Brussels).

Hyman, H. H. and Sheatsley, P. B. (1947) 'Some reasons why information campaigns fail', *Public Opinion Quarterly*, 11, 412–23.

Inglehart, R. and Rabier, J.-R. (1978) 'Economic uncertainty and European solidarity: public opinion trends', *Annals of the American Academy of Political and Social Science*, 440, 66–87.

Jenkins, R. (1977) *Programme of the Commission of the European Community for 1977.* (Address by Mr Roy Jenkins, President of the Commission, to the European Parliament.) (Luxembourg: Office of the Official Publications of the EEC).

Mathew, D. D. (1980) *Europeanism: a study of public opinion and attitudinal integration in the European Community* (Ottawa: The Norman Patterson School of International Affairs, Carleton University).

Rabier, J.-R. (1966) *L'opinion publique et l'Europe: Essai d'inventaire des connaissances et des lacunes* (Brussels: Institut de Sociologie de l'Universite Libre de Bruxelles).

Titchenor, P. J., Donohue, G. A. and Olien, C. N. (1970) 'Mass media flow and differential growth in knowledge', *Public Opinion Quarterly*, 34, 159–70.

7 Public Opinion and European Union: Thatcher versus the People of Europe[a]

John Pinder, Visiting Professor, College of Europe, Brugge

MONNET, SPINELLI AND THE PUBLIC

The Schuman plan was one of history's dramatic moments. But the drama was played with a small cast: a few ministers, officials and their close collaborators. Schuman, in calling it the first step towards European federation, indicated its tremendous potential; and the neo-functionalists did Monnet an injustice if they gave the impression that he expected the further steps to be taken without political battles. But he probably did think in terms of repeated dramas with small casts: of battles to be fought through the corridors of power.

The French Assemblée Nationale destroyed any such illusion when it ditched the European Defence Community in 1954. Monnet then created the Action Committee for the United States of Europe, bringing together the leaders of political forces to ensure that further steps would not suffer a similar fate; and the next parliamentary contests were indeed won when the Treaties of Rome were ratified.

Then came an episode which widened the arena from parliaments to the public. During the abortive entry negotiations in 1961–3, Britain's 'anti-marketeers' ran a massive public campaign. Their success in persuading Labour voters provided a groundswell which encouraged the Labour opposition to turn against the negotiations. Since opinion surveys also showed that Labour was likely to win the next election, this served to strengthen the case for de Gaulle's veto on British entry in January 1963.[1] When Britain's Europeans fought the return match in 1970–71, which finally assured membership, they organized a still more massive public campaign, based on analyses for surveys commissioned for the purpose. The people intervened yet more directly in 1975, when British membership was confirmed by referendum after another great public campaign had turned an initial majority of two to one against in the surveys round to a vote of two to one in favour.[2]

Meanwhile, the voters began to become more directly involved on the

101

Continent too in decisions on steps in the Community's development. A setback in the first round of the French presidential elections late in 1965 induced de Gaulle to moderate the attack on the Community that he had launched in that year. Pompidou held a referendum in April 1972 to confirm French acceptance of British accession. More recently, the Danes and Irish held referenda before the Single European Act was ratified in 1987.

If the facts of democratic politics imposed themselves by stages on Monnet's concept of stepwise Community development, the people had their place from the start in Spinelli's federalist idea, even if, still influenced by his political origins in the Italian Communist Party, he saw them as masses 'waiting to be guided'.[3] He reacted to the failure of the European Defence Community by attempting to organize a Congress of the European People to promote the convening of a constituent assembly in which the people's representatives would draw up the constitution of the European federation. Although the European people did not live up to his hopes then, they did elect their representatives a quarter of a century later when the first direct elections to the European Parliament were held in 1979 – thanks, ironically enough, to the provisions of Monnet's Community Treaties which Spinelli had earlier denounced as a cosmetic substitute for real unification. Spinelli persuaded the Parliament to play a constituent role by drawing up its Draft Treaty for a European Union, which would convert the Community into a federation in all essentials but for the integration of the armed forces of the member states.

When the governments reacted to the Draft Treaty with the more modest Single European Act, Spinelli reverted to the idea of popular pressure, expressed through referenda, to cause governments to agree to a mandate for the European Parliament to draw up the European constitution. Italy was the first country in which such a referendum was held. Meanwhile, the European Parliament, fortified by evidence of preponderant public support for the idea, has continued to prepare itself for the constituent role.

Thus both the Monnet and the Spinelli ways of unifying Europe lead to the need for knowledge about public attitudes towards the various aims and the methods of achieving them.

EUROPEAN UNION AND EUROBAROMETER

Since July 1974, Eurobarometer has provided a unique source of such knowledge. It not only shows how opinions fluctuate in response to events, giving the equivalent of weather reports that the name implies;[4] it also charts the more stable basic attitudes that form the climate within which those who want to develop the Community into a Union must work.

There has always been majority support in the Community, particularly

strong and consistent in the founder members, for the aim of a federal
Europe, whether presented as the United States of Europe, or (when the
European Parliament's Draft Treaty was being debated in the Community)
as a European Political Union, or in other ways. At least three to one have
been in favour of these two, when asked in recent years (see 3/87 A4 and
6/85 T28). (The references to Eurobarometer tables are given throughout
in this abbreviated form. First the month and year of the issue of Eurobarometer are given; thus 3/87 refers to March 1987 and 6/85 to June 1985.
Then the numbers of the tables are given: T24 is the table numbered 24 in
the text of that issue; the prefix A or B refers to the respective series with
those prefixes at the back of the issue.) A majority of four to one would
like the European Parliament to draft a European constitution, although
this falls to two to one when people are asked more precisely whether the
Parliament should vote laws or form a government (6/88 T15). Eight times
as many are for a referendum on the subject as against it (6/88 A18).

The obvious question for sceptics is: if the people want these things so
much, why are the governments so reluctant? Or, from the federalist side,
how can the support be mobilized so as to get the governments to act?
Here the Eurobarometer can help the would-be mobilizers to know what
arguments to present to which sectors of society. For example, those who
respond most positively to the words European Community are the young,
educated materialists (6/87 A8, 9); building the Community is the way to
present the idea of European Union to them. On the other hand it is the
older, educated Postmaterialists who most want a European government
responsible for currency, and the older, less-educated, right-wing materialists who want the same for security (12/87 A11).

On the whole, however, the differences among social groups are modest
compared with some of the differences among the member countries. Thus
the British have been cooler than the Community average in their attitudes
to many aspects of the Community and of its potential development,
standing halfway between the Danes, who have been the coldest, and the
more positive populations of the six founder members. When the British
government, so far from minimizing these differences, appears to exaggerate
them, the question arises whether a sufficient core of member states where
attitudes are positive could proceed towards Union, leaving the British and
some other reluctant partners to follow later. Such a two-speed solution
could be applied to particular steps, as for example in the Exchange Rate
Mechanism of the European Monetary System, or to the establishment of
European Union itself, as envisaged in Article 82 of the European Parliament's Draft Treaty. Thus the differences between the British and the
average of Community attitudes (which will on occasion be called 'Continental' attitudes for short) are not only a most interesting aspect of the
Eurobarometer material, but also crucial for the designing of strategies to
create the Union. The rest of this chapter is devoted to their analysis.

THE BRITISH AND THE UNITED STATES OF EUROPE

British attitudes towards the general idea of European unification have
been very stable since the early 1950s, apart from a few dips when relations
with the Community were most fraught (6/88 B4). Since 1982, when the
worst effects of Mrs Thatcher's quarrel about getting her 'money back'
were wearing off, the proportion in favour has not moved out of the range
of 60–70 per cent, with 15–25 per cent against. As the survey made in the
spring of 1988 shows in Table 7.1, the difference between the British and
the Community average is a little over 10 per cent, with more of the
Continentals in favour and fewer against.

The difference of about one-tenth recurs so often in the tables that
reflect British attitudes to the Community and its development, that it will
be called for short in the rest of this chapter Britain's standard deficit. If
one-tenth of the respondents were to shift from the anti to the positive
side, the deficit would in all these cases be removed. This applies, for
example, when the British are asked whether European unity protects or
impairs national identity: more feel that it protects than that it impairs, but
one-tenth would have to shift from the negative to the positive view, for
the British to align on the average (6/88 A4).

The degree to which the British diverge depends, however, on the
question at issue. When asked about the different ways of feeling European, the divergence is less than the standard deficit with respect to the
most prevalent feelings: putting past rivalries behind and living in peace;
and travelling without difficulties. But it exceeds the standard with respect
to more ideologically explicit statements: fewer sympathizing with 'adventure: the United States of Europe', and more with 'only a geographical
fact' (6/87 A13).

When asked directly in 1987 about the United States of Europe (see
Table 7.2), a majority of the British nevertheless approved, with no more
than the standard deficit. The difference between Britain and the Continent was, however, greater in the proportion against than in the proportion
for. This raises the question whether the term United States of Europe
(USE) has the same connotations on either side of the Channel. What does
it mean to the respondents? Some light is shed on this by another question
asked a few weeks later (see Table 7.3).

Here the respondents faithfully reflect Britain's standard deficit. One-
tenth more of the British want to dissolve the Community. One-tenth
fewer want a federation, precisely defined as having a federal government
with responsibility in certain important areas, or a 'single large country'
within which frontiers have completely disappeared. If those who want
'intensification', defined as an EC 'within which economic, scientific and
cultural exchanges between Europeans are more and more dense', are
added to those who want federation or a single country, we come remarkably close to the percentages wanting a USE.

TABLE 7.1: *Attitudes to the unification of Western Europe, Spring 1988*

	for		against
	percentages		
EC	73		14
UK	60		25

SOURCE: Eurobarometer, June 1988, Table B4

TABLE 7.2: *Are you for or against the European Community developing towards becoming a 'United States of Europe'?*

	for		against
	percentages		
EC	63		20
UK	52		37

SOURCE: Eurobarometer, *Europe 2000* (Special 30th Anniversary Edition), March 1987, Table A14.

TABLE 7.3: *Options for the European Community's future*

	federation or single country	EC intensification	status quo	dissolve
		percentages		
EC	35	31	16	5
UK	24	33	17	15

SOURCE: Eurobarometer, June 1987, Table A17.

A few of those who opted for 'intensification' of the EC spilled over to join those who preferred the status quo or dissolution, in opposing the USE. But the supporters of the USE included most of those who took a dynamic view of the Community's development.

In order to dig behind reactions to the slogan of the USE, Eurobarometer asked a more precise question which, in effect, defined its political content and explored the time-scale in which it was envisaged (see Table 7.4).

Here again, Britain and the Continent would be almost exactly alike but for the standard deficit at both ends of the scale: one-tenth fewer British who would entrust a European government with the main powers of a federation within ten years, and one-tenth more who would never do so. For both British and Continentals, the supporters of the USE (see Table

TABLE 7.4: *After what period of time would you entrust the government of Europe with the responsibility for economy, foreign affairs and defence?*

	within 10 years	10–20 years	20–30 years	several generations	never
			percentages		
EC	30	17	11	7	9
UK	19	17	12	8	17

SOURCE: Eurobarometer, *Europe 2000*, March 1987, Table 15.

TABLE 7.5: *Percentages giving no reply about USE, future EC options, European government*

	USE	future EC options	European government
EC	11	13	26
UK	17	11	27

SOURCE: see Tables 7.2, 7.3, 7.4 above

7.2 above) evidently included all of those who would entrust a European government with such powers within thirty years, and some of those who would want to wait 'several generations'. About a quarter on both sides on the Channel had no answer to this more complicated question, compared with just over a tenth, again on both sides, who failed to choose one of the relatively straightforward options for the EC's future. It was the slogan of the United States of Europe that provoked some of these British 'don't knows' into negative answers: the difference of 6 per cent between the proportion in Britain and in the EC as a whole who failed to pronounce on the USE was almost exactly equal to the excess above the standard deficit in the percentage of British who pronounced against (see Table 7.5).

Earlier evidence that the British have reacted better to more precise propositions than to the USE slogan came from Eurobarometer in 1983, when 60 per cent of the British, slightly more than the 57 per cent for the EC as a whole, agreed that a main aim for the MEPs to be elected to the European Parliament in the following year should be to work for a political union of the member states with a European government responsible to the European Parliament (12/83 T26). This came during a period when the number of British in favour of the USE was shown as between a third and a half. From 30 per cent for and 48 per cent against in 1970, the proportion in favour had risen to near balance with those against in 1978, only to fall back again to a minority, almost exactly the same in 1985 as it had been in

TABLE 7.6: *What comes to your mind if you hear 'European Community'?*

CAP mentioned:	positively	negatively
	percentages	
EC	3	12
UK	5	23

SOURCE: Eurobarometer, June 1988, Table A3

1970 (12/85 T40; 3/87 graph 8 and p. 28). With the progress to a substantial majority in favour by 1987, it can be seen that British views of the USE have fluctuated widely over the years. Why?

British perceptions of the most striking European developments in recent decades may give a clue. Both British and Continentals, when asked about this in 1987, gave a high rating to 'mutual trust'. But over twice as many Continentals as British mentioned 'EC Institution', while twice as many British as Continentals were struck by 'food surpluses': third most significant for the EC as a whole, but by far the most salient impression for the British (6/87 A14). The Community and its agri-budgetary problem has indeed loomed large in British attitudes to Europe.

BRITAIN AND THE EC: FROM AGRICULTURAL COMMUNITY TO SINGLE MARKET

This difference between British and Continentals was confirmed when they were asked what came to mind if they heard 'European Community' (see Table 7.6). While not many mentioned 'fundamental values and goals', the percentages on both sides of the Channel were similar, and both reacted positively. But when it came to the common agricultural policy, although both sides reacted negatively, it was twice as salient for the British, by far their most common reaction.

This British preoccupation with the CAP carried some other concerns in its wake. Thus 'reply related to own country' and 'EC internal political process' were also particularly salient for the British, and the view of the effect of the EC on Britain was predominantly negative. This can clearly be attributed to the CAP. British reactions to 'other EC policies' were positive; and almost as many reacted positively as negatively to the EC's internal political process – matching the balance between positive and negative on the Continent, although the political process was only half as salient for the Continentals. Thus although the political process has achieved its salience in Britain as a result of the CAP, which is widely seen as damaging to Britain, the balance of opinion about the merits of the process itself is much the same on both sides of the Channel.

   The CAP and the associated quarrel about the budget have nevertheless
at times generated very bad feelings toward the Community in Britain.
Eurobarometer has since the 1970s measured attitudes both to membership of the Community and to the eventuality that 'the common market
had been scrapped' (6/88 B5 and B7). As might be expected, the views that
the EC was a 'bad thing' and that the respondent would be 'relieved if
scrapped' were closely related; and both reflected the link between British
attitudes to the EC and the history of political relations between Britain
and the Community, themselves mainly centered on the agri-budgetary
issue. After the party-political battle over membership, which culminated
with the referendum in 1975, the proportions with these negative views
averaged one-third, and seldom rose above two-fifths, until Mrs Thatcher
began her campaign for 'money back' in 1979. Those who thought the
Community a bad thing and would be relieved if it was scrapped then shot
up to about a half, and stayed there for a couple of years, with the others
divided between those who thought it a good thing, or would be 'very
sorry' if it was scrapped, and those who were indifferent. By the end of
1981, the effect of the quarrel evidently began to subside, and the percentages with negative views declined to the low forties. From early in 1983 to
early in 1985, they averaged about a third. Then, following the agreement
about the budgetary rebate for Britain, the negative proportion fell by 1986
to about a quarter, compared with a tenth for the Community as a whole.
There it remained for the next two years, with the proportion of British
now thinking the Community a 'good thing' at around two-fifths, comfort-
ably exceeding the negative view, but still well below the three-fifths
prevailing in the Community as a whole. Thus the most recent survey
available at the time of writing, taken in the spring of 1988, still showed
that British views of the Community suffered somewhat more than the
standard deficit for British attitudes to other aspects of European unification. But, despite a modest setback to European sentiments which was
general in the Community at that time, it remains true that the British
public had shown, as Eurobarometer has put it, a 'slow but steady growth
of support for the Community' (12/87 p. xvi).
   The fluctuations in the British reactions to the 'United States of Europe'
seem to have followed the same path as attitudes towards the Community.
Views of the Community in 1970, when the balance of opinion was against
the USE, had been soured by de Gaulle's second veto, when the Labour
government sought membership. By 1978, when favorable views of the
Community had been restored, opinion about the USE was balanced.
After the quarrels of the early 1980s had put the Community in bad odour
among the British, attitudes towards the USE were back where they had
been in 1970. But by 1987, after the agreement on a fair deal over the
budget had sunk in and the Community was well viewed again, there was a
clear British majority for the United States of Europe.

The argument of counsel for the defence of the British people's European credentials could, then, run something like this. The two successive vetoes on Britain's attempts to join the Community in the 1960s had made the public suspicious of its good will. It was understandable, in these circumstances, that the opposition party in a bipolar political system should swing into opposition to entry on the terms negotiated by the government, and that the resulting party conflict should impair the view taken of the Community by many voters, particularly as entry coincided with the oil shock and the time of economic troubles that ensued. By the time, in the late 1970s, that the British were recovering from these events, the agri-budgetary problem, which was a time-bomb set in the early 1970s when the common agricultural policy was only feebly reformed and the terms of British entry were agreed, was reaching the time when it would explode. The two statesmen who were then the Community's leaders, Valéry Giscard d'Estaing and Helmut Schmidt, agreed to make an inadequate offer to Britain, and presented it in a patronizing way to the new British Prime Minister, Mrs Thatcher, at the Dublin meeting of the European Council in 1979.[5] Mrs Thatcher over-reacted and, lacking any background of European experience or sentiment, carried out a necessary negotiation in a manner that emphasized the worst aspects of relations between Britain and the Continent, thus turning British opinion against the Community again. That period of turbulence past, however, the British started their move towards a view of the Community that better reflects their long-standing support for the general idea of the unification of Western Europe. Although more still think that Britain has not benefited from the Community than the reverse, more see the Community as a good thing than as a bad one (6/88 B5, 6). Thus it is seen in terms beyond those of narrow national interest; and, as we have noted, a majority differ from Mrs Thatcher in favoring the idea of the United States of Europe.

We find, moreover, that the British react positively when presented with a major Community project which, unlike the CAP and its financing, does not seem to be biased against British interests: the programme to complete the single market by 1992 (Table 7.7). The British evidently favor the single market, even if with something more than the standard deficit compared with the EC as a whole. The standard deficit also applies to the negative view of the job market. But there is parity in the majorities seeing advantage for employees on both sides of the Channel; and the British are more sanguine than the people of any other member country in seeing advantages for problem regions. They also join the French and Germans in seeing the two most significant advantages of the single market as being the ability to carry money and make payments throughout the Community (6/88 T4).

Counsel for the prosecution, seeking to throw doubt on the European commitment of the British, might well say that he never questioned their

TABLE 7.7: *Attitudes on the single common market in 1992*

	good or bad thing		implications for job market for employees		implications for regions with economic problems	
	good	bad	advantages	disadvantages	advantage	disadvantage
			percentages			
EC	53	8	59	18	50	26
UK	39	19	59	28	62	22

SOURCE: Eurobarometer, June 1988, Tables 5, A7, A8

ability to identify an economic advantage for themselves, such as that offered by the single market. His concern, rather, was what the British might see the single market as leading towards; and here, Eurobarometer is downright disquieting. When asked whether they were in favour of 'going farther than the single common European market', 57 per cent of the British were against but only 24 per cent in favour, whereas in the EC as a whole those for outweighed those against by 44 per cent to 31 per cent (6/88 A15). Even if, moreover, the British have expressed themselves more positively than their Prime Minister about such things as a United States of Europe or a future European government, they have also followed her in her last vendetta against the Community, over the budget, so they will probably do the same again as she inveighs against monetary union, open frontiers, tax harmonization, stronger European institutions: in short, against all the important ways of proceeding beyond the single market.

Counsel for the defence might reply that 'going farther than the single market' does not evoke the vision of the good things that European unification should bring. If you compare the responses for the EC as a whole with those given regarding the United States of Europe (Table 7.2 above), you will find that people were much less attracted and more repelled by the concept of going farther than the single market than they were by the USE. The loss of enthusiasm as you move from one question to the other was, admittedly, rather greater on the part of the British, but this is understandable when the British have been favoured less than most by Community policies, and feel that they have lost as a result. What if 'going farther than the single market' should be in the direction of more like the CAP? Let us look, ladies and gentlemen of the jury, at British attitudes towards the main elements of a European Union, rather than at their answers to a question whose connotations take them closer to an experience which has not been altogether happy for them. Eurobarometer gives us a rich crop of evidence on this as well.

TABLE 7.8: *Role of the Court in European Community decision-making*

	perceived as important		desired as important	
	per cent	rank order	per cent	rank order
EC	18	5	13	=4
UK	30	1	14	3

SOURCE: Eurobarometer, June 1988, Table 4 and Figure 5

THE BRITISH, THE CONTINENTALS AND THE INSTITUTIONS OF EUROPEAN UNION

The institutions of the European Union would, according to the European Parliament's Draft Treaty, require a reform of the EC institutions to make the Parliament and the Council the two chambers of a legislature, with the Council voting generally by majority and sharing its legislative power with the Parliament; to make the Commission a government with adequate executive competences; and to strengthen the Court of Justice. Let us see how the British and the Continentals might react to these reforms.

The rule of law, in place of the power relationships that prevailed in Europe in the past, is fundamental to the European Community; and counsel for Britain's defence might be forgiven for putting the Court first, since Britain has a good record in the implementation of Community law, and this is reflected in the view of the public on the role of the Court. Eurobarometer asked people for which institutions they perceived or desired a 'really important role' in the Community (see Table 7.8). They were given a list of nine institutions: the Commission, the Council of Ministers, the European Council (called 'European Summit'), the European Parliament, the European Court of Justice, the national Parliament, the national government, professional organizations, political parties. Among the two-thirds or so on both sides of the Channel who gave answers to this rather complex question, the average number of institutions mentioned on both sides was rather more than two of perceived importance and rather less than two desired. Only the British perceived the Court as the most important institution, while the Continentals as a whole, including in particular the Dutch, French, Germans, Greeks and Spaniards, saw the 'Summit' as the most important. In all the Continental countries the Court was ranked between fifth and seventh, while the Irish placed it third.

While prosecuting counsel might accuse the British of ignorance as to who really counts in EC decision-making, defence could reply that the British appreciate better than the Continentals the importance of the rule of law, and hence of the Court's role, and could observe in support of this hypothesis that the British want the Court to be more important than the

TABLE 7.9: *European Parliament: impact, impression, perceived and desired importance*

impact (recently seen or heard on media)		impression given good bad percentages		perceived importance important not		desired importance more less	
EC	46	44	20	52	31	49	9
UK	37	27	46	50	36	37	22

SOURCE: Eurobarometer, June 1988, Tables B8, 9, 10, 11, survey of Spring 1988

'Summit', whereas the Continentals, if only by a small margin, want the reverse.

If the British gain a point in that round, they also start quite well if the same measure is taken of attitudes towards the European Parliament (see Table 7.9). Both British and Continentals rank the EP among the institutions for which a more important role is desired (6/88 T4, Figure 5). From a more detailed analysis the British also emerge quite creditably, but still with a standard deficit. The British suffer a standard deficit in the amount they see or hear about the EP in their media, even if in the run-up to the 1984 election about three-quarters had seen or heard something on both sides of the Channel. But the impression their media give the British is heavily negative, with a deficit of good impressions well above the standard, and the bad impressions at 46 per cent compared with 20 per cent in the Community as a whole. Despite this soaring deficit, British perceptions of the EP's importance are quite close to those of the Continentals; and, more significant for Britain's European credentials, the British who want a more important role for the EP substantially outweigh those who want it to be less important (even if there is here again a standard deficit in comparison with the Continent). This positive view has, indeed, always outweighed the negative one since Eurobarometer started asking this question in 1983. The average wanting the more important role has during those five years been 39 per cent, while those wanting less importance have never been more than 31 per cent, even between 1983 and 1986, when the impression received by the British from their media was even worse than it has been since (6/88 B9, 11).

The 1984 elections fell during the period when the British public's view of the Community was still vexed by the quarrel about 'money back'. Yet more British than Continentals saw those elections as an event 'with important consequences which is certain to make Europe more politically unified' (UK 44 per cent, EC 42 per cent); more, as we have seen, thought that MEPs should, as a main aim, work towards a political union with a European government responsible to the EP; and a majority, if this time

TABLE 7.10: *New powers for the European Parliament*

	draft a constitution for European union		*form a government*		*vote laws*	
	for	*against*	*for*	*against*	*for*	*against*
		percentages				
EC	57	15	49	24	49	28
UK	43	28	31	44	29	54

SOURCE: Eurobarometer, June 1988, Table 15

less than on the Continent, thought the EP should have more control over the functioning of the common market and the EC budget (UK 59 per cent, EC 67 per cent) (12/83 T26, 27).

With these fine answers before the 1984 elections, what a pity that so few of the British turned out to vote; and, with the fairly creditable balance in favour of a more important role for the EP, what a pity, again, that the British equivocated when asked, in 1988, about new powers for the Parliament (see Table 7.10).

Despite their lack of familiarity with the process of drafting a constitution, many more of the British favored than opposed the idea of the EP drafting a constitution for European union, even if with somewhat more than the standard deficit compared with the Continentals. But when asked whether the EP should have the key powers to form a government or to vote laws, the British swung round against. The Continentals, too, were less enthusiastic about these specific powers than about the drafting of a constitution; but they still had a substantial balance in favor.

Prosecution can, then, charge the British with favoring vague propositions such as a 'more important' role for the EP, or the drafting of an undefined constitution, but reneging when confronted with the idea of real powers for the Parliament. Defence might remind the court that the British had previously strongly favored a European government responsible to the EP (12/83 T26) and recently appeared to favor a European government with defined powers (see Table 7.4 above); plead in mitigation that the British react badly to governments in general, preferring parliaments and courts; and suggest that if the respondents had been asked if they favoured co-legislation by the EP with the Council, as the EP's own Draft Treaty had proposed, they would have given a different answer about the law-making power. But the court might not find these arguments sufficiently convincing. Defence would have to produce further evidence. The case proceeds.

Legislative power for the EP would, of course, lose much of its meaning if the Council, as co-legislator, continued to fight shy of voting by majority. Eurobarometer asked people if they favored voting by majority or by unanimity. Although the question was put in the autumn of 1985, before the British had recovered from the sour mood of the years of 'money back',

TABLE 7.11: *Voting by majority or unanimity*

	majority	unanimity
	percentages	
EC	51	32
UK	53	38
Italy	48	40

SOURCE: Eurobarometer, December, 1985, Table 33

TABLE 7.12: *More important role desired in Community decision-making for European Council, Council, national government, national parliament*

	national government	European Council	Council	national parliament
		rank order		
EC	2	3	=4	=6
UK	2	=5	=5	4

SOURCE: Eurobarometer, June 1988, Table 4 and Figure 5

and when they were still predominantly against the concept of the United States of Europe, 53 per cent of them favored majority voting, slightly more than for the EC as a whole (see Table 7.11). Although more of the British than of the Continentals preferred unanimity (fewer, by the same token, being unable to respond), the Italians were less 'European' than the British on both counts: fewer wanting majority and more wanting unanimity.

Could the British claim, then, that more of them accept the reality of what it takes to work together, while more of the Continentals prefer the rhetoric? That would be too heavy a load for a small difference in one survey to bear. But the Continentals did rank the institutions representing the member governments higher than the British, among those for which they wanted a more important role in Community decision-making (see Table 7.12).

Both British and Continentals put the national government second, after the European Parliament. The EC as a whole then put the European Council (called Summit) third, where the British, as we have seen, put the Court; the EC also ranked the Council higher than the British did, because the British preferred their own Parliament. As with the majority voting, then, the British seem to gain points in the balance of their preferences among the institutions, wanting, contrary to the Continentals, a more important role for the Court than for the Council and the European Council, both dominated by the member governments. More significant, however, are the similarities on both sides of the Channel: both placing the

TABLE 7.13: *Awareness and impression of the Commission*

percentages	heard or read recently	impression favourable	unfavourable
EC	44	39	24
UK	37	26	45

SOURCE: Eurobarometer, June 1988, Table A5

EP first and the national governments second; and both relegating the Commission to one of the two bottom places.

The media treat the Commission much as they do the EP, both in Britain and on the Continent (see Table 7.13). Despite the almost exact similarity between the impressions conveyed by their media about the EP and the Commission, the conclusions drawn by the British about the two institutions are at opposite poles: the EP comes top of their list for a more important role, the Commission bottom. For the Community as a whole, despite the much more favorable impression given by the media, the Commission comes only one from bottom of the list.

We have seen that the British reaction to the idea of European government can be perverse compared with their reaction to European Parliament and European Court, and speculated whether this may have something to do with an ambivalence about governments in general, leading them to give one answer in one context and an apparently contradictory answer in another. Such a general attitude could spill over onto the Commission; and a poor view of the Commission could impair the attitude toward the idea of a European government. But regardless of such speculations, the British have shown themselves more sanguine about a European government when asked if there is likely to be one by the year 2000 (see Table 7.14).

Thus in thinking about a European government in the not-so-distant future, the British come much closer to the Continentals. Of course it is not the same to expect that a European government is likely, as actually to desire one. But if you expect to be called to elect a government head (not what the British in fact do in their own country, but most respondents would probably interpret the question as asking about elections which resulted in the formation of a government), you expect that your country will have agreed to such European elections, which indicates a degree of acceptance of the idea of a European government.

Despite some positive British attitudes to the European Parliament and Court, then, and at least no greater attachment to the roles of the member governments, Council and European Council, there remains a deficit as regards reforms that would be needed to create the European Union,

TABLE 7.14: *Likelihood of a European government by the year 2000*

Will you, your children, be called upon to vote in an election to choose the head of government of Europe?		Will the head of government of Europe speak on equal terms with the leaders of the US, Soviet Union, etc.?	
		percentages	
	yes	no	yes	no
EC	50	30	44	35
UK	45	42	42	42

SOURCE: Eurobarometer, *Europe 2000*, March 1987, Table A12, 13

particularly with respect to the idea of a European government. Public opinion on the Continent is readier to accept the institutions of union, while the British still need more persuasion.

THE BRITISH, THE CONTINENTALS AND THE POWERS OF EUROPEAN UNION

The basic powers of a federal state are over trade, money, budget and armed force; and the European Parliament's Draft Treaty endowed the Union with full powers over the three former, while envisaging a more intergovernmental system for armed forces and security, at least for an indeterminate initial period.

We have seen that the British are quite favorable to the single market, which will complete the Community's powers over trade up to the level required by the union. The worry here is, rather, about German opinion, where only 41 per cent of manual workers see advantages in the job market, compared with 57 per cent of manual workers in Britain and 58 per cent in the EC as a whole. As regards the free movement of people, the British, unlike their Prime Minister, have higher expectations than the Continentals (see Table 7.15).

At least two thirds of all those who told Eurobarometer that they wanted to 'go farther than the single common market' wanted to do so in the field of currency; and this was so in every member country, although the force of this is reduced by the proportions who actually did say they wanted to go farther in general: one-half in the EC as a whole and one-third in Britain. In each country, more wanted to go farther in the fields of environment, science and technology, and external relations (6/88 T10, A15). The same message came from a question about the powers wanted for a European government, to which in the spring of 1988 only 43 per cent responded 'currency' (6/88 Figure 11). Even if the sort of people who, one may hope, are reading this book – the educated, opinion-forming Postmaterialists –

TABLE 7.15: *Do you expect you, your children, to travel, study, work, live in any European Community country in the year 2000 as you can now in any part of your own country?*

	yes	*percentages*	*no*
EC	62		24
UK	69		24

SOURCE: Eurobarometer, *Europe 2000*, March 1987, Table A9

TABLE 7.16: *Do you expect that you, your children, will use bank notes and cheques in the European currency in the year 2000?*

	yes	*percentages*	*no*
EC	50		33
UK	45		46
Netherlands	39		46

SOURCE: Eurobarometer, *Europe 2000*, March 1987, Table A4

are more enthusiastic than the average (12/87 A11), a European power over money is evidently not the most popular cause. Yet as far as expectations are concerned, the British are fairly close to the Community average; and if they have somewhat more than a standard deficit among those who do not expect it, they can at least claim that they are less unenthusiastic than the Dutch (see Table 7.16).

The budget is the other main arm of economic and monetary union, without which no Union or federal institutions would have significance. Here, the EC already has significant power to raise revenue: and the EP is closer to having a power of co-decision with the Council than it is with respect to legislation. It is reassuring that a majority both in Britain and on the Continent have expressed the wish, as we have seen, that the Parliament should have more control over the budget.

When we come to powers in the field of defence or security, where the EP's Draft Treaty trod so warily, the public in the Community as a whole is as positive as it is about currency, and the British much more so. Indeed, a substantial majority of British expect the EC to organize its defence in common and use the same equipment by the year 2000; and an overwhelming majority in Britain, reflected in an only modestly less preponderant majorit; on the Continent, want a common struggle against terrorism, in which suspects could be arrested and tried in any EC country (see Table 7.17).

TABLE 7.17: *Likelihood of common security by the year 2000*

Do you expect that our soldiers will have the same type of arms and equipment and assure together the security of the EC against threats from outside?		*Do you expect that we will fight in common against terrorism, for example, it is possible to arrest and bring to trial anybody accused of a serious crime no matter which country of the EC she or he has fled to?*	
yes	*no*	*yes*	*no*
		percentages	
EC	49	30	71	15
UK	58	29	83	10

SOURCE: Eurobarometer, *Europe 2000*, March 1987, tables A8, A10

   Granted that the expectation that one's country will have agreed to pool its defence effort with the other EC members by the year 2000 is not the same as wanting it to happen, the link seems close enough to conclude that the British in particular, and the people of the EC as a whole, would favour a genuine integration of security instruments and policies by then.

   The indications from Eurobarometer are, then, that the EC citizens are ready to accept that the Community be given the essential powers of the European Union, and indeed with the inclusion of security, of a federation, during the coming decade. The British appear to be more positive about common security and not much less positive about the economic powers; but that must be seen in relation to their more equivocal attitude to some aspects of Union institutions, and in particular to the idea of a European government, without with which the powers cannot, of course, be effectively exercised.

THE BRITISH, THE CONTINENTALS AND THE EUROPEAN UNION

Despite the lack of encouragement from their media and most of their political leaders, the British public do not seem likely to oppose steps towards European union in the Jean Monnet tradition. The obstacle is, rather, their Prime Minister. Following the example of the Single European Act, she might go along with such steps if they are initiated on the Continent. Their attitude to the single market, which was the centrepiece of the Single Act, indicates that the British public would favour this. If, on the contrary, she digs in her heels and quarrels with the Continentals about it, would the British turn against the Community as they did during the row about 'money back'? Probably not. The CAP and the raw budgetary deal for Britain that ensued from it were most unpopular in Britain, whereas the EC's other policies, and most of the steps that could be taken toward

European Union, are relatively well favored. The profile of British attitudes towards the Community does not indicate blind loyalty to a Prime Minister whose views on most such steps are pronouncedly more negative.

Nor have British opinions about the general idea of European Union and a constitution for it been anything like as negative as hers. But they have been ambivalent, confused, contradictory and fluctuating. We have seen that after wide fluctuations, the idea of the United States of Europe was favoured by a majority of the British in 1987, and that in 1983 a majority wanted the Members to be elected to the European Parliament to work for a European political union. But in 1985 the political union evoked a more even balance (6/85 T28), though still a more favourable reaction than was then accorded to the USE. Then again, the contradictory but on balance negative reactions to the idea of the European government have to be set against the recent warmth towards that of the United States of Europe.

We have also seen that the balance of British opinion in favour of the EP drafting a constitution for European Union was countered by a balance against giving the EP powers to form a government or vote laws. (See Table 7.10 above.) But when asked if they expected to be called to vote, by the year 2000, on a European constitution proposed by the EP, a majority of the British, almost exactly equal to the majority in the EC as a whole, said yes (UK 52 per cent, EC 53 per cent); and we have seen that over two-fifths of the British expected that there would be a European government by then (3/87 A11, A12, A13). The British also came down 76 per cent for and only 9 per cent against a referendum for or against the European Union, marginally more favourable than for the EC as a whole (6/88 A18).

If the British people seem to be persuadable about the merits of a constitution for European Union drafted by the European Parliament, Mrs Thatcher is certainly not going to try to persuade them in that direction. On the contrary, she has made it clear that she will oppose such ideas vehemently. This, coming on top of a lengthy period of quarrelsome and restrictive behaviour in the Community, has provoked thoughts about a core group going ahead towards European Union without waiting for Britain. The European Parliament's Draft Treaty, which provided for European Union to be reestablished after ratification by a majority of the Community's member states containing at least two-thirds of its population, was an example. In order to test public reactions to this, Eurobarometer asked whether a majority of the member countries, agreeing on the formation of a European Union, should create it even if 'two or three countries disagree', or whether they should 'abandon the project' (see Table 7.18).

The Continent as a whole thought predominantly that a core group should proceed. The Germans on balance thought the same, but less firmly. The British were not favorable, but the balance against was less

TABLE 7.18: *Whether to create a European Union even if two or three European Community members disagree*

	create it		abandon it
		percentages	
EC	54		27
FRG	45		32
UK	36		48

SOURCE: Eurobarometer, June 1988, Table A17

than might be expected, since it is fairly clear that the British would be among those left behind.

The British have, indeed, shown a certain realistic modesty when asked whose participation in a European political union would be necessary for the project to have some significance. Whereas around nine-tenths, both in the UK and in the EC as a whole, thought that France and the Federal Republic of Germany were necessary, only about two-thirds, both in the EC as a whole and in Britain itself, found the UK to be essential. The only important exception to this rating of the British role was in Germany, where three-quarters thought the British necessary. Thus there is, among the British, a certain level of awareness that a European union could be created without them (more, it seems, than among the Luxembourgers, 95 per cent of whom felt that the Grand Duchy was an essential element!: 6/85 T31). Yet there was enough of a majority, both in Britain and on the Continent, who saw Britain as an essential part of the political union, to warn that care would have to be taken not to present the action of a core group as divisive, if potentially dangerous repercussions in public opinion were to be avoided; and this seems to be particularly true of the Federal Republic.

This points towards the conclusion that the action by a core group to create the European Union is more likely to succeed if it is seen, not as breaking the Community to make the Union, but as building the Union on top of the Community: a two-speed Community, with the slower-speed members concentrating on the single market, until they catch up with the faster speed which includes the other essential elements of Union such as monetary union, security integration and institutional reform. Ingenuity would be needed, to devise a way of retaining the existing EC institutions for managing the present activities, centred on the common market, with all the present members (perhaps to be joined by new ones), while enabling the core group to adapt the institutions, reformed in a federal direction, to exercise the other powers of the Union. But if a convincing arrangement of this sort can be devised, it is likely to attract wider public support on the Continent and less divisive reactions from the British.

If the British were clearly against the European Union, such ingenuity would not be required. The core group would have to proceed regardless. But if it has been established that the British are not so much hostile as confused and uncertain, showing fair support for many aspects of Union despite media and political leadership pointing in the other direction, then the idea of a two-speed community/union, making it technically and psychologically easier for the British and others to catch up if they remain in the slow track at first, seems both juster and more likely to be supported by opinion on the Continent.

This assessment of British opinion may be contested. Perhaps the European jury will not be convinced that the British, despite some unfortunate experiences in relation to the Community and despite being so much misled by their media and politicians, are feeling their way towards a European destiny, embodied politically in the institutions and powers of a Union. The great merit of Eurobarometer is that it provides bases for an objective discussion of such aspects of the climate of opinion which, in our democracies, will condition the ways in which the European Union can best be created.

NOTES

(a) This chapter was completed at the end of 1988, since when the Eurobarometer surveys have shown further development of British opinion and significant political events have occurred. But the trends in the underlying attitudes which the chapter brings out still appear valid.

1. See Windlesham, Lord (1966) *Communication and Political Power* (London: Jonathan Cape) Chapter 6, and Jeremy Moon, *European Integration in British Politics 1950–1963: A Study of Issue Change* (Aldershot: Gower, 1985), pp. 156, 207.
2. Kitzinger, Uwe (1973) *Diplomacy and Persuasion: How Britain Joined the Common Market* (London: Thames and Hudson) Chapter 7 and pp. 412, 415.
3. S., A., and R., E., (1985) [Altiero Spinelli and Ernesto Rossi], 'The Ventotene Manifesto', reproduced in English translation in Walter Lipgens (ed.), *Documents on the History of European Integration Vol. 1: Continental Plans for European Union 1939–1945* (Berlin and New York: de Gruyter, p. 483.
4. *Eurobarometer* 1, July 1974, p. 2.
5. Tugendhat, Christopher (1986) *Making Sense of Europe* (Harmondsworth: Penguin) pp. 121ff.

8 The Role of South European Interest Groups in the European Community:[1] a comparative approach

Dusan Sidjanski
University of Geneva

The transition from authoritarian regimes to democracy and pluralism is the new trend in world politics. It began in Latin America and in Southern Europe and is spreading rapidly among the socialist countries of Eastern Europe. The South European countries, Greece, Spain and Portugal became members of the European Community (EC) in order to consolidate and develop their new or recovered democratic regime. Their adaptation to the Community's system was facilitated by their market economy and the quick integration of their political parties and interest groups in the network of European institutions and associations. In fact, one of the characteristic features of the EC is its large pluralistic network of different organizations, groups and autonomous centres of decision. At the political stage this pluralism is examplified by the presence of various political parties and free elections, at the socio-economic stage it is symbolized by the diversity of groups which reflect a variety of activities, interests and values.[2]

The Community, endowed with powers of a political nature but limited in scope and essentially economic, governs not only certain aspects of the behaviour of Member States but also groups and individuals. In fact, this emerging European authority presents an entirely original trend with its capacity to take decisions which affect groups, enterprises and people as well as the Member States. By directly influencing the actors of the socio-economic scene, the EC incites a vast movement of re-groupment of, in particular, the interests which have already been organized at the national level. As a consequence of this a network emerged consisting of interest groups, at the Community level around the principal decision centres of the EC. Obviously, these European groups, about 600 of them, have neither the structure nor the capacity comparable to their national

123

TABLE 8.1: *Inclusion of the South European interest groups within the groups of the Community*

Country	Integration	1970	1975	1980	1986
Greece	1980	–	2	66	154
Spain	1986	–	5	167	189
Portugal	1986	–	–	85	113
Total number of interest groups in the Community		308	346	431	515

counterparts, but all the same, they are better organized and more efficient than the international organizations of the same nature. Their actions are more intensive and tangible, corresponding, in principle, to domains at which the EC takes decisions and formulates common policies. From a different angle, this European network of organizations, their structures as well as their governing organs' formation and their membership are, in fact, the indicators of the real power of the Community and the intensity by which the informal socio-economic integration has been achieved in the EC.[3]

The coming into force of the European Single Act on 1 July 1987, has vigorously accelerated the activities at the Community level in which the interest groups have been actively involved. It is assumed that the interest groups have found their structures and functions strengthened by the idea of a Europe without internal frontiers as well as by the developments of common policies and structural funds.

The Greek interest groups' integration proceeded rather slowly and in a manner not conforming with the trend so far followed. If we compare this situation with the entry of Portuguese and Spanish groups of interest, we can see that the latter countries' groups have established organic and substantial relations with those of the Community much earlier than their formal entry and much more intensely than their Greek counterparts. How to explain this inconsistency? Are the Greek groups insufficiently disposed regarding necessary personnel or means for representation at the European level? Do the cost, the distance or the language form barriers in the way of their participation in the activities of the European groups? On the other hand, are the Greek groups simply less in number, less well-structured or more turned inward compared to the groups of the other two South European countries?

The groups of the new members of the European Community follow, more or less, the same route that the groups of the founding countries have followed: the groups which are most interested in and most motivated by the European Community establish relations first with the groups of interest at the Community level and others gradually follow depending on how well they feel their interests are represented. This process takes a relatively long period of time, somewhere about five years, to reach a sufficient level of representation. For example, the agricultural groups of interest of the Community, on account of the formulation of a common agricultural policy, have established organic relations first. The industrial sector and the services attract the recently adhering groups to the EEC according to their sectors and type of interest.[4] In the case of Greek and Portuguese interest groups, after the agricultural groups it was mainly the liberal vocational groups and trade unions which sought representation at the European level.

Concerning the Turkish interest groups, one can observe a certain hesitation on the side of the Community groups of interest. At the present time, four Turkish groups are members of the Community groups. They take part in the Permanent Conference of the Chambers of Commerce and Industry of the EEC, the European Confederation of Trade Unions and the Committee of Professional Agricultural Organizations of the EEC. The Turkish Confederation of Employers, which was a member of the UNICE, resigned later on account of conflicts regarding assignment of quotas, but has recently been re-integrated following Turkey's demand for entry into the EC.

The comparison of the interest groups of South Europe is not easy because of differences that exist between the three countries, although they are situated in a part of Europe which is more or less homogenous in many respects. Regarding their histories, their traditions of cooperation, the evolution of the interest groups are different and also the legal frameworks and socio-economic environments vary from one country to the other. In the meantime, these countries which belong to similar parts of Europe can also be associated with Ireland, a country with an economic level within the lower group in the EC.

According to the statistical data concerning the EC (European Parliament), *Les Progrès de la construction européenne*, 1987 (p. 9) the per capita incomes were in 1985, roughly 2 600 ecus in Portugal, 4 500 ecus in Greece and 5 500 ecus in Spain. This difference becomes less vivid when purchasing parities (PP) are compared; the difference which is very small between Greece (about 7 000 ecus) and Portugal (about 6 500 ecus) is rather high in the case of Spain (about 9 000 ecus).

Taking into account all these differences, we find ourselves in a position to compare these interest groups between themselves and with the European groups with respect to three dimensions: the organizational and functional dimension; the decision-making dimension and the Community dimension.

Regarding the *Community dimension* the approach to matters pertaining to the Community in general of the interest groups of the South European countries is mainly governed by three factors. First of all, their interest is the main factor which determines their behaviour. The second factor has to do with their financial and administrative capacity. The large central organizations of the South European countries were the first to participate in the activities of the Community groups, as associate members in the beginning, gradually becoming corresponding members and then full members. They are usually the employers' organizations acting in the fields of commerce, industry, agriculture and also in the capacity of employers' unions. The last factor is the advantage of obtaining first-hand information from the EC without passing through the official channels. This priority in obtaining information is particularly important when the sector in which the group acts is involved in matters concerning the Community. These three factors, organizational, decision-making and Community dimension, not only guided the formulation of our questionnaire but also influenced the orientation of our studies.[5] But it is also necessary to add another factor: European socialization accomplished by a common learning process of group leaders and members of the European Parliament also plays a decisive role in determining the behaviour of the South European interest groups when faced with questions concerning the Community.

THE INTEREST GROUPS AND TRANSITION TO DEMOCRACY

Contrary to Spain and Portugal, Greece has suffered only one interruption in the democratic process after the war, between 1967 and 1974 under the colonels' regime. This interruption did not have major effects on the interest groups, whose structures or management had in fact enjoyed a certain stability under the dictatorship which practised a liberal economic policy. The trade unions, on the other hand, which were already weak under democracy, suffered a further setback and marginalization under the military regime.

From the point of view of the interest groups, the return to democracy in 1974 did not bring any significant changes at the structural level; however, it emphasized the autonomy of the organizations and caused changes at the management level. This continuity of structure and administrative style of the professional organizations is also one of the reasons for the rigidity of the Greek groups which, despite the long period elapsed since their application and acceptance, still require very little support from the Community groups to improve their standing at the national level. This may be one of the reasons for the slow progress of the process of adaptation of the Greek groups to the Community environment.

The evolution in the two Iberian countries has been quite different. Paradoxically, the socio-economic groups of these countries had not reached a development which could have been expected under a corporatist system. In fact, in that context, the political authority had been seeking means of slowing down or controlling the progress towards autonomy of employer or labour groups, imposing on them vertical organizational systems. This State intervention had given rise to the development of underground or parallel systems, especially the Communist oriented trade unions (the Portuguese *Intersyndicale* and the Spanish Workers' Commissions). The socio-economic structures, as they are today, had begun to emerge and to establish themselves progressively with the implementation of a gradual opening and liberalization programme of the economies of these two countries: see the role of the Opus Dei, of the sixties in Spain during which time the exceptional economic growth was accompanied by in-depth changes in the economic structure; also the liberalization policy implemented by the Gaetano government during the years preceeding the Portuguese Revolution. This Revolution of 1974 has, in reality, caused a break much sharper than that which took place in Spain with the coronation of Juan Carlos I in 1975; from then onwards, despite a slight setback due to the revolutionary, unstable period between 1974 and 1976 in Portugal, both countries have taken decisive measures towards the democratization of their socio-political structures.

With the transition to democracy in Portugal, the trade unions came up from their clandestine positions. By 1976, the hegemony of the *Intersyndicale* had been overcome by the tertiary sector unions, supported by the SP and SDP. A second central labour organization, the UGT, with socialist and social democratic leanings was established as a result of dissident movement at the heart of the *Intersyndicale*. A similar chain of events took place in Spain after the enactment of the law recognizing the freedom of unionist activities in 1977, which allowed groups of trade unions to organize at the expense of the vertical unions of the old regime and to form two main branches, the UGT, which had socialist leanings, and the Confederation of Unions of Worker Commissions which sympathized with the PCE.[6]

The employer organizations were somewhat slower and were established from 1975 on, in reaction to the socializing policy of the pro-communist Portuguese government. The Confederation of Portuguese Industry (CIP) was founded in 1975 and the Confederation of Portuguese Trade (CCP) in 1976. During negotiations with the IMF, they gained influence due to the fact that the minority government of the socialist Soares needed their support to be able to come to terms with the IMF. On the other hand, following the launching of the agricultural reform and the nationalization in 1975, the Confederation of Portuguese Farmers (CAP) was established. Both the CIP and CAP supported the SP and the SDP to put an end to the revolutionary period. The three confederations met regularly in order to coordinate their activities in favour of a liberal economic policy which, in fact, corresponds to the EC's orientation. Their legitimacy and their influence have since been enhanced with the institution in 1983 of the Permanent Council for Social Cooperation and their affiliation to groups at the Community level. The attachment of Portuguese professional groups to the EC organs has also reinforced their standing at the national level.

The Spanish employers' organizations have been formed and recognized following the enactment of the law of 1977. The Spanish Confederation of Employers' Organizations (CEOE) was founded in 1977 along with the other organizations of the CEPYME and the AEB. The National Confederation of Farmers and Breeders was also established at the same time. At the beginning of the transition period, a certain confusion reigned concerning the respective roles of the political and socio-economic leaders, due in part to the fact that the new political personalities were, to a significant proportion, also responsible for professional groups. The leaders of employers' and labour organizations also assumed leading political functions especially as a result of their representation at the Parliament during the first legislative periods of the new regime.[7] This situation changed following the signing of the 'Pact of Moncloa' in 1977 and the birth of the principal parliamentary parties, from which members of unions and employer organizations have been excluded. After this division of responsibilities, the employers' and trade unions' leaders gradually began to manifest their group desires to establish their autonomy with regard to the State and the political parties. A desire to pursue common views and interests both from the point of view of groups and of the political parties was no longer evident or necessary as it was during the beginning of the transition to democracy.

As compared to the other two countries of the South, Spain displays a peculiarity due to its autonomous regions like Catalonia. Its status of autonomy (gained in 1979) could suffer from entry into the EC, due to certain restrictions concerning the role assigned to the central government in activities at the Community level. While supporting European integration and the 'Europe of the Regions', the Catalan authorities seek to preserve or increase their autonomy by applying measures which abide by the rules, and by executing decisions of the Community that are within their competence (art. 27 al 3 of the Status of Autonomy), and by supporting the actions of the regional groups. In 1982, the government established the 'Patrona Catala, Pro Europa' to facilitate the integration of various sectors to the EC. By 1986, it had installed a Catalonian office in Brussels to serve Catalan interests and also to provide a seat for the officials and private representatives of the region. Thus, the Catalan employers associations are in direct contact with Brussels. Sometimes, a regional association like the Catalan Confederation of Commerce participates directly at the level of European Confederation of Retail Trade. This tendency towards regional representation gained force by the presence of certain German 'Länder' and certain regional interest groups, and is likely to become more widespread with the realization of a single borderless market for 1993.

The foremost industrial region of Spain, Catalonia accommodates thirty-eight (20 per cent) of the 189 national Spanish interest groups represented at the Community level. Another sign of the presence of the region is manifest in the predominant role it plays in the national interest groups. Examples are: the Spanish Intertextile Council created in 1980 in view of integration, which is a member of the Comitextil; the Spanish Association of the Mesh Industries, a member of *Mailleurop*. These organizations, most of the leaders of which are the former leaders of regional organizations, have now undertaken the representation of the national interests in Brussels.

Even if Turkey does not have a quite comparable pattern, its case is studied in the double perspective of its process of democratization and of its demand for integration into the EC. After many interruptions in the democratic process and three years of military regime, Turkey has once again returned to the democratic path since 1983. In this new context, the interest groups, whose activities had been suspended during the military regime, have regained their functions following the parliamentary elections in 1983 and within the framework of the liberal economic policy of the Özal Government. The aim was the modernization of the economic structure by the introduction of the competitive market system and opening up of the economy to the outside, and particularly to the EC. Before that, the Turkish economy had been a protected economy since the establishment of the Republic, where the state enterprises which were created about fifty years ago for the promotion of industrialization, continued to occupy a central place. In fact, they employ more than half of all the workers in the manufacturing industries, and the state investments constitute 55 per cent of the total of investments. In this situation, the definition and readjustment of the role of the State in the economy becomes a priority. In this sense, a series of measures have been taken to adapt the public enterprises to the laws of the market economy. Evaluating the attitudes of the principal Turkish interest groups in view of adaptation to a liberal economy and opening up to international competition, one has the impression that the process may be slow as the majority of these groups are in favour of a halfway policy between a liberal and a state-controlled economy. The most outstanding exception to this situation is the truly liberal position of the Textile Employers' Union and of MESS (Metal Industries Employers' Union). Textiles represent more than a third of all the exports of Turkey, and the Union mentioned is the unique representative to the EC Commission. An important point is the centrist position of the principal workers' union Türk-Is, which is in favour of the EC in its expectation of its influence on the stabilization of the democracy and attainment of a higher level of protection of the rights of workers. Opening themselves to competition and to the conditions of market economy, Turkish interest groups are preparing for participation in Community activities.

THE ATTITUDES OF THE INTEREST GROUPS TOWARDS THE EC

From the political point of view, the perception of the integration process of the Spanish socio-economic groups is, in general, positive. Both the employers' groups – the majority of which hold a positive view with none against – and the spokesmen for the unions consider Spain's entry into the EC a positive move and in support of the development of the democratic political system. The views on the economic consequences, however, vary; the leaders of the employers' organizations express more optimistic views than those of the unions, the more optimistic ones being nearer to the government. On the other hand, the more pessimistic organizations are mostly sectoral ones or those farther away from the governmental position.

A similar attitude is found among the Portuguese interest groups. With the exception of the groups in alliance with the PCP, most of the groups express views which converge towards a positive attitude. Consensus exists that the EC would contribute to the stabilization of the democracy. This general positive attitude was much more *nuancée* at the period of negotiations with the EC, during which time the interest groups had been confronted with various substantial problems. Since then, the employers and their various sectors have expressed reservations and assumed a position for better claiming protection of their interests. In the meantime, following the integration of Portugal, this circumspect attitude has been transformed to a more positive attitude recognizing the reality of integration and the need to take as much advantage as possible of this new situation.

In Greece, the principal political advantages of integration are the services rendered in support of the general interests of the country and its contribution to institutional and juridistic modernization. Most of the representatives of the employers' organizations still dwell on its economic advantages and disadvantages. For certain groups like the Greek merchant marine, the integration brought neither gains nor losses. Many groups appeared to fear the adverse effects of external competition, especially on account of the more advanced technological level of some of the EC countries. Nevertheless, none took a general stand against the EC. The farmers' organization Paseges, which always stressed the danger of external competition, keeps a positive balance: however, this is mainly due to the Integrated Mediterranean Programmes, modernization of the agricultural sector and various aids.

On the side of the trade unions, despite the relatively favourable opinion of the General Confederation of Greek Workers (GSEE), their perception of integration is in general less positive than the employers'. The trade unions which are nearer to the Communist Party or the left wing of PASOK carry still less favourable opinions. An example is the Athens Labour Exchange which is controlled by the Communist Party.

Altogether, the Greek interest groups manifest less favourable attitudes, with a more pronounced cleavage between employers and trade unions, and also in general a higher level of indifference and distance towards the EC. This general observation does not apply to the central employers' organizations but is more in relation to certain sectoral organizations and trade unions.

Most of the Turkish organizations regard the Association Agreement in a negative perspective, with the exception of the Textile Organizations, the ISO (Istanbul Chamber of Industry) and the ATO (Ankara Chamber of Commerce). The overwhelming majority are in favour of immediate integration and expect that as a result of this the Turkish economy will gain in dynamism. Certain groups like the TGS (Turkish Journalists' Association) and the TESD (Associations of Turkish Artisans and Tradesmen) are of the opinion that the application for membership in the EC should have been made under more favourable economic circumstances.

ADAPTATION TO AND PARTICIPATION IN THE ACTIVITIES OF THE COMMUNITY GROUPS

The Greek central employers' organization has progressively established and developed relations at the European level since 1962, the date of the enactment of the Association Agreement. Since the entry of Greece into the EC, these relations have been intensified. Becoming a member of the UNICE after many years of contacts, the SEV is now a participator in the activities of the UNICE and in its working groups and keeps a permanent representative office in Brussels. It is also represented in a series of advisory organs. This institutional participation is reinforced by a network of informal contacts. In addition to that, the SEV has established close relations with the employers' groups of many member countries, with those of Germany in particular. This multi-faceted participation is carried out by many SEV leaders, especially its President.

Participation in sectoral organizations vary according to sectors. For example, the Union of Greek Shipowners takes part in the Council, and also in the working groups of the Committee of Shipowners Association of the EC (CAACE) as well as in the Economic and Social Committee since the entry of Greece into the EC. They maintain regular and frequent contacts with the Commission. On the other hand, the approach of the Union of Greek Cotton Industrialists and that of the Union of Greek Wool Mills display significant differences. While the cotton people participate actively in the activities of COMITEXTIL and of the Eurocoton, collaborate with the Commission and develop bilateral relations especially with their French and Italian counterparts; the wool people have only occasional contacts with the COMITEXTIL – which they consider an 'overgrown monster' – to the degree in which it can provide them with useful

information at reasonable cost.[8] These two forms of participation reflect
the modernistic-traditional dichotomy.

In different cases the participation is made difficult by an absence of
equivalent structures at the EC level: the Union of Exporters of Industrial
Products, for example, is represented sometimes through the Panhellenic
Association of Exporters, or SEV or through the Ministry of Commerce.
PASEGES, member of COPA and of the COGECA, works through a
permanent representative office in Brussels which facilitates contacts with
the Commission as well as its various committees or working groups.

The level of participation is also high on the part of the organizations of
architects, engineers, lawyers, medical doctors and especially on the part
of the travel agents (Group of National Unions of Travel Agencies of the
EC – under Greek chairmanship). Nevertheless, many other groups do not
express as much need for pursuing relations or being involved in organic
cooperation with their counterparts in the Community.

The participation of the trade unions is marked by a considerable delay
according to the GSEE and the Athens Labour Exchange themselves. The
GSEE takes part in the activities of some commissions of the ECTU-
European Confederation of Trade Unions as well as in certain international sectoral organizations (eg. restaurant and tourism workers). The
Federation of Textile Workers, although formally a member of the European Committee of Textiles, Garments and Leather Unions, declares that
they are not participating in any unionist activity at the European level
which they consider lacking in class-consciousness and class politics.

The consequences of the entry of Spain to the EC, as evaluated by the
Spanish interest groups, are considered positive by the majority of representatives, both at the level of employers and of the trade unions. One of
the signs of the adaptation of the Spanish groups is the numerous surveys
and analyses made by them concerning the EC, carried out for the purpose
of assuring a more efficient representation at the EC level (three-quarters
of the twenty interviewed). The structural adaptation has not created any
problems; many of the organizations which were recently established have
taken into account the European dimension and many of them have found
there a stimulating factor or seen possibilities of support. From this point
of view also the comparison between Spanish and Portuguese interest
groups is obvious, due to their parallel emergence and development.

Spain is the leading country among the new members and even among
some older members, owing to its high number of groups already integrated in the Community network. Almost all the employer or trade union
groups of any importance at the national level take part in one or more
European organization. The effective participation in European associ-
ative life is growing on a par with the increasing participation of Spain in
advisory or decision-making organs. All the interviewed employers' groups
encourage their affiliates to become members of at least one European

organization; almost a third of them are members of two or three Community organizations. Unions which sympathize with the SP or the SDP have good connections in the unionist groups at the Community level; the two other unions, the CNT and the Workers' Commissions, even if more internationalistically oriented, wish to participate in the ESC. Altogether, participation in one or the other aspect of the Community by this or that group is being pursued actively with the aim of coordinating action at the European level.

The employers' organizations also maintain bilateral relations with their counterparts in other member countries, either directly or through the related European groups. One representative stated that these contacts were of decisive importance for his organization. Other spokesmen declared these relations were complementary, serving to update information.

In nine cases out of ten, the participation is evaluated as positive, the appraisal of the employers' groups being slightly more positive than the unionist groups. In general, the participation of Spanish delegations in Brussels is, for the majority of groups, periodic but of a very high frequency and regularity. They vary depending on several factors: the importance and efficiency of the Community group, its power of influence as well as its level of intervention, the role of the EC in various sectors of the economy[9] and above all the budgetary means, which, rather low for Spanish groups, are limiting their levels of participation. This last argument is also underlined with more emphasis by the spokesmen of the Portuguese groups. These evaluations appear in fact more relative if compared with the even lower level of participation of Greek groups in general. Nevertheless, as a general rule, the interest groups are inclined to complain of the insufficiency of means at their disposal.

In Portugal, the principal organizations have reinforced their structures and their capacities following entry into the EC. This led to the recruitment of additional staff and helped accelerate modernization of the equipment of certain groups. For example, the CCP has installed a permanent post in Brussels (1987) where it has representatives in about fifteen advisory committees. Since 1986, it has become a member of the Federation of European Associations of Wholesale and Foreign Trade; notwithstanding its activities rest mostly on its sectoral associations, affiliated to European commercial groups. In the domains of industry and agriculture, participation is mainly accomplished by the two central organizations, the CIP and the CAP, and some sectoral groups oriented towards exportation, like the ones concerned with textiles. The degree of participation depends normally on the budgetary means of the national groups which they are endeavouring to expand since 1986, this leading the way also to a general reinforcement of the groups themselves. The first of these organizations to establish contacts at the European level has been the CIP, becoming first an associate and then a full member of the UNICE; it also installed a permanent representative office in Brussels in 1982. The CAP has also reinforced its representation by becoming a member of the COPA in 1985, assuming its vice-presidency in 1987 and establishing a permanent representative office in Brussels.

The situation at the level of the trade unions reflects a well-known conflict; the entrance of the UGT to CISL since its creation has facilitated its subsequent affiliation to the ETUC, giving it an advantage over its rival, the CGTP-IN, whose several attempts for acceptance have remained fruitless. This inequality of access between the two confederations is partially neutralized by an equal representation by both of them at the Economic and Social Committee. In these circumstances, it is quite normal that the CGTP-IN attaches great importance to its participation in the ES Committee, as it is kept outside the European Trade Unions Confederation.

Since the country's membership in the EC, all the important Portuguese groups have intensified their activities at the Community level. The delegations representing all the groups travel regularly, about once a week, to Brussels in order to take part in various meetings, and especially in those of the Economic and Social Committee. The Portuguese groups which have only recently established contact with the Community organs appear to assign greater importance to the Economic and Social Committee than the other groups. This is also the case for the CGTP-IN for the above-mentioned reason.

The membership of the Turkish groups in the Community organs are at the level of 10 per cent as compared to the groups of the other three countries of Southern Europe, totalling up to only fifteen in 1986. This level is below that of Spain at the time of its application for entry into the EC, and roughly comparable to that of Greece in a similar period. The TISK (Turkish Employers' Confederation) which had suspended its membership in the UNICE on account of financial deficiencies, has meanwhile re-assumed its place there. An exceptional case which requires mentioning is the case concerning the Turkish representative of the textile industries, who plays a prominent role as the only spokesman in the negotiations with the Commission, and who is also responsible for the distribution of annual quotas between the Turkish textile enterprises. The evolution of the Turkish groups' activity will probably follow a similar pace to that of the Greek groups in their participation in the Community organs, which gained momentum after Greece's entry into the EC. On the other hand, the process of integration of the Spanish and Portuguese groups took place much earlier and faster, already before 1980.

Our survey in Greece indicated the existence of two conflicting approaches towards European integration in the industrial sectors; the food industries are better integrated than the other industrial branches; on the other hand, the textile industries (with the exception of cotton), chemistry and metallurgy appears to be insufficiently integrated in the Community groups. The inverse practice is observable in Spain, where most of the industrial groups are well integrated with the European groups with the exception of the food industries sector. In Portugal, the industrial groups are integrated unequally and on the average despite the recent progress made on the part of the central interest groups. In principle, the degree of participation corresponds to the level of membership, taking in account that Greek and Portuguese groups suffer comparatively more from lack of sufficient means.

In the three countries the liberal professions, services and commerce are well represented, with the exception of the Spanish craftsmen, the intensity of participation varying in terms of the impact of the Community policy on the sector, and the relative importance of the sectors concerned, as well as the means at their disposal. This observation, which could be extended to other sectors, must be interpreted in the light of the perception that the leaders of the groups are concerned regarding their relations with the Community groups and the institutions of the EC in terms of a cost-benefit analysis. In the same line of thought, we have observed that the agricultural groups are, in general, well-integrated and more active as agriculture remains an important field of activity in the three countries, and in the Community: agriculture is the object in relation to a substantial form of encouragement within the framework of the CAP special contributions made to the farmers of the South European countries. These inputs have sometimes also a significant political dimension, as in the case of Greece.

THE FUNCTIONS OF NATIONAL INTEREST GROUPS AS RELATED TO THE EC

Among the principal functions of the interest groups with relation to the European integration, the following are the predominant ones: information studies and analysis, representation and coordination, influence, promotion or defence of interests. As elaborated in the past in our previous work,[10] the information function comes first in importance among the activities of the European groups. Progressively, with the development of the integration process, other functions also begin to assume more importance. In the South European countries and especially in Spain and Portugal, their processes of democratization brought forward the legitimization function of national groups through membership in the Community or international organizations. Their belonging to the European associations is, in a way, the recognition of their representativity and consequently of their legitimacy, which mostly results in the reinforcement of their status and their influence at the national level.

In Greece, all the groups utilize the traditional channels of information –

circulars, bulletins, reports etc. to keep their members abreast of current European problems; in addition, the exporters also operate a databank. The information is concentrated on specific questions like industrial development under SEV. The Technical Chamber and PASEGES furnish rich and regular information on the integrated Mediterranean Programmes. On the other hand, the information provided appears insufficient in the opinion of trade unions, with the exception of the textiles trade union. In Spain as well as in Portugal the demand for information has significantly increased since their integration. The dissemination of information is accomplished through the regular and periodic means to which publications and up-to-date reports are added. The primary function of the groups, it appears, is to act as instruments for the retrieval and dissemination of information concerning the EC. They constitute a means of reducing the distance between their members and the EC, as well as of facilitating the action of their members in European matters. Thus, for example, the members of Portuguese organizations interviewed mostly regard their organizations more and more like a conveyor belt of information – evaluated as more efficient than national administrations – rather than real pressure groups. Moreover, in the three countries, the great majority of leaders of the groups interviewed are of the opinion that the national administrations furnish incomplete information parsimoniously, and that it is through their contacts and their participation at the Community level that the interest groups are informed of the prevailing problems and decisions taken in the Community. According to the principle of division of work, the general information is disseminated through the central organizations, the specialized organizations being responsible for sectoral information.

Other functions of the groups tend to develop as the impact of the EC on the tangible interests of their members increases: aggregation of the interests of its members and of definition of common attitudes; representation and negotiation within groups or advisory organs of the EC; elaboration of strategies and their coordination with those of other national groups; protection of the interests of their members; pressure in order to influence the positions of the Community groups as well as the decisions of the EC. In addition to these functions of pressure group or lobbying, the interest groups assume also a more general role: they contribute by the diversity and richness of information to the transparency and through the plurality of the decision centres to the democratization of the socio-political system. This role of the national groups is reinforced by their integration within the network of European groups. Finally, altogether and in their various levels and degrees they bring their contributions to the process of 'European socialization' of their leaders and their members.

The means and accesses used by the socio-economic groups of the three countries are not fundamentally different from those available to their European counterparts: the principal means are the advice, the reports and the positions the groups transmit to their European organizations, and which they seek to have prevail at national or Community level. It is only occasionally that groups use other means like the media or exceptional manifestations (eg. manifestations of European farmers organized by the COPA). The difference, according to the leaders of South European groups, as expressed in interviews with them, lies mainly in the magnitude of means available to them in the form of financial resources, the level of competence or the number of delegates or experts available. As referred to before, the Greek and Portuguese as well as Spanish leaders emphasize the insufficiency of their financial resources as an obstacle in the way of keeping an active and continuous participation within the professional and official organs of the EC.

EVALUATION OF THE INFLUENCE OF THE NATIONAL INTEREST GROUPS AT THE COMMUNITY LEVEL

The basic issue, and also the most difficult one, concerns the evaluation of the influence of the socio-economic groups on the process of decision-making both at the national and at the Community levels. In our previous studies devoted to this subject, we had to analyse and evaluate the weights of various indicators of power, investigate the various accesses and means available to obtain results and through these various approaches, try to reach an appraisal of the potential capacity of influence of interest groups.[11] This method which consists, to begin with, of approaching and surrounding a central problem by means which are easy to observe, is finally completed by an analysis of certain cases of influence. In full consciousness of the deficiencies of this approach, we have found it pertinent to extract certain general conclusions based on our observations, inquiries and our knowledge of the subject.

Without carrying a general judgment, one can conclude that the predominance of specialized organizations is a sign of efficiency of technical action. General action, on the other hand, is difficult to define; a general agreement is mostly in the form of a compromise of approaches or ideas. When the decision rests on general problems, pressures are imprecise and indistinct and have less chances of exerting any real influence. On the other hand, technical action is more limited, but also much more precise. A draft regulation concerning beer or jam suggested by European organizations has a much better chance of approval by the EC authorities than a commercial or antitrust policy proposed by a central organization. At the present stage of European integration it appears that specialized, limited or technical influence will have an upper hand over general influence. This observation seems quite plausible, as it is much more difficult to evaluate the general influence of organizations like the UNICE or the ETUC as compared to the more precise and incisive action of COPA, for example. However, this observation is not meant to give an exaggerated impress- ion of the influence of specialized or technical groups.[12] A general evaluation of the influence of the interest groups is a hazardous exer- cise: it implies analyses of a multitude of factors in a chronological perspective as well as an appraisal of a complex model of inter-influences somewhat akin to a polygon of forces, of decisions and of pressures evolving from the framework of a special process which is in general inseparable from the overall national or Community level processes.

Due precautions having been taken, a concrete distinction, however, could be established between the general and the sectoral or specialized influence. The representatives of the Spanish groups, in general, value sectoral influence as much more effective and important than general influence. The responses to these questions are inversely proportional, with 70 per cent of the interviewed rating sectoral influence maximum, and about 65 per cent judging general influence minimum. The majority of the Spanish groups, subject to our research, are of the opinion that the capacity for influence of the groups is increasing following Spain's entry to the Community. The effect at the national level is evident, as perceived from the responses of the majority of our interviewees whether from the trade unions or the employers that the influence of the professional organizations have increased since the entry of Spain into the EC.

This dimension occupies an important place in the views of the Portu- guese and Greek socio-economic leaders. It is significant that being part of a European group greatly facilitates intervention in the decision-making process concerning Portugal. In the same way, for the representatives of the employers' organizations the integration of Portugal in the EC contrib- utes to the reinforcement of the engagement of the country in a market economy system and obliges it to revise the constitution in that sense. This is, at least, their expectation, which also coincides with the efforts deployed by the SDP government.

The experience of the Greek groups deserves further attention. It is interesting to note that the evaluation of the principal Greek employers' groups of the European groups' influence, although quite laconically expressed, is positive and quite effective in general. Only the exporters are of the opinion that their influence is weak and the real power passes through the government and the European Parliament. This reference to the European Parliament suggests that the evaluation is largely a function of the relations and views of the interviewees, and that it should be moderated by the real weight that the European Parliament has in the Community system.

The Technical Chamber, the liberal professions and the PASEGES perceive the influence of the European groups differently, although the majority agree on attributing to them a real or potential part of influence.

According to most of them, this influence is a function of the capacity of the European groups in formulating tangible and sectoral proposals. Only the PASEGES made a critical evaluation of the influences of the COPA and the COGECA on common agricultural policy. Nevertheless, this affirmation is greatly toned down by its following observation according to which the Commission takes back or modifies its proposals each time a strong majority of member groups of COPA opposes it, indicating thus their 'veto power'. When it comes to trade unions – as could be judged from their level of participation – they are mostly sceptical in this respect.

If it is important to find out how the national groups evaluate the capacity of influence of the European groups, it is also significant in this context to analyse their opinions on their own influence within the European socio-economic groups. In this respect, one can assume in principle that those who attribute a high degree of influence to the European groups of which they are members, usually tend to evaluate their own influence positively within their European groups. Such is the case with the modernistic employers' fractions – SEV, EEE, Cotton – who claim to have a certain influence within the organizations of which they are members. Taking into account its resources and the dimensions of its membership, the SEV admits to be not as influential as the great European employers' organizations, while the EEE claims to have a great influence as it represents the most important merchant fleet in the EC. Various other groups like the PASEGES declare themselves influential within the European groups, like the COPA. The PASEGES emphasizes that it is essential, for the protection of the interests of the group, to seek alliances with its counterparts of the other member countries. Finally – with surprise – one finds that the majority of the representatives of the workers consider themselves as influential in the Community groups of which they are a member. This statement raises doubts and one tends to suspect wishful thinking on the part of certain groups. It is a general tendency observed regarding various groups, to overrate their influence in an attempt to increase their importance in front of their members and the decision-making bodies.

The principal Greek groups mainly agree that their affiliation to European organizations has had a positive effect on their relations with the government. For example, the Association of Medical Doctors declares that their affiliation to the European organization renders them able to criticize the government policy whenever it deviates from the decisions taken at the Community level. The Bar's representatives declares that their relations with the government and the Ministry of Justice are quite good, so that there is no reason to criticize the government. While many other groups complain of a lack of consultation on the part of the government, the PASEGES, on the contrary, claims that its exchange of information and assistance with the Ministry of Agriculture and its participation in the

Community groups, has gained it the advantage of informal but continuous collaboration with the Ministry of Agriculture.

This collaboration in the agricultural sector is not particular to Greece but is encountered in most of the EC countries: in France, in Germany, in Denmark or in Italy but mostly in Spain and in Portugal. Many arguments have been raised in explanation of this phenomenon, especially stressing the fact that agriculture – often in difficulty or regression – remains as a sector politically and socially worthy of attention, or of some sort of special protection by the governments. Some workers' organizations appear to draw certain benefits from their international or European affiliations, especially in the form of support for their claims at home.

On the whole, with the exception of certain Greek groups, the groups from Southern Europe are of the opinion that the governments keep them out of the process of decision-making. Contrary to what happens in the other European countries, the practice of consultation with socio-economic groups does not appear to be a general tendency. Probably, the integration of a country into the EC and of its national groups into the European groups, contributes to the development of the process of consultation which many governments practise regardless of their political colour. Finally, one can wonder if other substitutes or additional relations exist, especially in the form of personal relations. Already there is good reason to believe that the foreseeable evolution in the countries of Southern Europe will progressively increase the transparency of relations between the enterprises and their groups on one hand, and the governmental bodies on the other.

CONCLUSIONS

Despite the structural differences among them and a certain degree of difference in their timing of affiliation to European groups, the interest groups of the three new member countries display comparable modes and often convergent behaviours. With their return to democracy, the emerging interest groups of the three new members have found themselves stronger and with more autonomy with regard to the government and the political parties. In this way, they contribute to an increase in the representation of diverse socio-economic interests and to the revival of social pluralism.

Taking as an example the general process of creation of the Community groups, the central national organizations were the first to adhere to the large European organizations like the UNICE and the COPA. The *process of integration* of the sectoral groups also conforms with the general trend observed in the EC: the interests most affected by the policies and decisions at the Community level tend to integrate first, the others follow gradually in relation to the rate at which Community level action penetrates their field of activity. In Greece and in Portugal, first the central and then the sectoral national groups affiliated to the EC groups, while in Spain – as a result of the autonomy of regions – this process at the national level was followed by affiliation of a certain number of regional groups. This regionalization is also reflected within the national groups, in the composition of their leaders and in the distribution of authority.

An *analysis of the attitudes* of the principal leaders of the interest groups taken as basic factors of behaviour, leads to the conclusion that their attitudes are in general positive from the viewpoint of general policy. In fact, the groups are of the opinion that the entry of their countries to the EC would constitute a firm anchorage to the democratic Europe reinforcing the stability of their young democracies. On the other hand, as one investigates further in individual domains and especially within various sectors, one finds that the attitudes become more subtle, more prudent and even more reserved. The fear of unequal competition from enterprises better-equipped and technologically much more advanced begins to emerge. However, following the adhesion to the EC and direct experience within the EC, these apprehensions begin to subside and turn into an attitude which is more positive and active in pursuit of profit from the opportunities and the advantages offered by the EC.

This upwards evolution corresponds, in general, to the trends of *public opinion* in the three countries; the initially less favourable public opinion about integration with the EC in Greece since 1981, has turned up following 1983 reaching the 50 per cent limit by 1987 and a little over that in 1988; in Portugal, the ratio of those in favour of integration was about 30 per cent between 1980 and 1985. It made a jump between 1985 and 1987, attaining a value of about 60 per cent in 1987; with a small decrease, it was slightly over 50 per cent in 1988. The opinions concerning the beneficial consequences follow the same evolution between 1986 and 1988 and remain slightly below those in favour of integration; in Spain, the public opinion in favour of integration has remained relatively stable and increased only slightly between 1980 and 1988, exceeding the 60 per cent mark; but contrary to the other two countries, opinions concerning beneficial consequences display a considerable difference compared to the opinion on entry: while remaining at a much lower level, it rises by 15 per cent in 1986 to near 25 per cent in 1988.[13]

By comparison, the *adaptation* of the Greek interest groups appears quite slow, and their *participation* in the Community level activities less effective, with the exception of the central employers' organization and the shipowners. Although it became a member six years later, Spain has reached the level of 167 in 1980 and of 189 in 1986, numbers much above the number of Greek groups taking part within Community level groups. The dimensions and diversification of its economy, which is much beyond those of the Greek economy, are probably the decisive factors in this development. The comparison of the rates of affiliation of the Greek and Portuguese groups is interesting to note; in 1980 the number of Portuguese groups affiliated was 85 as compared to 66 from Greece; however, Greece has caught up with and surpassed Portugal in 1986, with 154 against 113. It appears that the constitution or rather reconstitution of the Spanish and Portuguese interest groups, with the return to democracy of these countries, enables their adaptation to be faster and their need for affiliation to and their participation in the Community groups larger. In a lesser degree, these factors are equally valid for Greece.

The employers-trade unions *conflict*, which is more pronounced in Greece as compared to the other two countries, is also discernible in the attitudes as well as in the degrees of participation of the interest groups. The intensity of participation appears, in a way, less than that which prevails in Spain or Portugal; the trade unions close to the governmental parties are participating more actively within the ETUC. However, the intensity of participation, although indicative of the influences of employers/trade unions and communist/socialist cleavages and conflicts, equally depends on the respective weights of other factors like the impact of the Community policies and decisions on the interest groups, the importance of the sectors affected, their opening up to the EC and on the resources available to the interest groups concerned.

An *analysis of the functions* of the interest groups reveals a confirmation of the results previously obtained: to begin with, access to information plays a predominant role: next to that come functions of representation, common strategies and the protection which increase as the field of influence of the EC grows. Also of importance is the fact that the more the impact of the EC becomes tangible and immediate, the larger is the spectrum of functions with regard to Community affairs that the interest groups assume.

The *real degree of influence* of the interest groups is also rather difficult to assess, as the groups tend to manifest a general inclination towards overestimating their influences. In this perspective, it is quite probable that they slightly exaggerate the importance and influence of the Community groups also, to emphasize their own weights at the European level. Despite all these overevaluations, all the groups confirm that their joining the Community groups and their participation at that level increased their capacities of access and their influences within their governments. In this context the Turkish textile groups constitute an extreme case.

As a rule, the national interest groups are directly in touch with the Community echelons without passing through the channels of the national administrations. This direct access at the European level also reinforces their positions in negotiations at the national level. However, there is another mode of approach also observed as regards the national groups, which involves using their access at the level of national administrations as an additional means of influence to affect the decisions of the Council where national ministers sit and vote.[14]

All the experience gained from studies on the interest groups indicate that the global and general influence of the groups is more difficult to ascertain as a result of the various factors and actors which enter the play, to say nothing of the other pressures, informal influences due to certain situations, to the atmosphere or to the dominant ideas of the moment as well as the 'invisible' interaction of people, of groups and of officials. The complexity of the global socio-political processes makes it difficult to assess the parts of influence attributable to various actors. On the other hand, our inquiries confirm most of our previous conclusions, and especially the one that in the present state of the European integration, the sectoral influence which is more specific, more technical and somewhat more striking is also more easily distinguishable by the available techniques of observation.

By concentrating our analysis on the interest groups themselves, we ought to keep ourselves away from fallacies which may lead to overemphasizing their weights on the European and national level decision-making processes. In reality, as a result of our work, we reached the conclusion that the weights of the European as well as the national groups of interest on processes of decision-making and management at the Community level remain relatively modest as compared to those of the governments and their representatives. But we have to take into account that, in turn, the governments can be influenced by their national groups, the weight of which varies from country to country. The fact remains that alongside institutional centres of decision, the political parties and the electors, the groups – reflecting a multitude of socio-economic interests – assume a variable but effective role in their national communities and also in the European Community.

NOTES

1. This synthesis reproduces the results of research on the political parties and interest groups in their relations with European units and groups performed under my direction in collaboration with Dr. U. Ayberk and with the aid of the Volkswagenwerk Foundation. It is based on the following papers: Carlos Garcia, 'Les groupes socio-professionnels espagnols et la Communauté', University of Geneva, October 1987; Anna Melich, 'Problématique centre-périphérie en Espagne: Intégration à la CE des groupes dont le siège n'est pas dans la capitale', University of Geneva, October 1987; Maximos Aligisakis, Ioannis Papadopoulos, with the collaboration of Marianna Cossina, 'Aspects de l'insertion des groupes d'intérêts grecs dans la Communauté Européenne: la perception des élites en tant qu'indicateur d'intégration', University of Geneva, October 1987; Guilhermina Marques, 'Quelques aspects de l'intégration des

groupes d'intérêts portugais au niveau européen', University of Geneva, March 1988; Ural Ayberk, Emre Boduroglu, 'Les groupes d'intérêt turcs face à la Communauté Européenne', University of Geneva, October 1987.

2. Sidjanski, D. (1979) *Europe élections: de la démocratie européenne* (Paris: Stanké).

3. Meynaud, J. and D. Sidjanski (1971) *Les groupes de pression dans la Communauté européenne 1958–1968* (Bruxelles; Editions de l'institut de Sociologie).

4. Sidjanski, D. and Ural Ayberk (1987) 'Bilan des groupes et du processus de décision dans la Communauté européenne des Six', *Rex Publica* No 1, 1974 and 'Le nouveau visage des groupes d'intérêt communautaires', *Revue d'intégration européenne*, 2 and 3.

5. The collection of data on the groups of the south of Europe has been completed following eighty-four in-depth interviews with the leaders of central employers' organizations, industrial and commercial, agricultural organizations, trade unions as well as with some sectoral organizations. Cf. Sidjanski, D. and U. Ayberk (1989) *Rapport sur les partis politiques et les groupes d'intérêt en Europe du Sud dans leurs relations avec les formations et groupes européens*, Stiftung Volkswagenwerke/SVW, October.

6. In the final elections the Spanish UGT has obtained the greatest number of delegates followed by the CC.OO. which has the majority in various cities and large industrial enterprises.

7. Condomines, J. (1984) 'Les syndicalistes parlementaires en Espagne', Department of Political Science, Geneva.

8. The contacts are considered difficult on account of cost and therefore not established except on an occasional visits of individual members of the Union.

9. See Sidjanski, D. and U. Ayberk (1974) 'Bilan des groupes...', *Res Publica*, which emphasises the parallelism between the impact of Community policies and actions on the one hand and the emergence or importance of the Community groups on the other.

10. Meynaud, J. and D. Sidjanski (1967) *L'Europe des affaires* (Paris: Payot) and *Les groupes de pression dans la Communauté européenne*, op. cit; D. Sidjanski and U. Ayberk 'Le nouveau visage des groupes d'intérêt communautaires', op. cit.

11. See our works realized mostly with Jean Meynaud, Ural Ayberk, José Barroso and Jonas Condomines. In our analyses we have made reference to indicators of the capacity to influence such as: 1. The importance of the sector and the grouping in the sector in terms of turnover, per cent of workers and the sales; 2. the importance and the validity of the cause or interests defended; 3. the representivity and the number of its members, eg. unions, farmers, enterprises; 4. financial assets; 5. organization and efficiency: a) actual number of staff, b) competence of administrators, c) their authority and prestige; 6. image and reputation of the group; 7. homogeneity or divisions; 8. relations with other groups (coalitions, rivalries); 9. means of contact with or access to institutions and centres of decision.

12. Sidjanski, D. (1982) 'Les groupes de pression dans la Communauté européenne' *Il Politico* 3, 559 and 560.

13. Eurobarometer 29, June 1988.

14. See the general action diagram of Community and national groups in our article 'Les groupes de pression dans la Communauté européenne' in *Il Politico*, 3, 1982, pp. 553–5.

9 Trust between Nations: Primordial Ties, Societal Learning and Economic Development

Ronald Inglehart, University of Michigan

ABSTRACT

Though widely criticized in recent years, the concept of political culture is useful in understanding the nature and sociopolitical impact of interpersonal trust. For trust – both in others of one's own nationality, and toward other nationalities – seems to be an enduring characteristic of given cultures that can, partly, be traced to long-term societal learning. Trust is also strongly related to a given society's level of economic development. Primordial ties, such as race, religion or geographic proximity, have surprisingly little impact on trust, when we control for the effects of economic development and shared historical experiences. Trust ratings of seventeen nationalities, made by ten Western publics, show a remarkable cross-cultural consensus that certain nationalities can be trusted more than others. The evidence suggests that economic development is conducive to trust – but that inter-personal trust may also be a prerequisite for economic and social modernization.

INTRODUCTION

Interpersonal trust plays an important role in economic and political cooperation, as has long been recognized (Wylie, 1957; Banfield, 1958; Almond and Verba, 1963; Easton, 1966; Hart, 1973; Luhman, 1979; Hill, 1981; Miyake, 1982; Abramson, 1983; c.f. Miller, 1974; Citrin, 1974; Marsh, 1977). Nevertheless, little empirical research has dealt with trust between different nationalities; the most relevant work is Deutsch, 1952; Buchanan and Cantril, 1953; Deutsch, *et al.*, 1957; Merritt and Puchala, 1968; Nincic and Russett, 1979.

Trust or distrust help shape one's expectations under conditions of imperfect information; they can be crucial factors when the leaders of one nation interpret the actions of another nation. Trust is the expectation that another's behavior will be predictably friendly; distrust is the expectation that another's behavior will be harmful or unpredictable (Pruitt, 1965). Thus, trust or distrust predispose one to interpret another's actions as friendly or threatening when ambiguity exists. The consequences can be vitally important.

In the early 1980s, for example, the United States and the USSR seemed to be engaged in an arms race, with both sides pouring trillions of dollars into the development and implementation of potentially devastating weapons systems, targeted on each other and their allies. Expectations of war were rising (a fact that was reflected in the Eurobarometer surveys of those years). As we enter the 1990s, the arms race has leveled off and some weapons systems are actually being dismantled. The prospects for peace have rarely looked better. From a purely geopolitical perspective, the two nations have not changed much since the early 1980s: they are still the world's two leading military powers, with contrasting ideologies and political systems, and occupying the same geographical and strategic positions as before. But one thing has changed: their subjective perceptions have evolved; with a key aspect of this change being a marked rise in mutual trust.

When Western decision-makers perceive Soviet actions as threatening, they will feel they must take counter-measures; if the Soviet leaders, in turn, interpret Western measures as motivated by hostile intent, it can become a vicious circle of mutual paranoia. Objectively, the US and the Soviet Union have no trade rivalries, no border conflicts, complementary economies and an immense common interest: a mutual stake in avoiding World War III. If it is true that their ideological differences are fading, the main thing that separates them may be simply a matter of trust – but this may turn out to be a question of life and death.

Distrust tends to become a self-fulfilling prophecy, as history has shown repeatedly. From 1866 to 1945, each generation of Frenchmen and Germans anticipated the coming war between their two nations – eagerly or with foreboding, but with the conviction that it was inevitable, virtually a law of nature. Dramatic changes have occurred since 1945: such 'laws of nature' can be abolished. But the process is not easy, for trust or distrust between two mutually salient nations tends to be persistent – especially if it is rooted in cultural differences. Since political elites are socialized within a given political culture, their outlook is likely to reflect the stereotypes of trust or distrust prevailing within their culture.

The tendency for given nations' actions to be interpreted differently within different cultural zones is illustrated vividly by the Falkland Islands crisis of the early 1980s. To a remarkable extent, Spanish-speaking regimes located all along the political spectrum from extreme left to extreme right supported an Argentine military dictatorship in the conflict; while Great Britain's partners in the European Community, together with English-speaking nations such as Canada, Australia, New Zealand and the United States, supported Great Britain.

Trust between nationalities may be vital – but can anything be done about it? In so far as it is linked with primordial ties such as race and ethnic ties, it is relatively intractable. But geographic proximity and race seem to be declining influences on cross-national trust or distrust; and, though language is important, its significance lies more in the fact that it can be a channel of communication or a barrier to communication flows, rather than as a fixed ethnic characteristic. Trust or distrust between nationalities shows an impressive tendency to persist over time; but it is a variable not a constant, and hence is subject to human intervention.

What factors influence international trust? A great many possibilities suggest themselves; they can be grouped into four main categories:

Primordial Ties

Fear of the unknown is widespread. If one is inexperienced in dealing with other kinds of people, one tends to trust those who seem similar more than those who seem different. Similarities of race and religion are among the most obvious primordial ties. Often, the myth of a common race is based on a common language – in which case, language too seems like a primordial tie: something one is born into, part of one's basic identity, rather than something one chooses to learn. But language also serves another function: it set boundaries between those with whom one can communicate, and those with whom one can not. In this respect, it plays a major role in social learning processes.

The geographical location of a given nationality is also more or less fixed, rather than chosen; and prior to the development of modern communications technology, it too limited interactions between peoples. Trust is an expectation that another's behavior will be non-hostile, so it requires predictability; predictability, in turn, presupposes a certain amount of information about the people in question. With a low level of technology, one can become familiar only with those who are nearby – and hence, one trusts only nearby peoples (if any). Thus, in pre-industrial societies, proximity and primordial ties set the limits to whom one trusts: the old adage that 'Blood is thicker than water' sums up this perspective. But with higher levels of technology and education, it becomes possible to know enough about very distant and very different peoples, so that one may trust them. We hypothesize, then, that if economic development leads to rising levels of education and communications technology, it makes trust between nationalities less dependent on proximity or primordial ties, and more a question of societal learning and communications flows. Communication, of course, does not guarantee that trust will result – but it at least opens up the possibility.

Societal Learning

In contrast with the ascriptive and largely immutable nature of primordial ties, societal learning reflects the impact of specific historical experiences on a given nationality's outlook. Probably the most dramatic such experience is a war between nations. War can leave lasting expectations of hostile behavior, creating a vicious circle that leads to future hostility. On the other hand, positive interactions that persist long enough to become predictable patterns, lead to mutual trust: thus, long-term alliances, whether military (such as NATO) or economic (such as the European Economic Community) should be conducive to trust. Even a long-term pattern of benevolent neutrality could lead to the perception that the given nation is predictably non-hostile. Moreover, small nations are inherently less threatening than large ones: they do not have the *means* to be threatening, and thus may be trusted. Conversely, nationalities that are perceived as violence-prone would tend to be distrusted.

The work of Karl Deutsch and his colleagues (Deutsch, 1952; Deutsch *et al.*, 1957) emphasizes the importance of communications flows in international relations. A relatively high frequency of exchanges is conducive to a sense of mutual responsiveness and trust – provided the exchanges are perceived as rewarding. War, no doubt, is *not* normally viewed as rewarding; but most other forms of exchange probably are, particularly those from which one is free to withdraw if they seem unrewarding. Thus, with increasing rates of trade, diplomatic exchanges, student exchanges, tourist flows and other types of interaction, different nationalities find each other increasingly predictable and hence trustworthy; it is a learning process in which positive reinforcement lead to positive expectations and behavior.

In so far as a common language facilitates these communications flows, it is conducive to trust and a sense of community, quite apart from any myth of blood ties. A common ideology is like a common language. It provides a set of shared symbols that facilitate communication. In addition, a common ideology may give rise to feelings of similarity and common interest – though this is not inevitable, as the violent conflicts between the Soviet Union, China, Vietnam and Kampuchea illustrate. Thus, language and ideology may be intractable variables, but they are by no means immutable. One can learn another language in a matter of months. Even without doing so, continuous communication across language or ideological borders may develop close approximations of foreign concepts within one's own language. Predictability is an essential aspect of trust; and predictability is enhanced by open communication.

Economic Development

In their class study, Almond and Verba (1963) concluded that interpersonal trust is a prerequisite to the formation of secondary associations, which in turn is essential to effective political participation in any large democracy. Their Italian respondents ranked relatively low, both on subjective political competence and on interpersonal trust; to some extent, these findings could be attributed to a relatively low educational level, but in part it seemed linked with a specifically Italian cultural heritage (the result of societal learning).

Still earlier, Banfield (1958) had also found that Italian society was characterized by relatively low interpersonal trust, reaching pathologically low levels in the South where the prevailing outlook was 'amoral familism', the absence of feelings of trust or moral obligation toward anyone outside the nuclear family. Banfield attributed this phenomenon to a long history of dire poverty and foreign domination. Trusting others is gambling on the expectation that they will reciprocate, rather than abuse your trust. But under conditions of extreme poverty, one has no margin for error: one can not afford to gamble, because if one's trust is abused – if a loan is not repaid, for example – it may drive one's entire family below the subsistence level. Only if such a culture has strong and reliably enforced norms of reciprocity is it rational to trust others. The South Italian culture apparently lacked such norms. A contributing factor was the fact that Southern Italy has an intense distrust of authority resulting from a long history of exploitative foreign domination. Thus, Banfield's explanation is based on an interaction between economic development and societal learning.

Banfield's interpretation was controversial. Pizzorno (1966) traced the lack of trust and interpersonal cooperation to the Italian social structure, rather than to a specific cultural heritage. Similarly, Lopez Pintor and Wert Ortega (1982) found that the Spanish public consistently displayed low levels of interpersonal trust, in a series of surveys carried out from 1968 to 1980; they argued that distrust tends to characterize traditional societies in general. While traditional societies can survive even if one trusts only those one knows personally, modern society can function only if people do not assume that strangers are enemies. The large-scale enterprises and bureaucracies that make modern economic and political organizations possible depend on predictable and reliable standardized patterns of interaction between people who may be total strangers. Since Southern Europe began to industrialize much more recently than Northern Europe, to a considerable extent it still manifests the characteristics of traditional society.

The relationship between a culture of distrust and the presence or absence of modern social structures has the ambiguity of the chicken versus egg question: does Southern Europe have low levels of trust because it has not yet developed modern organization structures? Or (in a variation on Weber's thesis of the Protestant ethic), did Southern Europe industrialize and develop modern organization structures later than Northern Europe because its traditional culture was relatively low on interpersonal trust?

We cannot answer this question conclusively with the available data. Banfield's interpretation implies that low levels of trust are a distinctive and persisting feature of given cultures or regional subcultures. His critics tend to emphasize the impact of economic development on societal learning. In our view, a reciprocal causal relationship seems likely. In any case, economic development seems linked this interpersonal trust.

But what is the relationship between economic development and trust toward *other* nationalities? Two quite different models seem plausible:

Economic Development Plus Projection

On the one hand, we might suppose that trust toward other nationalities is primarily shaped by what one experiences within one's own society: in societies with high levels of trust, one *projects* experience with one's own nationality onto other nationalities and trusts them also. If it is true that the publics of economically more developed nations have relatively high levels of trust toward their own nationality, they would show high levels of trust in other nationalities as well. Trust between nations would be a direct result of economic development, with the populations of wealthier nations being relatively trusting.

Economic Development Plus Societal Learning

On the other hand, one might suppose that trust for other nationalities results from a societal learning process in which, through an accumulation of both first-hand and second-hand experiences, given nationalities come to perceive other nationalities as relatively predictable and reliable – and therefore trustworthy. Since cultures in which people behave in the predictable, standardized patterns required by large organizations are a prerequisite to industrialization, the nationalities of more developed nations would be more highly trusted than those of less developed ones.

Which of these two patterns actually prevails – the one in which economic development leads to *projection* of trust onto the international scene, with wealthier nationalities being more trust*ing*; or the one in which economic development leads to societal learning, so that wealthier nationalities are more trust*ed*? In this chapter, we will test these two models against survey data from ten Western nations at various levels of economic development. As we will see, the evidence provides an unequivocal answer to this question.

All of the above factors seem relevant to trust between nationalities. But we suspect that the importance of primordial ties has been declining, and societal learning has become more important, as economic and technological development take place. As communications technology improves, one immutable factor – geographic proximity – becomes less meaningful. By telephone, New York is almost as near to Berlin as to Buffalo: the price of a phone call to the two places is surprisingly similar. And with rising educational levels and improved information flows, simplistic notions of race become less important: unpredictable barbarians who speak incomprehensible gibberish turn out to be people whose goals and values may differ, but whose behavior is reasonably predictable. Finally, at a high level of economic development, one's margin for survival becomes broader. In a subsistence economy, if one mistakenly trusts another, the consequence may be starvation; in advanced industrial society, billions of dollars can be written off without grave danger.

But technological development also brings immensely enhanced means of destruction. Economic survival may no longer be at stake, but physical survival may depend on trust between nations more than ever. Let us examine some empirical evidence about where it exists and the factors that shape it.

THE PSYCHO-GEOGRAPHY OF TRUST AS SEEN FROM WESTERN EUROPE

In 1970, 1976, 1980, 1982, and again in 1986, representative national samples of the publics of the European Community countries were asked in a series of questions about how much they trusted or distrusted peoples of various other nationalities. These Eurobarometer surveys included those nations that were members of the European Community at the time of the survey: in 1970, they were carried out in West Germany, France, Italy, Belgium, Luxembourg, and the Netherlands; in 1976, Great Britain, Denmark, and Ireland were added; in 1980 Greece came in, and in 1986 Spain and Portugal joined the group. In each of these surveys, the publics were asked:

Now I would like to ask about how much you would trust people from different countries. For each country please say whether, in your opinion, they are in general very trustworthy, fairly trustworthy, not particularly trustworthy, or not at all trustworthy.

The questions were asked in the context of surveys dealing with international relations. The key word 'trust' was translated in German and Luxembourgeois as *Vertrauen*, in French as *confiance*, in Danish as *trovaerdige*, in Italian as *Fiducia*, in Dutch as *vertrouwen*, and in Greek as *epistosuni*. (For detailed information about fieldwork, see the ICPSR codebooks for these surveys). Table 8.1 shows the overall ratings of each of seventeen nationalities, based on the responses of the ten European

TABLE 9.1: *Trust in other peoples (average of replies from people in Community countries)*

	Very trust-worthy	Fairly trust-worthy	Not parti-cularly trust-worthy	Not at all trust-worthy	Don't know	Total	Trust Index*
Swiss	30%	41%	9%	5%	15%	100%	.68
Danes	17	41	10	4	28	100	.62
Luxembourgers	15	41	11	4	29	100	.59
Dutch	19	43	11	5	22	100	.58
Belgians	15	46	13	4	22	100	.54
Americans	24	43	16	8	9	100	.47
West Germans	18	42	17	12	11	100	.32
British	13	46	22	9	10	100	.29
Irish	10	35	19	10	26	100	.17
French	14	39	23	13	11	100	.17
Japanese	15	33	19	14	19	100	.15
Greeks	6	32	24	11	27	100	−.02
Spanish	7	34	29	13	17	100	−.07
Portuguese	5	28	25	12	30	100	−.11
Chinese	13	19	12	27	29	100	−.23
Italians	5	32	31	18	14	100	−.23
Russians	4	16	23	41	16	100	−.61

* This index adapted from Merritt and Puchala (Western European Perspectives on International Affairs, Praeger, 1968, pp. 115–17), uses the following formula:

$$I = \frac{G - B}{G + B},$$ where G is the total of weighted positive replies ('very trustworthy' = 2, and

'fairly trustworthy' = 1), and B is the total of weighted negative replies ('not very trustworthy' = 1, and 'not trustworthy at all' = 2). Scores on the index range from −1.00 to +1.00. Differences between national scores of less than .10 should not be regarded as significant.
SOURCE: Eurobarometer 14 sponsored by the Commission of the European Communities (fieldwork carried out in October 1980).

Community publics in 1980, a year in which an unusually extensive battery of trust questions were asked.

The seventeen nationalities include the twelve peoples of the European Community, four major non-European nationalities (the Americans, Russians, Chinese, and Japanese) and one prominent neutral (the Swiss). Most people felt able to express an opinion about the trustworthiness of these nationalities, but the percentage saying 'I don't know' varied widely from nationality to nationality. While only about 10 per cent of the European Community publics failed to rate the Americans or Germans, about 30 per cent gave no rating for the Portuguese or Chinese.

In general, 'don't know' responses were highest about small nations, but the Chinese constitute a striking exception: despite their massive numbers, relatively little was known about the Chinese, and West European publics, accordingly, seemed uncertain about how much trust to place in them. Low

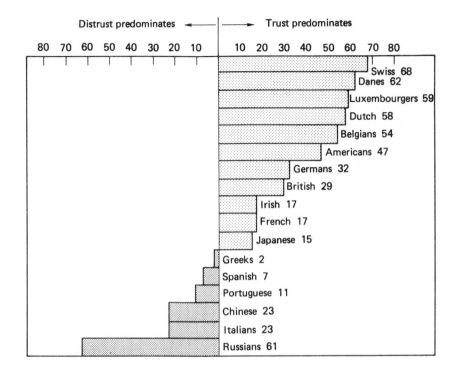

FIGURE 9.1: *Levels of trust toward seventeen nationalities.* (Trust Index is based on weighted positive ratings minus negative ratings among the ten European Community publics surveyed in October, 1980)

salience seems conducive to relatively sudden changes in trust ratings; at any rate, the most dramatic change observed during the periods covered by our surveys; was a striking increase in the trust ratings of the Chinese, from 1970 to 1986.

It is difficult to deal with the mass of detailed information in Table 9.1, and the problem is multiplied many times over when we examine the trust ratings of each of the seventeen nationalities by each of these publics. In order to condense this information into a more manageable form, we constructed a trust index, using a procedure developed by Merritt and Puchala (1968) which is described at the foot of Table 8.1. The result is fairly similar to what we would obtain by simply subtracting the percentage of non-trusting responses from the percentage of trusting responses, except that it takes the intensity of one's ratings into account, and controls for non-response. Figure 9.1 shows the relative levels of trust that West European publics place in each of the seventeen nationalities, on the basis of our trust index. A detailed nation-by-nation breakdown appears in the ICPSR codebook for Eurobarometer 14.

The Swiss are the most highly trusted nationality in Europe. A nation with a long history of benevolent neutralism, Switzerland is too small to threaten her neighbors and is characterized by domestic order. Her association with the International Red Cross and other international organizations probably enhanced her image. But she has yet another advantage: she shares common languages with each of her neighbours. As we will see below, these countries give the Swiss particularly high ratings. Interestingly, the Swiss themselves rank other nationalities in almost exactly the same order as that shown in Figure 9.1 (ISOP, 1982).

The other most trusted nationalities all have in common the fact that they are small, not noted for domestic conflict, and tend to be multilingual. Though most Luxembourgeois speak a dialect of German, the official language is French. In order to graduate from a Dutch secondary school, until recently, one needed a knowledge of English, German, and French. Most educated Danes are conversant with English and German. Though Belgium is both small and bilingual, she lags a little behind the others; her image may suffer somewhat from recent conflicts between her two main ethic groups.

All five of the most-trusted nationalities live in small nations, but smallness alone is not sufficient to generate trust, for the people of some small nations, such as the Greeks and the Portuguese, rank far below those of larger nations. Both of the latter nations had only recently completed a stormy transition to democracy, and their internal politics were still somewhat unpredictable in 1980. Moreover, because of relatively low educational levels, their populations are largely monolingual despite their small size. Apparently, the ideal combination is to be small, economically developed, multilingual *and* have a long history of both international and domestic tranquility.

It seems highly significant that racial differences are *not* necessarily a barrier to trust between nationalities. For in 1980, the people of the European Community placed distinctly more trust than distrust in the Japanese; indeed, they ranked them above four of the European peoples included in this survey. And the Chinese – though still more apt to be distrusted than trusted – ranked slightly above the Italians and far above the Russians. Trust in the Chinese rose rapidly from 1970 to 1980; by 1980 it was clear that racial differences are not necessarily a barrier to international trust.

Similarly, the fact that West Europeans trust both the Americans and the Japanese more highly than many nearby European peoples is evidence that geographic proximity is not necessarily decisive. Together with further evidence presented below, these facts indicate that the 'Primordial' category, consisting of immutable national characteristics, is not a decisive influence on trust between nationalities.

But now, let us turn to some evidence that *does* suggest that cultural,

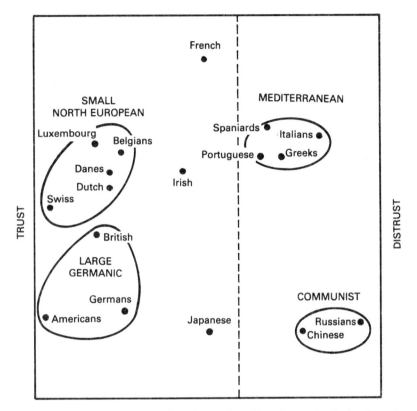

FIGURE 9.2: *The psychogeography of trust.* (Smallest Space Analysis of trust ratings of seventeen nationalities, by combined ten-nation sample of European Community publics, October 1980).

racial and regional proximity play an important role. Figure 9.2 shows the results of a smallest space analysis based on trust ratings of the various nationalities.

In this analysis, nationalities that receive similar ratings are located relatively near each other, while those that receive dissimilar ratings appear relatively far apart. Thus, those nationalities that are highly trusted are located toward the left side of Figure 8.2, while those that are distrusted are located toward the right. The dotted line is a sort of 'equator', showing the boundary between predominantly trusted and predominantly distrusted nationalities. But the information conveyed by Figure 9.2 goes beyond this. It indicates which nationalities are perceived as *similar*, not simply how much trust is placed in them. As one would expect, nationalities that are perceived as similar tend to receive similar trust ratings, but there is no one-to-one relationship between the single dimension shown in Figure 9.1 and the two-dimensional space shown in Figure 9.2, for the latter figure also reflects the impact of other factors, such as regional and cultural proximity.

Overall, our West European respondents tend to perceive the seventeen nationalities as falling into four coherent clusters, with three intermediate cases. In the upper left-hand quadrant, we find a cluster of five small North European nationalities, which includes the five most trusted peoples among those rated. The Irish – citizens of another small North European country – are located nearby. By expanding the boundaries they could be included within this cluster, though they rank several places below all five nationalities in this group. Three peoples living in large Germanic-speaking nations form a cluster in the lower left-hand quadrant; this is the second most-trusted group. Four Mediterranean peoples from another compact cluster in the upper right-hand quadrant; this group tends to be viewed with more distrust than trust. The French (living in a nation that borders on the Mediterranean but extends much farther north than the others) are an outlier, located in the general vicinity of the Mediterranean cluster but some distance apart. Two Communist giants, the Russians and Chinese, are in close proximity, in the lower right-hand quadrant. West European trust in them tends to be very low; and (despite Soviet-Chinese hostility) European publics react to them as if they were similar.

Clearly, the horizontal dimension reflects trust versus distrust. To some extent, the vertical dimension might be described as tapping a large-small dimension but this is somewhat oversimplified. The five largest nations (in terms of both population and gross national product) constitute a bottom tier. The British are located higher and somewhat apart from the five economically most powerful (and therefore potentially threatening) nations on the bottom tier. The nations represented in the upper half of Figure 9.2 are all much smaller, with one anomaly: France. Though their economic strength ranks immediately after the five giants, the French are located nearer to the top of Figure 9.2 than any other nationality. In part, this is because the European Community publics view the French as somewhat similar to the other nationalities that speak Romance languages; her nearest neighbours on Figure 9.2 are the Spanish, Portuguese and Italians, on one side; and the Belgians and Luxemburgers, on the other. This, together with an intermediate level of trust (probably linked with the solitary and sometimes unpredictable role France formerly played in NATO and the European Community), placed the French in an isolated position near the upper-center. Conversely, the Japanese location near the lower centre reflects not only her economic might, but also a pervasive tendency for all nationalities to see them as proximate to another Asiatic people, the Chinese; *and*, at the same time, relatively near to her World War II ally, the Germans. Interestingly enough, the Germans themselves give the Japanese a higher percentage of positive trust ratings than any other European Community public: the remembrance of past alliance, rather than enmity, seems to have left a residue that had not completely faded out thirty-five years after the end of World War II.

Finally, the isolated position of the Irish, midway between the small north-European cluster (in which she logically might be located) and the Mediterranean group, may reflect a contamination of the Irish image, from the persisting conflict in Northern Ireland: though the Republic of Ireland has enjoyed a long period of domestic tranquillity, reports of violence in Northern Ireland may influence some segments of European publics to perceive them as less orderly and more violent than the Danes, Dutch, Swiss, or Luxembourgers.

REGIONAL AND DEVELOPMENTAL FACTORS

The results of the smallest space analysis depicted in Figure 9.2 make it clear that West European publics tend to perceive certain clusters of nationalities as similar and evaluate them similarly in judging how trustworthy they are. But the reasons *why* they are seen as similar are not entirely clear. At first glance, one might be tempted to ascribe much of the variance to simple ethnocentrism: North Europeans have a relatively favourable image of themselves, and a negative image of South European peoples; and since the Northern Europeans constitute a majority of the Community's population, their image tends to prevail.

This interpretation seems mistaken. The pattern shown in Figure 9.2 does *not* merely reflect the ethnocentrism of the North Europeans. On the contrary, this pattern has a remarkable degree of cross-national reliability; to an astonishing degree, it reflects the world view of the South European peoples, as well as the North Europeans. Table 8.2 provides some evidence on this point.

The available data indicate that the low sense of trust for South European peoples is shared by the South Europeans themselves. They tend to perceive other South European peoples as similar to themselves – but *not* to trust them. Surprising as it may seem, the South Europeans' trust ratings of South European peoples are no higher than that of the Northern Europeans – if anything, they are a trifle lower.

The Italians constitute a particularly striking case. In addition to rating other peoples, each public was also asked how much they trusted people of their *own* nationality. As one would expect, in virtually every country people tend to trust those of their own nationality more than they trust foreigners. But the Italian response was unique: not only did they express little trust for other Mediterranean peoples, they even displayed a remarkably low level of trust for their own countrymen. In 1980, 39 per cent described the Italians as either 'not particularly trustworthy' or 'not at *all* trustworthy'. This is an exceptionally high figure. The Greeks showed the

158

TABLE 9.2: *Trust toward the peoples of Southern Europe, in North European and South European countries, 1980*

NORTHERN EUROPE

Mean Trust Index toward:	Belgium	Denmark	West Germany	France	Ireland	Luxem-bourg	Nether-lands	United Kingdom	MEAN
The Italians:	-.26	.01	-.46	-.07	.24	-.03	-.36	-.10	-.13
The Greeks:	-.16	.13	-.14	.29	.20	-.16	.09	.03	.04
The Spaniards:	-.10	.03	-.09	.10	.25	-.23	-.19	-.20	-.05
The Portuguese:	-.16	.06	-.26	.04	.18	-.25	-.05	.15	-.04
MEAN:	-.16	.06	-.24	.09	.22	-.17	-.13	-.03	-.05

SOUTHERN EUROPE

Mean Trust Index toward:	Italy	Greece	MEAN
The Italians:	–	-.17	-.17
The Greeks:	-.19	–	-.19
The Spaniards:	-.10	.20	.05
The Portuguese:	-.38	.14	-.12
MEAN:	-.22	.06	-.08

next lowest level of trust in their own nationality, with 20 per cent giving negative ratings. In the other countries, the figure ranged from a low of 6 per cent in Denmark, to a high of 15 per cent in France.

Over thirty years ago, Banfield (1958) argued that Italian society was characterized by a distinctively low level of interpersonal trust, and that this pattern was particularly strong in Southern Italy. Whether his interpretation of 'amoral familism' is correct or not, the empirical phenomenon he perceived was still present in 1980, and is more pronounced in Italy than elsewhere (though it does seem to characterize Southern Europe as a whole). Moreover, in 1980 as in 1955, interpersonal trust was far lower in Southern Italy than in the North. In 1980, 28 per cent of our respondents from the Northwest region of Italy described Italians as 'not particularly trustworthy', or 'not at all trustworthy'. In the Northeast, the figure was 36 per cent; in Central Italy it was 42 per cent; in the South it was 45 per cent; and in Sicily and Sardinia, the figure was 49 per cent. In the 1976 survey, North-South differences were equally strong. But a comparison of the 1976 and 1980 figures shows an encouraging trend. In 1976, 51 per cent of the total Italian sample gave negative trust ratings of their countrymen. In 1980, this figure had declined to 39 per cent.

Though the Italians display low levels of interpersonal trust, their ratings of other nationalities are *not* simply a projection of what they perceive in their immediate surroundings – for they can and do differentiate between various nationalities. Though they place limited trust in their countrymen, they express relatively high levels of trust toward certain foreign nationalities. In 1980, only 26 per cent of the Italians expressed distrust for the Americans, while 68 per cent gave positive ratings; Italian ratings of the Swiss and the Dutch were almost equally high.

Relatively low levels of trust are registered not only *toward* the Mediterranean peoples, but *by* them. We hypothesized that this may reflect relative levels of economic development, in part: Southern Europe began the process of industrialization much later than Northern Europe, and the South still has, on the whole, a markedly lower level of income. At low levels of income, one's margin above the subsistence level is relatively small; one cannot afford to take risks as readily as when one has a good deal of discretionary income – and trust implies accepting the risk that the other person or nation may, in the long run, fail to reciprocate. Though most of Southern Europe, today, is well above the subsistence level, the effects of earlier poverty may persist to some degree in current cultural patterns.

To what extent is trust linked with economic development? At the individual level, we find a consistent tendency for trust in other nationalities and in one's own nationality to be higher among the economically more secure and better educated. And when we turn to cross-national comparisons, we find a similar pattern. Table 9.3 shows the relationship between current economic level and three aspects of trust.

TABLE 9.3: *Trust and economic development among European Community publics (Cell entry is Trust Index)*

	GNP per capita in 1979 (in dollars)	Trust in own nationality	Trust in 16 other nationalities	Trust by 9 other EC nationalities
1. Luxembourg	12,820	90	22	59
2. Denmark	11,900	78	67	62
3. West Germany	11,730	91	34	32
4. Belgium	10,890	80	44	54
5. Netherlands	10,240	84	50	58
6. France	10,030	74	44	17
7. United Kingdom	6,331	88	37	29
8. Italy	5,240	24	22	−13
9. Ireland	4,230	75	54	17
10. Greece	3,890	62	12	−2

SOURCE: Trust indices based on October 1980 survey sponsored by the Commission of the European Communities (Eurobarometer 14).

It seems clear that the people of wealthy nations tend to be trusted, and to trust, more than those of less wealthy ones. But the relationship is not equally strong with the three types of trust. For we find a relatively good fit between economic development and trust in one's own nationality; and the extent to which one's nationality is trusted by others. There is a much poorer fit between a nation's level of economic development and the extent to which it trusts *other* nationalities.

Trust in one's *own* nationality closely reflects economic development levels, while trust in other nationalities does not. This is true because both the relatively affluent North Europeans *and* the less wealthy South Europeans tend to view the former with relatively high trust. Two of the three richest nations – Luxembourg and West Germany – have high trust in their own nationality, but relatively low levels of trust toward the various other nationalities. At the other end of the scale, the publics of the three least wealthy nations, Italy, Ireland, and Greece – tend to rank lowest on all three types of trust; but the Irish manifest one of the highest levels of trust in *other* nationalities. In short, there is a fairly clear cross-national consensus, among the ten European Community publics, about which nationalities are most trustworthy: to a surprising extent, both rich and poor agree that it is the richer nationalities. Which nationalities actually *are* more trustworthy is beyond the scope of this study. The prevailing perception may well be false. But a prevailing perception clearly does exist and it is linked with relative levels of economic development. Furthermore, the evidence supports the interpretation that trust in other nationalities is shaped by economic development plus societal learning, rather than by economic development plus projection. The nationalities of more developed countries are most trust*ed*; they are not necessarily more trust*ing*.

The causes of this linkage between trust and economic development seem complex. Economic security probably is conducive to interpersonal trust. But it may also work the other way around: a relatively high level of interpersonal trust permits large-scale modern economic enterprises to develop and function effectively, and hence is conducive to economic development. If it is true that relatively high levels of interpersonal trust have been a long-term cultural characteristic of the North-West European nations, this could help explain their relatively early industrialization and their contemporary economic lead by comparison with Southern Europe. Since our data only go back as far as 1970, we cannot test this hypothesis; during the relatively brief span for which we do have data, the cross-national trust rankings have been reasonably stable; the evidence is compatible with the thesis that long-term cultural patterns are involved. But, as we will see below, certain rather dramatic changes did occur during 1970–86. Trust between nationalities is linked with economic development, but it seems clear that other historical events are also involved. These factors emerge more clearly when we examine patterns of trust from the distinctive perspective of each nationality.

THE PSYCHOGEOGRAPHY OF THE WORLD: TEN NATIONAL PERSPECTIVES

Thus far, we have mainly dealt with overall patterns of trust between peoples. In order to examine the possible impact of a given nation's culture and historical experiences, let us examine the perspectives of each nationality. Figures 9.3(1) through 9.3(10) present the results of smallest space analyses based on data from each of the ten respective national samples. Figures 9.3(1) and 9.3(2) show the results from two large Germanic nations, the Federal Republic of Germany and the United Kingdom.

In these analyses (unlike that presented in Figure 8.2), we included each public's rating of its *own* nationality, as well as their ratings of others. The British and Germans – like most peoples – express considerably more trust in their own nationality than in any other. Consequently, the resulting maps can be interpreted as ethnocentric: for example, the Germans themselves constitute the positive pole in Figure 9.3(1) with other nationalities located around them according to how strongly they are trusted or distrusted; the nearer a given people are to the Germans, the more highly they are trusted. The space is not unidimensional – cultural, racial and ideological similarities seem to influence the location of given nationalities. Hence concentric circles are shown, to help one compare the distances of

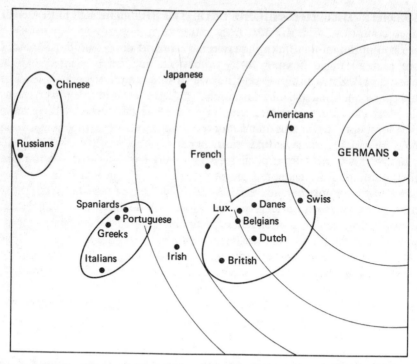

FIGURE 9.3(1): *The psychogeography of the world as seen by the Germans*

various peoples from the positive pole. The outermost circle constitutes a sort of equator, showing the boundary between positive trust and negative trust; those nationalities located beyond the outermost circle are distrusted more than they are trusted.

From the German perspective, the Swiss are the most highly trusted of the sixteen foreign peoples rated in 1980: 83 per cent of the Germans viewed them as 'very trustworthy' or 'fairly trustworthy'. The Americans ranked second. Conflicting German and American views about installing intermediate-range missiles, about the Soviet invasion of Afghanistan, and the repression of Solidarity in Poland, gave rise to widespread concern about neutralism and anti-Americanism in Germany at that time. In fact, the long-term images persisted: as of October 1980, 78 per cent of the German public expressed trust in the Americans, with only 18 per cent indicating distrust. The Russians ranked at the opposite end of the scale: 13 per cent of the West German public expressed trust, and 78 per cent distrusted them. This was hardly a neutralist position. Genuine policy differences existed, but they existed in the context of a clearly pro-Western orientation among the West German public: feelings of trust heavily outweigh distrust toward the Danes, Dutch, Belgians, Luxembourgers,

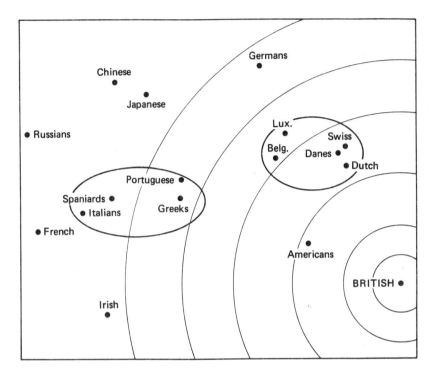

FIGURE 9.3(2): *The psychogeography of the world as seen by the British*

British, French, Irish and Japanese. The Franco-German hostility that persisted for generations and was still manifest in the 1950s had been overcome: the French were trusted almost as much as the Danes and the Dutch, two peoples with whom the Germans have long had close cultural and economic ties. The four South European nationalities tend to be distrusted, though in the case of the Spanish and Greeks, positive and negative attitudes are rather closely balanced. The two Communist nationalities are viewed with overwhelming distrust.

Figure 9.3(2) depicts the psychogeography of the world in 1980, from the British perspective. It is basically similar to that of the Germans, but the details in which it differs are instructive. First, the Americans, rather than the Swiss, are the nearest and most trusted nationality. While the Germans share a common language with (most of) the Swiss, the British share one with (most of) the Americans. A common language and long-standing alliance seems more important than geographic proximity, for the Americans are geographically further from the British than most of the other peoples, yet subjectively they are much nearer. But a common language by itself does not ensure trust, for the Irish are viewed with somewhat more distrust than trust – probably a spill-over from the conflict in Northern

Ireland. The Danes, Swiss, Dutch, Belgians, and Luxembourgers constitute a compact cluster of peoples who are perceived as similar, and trusted
highly; the Germans also are predominantly trusted. The British differentiated between the Mediterranean people, expressing trust for two old
allies – the Portuguese and the Greeks – and distrust for the Spanish and
Italians. The British were unique in that they trusted the French even less
than the Italians – but here, again, the cause seems fairly obvious; General
DeGaulle's two vetoes of British admission to the European Community
were unexpected and viewed as treacherous by many of the British.

Though the locations of the Russians, Chinese, and Japanese are very
similar in Figures 9.3(1) and 9.3(2), there is a subtle difference. For the
British, the Japanese were viewed with more distrust than trust, and
located in a position proximate to the Chinese (and somewhat near the
Germans). For the Germans, the Japanese were trusted positively and are
more clearly differentiated from the Chinese. The difference may be
derived from the contrasting alliances in World War II; though the effects
of that war have been overcome to such an extent that predominantly
positive feelings prevail between the British and German peoples, some
secondary effects still persist in 1980.

Figures 9.3(3) and 9.3(4) show the psychogeography of two nationalities
who are not grouped in any of the four clusters in Figure 8.2. For the Irish,
the relative positions of the various nationalities is quite similar to that of
the British, but the *levels* of trust in other peoples is much higher: the Irish
trust everyone but the Russians and Chinese; overall, only the Danes
register a higher level of trust in other nationalities. Like the British, the
Irish trust the Americans more than any other foreign nationality. Another
primarily English-speaking people – the British – rank second. Though for
some Britons, the word 'Irish' may evoke images of strife in Northern
Ireland, or bombings in England, the reciprocal type of confusion is
unlikely for the citizens of the Republic of Ireland. Trust for the Germans
is relatively high; they rank at least as high as the Swiss, Danes, Dutch, and
Belgians; the Japanese also rank relatively high. Both could reflect the fact
that Ireland was neutral during World War II.

If so, the French perspective demonstrates that the impact on trust of
even such a gigantic historical event as World War II can be undone in the
long run. For the French, the Germans are closer than any people but the
Swiss. This is impressive. The French tend to think of the Swiss as
Francophone, since when they visit Switzerland, they generally visit the
French-speaking region. Moreover, as we have noted, the Swiss have all
the attributes of the ideal-type of highly-trusted nationality. Though
neither Francophone nor small and with a long history of hostility toward
France, the Germans now are trusted immediately after the Swiss. This
seems to be the result of a successful Franco-German rapprochement that

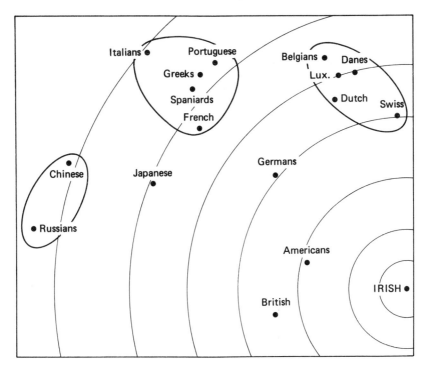

FIGURE 9.3(3): *The psychogeography of the world as seen by the Irish*

has taken place on many levels, with the most important and salient setting being the European Community.

Figures 9.3(5) and 9.3(6) show the psychogeography of the world from the perspectives of two Mediterranean nationalities, the Italians and Greeks. The results are highly distinctive. In contrast with the eight other nationalities, these cognitive maps *cannot* be interpreted from an ethnocentric perspective. For the Italians, the most trusted nationality is *not* the Italians, but the Americans – followed closely by the Swiss and the Dutch. Hence, the positive pole is *not* located at the point occupied by the Italians, but at the point indicated between the Americans, Dutch, and other North European nationalities – all of whom (apart from the Irish) are more highly trusted than the Italians. The Italians see the other South Europeans as similar to themselves, particularly the Spanish (whose language is closest to Italian). But they tend to distrust these peoples, especially the Greeks.

The Greeks have a rather similar outlook. Though they trust the Greeks more than any other nationality, they do not perceive *any* nationality as very close; the nearest nationality is the Italians, and they are predominantly

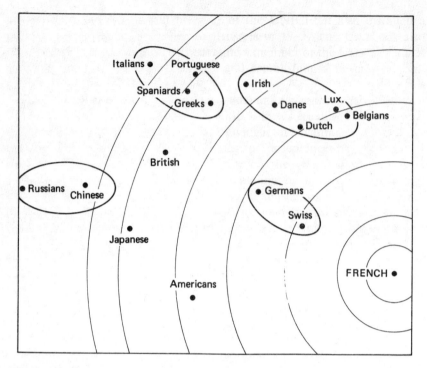

FIGURE 9.3(4): *The psychogeography of the world as seen by the French*

distrusted. Instead, the Greeks have a secondary centre of trust, based on the tight cluster of small north European peoples, and those located nearest this cluster: thus the Spaniards and Portuguese get mildly positive ratings, though they are located much nearer to the Belgians or Irish than to the Greeks. The British, Germans and Americans are distrusted by the Greeks. The Greeks were the *only* people in the European Community to register negative attitudes toward these peoples in 1980, with a single exception (the Luxembourgers showed slightly more distrust than trust toward the British). Moreover, the Greeks are the only people who trust the Russians more than the Americans: both attitudes are predominantly negative, but only 33 per cent of the Greeks trust the Americans, while 35 per cent trust the Russians. The failure of the Americans and other Western powers to support them more strongly during the Turkish invasion of Cyprus was intensely resented in spite of the arms embargo imposed on Turkey. These and earlier events seem to have left persisting effects. When one's allies fight each other, one can only lose.

   Figures 9.3(7) through 9.3(10) depict the geography of trust as seen from the perspective of the four nationalities in the 'Small North European' group. Like Figures 9.3(1) through 9.3(4) the perspective is ethnocentric: one's

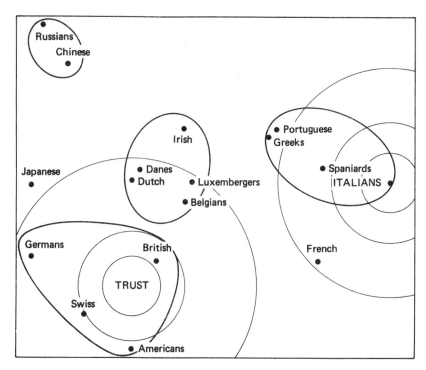

FIGURE 9.3(5): *The psychogeography of the world as seen by the Italians*

own nationality is most highly trusted, and defines the positive role. The Danes, Luxembourgers, Belgians and Dutch see each other as a group: the other members tend to be nearest and most highly trusted. But the Danes rank highest of the ten European Community publics in trust for other peoples; they perceive many other nationalities as quite close to themselves (and if the other Scandinavians had been rated, the number of peoples near the Danes would almost certainly be even higher). The Danes are the only people to give the Chinese a predominantly positive trust rating. On the other hand, the Luxembourgers have relatively low levels of trust toward other peoples (but higher trust in their own compatriots). Moreover, though most other peoples consistently place the Luxembourgers closest to the Belgians, the Luxembourgers themselves do not. They trust the French slightly more: the fact that French is the official language reflects a deep-seated cultural affinity.

The Belgian and Dutch maps are quite similar: their patterns of relative trust are parallel, though the absolute levels are higher in the Dutch case. The role of language ties is illustrated once again by the fact that the Belgians accord relatively high trust to the French, with whom they share a common language. Conversely, German is so closely related to Dutch that

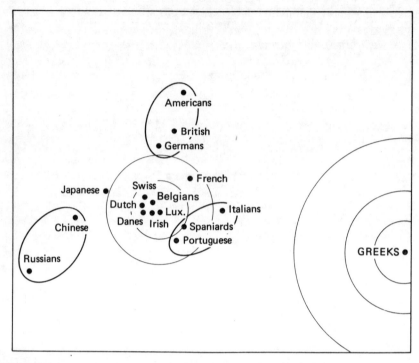

FIGURE 9.3(6): *The psychogeography of the world as seen by the Greeks*

it is understood by most of the Dutch; and the Dutch trust the Germans more than the Belgians do. Both nationalities locate the Japanese relatively near the Germans.

STABILITY AND CHANGE IN TRUST FOR OTHER NATIONALITIES

We noted earlier that the Italians' sense of trust for their own nationality showed a pronounced increase from 1976 to 1980. This seems to have been part of a general upward movement of trust in European Community publics during this period, for the overall ratings rose for all nine publics rated at both time points. The cause of this upward trend is unclear, but it was pervasive. Figure 9.4 shows the changing levels of trust toward nine nationalities during the period from 1970 to 1982. It uses only the ratings from the six original member nations of the European Community, since only these countries were surveyed in 1970; moreover, fewer nationalities were rated in the 1970 survey than in 1980; and in the April 1982 survey (Eurobarometer 17) only four nationalities were rated: the Americans, Russians, Chinese, and Japanese.

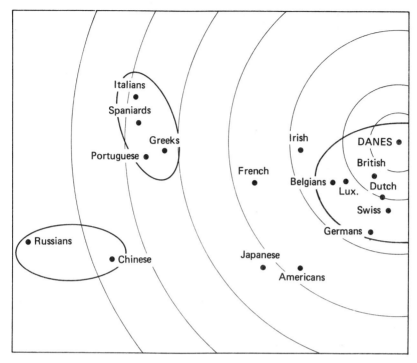

FIGURE 9.3(7): *The psychogeography of the world as seen by the Dunes*

As Figure 9.4 reveals, there was a downward movement in trust for some nationalities from 1970 to 1976, followed by an upward swing from 1976 to 1980. This pattern applies to the Swiss, Americans and British; attitudes toward the French and Italians were constant during the first period, and rose sharply during the latter period. These shifts were probably linked with the worldwide economic recession of 1974–5, from which recovery was taking place in 1976. If this is the case, it would be further evidence of the linkage between prosperity and international trust. But such effects, obviously, are only part of the story, for trust toward both the Germans and the Chinese showed a dramatic increase from 1970 to 1980.

In the 1970 survey, the Germans were viewed with slightly more distrust than trust by the public of the other five nations then in the European Community. Earlier data, based on responses to a question concerning whether one had a good opinion or bad opinion of other countries, indicates that negative feelings toward the Germans were overwhelmingly preponderant during the 1950s, but shifted toward a much more positive state during the 1960s (Merritt and Puchala, 1968; pp. 111–41, 235–48). It appears that during the 1970s, the Germans were completing a long march from the status of a pariah nationality to becoming one of the highly-trusted peoples of Europe, on a plane with the British and French. The fact

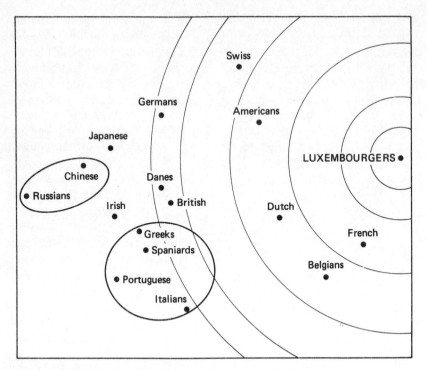

FIGURE 9.3(8): *The psychogeography of the world as seen by the Luxembourgers*

that the German economy functioned relatively well during the 1974–5 recession, while other countries were severely disturbed, may have enhanced the German image during the period.

The rise of trust in the Chinese people was even more dramatic. In 1970, the Chinese were the least trusted nationality among those rated, ranking far below the Russians. By 1980, they ranked far above the Russians, and even slightly above the Italians. This remarkable change in image is probably linked with the end of the violent upheavals associated with the Great Proletarian Cultural Revolution and the coming of power of the pragmatists immediately after the death of Mao in 1976. The subsequent period of moderation and of opening to the West was also a period of sharply rising trust in the Chinese. The exceptionally rapid change in attitudes toward the Chinese may have been facilitated by the fact that attitudes were relatively fluid: West European publics were much more likely to say they didn't *know* how trustworthy the Chinese were, than was the case with any other major nationality. Though there was a decline in 1982, the overall rise in trust toward the Chinese was remarkable, and constitutes a major change in the psychogeography of the world.

This reorientation toward the Chinese was not limited to Western

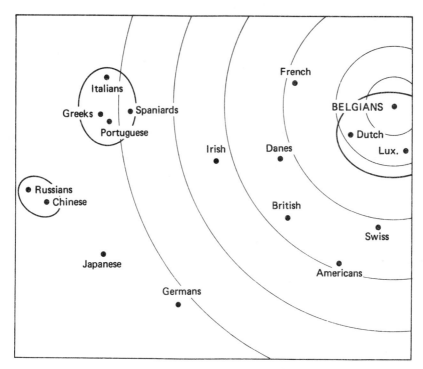

FIGURE 9.3(9): *The psychogeography of the world as seen by the Belgians*

Europe. In 1974, only 17 per cent of the American public viewed the Chinese as friendly; by 1982, fully 74 per cent considered them friendly, and only 17 per cent described them as unfriendly. But at the same time, only 9 per cent viewed the Soviet Union as friendly (Harris Survey, 1982). A similar pattern prevailed in Japan: in 1982, 73 per cent of the Japanese public had friendly feelings toward China – and only 16 per cent felt friendly toward the Soviet Union (Prime Minister's Secretariat, 1982). The rapid rise of trust toward the Chinese demonstrates that neither racial nor ideological differences constitutes an insurmountable obstacle to the development of international trust. The Chinese system became more open and more predictable after 1976. The impact on the outlook of other peoples was remarkable.

The Japanese themselves were not rated in the earlier surveys, unfortunately, so we have no direct measure of changes in trust toward them; but the relatively high levels of trust toward them registered in 1980 almost certainly reflect a long-term upward movement, like the one that characterized ratings of the Germans and Chinese.

While trust was rising toward all of the other nationalities during 1976–80, trust toward the Russians declined. In 1980, they ranked far

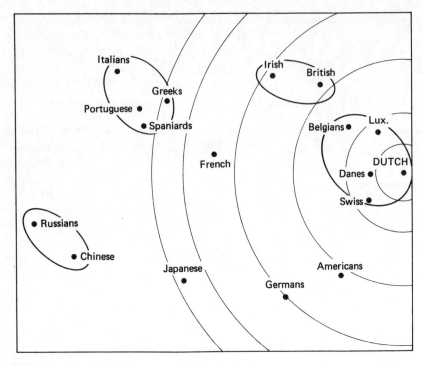

FIGURE 9.3(10): *The psychogeography of the world as seen by the Dutch*

below any other nationality. The Soviet invasion of Afghanistan in December, 1979 probably helped maintain the strong sense of distrust felt toward them throughout Western Europe, though it did not move the level much below where it already was in 1976.

The 1982 survey shows a sharp decline in trust toward the Americans, Japanese, Chinese, and Russians (the only four nationalities included in 1982). The available evidence does not enable us to determine the precise causes of this decline, but it seems likely that it reflected the severe economic recession that followed the OPEC oil price increase in December 1979, and growing East-West tensions, in which declining trust for the Americans and Russians was generalized and applied to the Chinese and Japanese as well.

Trust toward the Russians showed the *smallest* decline among the four nationalities. This may seem surprising, in view of the events taking place from 1980 to 1982. The war in Afghanistan continued, with no sign of abatement, and in 1981, the Polish army seized power, apparently acting from fear of Soviet military intervention if they didn't crush Solidarity. But meanwhile, the leaders of the NATO nations agreed to install American middle-range nuclear missiles in Western Europe, unless agreement were reached to withdraw similar new Soviet nuclear missiles. The NATO

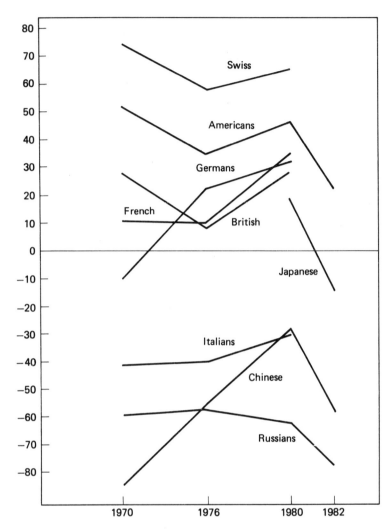

FIGURE 9.4: *Changes in levels of trust toward nine nationalities, among the publics of the six original European Community member nations, 1970–82*

'double decision' led to the mobilization of a massive peace movement throughout the NATO nations, accompanied by a general decline in international trust.

The decline registered from 1980 to 1982 proved to be transient, however. Short-term factors, such as the reaction to Afghanistan and the cruise missiles, tend to have only a short-term impact, and when their effects have been dissipated, relatively enduring national stereotypes reassert themselves. Thus, by 1986, feelings of trust had recovered to their 1976 levels – and indeed, were almost identical to ten years earlier.

Table 9.4 shows the relative levels of trust toward various other nation-

TABLE 9.4: *Trust in other nationalities among nine West European publics, in 1976 and 1986. (rank and mean* rating of each public, by the combined nine publics)*

1976		1986		Shift, 1976 to 1986
1. Swiss	.68	1. Swiss	.70	+.02
2. Dutch	.65	2. Danes	.66	+.02
3. Danes	.64	3. Dutch	.65	.00
4. Germans	.64	4. Luxemburgers	.64	+.01
5. Luxemburgers	.63	5. Germans	.63	−.01
6. Belgians	.62	6. Belgians	.61	−.01
7. Americans	.59	7. Americans	.58	−.01
8. British	.57	8. British	.58	+.01
9. French	.55	9. French	.57	+.02
10. Irish	.45	10. Irish	.53	+.08
11. Italians	.42	11. Italians	.51	+.09
12. Chinese	.31	12. Chinese	.48	+.17
13. Russians	.30	13. Russians	.38	+.08
mean:	.54	mean:	.58	+.04

* Mean score is based on overall ratings for each nationality, with 0 = 'not at all trustworthy', .33 = 'not very trustworthy', .67 = 'fairly trustworthy' and 1.00 = 'very trustworthy'. Thus, a mean score of .50 is the neutral point where positive ratings equal negative ratings.

SOURCE: pooled data from representative national samples of publics of France, Britain, West Germany, Italy, the Netherlands, Belgium, Luxembourg, Ireland, and Denmark, surveyed in November 1976 (Eurobarometer 6) and in April 1986 (Eurobarometer 25), with results from each country weighed according to population.

alities that were expressed by the publics of the nine countries that were members of the European Community in 1976, and the levels of trust expressed by these same nine publics a decade later in 1986. On the whole, both the absolute and relative levels of trust that West European publics have for other nationalities have been extremely stable. Indeed, the rank orders of all thirteen nationalities that were asked about in both surveys remain virtually identical across the ten years from 1976 to 1986. The Swiss were the most trusted nationality and the Russians were the least trusted, both in 1976 and 1986. The eleven nationalities in between also maintain virtually identical positions, apart from slight shifts for the Dutch and the Danes, who were ranked second and third respectively in 1976; but ranked third and second respectively in 1986. The Germans and Luxembourgers show a similar slight shift; while all other nationalities show *exactly* the same rankings in 1976 and 1986. Table 9.4 presents the results from nine European Community publics as a whole, but the ratings made by given publics within the Community show a similar stability: relatively trustful or

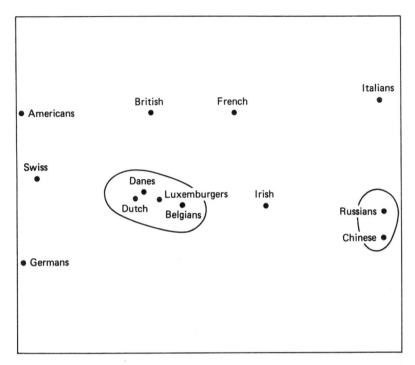

FIGURE 9.5: *Trust ratings of thirteen nationalities by the publics of nine European nations, 1976 (N=9, 210)*

distrustful predispositions toward specific nationalities are a stable feature of given political cultures.

This is true not only of trust toward specific nationalities, but of entire configurations of trust toward other peoples, as Figures 9.5 and 9.6 demonstrate. These figures present the results of Smallest Space Analyses based on the correlations between trust ratings of various nationalities. In these diagrams, those nationalities whose ratings are closely correlated are located nearby each other. The results reveal that those who gave relatively high ratings to the Russians, for example, were likely to give similar ratings to the Chinese as well: the fact that both societies were governed by Communist systems probably accounts for the tendency for them to receive similar ratings in every year for which we have data. Since both nationalities were ranked relatively *low* on trustworthiness, they are located at the *low* trust pole (the left side of these figures); the Italians also tend to receive low ratings, but are perceived as culturally different, so they also appear on the left, but as some distance from the Russians and Chinese. Another group that is perceived as similar consists of the Danes and the Dutch, and the Belgians and Luxembourgers as well: West European publics tend to see them as similar, and give them similar ratings. The same

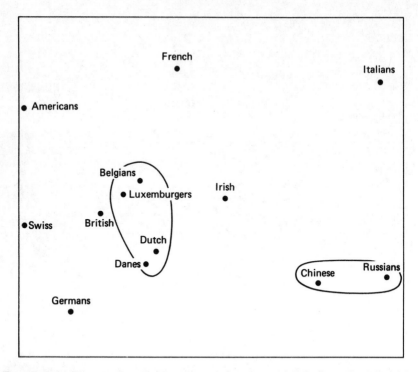

FIGURE 9.6: *Trust ratings of thirteen nationalities by the publics of nine European countries, 1986 (N=8, 823)*
Smallest Space Analyses based on representative national samples of publics of France, West Germany, Italy, Netherlands, Belgium, Ireland, Netherlands Denmark and Luxembourg in Eurobarometer 6 (1976) and 25 (1986). Kruskal's stress for 1976=.09; for 1986=.12.

is true, to a somewhat lesser degree, of the Germans and Swiss. Indeed, the entire cognitive map of which nationalities can be trusted and how the ratings of one nationality go together with ratings of others shows remarkable stability across the decade: the overall pattern for 1976 is virtually identical with that for 1986. Moreover, both of these maps are very similar to the one shown in Figure 9.2, although it is based on a larger number of nationalities.

Trust and distrust for given nationalities seems to be part of a stable cognitive map in the minds of given publics. But these patterns are not immutable. If we turn again to Table 9.4, we notice a very interesting phenomena: the ratings of most nationalities tend to be slightly higher in 1986 than they were in 1976. Though the rank order remains very stable, nine of the thirteen nationalities received higher ratings in 1986 than they had in 1976; one remained unchanged and three received slightly lower ratings; the overall mean rating rose by +.04 points and two nationalities that had received predominantly negative ratings in 1976 (below .50) rose above this threshold, with both the Irish and the Italians receiving predominantly positive ratings in 1986. The Chinese showed an unusually steep rise, moving near this threshold in 1986; and the Russians also made impressive gains. The Americans were one of the three nationalities that declined, moving against the overall upward trend. Though the amount of change that took place from 1976 to 1986 was very slight, this decline seems to be part of a long-term trend. Data from other surveys indicates that favorable opinions of the United States declined sharply from 1964 to 1976 (the era of the war in Vietnam) and then showed a recovery that was offset by another decline in the early 1980s, followed by a partial recovery in 1985–7. Thus, there is a mild absolute decline in ratings of the US since the late 1950s and early 1960s – and a very sharp *relative* decline. For in the 1950s, the United States received much more favorable ratings than did Britain, West Germany or France – and incomparably more favorable ones than Italy, China and the Soviet Union, all of which were predominantly negative (Inglehart, 1990: Chapter 13).

The trust ratings shown in Table 8.4 are not directly comparable to these overall good or bad opinion ratings, but they seem to follow a common trajectory. Already in 1976, the level of trust felt toward the Americans was well below that felt for the Germans – almost certainly a sharp reversal of what we would have found if this question had been asked in 1954–5. The Americans still ranked .02 points above the British and .04 points above the French in 1976; but by 1986, the Americans were exactly tied with the British and only .01 point above the French. Mass opinions of the United States and trust in the American people remain predominantly positive. But their absolute level has declined slightly; and the relative position of the United States has declined greatly, which means that her position as natural leader of the Atlantic Alliance has deteriorated. In the 1950s, the alliance was inherently and almost inevitably American-centered; in the 1980s, some intra-European bonds have become stronger than the Atlantic tie – while the psychological gulf between East and Western Europe has become narrower.

TRUST BETWEEN NATIONALITIES: A MULTIVARIATE ANALYSIS

The changes observed from 1970 to 1976 make it evident that current political and economic events can have a major impact on trust between nationalities. But there is also strong evidence of an underlying stability in patterns of trust: absolute levels may go up and down, but the relative rank orders tend to remain stable. Certain nationalities persistently tend to see each other as relatively trustworthy: the correlation between trust levels for the various nationalities measured in different years is consistently better than .90. In the long run, major changes can take place, such as the shift from distrust to trust that seems to have taken place in attitudes toward the Germans; and the gradual decline in the *relative* position of the Americans.

Though long-term patterns exist, trust between nationalities does not necessarily reflect immutable geographic or primordial characteristics. The Japanese provide a particularly striking illustration. Remote from Western Europe geographically, culturally and racially, the Japanese are, nevertheless, more highly trusted by Europeans than a number of much nearer and more similar nationalities.

In order to probe further into the relationship between communication and trust, we analyzed the proportion of persons saying they 'don't know' how trustworthy given peoples are. This, presumably, tends to reflect how well-informed one is about that people. As noted above, this percentage varies greatly. The lowest proportion was found in the rating of the Germans by the Luxembourgers, where only 2 per cent said they didn't know. The Luxembourgers also gave very low proportions of 'don't know' responses in their rating of the Belgians and French (4 per cent in each case). This seems intuitively very reasonable: a tiny country, the capital of Luxembourg is within a half hour's drive of Germany and France or Belgium; and contacts with these nations are extremely frequent. Another instance of extremely low 'don't know' responses is found in the German ratings of the Americans – where the proportion again is only 4 per cent. Though the United States is geographically remote, the Germans have a high rate of exposure to Americans via military, student and tourist exchanges; to American television, books and films; and to news reports about the United States. In each of these cases of extremely low non-response rates, high trust ratings are present.

At the other extreme, the highest proportions of 'don't know' responses are found in the Danes' ratings of the Portuguese and the Luxembourgeois (in both cases, 54 per cent say 'don't know'); and in the Irish ratings of the Portuguese, where 59 per cent give no response. Communication flow between these countries is minimal, so a low salience level is what we would expect.

We constructed an index of salience similar to our trust index, using the procedure developed by Merritt and Puchala (1968). Our initial expectation was that salience would be positively correlated with trust. This expectation was *not* confirmed in any clear cut fashion. We find only a modest correlation between salience and trust of .08. The absence of a strong positive correlation, in part, reflects the fact that the peoples of small nations often rank low on salience, but receive high trust ratings. But this is only part of the story. For, as Deutsch argues, communication is conducive to a sense of responsiveness and trust, *provided* that the interactions are positive. A common language may facilitate economic and cultural interactions that are usually positive. But it is also possible for a nationality to achieve high salience *without* such exchanges, simply by figuring prominently in the news. And the dominant news medium today is television – a type of medium that tends to focus on violent confrontations, far more than on peaceful economic, cultural or diplomatic exchanges. The print media may provide accounts of conferences, trade and agreements; but television favors pictures of dramatic physical confrontation, rather than quiet bargaining. In this context, the old adage seems particularly appropriate that 'No news is good news'. Previous research has found that high television viewing tends to be linked with a fearful, distrusting attitude toward society (Gerbner *et al.*, 1980). It may be that the focus on violence that seems to characterize television has a significant impact on trust between nationalities, neutralizing the effect that increased communication flows would otherwise be expected to have.

MULTIVARIATE ANALYSIS

We have identified a number of factors that seem to influence trust between nations. Which are the most important? In order to measure the relative impact of various explanatory variables, we constructed a second-order data set in which the unit of analysis is each nationality's rating of each of the *other* nationalities. Since our 1980 surveys provide ratings of sixteen nationalities (besides one's own), by ten different publics, we have a total of 160 cases.

Using each nationality's mean rating on the Merritt-Puchala Trust index as our dependent variable, we examined the linkages with a variety of macroeconomic and societal characteristics, ranging from the GNP per capita of the rated nationality, to the annual imports per capita from the rated nation, and whether the two nationalities were on the same side in World War II. Table 9.5 presents the zero-order correlations for a number of characteristics. As we noted above, salience had a correlation with trust of only .080. The strongest correlate of trust was an indicator of economic development – the GNP per capita of the nationality that was rated. The economic level of the nationality *doing* the rating, on the other hand, showed no significant linkage: this confirms the findings in Table 9.3 (based on more highly aggregated data, with an N of only 10), that wealthier nationalities are more highly trust*ed* by other nationalities, though not necessarily more trust*ing* toward other nationalities.

Our second strongest predictor of trust is a dummy variable based on whether the two nationalities belong to the same language group (e.g., the Germanic or Romance groups). As our impressionistic overview indicated, this relationship is very strong and probably reflects the relative ease with which a Dutchman (for example) can learn German or English,

TABLE 9.5: *Correlates of trust between nationalities* (Product-moment correlations with Trust Index, based on ratings of seventeen nationalities by ten West European publics)*

	r =	significance
Gross national product per capita, of nationality being rated	.701	.0001
Gross national product per capita, of nationality doing the rating	.040	n.s.
Do rated and rating nationality belong to same language group?	.588	.0001
Do rated and rating nationality share a common language?	.318	.0001
Are rated and rating nationalities primarily of same race?	.255	.001
Are rated and rating nationalities primarily of same religion?	.416	.0001
Does rated nationality live under a democratic political system?	.567	.0001
Distance between capitals of the two nations	−.421	.0001
Were both nationalities on same side in World War II?	.222	.005
Were both nationalities on same side in World War I?	−.096	n.s.
Exports per capita to rated nationality	.213	.01
Imports per capita from rated nationality	.166	n.s.
Student flow per capita to rated nationality	.215	.01
Student flow per capita from rated nationality	.119	n.s.
Percentage age group in higher education	.053	n.s.

* The total number of pairs for which Trust Indices are calculated is 160, since each nationality's rating of itself is excluded from this analysis.

SOURCE: Based on October, 1980 EC surveys (Eurobarometer 14) plus aggregate statistical data from UN sources; sides taken in World War I and World War II were coded by authors.

as compared with French or Spanish – and the facilitating effect this has on communication flows. Interestingly enough, a shared language *group* has a decidedly stronger correlation with trust than does the fact that two nationalities share precisely the same language. There are relatively few instances of the latter (the English-Irish-American cases; and the French-Belgian-Swiss cases, for example); and while these relationships clearly tend to show high trust, overall the levels are no higher than relationships within the same language group (such as the German-Danish-British-Dutch-Swiss cases).

The presence of a similar political system is also strongly related to trust levels. We coded each nation as democratic or non-democratic, with only the Soviet Union and China falling into the latter category. This variable shows a powerful relationship with trust levels. A similar ideology and political institutions – like a common language – probably facilitate communication and mutual predictability. And the historical experiences of the past few decades, particularly the various phases of the Cold War, seem to have instilled a strong sense of distrust toward the peoples of the two leading Communist nations. Clearly, this is the product of societal learning, rather than a reflection of primordial characteristics. But we must note that religion, race and geographical proximity *also* seem to be important factors in so far as their zero-order correlations with trust are valid indicators.

Finally, whether or not the two given nationalities were on the same side in World War II also showed a significant relationship with the level of trust between them thirty-five years later, in 1980: societal learning of trust or distrust seems remarkably persistent. (In ambiguous cases, where a nation changed sides or entered the war after a period of neutrality, our criterion was whether the two nations were on the same side for more than half of the time from 1939 to 1945.)

Some indicators of communications flows showed only marginal linkages with trust, though they were in the expected direction: exports *to* the rated nationality had a moderate but significant linkage with trust, but imports from that nationality did not: apparently, one trusts one's customers more than one's suppliers. Similarly, student flows *to* the rated nationality showed a significant relationships, but student flows *from* the rated nationality did not: apparently one goes to study among people one trusts to a greater extent than one trusts those who come to study in your own country. We included those indicators showing strong zero-order relationships with trust, in a preliminary regression analysis. The variables used were limited to those shown in Table 9.6, in order to minimize multicolinearity: thus we used 'Common Language *Group*' but not the closely related variable 'Common Language'.

Only four variables showed significant effects in this analysis, but in each case the relationship was statistically significant at a very high level. Economic development is clearly a major factor in international trust. Belonging to a common language group comes next – and it may reflect a sense of primordial ties, to some extent, as well as facilitating international communications. Whether the rated nationality lives under a democratic political system also has significant effects. Finally, the apparent impact of alliance or hostility in World War II is not only maintained, but slightly increased, when we take the other variables into account. Societal learning seems to be a genuine influence on trust.

On the other hand, the impact of religion, race and geographic proximity shrink to insignificant levels when we control for the effects of the other variables: their strong zero-order relationships with trust seem to reflect the fact that they are linked with the presence of similar language groups

TABLE 9.6: *Regression analysis: trust between nationalities*

	Partial r	Standardized Regression Coefficient	Significance
Gross national product per capita of rated nationality	.649	.551	.0001
Common language group	.296	.235	.0001
Democratic political system	.353	.173	.0001
On same side in World War II	.260	.153	.0005
Geographical distance between nations	−.153	−.055	n.s.
Exports per capita to rated nationality	.133	.080	n.s.
Primarily of same religion	.087	.099	n.s.
Predominately of same race	.062	.055	n.s.

Multiple $R = .849$ $R^2 = .722$

and economic levels. The role of exports also shrinks to an insignificant level in multivariate analysis. We performed a revised multiple regression analysis including only those variables having significant effects in Table 9.6. On the basis of these four variables alone, we can explain nearly 70 per cent of the variance among the 160 trust ratings made by ten Western publics (multiple $R = .833$); the four variables that were dropped explain only 2 per cent additional variance. Economic development, language group, and two societal learning variables (reflecting the impact of the Cold War and World War II, respectively) explain the great bulk of the variation in trust.

CONCLUSION

Trust between nationalities seems to be shaped by three main factors: economic development, societal learning and primordial ties – in that order. We suggested that primordial ties are of declining importance. We do not have an adequate time series base to demonstrate whether this is true, but our findings are consistent with this interpretation. Race, religion and geographic proximity all have surprisingly little impact when we control for other variables. One's language group is the only 'primordial' variable having a significant impact on trust, and this impact may be due to its function in facilitating or inhibiting communication, rather than as an ethnic characteristic.

On the other hand, economic development clearly does have a powerful relationship with trust toward other nationalities. This relationship seems to reflect societal learning, rather than a process of projection: the wealthier nationalities are decidedly more highly trusted, but they do *not* necessarily trust other nationalities, simply projecting onto them what they have experienced at home. Conversely, the less prosperous nationalities tend to show relatively low trust in their own nationality and in others of their region, but they often *do* show relatively high trust in given North European peoples. Trust toward specific nationalities seems to be learned, rather than reflecting the psychodynamics of the nationality doing the rating.

It is clear, however, that certain nationalities tend to show relatively high or low levels of trust toward other people in general and toward their own countrymen in particular. We lack the time series data needed to determine whether high levels of interpersonal trust are the result of poverty – or a prerequisite for economic growth. We suspect that causality flows in both directions. In any case, it seems clear that low trust has been a stable characteristic of certain cultures.

Twenty-five years ago, Banfield found that Italian society had distinctively low levels of interpersonal trust – a characteristic that was particularly evident in Southern Italy. A tremendous amount of economic development and modernization have taken place in Italy since Banfield's fieldwork in the 1950s. Nevertheless, levels of interpersonal trust remain strikingly low in Italy, especially in the South. These levels were even *lower* in 1958 (Inglehart, 1990: Chapter 1) – but, despite economic modernization, a sizeable trust deficit remains. Furthermore, the Italians show much lower levels of trust in their countrymen than do the publics of nations that are economically even *less* developed (such as Ireland and Greece). Poverty may be a contributing factor, but it cannot be the whole explanation. Relatively low levels of interpersonal trust seem to be a long-established aspect of the Italian political culture which is only gradually disappearing as economic development progresses.

The concept of 'political culture' became unfashionable in recent years (Almond, 1980; Verba, 1980). Partly, this simply corrected an earlier tendency to try to explain too much in terms of micropolitical variables, without reference to other types of variables and other levels of analysis. But the evidence examined here indicates that political culture *does* have a life of its own. As the residue of societal learning at a given point in time, it is by no means immutable. Such major events as World War II or the Cold War seem to have partially reshaped the orientations of trust/distrust prevailing in given nations, leaving impressions that are visible today. But the impact of such events, in turn, enters into a political culture that is also an independent variable that plays a role of its own.

REFERENCES

Abramson, Paul R. (1983) *Political Attitudes in America: Formation and Change* (San Francisco: Freeman).

Almond, Gabriel and Sidney Verba (1963) *The Civic Culture* (Princeton, NJ: Princeton University Press).

Almond, Gabriel A. (1980). 'The Intellectual History of the Civic Culture Concept', in Almond and Verba (eds), *The Civic Culture Revisited* (Boston, Mass.: Little, Brown).

Banfield, Edward (1958). *The Moral Basis of a Backward Society* (Chicago: Free Press).

Buchanan, William and Hadley Cantril (1953) *How Nations See Each Other* (Urbana: University of Illinois Press).

Citrin, Jack (1974) 'Comment: The Political Relevance of Trust in Government', *American Political Science Review* 68, 3 (September) 973–88.

Deutsch, Karl W. (1952) *Nationalism and Social Communication* (Cambridge, Mass.: M.I.T. Press).

Deutsch, Karl W. et al. (1957) *Political Community and the North Atlantic Area* (Princeton, NJ: Princeton University Press).

Easton, David (1966) *A Systems Analysis of Political Life* (New York: Wiley).

Gerbner, George et al. (1980) 'The "Mainstreaming" of America: Violence Profile No. 11', *Journal of Communication* 30, 3: 10–29.

Harris Survey (1982) 'Allies or Enemies? Americans Rate Foreign Nations' 104 (27 December).

Hart, Vivien (1973) *Distrust and Democracy* (Cambridge: Cambridge University Press).

Hill, David B. (1981) 'Attitude Generalization and the Measurement of Trust in American Leadership', *Political Behavior* 13, 3, pp. 257–70.

ISOP (1982) 'Uber das Vertrauen der Schweizer in die Bevolkerung von 16 Staaten', Zurich: Swiss Institute of Public Opinion (ISOP).

Lopez-Pintor, Rafel and Jose Ignacio Wert Ortega (1982) 'La Otra Espana: Insolidaridad e Intolerancia en la Tradicion Politico- Cultural Espanola', *Revista Espanola de Investigaciones Sociologicas* 19 (July-September).

Luhmann, Niklas (1979) *Power and Trust* (Chichester and New York: Wiley).

Marsh, Alan (1977) *Protest and Political Consciousness* (Beverly Hills, Ca. and London: Sage).

Merritt, Richard L. and Donald J. Puchala (1968) *Western European Perspectives on International Affairs* (New York: Praeger).

Miller, Arthur H. (1974) 'Political Issues and Trust in Government: 1964–1970', *American Political Science Review* 68, 3 (September) 951–72.

Miyake, Ichiro (1982) 'Trust in Government and Political Cleavages: A Cross-National Comparison', *Doshisha Law Review* 171 and 172.

Nincic, Miroslav and Bruce Russett (1979) 'The Effect of Similarity and Interest on Attitudes Toward Foreign Countries', *Public Opinion Quarterly* 43, 1 (Spring) 68–78.

Pizzorno. A. (1966) 'Amoral Familism and Historical Marginality', *International Review of Community Development* 15.

Prime Minister's Secretariat (1982) 'Public Opinion Survey on Diplomacy', (Tokyo: Foreign Press Center).

Pruitt, Dean G. (1965) 'Definition of the Situation as a Determinant of International Action', in Herbert C. Kelman (ed.), *International Behaviour: A Social-Psychological Analysis* (New York: Holt, Rinehart and Winston).

Verba, Sidney (1980) 'On Revisiting the Civic Culture: A Personal Postscript', in
  Gabriel A. Almond and Sidney Verba (eds), *The Civic Culture Revisited* (Boston, Mass.: Little, Brown).
Wylie, Laurence (1957) *Village in the Vaucluse* (Cambridge, Mass.: Harvard
  University Press).

10 Gender Differences in Sex-Role Attitudes: A Topic Without a Future?

Marita Rosch Inglehart, University of Michigan

INTRODUCTION

Will gender still be a significant variable for analyzing attitudes, opinions, and values in Western industrialized countries in the year 2000? Or will structural and individual changes towards the equality of men and women in these societies make such analyses superfluous? This chapter analyses the present state of gender differences in sex-role attitudes using Eurobarometer data, data from the World Value Study conducted in 1981, and Argentinian data from 1988. These analyses demonstrate that there are sizeable gender differences in the attitudes towards the role of men and women in the families, in the workplace, in politics, and in the sexual domain. But they also show that the gender differences found in these surveys are a function of (a) the year in which the survey was conducted, and (b) the nation that was studied. These differences show dramatic changes over time, and when we move from economically less developed to more developed societies. These finding suggest that the size of gender differences are declining over time, and that future research on gender differences in political and social attitudes may have a different focus from the one it has today.

CURRENT RESEARCH ON GENDER DIFFERENCES

Recent years have seen the rise of a vigorous debate in psychology concerning whether research on gender differences should be conducted at all. Proponents of a 'yes' to this question go so far as to demand that researchers should routinely test for gender differences in virtually all studies, and should report any such differences provided they can be replicated or are theoretically interesting (McHugh, Koeske and Frieze, 1986). Eagly (1987) even argues that sex differences should be reported in every possible publication, in hopes that this practice would end sex discrimination. On the other hand, proponents of a 'no' answer to this question argue that keeping separate records of female and male subjects in psychological studies is likely to perpetuate discrimination against women, and that it would not contribute in any important sense to knowledge about human behavior (Baumeister, 1988).

Three separate lines of arguments fuelled this debate on the significance of psychological research on gender differences. From a methodological point of view some researchers argued that psychology cannot be viewed as unbiased concerning gender roles if twice as many articles in personality journals used male subjects as female subjects (Carlson, 1971) and if 75 per cent of the articles in animal behavior journals used male animals (Hyde & Rosenberg, 1980). These researchers aim mainly at demonstrating that there is a masculinity bias in psychology that leads (male) researchers to study male subjects and then claim to have found general principles of human behaviour (McHugh, Koeske and Frieze, 1986; Rothblum, 1988).

From a political perspective some researchers warned that the mass media coverage of psychological research on gender differences can be detrimental to establishing equal opportunities for both sexes. Eccles (1982) documented for example how a 3 per cent sex difference in maths performance was presented by mass media nationwide as a huge difference, often with implications that women should not attempt to enter careers which demand quantitative skills. Apparently, findings of no gender differences are not newsworthy to mass media, and findings of small differences are subject to exaggeration. Politically, research on gender differences might thus be used to perpetuate and to legitimize discrimination against women (Baumeister, 1988).

Finally, on a scientific level some researchers argue that finding a gender difference does not really explain anything. Instead it raises the question what it is about the sexes that causes this difference (McHugh, Koeske and Frieze, 1986). And if this question is the really interesting one, then – one might argue – this question should have been studied from the beginning.

To some extent this ongoing debate in psychology about the relevance of research on gender differences relates to issues concerned with conducting psychological research. In this sense, social scientists from other disciplines might not see this debate as relevant at all for their own areas of research. Social scientists who use representative surveys to study gender differences might argue, for example, that their samples are representative of the population under investigation, and that the methodological concerns voiced against psychological research are inappropriate when evaluating their research on gender differences. But other aspects of this debate among psychologists about the merits or dangers of studying sex differences are definitely of general relevance. Political damage can result from using social scientists' findings of gender differences to perpetuate and legitimize discrimination against women, for example, in the workplace or in educational settings. From a scientific viewpoint, it is true that a gender difference *per se* does not mean much unless its underlying causation is understood.

When studying gender differences in political and social attitudes, the significance of both of these issues becomes apparent. Therefore, one might advocate abandoning gender research and instead aiming at understanding the dynamics underlying differences in social and political attitudes. Searching for those background and socialization factors which lead to a more liberal or conservative point of view, to a higher or lower level of interest in politics, or to a stronger or weaker involvement in political or social movements, seems a more appropriate approach to studying political phenomena than to look automatically for gender differences in these variables.

But there is one subset of attitudes in which gender research clearly should contribute to our understanding, because the gender variable is inherently related to the content of the attitude. These are sex-role attitudes. The study of gender differences in these attitudes is of clear interest in itself because being raised as a woman or as a man, and evaluating members of one's ingroup or of one's outgroup is actually significant for understanding differences in sex-role attitudes.

In this chapter, gender differences in sex-role attitudes will be studied by analyzing survey data from various industrialized nations and across time. These analyses are interesting in themselves, because they can be used to investigate, for example, the influence of the Women's Movement or the influence of structural variables. We will examine (a) trends over time, and (b) cross-national differences in how respondents reacted to these issues.

These analyses will also be used to illuminate the broader debate about the political and scientific aspects of conducting research on gender differences in the social sciences. Finally, we will address the question whether studying gender differences in social and political attitudes should or will be an important topic in industrialized societies in the twenty-first century.

SEX-ROLE ATTITUDES IN INDUSTRIALIZED SOCIETIES: IS THERE A GENDER GAP?

Undoubtedly one of the most significant social changes in the sixties and seventies of this century in industrialized nations concerned the role of women in these still largely male-dominated societies. These changes were reflected in shifts in political and social attitudes. In connection with these shifts, the term 'gender gap' was introduced into sociological literature. It referred to the finding that in the 1980s women – who previously had been more conservative than men – began to vote more for liberal or for more left-oriented candidates in the USA and Great Britain. Some authors even argue that these gender differences are a major new political cleavage in the politics of these countries (see Wirls, 1986, for an overview of the situation in the USA; see Norris, 1986a, 1986b, for the situation in Great Britain and the cross-national situation; see also Bennett, 1986; Rossi, 1983; Walker, 1988).

Gender differences in political and social opinions were documented consistently even before 1980. These differences are in line with the widely-accepted distinction that Parsons (1955) had introduced in his writings about the division of labour in most societies. Parsons (1955) had argued that in most societies men have mostly instrumental functions – they are responsible for supporting and protecting their families, and for managing their society's economic and political institutions. Women, however, have primarily expressive functions: that means that societal expectations are for women to be caretakers and nurturers of their families.

These functional differentiations led to clear gender specific expectations which in turn influenced political and social attitudes. Smith (1984) pointed out, for example, that there are rather striking and persistent gender differences in issues concerned with force and violence, both on the domestic front and in an international context (see also Jensen, 1987); Silverman and Kumka, 1987). And the editors of *Public Opinion* (Opinion Roundup, 1982) provide evidence that women are more supportive of 'compassion' issues, such as aiding the poor, the unemployed, the sick and others in need. In recent years, some authors argued that due to the Women's Movement women began to generalize their more traditional roles as caretakers to society as a whole and that this explains women's support for regulatory policies (such as environmental protection, consumer protection, other safety issues) that aim at protecting the public as a whole (see Shapiro and Mahajan, 1986, for an overview).

Not surprisingly, there were a number of studies that reported the existence of gender differences in attitudes towards women's roles in politics and society (see Erskine, 1971, for an overview of the research conducted between 1930 and 1970). Finally, numerous studies were interested in gender differences in sex-role attitudes in general and the changes that took place in recent years (see Spence, Deaux and Helmreich, 1985 for a summary).

This chapter investigates whether gender differences in sex-role attitudes still exist in industrialized societies, and if so, whether they are remaining consistent with the traditional societal expectations for men and women. Attitudes towards men and women's role in the family, the workplace, and in politics will be analysed as well as attitudes in the sexual domain.

METHODS

Data from the Eurobarometer Survey conducted in April 1987 in thirteen countries (Belgium, Denmark, France, Great Britain, Greece, Ireland, Italy, Luxembourg, Northern Ireland, Portugal, Spain, the Netherlands, West Germany; N=11 651), from the World Value Study conducted in 1981 in twenty-four countries, and a survey conducted in August 1988 in Argentina (N=1 006) are used here.[1] Data from nineteen countries (N=25 572) studied in the World Value Survey were included in these analyses. These countries were Australia, Belgium, Canada, Denmark, Eire, France, Great Britain, Hungary, Italy, Japan, Mexico, Northern Ireland, Norway, South Africa, Spain, Sweden, the Netherlands, USA, West Germany. The results from the Eurobarometer Survey from April 1987 were compared with the results from Eurobarometer surveys conducted in 1975, 1977, and 1983 by the Commission of the European Communities.

RESULTS

Table 10.1 presents some results concerning attitudes toward the husband's and wife's role in the family, based on responses from the Eurobarometer Surveys carried out in 1983 and in 1987. The possible responses ranged from an egalitarian position ('A family where the two partners each have an equally absorbing job and where housework and the care of the children are shared equally between them') to a traditional position ('A family where only the husband has a job and the wife runs the home') with one intermediate position ('A family where the wife has a less demanding job than her husband and where she does the larger share of housework and caring for the children').

Table 10.1 sums up combined results from the ten West European countries that were included in both the 1983 and 1987 surveys (Spain and Portugal joined the Community only in 1988 and were not included in the earlier surveys). In 1983, the responses made by the men in these ten countries were almost evenly divided among support for traditional, equalitarian and intermediate roles: about one-third supported each of the three roles. Among women, the most frequent choice was for the egalitarian role, though it was endorsed by only 39 per cent, far short of a majority. By 1987, the egalitarian role had moved into a clear lead among West European men, whose responses were now almost identical to those that West European women had shown four years earlier. But the women too had shifted in the same direction; with almost half now choosing the egalitarian option.

During the four years from 1983 to 1987, a significant shift of outlook

TABLE 10.1: *Gender differences in attitudes toward the husband's and wife's roles in the family: 1983 vs 1987* (Responses of combined sample from ten West European nations)

Question: People also talk about the changing roles of husband and wife in the family. Here are three kinds of family. Which of them corresponds most with your ideas about the family?

Response 1: Egalitarian roles.
Response 2: Intermediate roles.
Response 3: Traditional roles.

	April/May 1983 (Eurobarometer 19)		April 1987 (Eurobarometer 27)	
	Men	Women	Men	Women
Egalitarian roles	33%	39%	40%	45%
Intermediate roles	32%	29%	29%	27%
Traditional roles	29%	26%	27%	24%

took place among West European men. Figure 10.1 illustrates the overall results for both sexes combined. The egalitarian alternative moved into a clear lead, with an eleven-point margin over its nearest competitor, the intermediate option. A shift toward the egalitarian option took place among *both* men and women, but the movement was slightly greater among men than among women, so that the size of the gender gap diminished during this period. No one would describe these shifts as revolutionary. And indeed, it would be unrealistic to expect rapid changes in such basic social norms as the division of labor between the sexes. But for a period of four years, this is an impressive shift and it is all the more impressive because it was not an isolated fluke occurring in one country: shifts toward the egalitarian pattern took place in virtually every country studied here.

What is even more interesting is that the data suggest that this shift in outlook from 1983 to 1987 was apparently part of a long-term trend. For when we compare the responses of different birth cohorts, we find that even in 1987, the traditional role was the leading option among the older cohorts. Among those born before 1925 (aged sixty-two and older in 1987), both women and men were likelier to favour the traditional roles than either the intermediate or the egalitarian alternatives (40 per cent of the women and 45 per cent of the men were traditionalists). Among the younger birth cohorts, on the other hand, the egalitarian option was the leading alternative; indeed, among those born after 1945, it was supported by an absolute majority of *both* men and women (the figure being 51 per cent and 55 per cent respectively). Men have more traditional gender role orientations than women, but both seem to be moving in the same direction.

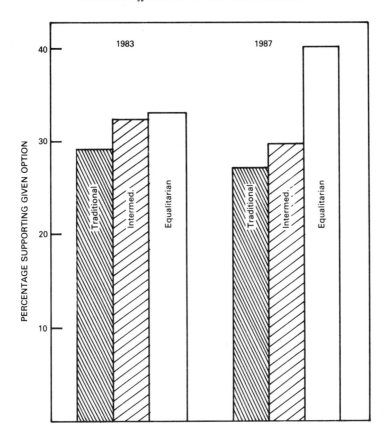

SOURCE: *combined data from ten nations surveyed in Eurobarometer surveys 19 and 27.*
FIGURE 10.1: *The balance between support for traditional and egalitarian gender roles among West European men in 1983 and 1987.*

A similar pattern is found in Table 10.2 which presents data from an Argentinian survey conducted in August 1988. In this survey, men were likelier than women to support the traditional statement 'The man is the head of the family and it is he who should make the decisions', but the modal response for both sexes was the 'strongly disagree' response.

The responses offered to question B in this survey again ranged again from a traditional position ('Women should not work outside of the home, but should dedicate themselves to taking care of the children') to an egalitarian position ('Women should not dedicate themselves solely to taking care of the children, but the possibility for them to work outside of the home should become equal to that for men') with one intermediate position ('Although women should not work outside of the home, present economic conditions may make it a necessary evil'). Again, both men and

TABLE 10.2: *Attitudes toward husband's and wife's role in the family in Argentina, 1988*

Question A: How strongly do you agree/disagree with the following statement: The man is the head of the family and it is he who should make the decisions. Answers range from 1 (strongly agree) to 4 (disagree totally)

Question B: Which of the following statements best describes your ideas about the family?
   B1. Traditional roles.
   B2. Intermediate roles.
   B3. Egalitarian roles.

Question:	The man is the head of the family (A)			(B)	
	men	women		men	woman
strongly agree	15%	6%	Egalitarian	42%	54%
agree	19%	13%	Intermediate	33%	29%
disagree	22%	20%	Traditional	25%	17%
strongly disagree	43%	61%			

women chose the egalitarian position most frequently, with women being even less traditional than men.

A comparison of these three alternatives presented in the Argentinian survey with the alternatives presented in the Eurobarometer Survey shows that less traditional attitudes towards men's and women's roles are supported by men and women both in Europe and in a South American country, with men being more traditional than woman. When making these comparisons one should note that the responses offered as alternatives in the Argentinian survey are less extreme: they do not include an equal distribution of housework or child care responsibilities in the egalitarian statement, so they cannot be compared directly with responses to the question used in Europe.

Indeed, though the difference in question formulation shows Argentine results toward the egalitarian pole, the gender gap – that is, the *difference* between male and female responses – is much larger in Argentina than in Western Europe. This is precisely what one would expect, if gender-role differences tend to decline as economic development takes place, for Argentina's gross domestic product per capita is only about one-quarter as large as that of the European Community as a whole.

Table 10.3 presents some results concerning attitudes of men and women in the workplace. In 1983 a considerable percentage of Europeans still had more trust in a man than in a woman in traditionally male professions such as driving a bus or train (41 per cent more trust in a man; 2 per cent more trust in a woman; 56 per cent the same), being a surgeon (39 per cent in a man; 2 per cent in a woman; 57 per cent same) or a lawyer (33 per cent in a

TABLE 10.3: *Attitudes towards men and women in the workplace*

Question: Generally speaking would you have more confidence in a man or a woman . . .

respondents:	in a man	1983: total in a woman	same	in a man	1987: total in a woman	same
. . . as a driver of your bus or train?	41	2	56	35	3	63
. . . as a surgeon to operate on you?	39	2	57	29	4	67
. . . as a doctor delivering your baby?	11	33	52	11	23	66
. . . as a lawyer to defend you in court?	33	6	59	26	8	66

man; 6 per cent in a woman; 59 per cent same). By 1987, a change had taken place towards more liberal sex-role attitudes. Women were clearly more liberal than men, in their attitudes, but both women and men showed significant overall shifts toward more egalitarian attitudes in their images of the relative competence of women as bus driver, surgeons and lawyers. The one exception was in regard to 'a doctor delivering your baby'. Here, there was no change from 1983 to 1987 – but both men and women had greater confidence in a *woman* to perform this task, at both time points.

Attitudes towards men's and women's involvement in politics are the third area that is considered here. In Table 10.4, the trend in men's and women's sex-role attitudes in this domain is illustrated by presenting the answers to three questions concerning whether 'politics should be left to men', the confidence in a male versus a female member of one's Parliament, and the expectation whether things would go better, worse or the same if more women were in Parliament. In regard to each item sex-role attitudes became more markedly liberal between 1975 and 1987; whereas in 1975, 36 per cent of West European men agreed that 'politics should be left to men', in 1987 only 27 per cent did so – while 77 per cent disagreed. And whereas in 1975, 42 per cent of the men said they had more confidence in a man as a member of Parliament, in 1987 only 27 per cent did so. Nevertheless, in each case, women were more liberal in their attitudes concerning these issues than men. This is especially interesting, because of the findings presented in Table 10.5 which shows data from the World Values Study conducted in 1981. Here, women indicated that they were less interested in politics than men, and that they discussed politics far less frequently than men: fully 42 per cent of West European women reported that they *never* discuss politics, as compared with only 26 per cent of the

TABLE 10.4: *Gender differences in attitudes towards women's and men's involvement in politics*

Question: It is sometimes said that 'politics should be left to men'. How far would you agree with this?

	Men			Women		
	1975	1983	1987	1975	1983	1987
agree a lot	15	8	9	9	15	8
agree a little	21	18	16	19	16	12
disagree a little	23	23	22	20	21	20
disagree a lot	37	48	53	41	51	60

Question: Generally speaking, would you have more confidence in a man or in a woman as your member of Parliament?

	Men				Women			
	1975	1977	1983	1987	1975	1977	1983	1987
in a man	42	47	34	27	33	33	27	19
in a woman	6	6	4	4	11	16	9	11
same	46	42	60	69	50	44	61	70

Question: Would things go better or worse if there were distinctly more women in Parliament?

	Men			Women		
	1975	1983	1987	1975	1983	1987
better	19	18	22	35	29	35
worse	25	12	18	12	6	10
same	42	60	60	36	53	55

SOURCE: *Eurobarometer surveys in years indicated.*

men. In their actual behaviour, women continue to differ significantly from men. Nevertheless, women do have egalitarian attitudes concerning women's and men's involvement in politics.

Now let us turn to another area in which women traditionally have been more conservative than men, and where these differences have persisted despite the change in women's attitudes toward politics. This area is the sexual domain (see Hendrick, Hendrick, Slapion–Foote and Foote, 1985 for an overview). Table 10.6 presents results from the 1981 World Value Study concerning sexual attitudes. When asked whether they thought that 'married men/women having an affair', 'sex under the legal age of consent', 'homosexuality', 'prostitution', 'abortion', and 'divorce' were 'never' ('1') to 'always' ('10') justifiable, an interesting pattern of results occurred. In regard to each issue other than that of 'homosexuality' men were clearly more liberal than women. The only statement towards which women held more liberal attitudes than men was the issue of 'homosexuality'.

TABLE 10.5: *Gender differences in attitudes toward political behaviour*

Question: When you get together with friends, would you say you discuss political matters frequently, occasionally or never?

	Men	Women
frequently	16	9
occasionally	58	49
never	26	42

Question: Which of these statements comes closest to describing your interest in politics?

	Men	Women
A. I take an active interest	8	4
B. I am interested in politics, but don't take any active part	42	32
C. My interest in politics is not greater than other interests	29	32
D. I'm not interested in politics at all	20	32

SOURCE: *World Values Survey, 1981–3 (combined cross-national data)*

TABLE 10.6: *Gender differences in attitudes toward sexual behaviour*

Question: If someone said that individuals should have the chance to enjoy complete sexual freedom without being restricted, would you tend to agree or disagree?

	Men	Women
tend to agree	26	19
tend to disagree	56	64
don't know	18	18

Question: Please, tell me for each of the following statements whether you think it can always be justified, never be justified or something in between. (percentage saying 'never')

	Men	Women
– married men/women having an affair	49	61
– sex under the legal age of consent	61	67
– homosexuality	54	49
– prostitution	49	61
– abortion	32	37
– divorce	19	22

SOURCE: *World Values Survey, 1981–3 (combined cross-national data)*

CONCLUSIONS

Three clear findings emerge in these analyses of gender differences in attitudes towards men's and women's roles in the family, in the workplace and in politics. The first finding is that egalitarian sex-role attitudes are apparently becoming the modal response in industrialized societies. Secondly, clear gender differences remain in sex-role attitudes, with women generally having less traditional sex-role attitudes than men. The only area in which men are still more liberal than women is the area of sexual attitudes. On the whole, women continue to hold more traditional sexual attitudes than men. The third finding concerns changes in sex-role attitudes over time towards more liberal sex-role attitudes.

An interpretation of these findings must address two issues. The first concerns the implications of these findings *per se*. The second issue goes back to the opening question of this chapter, whether research on gender differences in general is politically wise and scientifically fruitful. Concerning the first issue, the question arises: What are the implications of such findings in the real world? Do these changes in sex-role attitudes imply that discrimination against women in the workplace and in politics is decreasing and will disappear in the near future? Do these findings imply that the majority of men and women in industrialized societies are becoming less likely to show sexist biases against others? Do they imply that in future generations boys and girls, and men and women will have equal opportunities to live up to their potentials?

We cannot conclusively answer these questions here for two reasons. The first has to do with the limited data base available. Data are available from only a few time points, covering a relatively modest span of years. The analyses presented here can only provide a rough first impression of this topic. But they also demonstrate that at this point in time, social scientific analyses can go far beyond what is offered in this chapter. The availability of large cross-national data sets with data collected at several points in time – such as the Eurobarometer surveys – open up new possibilities. They allow social scientists to analyze trends in sex-role attitudes and other social trends in a more systematic way than has been possible before.

The second factor that makes it difficult to pinpoint the implications of these findings has to do with the relationship between social cognitions and actual behaviour in the real world. Even if we assume that the attitudes analysed here were measured reliably, validly and objectively, they do not necessarily influence our respondents' actual behavior. This leads to one suggestion for future survey research. In addition to social and political attitudes, data concerning behavioural intentions and concrete behavior related to these attitudes would be useful to have. For example, in addition to asking how housework and caring for children should be shared between a husband and a wife in a family, it would be interesting to also have data on the number of hours women and men spend doing housework and caring for children in the week before the survey was taken. The results presented here map out the respondents' thoughts about these issues. They do not demonstrate that the concrete situations in the families and in the workplaces changed to the same degree as the attitudes changed over time.

A second issue when thinking about the implications of these findings has to do with the future of research on these issues. The availability of cross-national time series data sets such as the Eurobarometers makes systematic analyses of these issues possible. What are the implications of these findings for research on gender differences in social and political attitudes in the future? From an optimistic angle one might argue that sex-role attitudes are changing towards more equality for men and women, and that women especially are enforcing more and more egalitarian views. Once the point were reached at which men and women are treated equally and hold egalitarian sex-role attitudes these issues would no longer be interesting. Social scientists can now work on documenting the changes in these attitudes in various countries and over time, but they should begin to reflect beyond the findings of gender differences to gain a clearer understanding of the underlying processes that lead to these findings. In so far as structural variables and individual factors change towards equality for men and women, the less interesting research on gender differences will be. In this sense, we hope that this will be a topic without a future in the coming century.

NOTES

1. I want to thank Marita Carballo de Cilly from the Argentinian Gallop Institute for providing me with access to the data from the Argentinian Survey conducted in August 1988. I also want to thank the principal investigators for the opportunity to use data from the World Value Study conducted in 1981, and from the Eurobarometer conducted in April 1987.

REFERENCES

Baumeister, R. F. (1988) 'Should we stop studying sex differences altogether?' *American Psychologist*, 43, 1092–5.
Bennett, L. L. M. (1986) 'The gender gap: When an opinion gap is not a voting bloc', *Social Science Quarterly*, 67, 613–25.
Carlson, R. (1971) 'Where is the person in personality research?' *Psychological Bulletin*, 75, 203–19.

Commission of the European Communities (1983) *European women and men in 1983* (Brussels: European Commission).

Eagly, A. H. (1987) 'Reporting sex differences', *American Psychologist*, 42, 756.

Eccles, J. (1982) 'Sex differences in achievement patterns' (Paper presented at the annual meeting of the American Psychological Association, Washington, DC).

Erskine, H. (1971) 'The polls: Women's role', *Public Opinion Quarterly*, 35, 275–90.

Hendrick, S., Hendrick, C., Slapion-Foote, M. J. and Foote, F. H. (1985) 'Gender differences in sexual attitudes', *Journal of Personality and Social Psychology*, 48, 1630–42.

Hyde, J. S. and Rosenberg, B. G. (1980) *Half the human experience: The psychology of women* (Lexington, Mass.: D. C. Heath).

Jensen, M. P. (1987) 'Gender, sex roles, and attitudes toward war and nuclear weapons', *Sex Roles*, 17, 253–67.

McHugh, M. C., Koeske, R. D. and Frieze, I. H. (1986) 'Issues to consider in conducting non-sexist psychological research: A guide for researchers', *American Psychologist*, 41, 879–90.

Norris, P. (1986a) 'Conservative attitudes in recent British elections: an emerging gender gap?' *Political Studies*, 34, 120–8.

Norris, P. (1986b) 'The gender gap: a cross-national trend?' In C. Mueller (ed.), *Politics of the Gender Gap* (Beverly Hills, Ca.: Sage).

Parsons, T. (1955) 'Family structure and the socialization of the child', In T. Parsons and R. F. Bales (eds), *Family, socialization, and interaction process* (Glencoe, Illinois: Free Press).

Public Opinion (1982) 'Opinion roundup: women and men: is a realignment under way?' *Public Opinion, April/May*, 21, 27–32.

Rossi, A. S. (1983) 'Beyond the gender gap: Women's bid for political power', *Social Science Quarterly*, 64, 718–33.

Rothblum, E. D. (1988) 'More on reporting sex differences', *American Psychologist*, 43, 1095.

Shapiro, R. Y. and Mahajan, H. (1986) 'Gender differences in policy preferences: A summary of the trends from the 1960s to the 1980s', *Public Opinion Quarterly*, 50, 42–61.

Silverman, J. M. (1987) 'Gender differences in attitudes toward nuclear war and disarmament', *Sex Roles*, 16, 189–203.

Smith, T. W. (1984) 'The polls: gender and attitudes toward violence', *Public Opinion Quarterly*, 48, 384–96.

Spence, J. T., Deaux, K. and Helmreich, R. L. (1985) 'Sex roles in contemporary American society', in G. Lindzey and E. Aronson (eds), *Handbook of social psychology* (New York: Random House) Vol. II.

Walker, N. J. (1988) 'What we know about women voters in Britain, France, and West Germany', *Public Opinion, May/June*, 49–52, 55.

Wirls, D. (1986) 'Reinterpreting the gender gap', *Public Opinion Quarterly*, 316–30.

11 Politicization and Political Interest

Jan W. van Deth, University of Nijmegen

INTRODUCTION

By any definition of democracy, citizen involvement in public affairs is central. In the continuing debate on the problems and prospects for democratic government, both normative and empirical questions have been raised concerning the modes and levels of participation and representation. An enduring 'paradox of mass politics' (Neuman, 1986) lies in the tension between the norm of an informed citizenry put forward by democratic theory, and the actual knowledge and attitudes of people revealed by survey research. However, it is agreed that some level of citizen involvement is a necessary condition for the distinction between democratic and non-democratic government. The debate focuses on the *degree* or *distribution* of involvement; not on the crucial role of involvement in this kind of discussions (c.f. Almond and Verba, 1963: 474ff; Berelson et al., 1954: 307). Direct attacks on vested interests or severe social conflicts may be major causes of citizen involvement. But even when their vital interests are not at stake, democratic citizens are expected to pay some attention at least to the political process. A kind of curiosity about politics should characterize these people regardless of their actual participation in that process. Thus, some degree of political interest is a forerunner to political action in democratic processes.

In this chapter I will examine the frequently reported observation that a clearly increasing trend in political interest is evident in Western societies in the last decades. First, an explanation of a change in political interest called 'politicization' is presented. Second, cross-national and longitudinal empirical analyses are performed to test the proposition of rising interest. Finally, attention will be paid to the disproportional impact of certain political ideas on the opinion climate. Empirical analyses will be limited to time-series data from eight older members of the European Community: Britain, France, Germany, Italy, Belgium, Denmark, Ireland, and the Netherlands.

POLITICIZATION AND INTEREST

The traditional voting studies of the 1950s depicted the average citizen in democratic society as not well-informed, not particularly active, and certainly not deeply involved in politics (c.f. Berelson et al., 1954: 305ff; Campbell et al., 1960: 539ff). This picture appears to have changed in the last decades. Restricting ourselves to the level of political interest, a clear trend of increasing interest is observed among the populace of many countries. The authors of *Political Action* note: 'One change that can be unambiguously demonstrated with survey data and is of major importance with respect to the structure of political action is the increasing political involvement of the citizenry' (Kaase and Marsh, 1979: 36). More recently Dalton summarizes the findings for the period between the early 1950s and the 1980s as follows: 'General political interest has grown most steadily in West Germany . . . Yet there are similar trends of expanding political interest in the United States, Britain, and France. The available evidence is often incomplete, and different survey questions are used in each nation, but the trend of increasing political interest is unmistakable' (1988: 22). A longitudinal study of political interest in the United States, West Germany, and the Netherlands results in the same conclusion (Van Deth, 1989). Despite all kind of historical, demographical, social, and political differences between the advanced industrial societies of the Western world, the trend of increasing political interest seems to be a universal phenomenon. This trend can be explained by referring to some other common characteristics of these countries. What can be noted is an ongoing and increasing intervention of political decision-makers in the economic process (especially dealing with aspects of macro-economic policies like inflation, employment, budgetary deficits, and the like), while the political process becomes dominated by these economic issues and by the conversion of social and political conflict into budgetary claims (the 'fiscalization of politics').

Although the exact nature of the relationship between the political and economic processes is still a controversial topic, there appears to be consensus on the *consequences* of these interferences.[1] As per capita real income increases, government will spend a higher proportion of national product than before ('Wagner's Law'). But not only the amount of money spent by government grows continuously; the number of distinct activities covered by government regulation, subsidizing, or taxation increases as well. The result is that democratic government in advanced industrial societies occupies a substantial part of the national product and is a party to such divergent aspects of social life as housing, education, transportation, social security, foreign trade, and health care. What happened is that new governmental tasks have been added to old ones without a reduction of these old tasks. With each increase in government spending and with each expansion of government tasks, however, the number of interests who organize around government grows. As Webber and Wildavsky remark: 'Big government breeds big pressures. Each new program creates interests who organize around it. More people make demands on politicians. Decisions must be made to satisfy them and to cope with the consequences of prior politics' (1986: 493).

The abandonment of the traditional laissez-faire doctrine of rising industrial capitalism in many countries followed the traumatic experiences of the Great Depression of the 1930s and the postwar economic chaos in the late 1940s. Although the dissimilarities between different countries and distinct points in time have always been evident, the processes led to considerable strengthening of the position of central government agencies in social-economic and cultural life. The average citizen, then, is confronted with the ever-growing invasion of government intervention in many areas, and the continuing 'fiscalization' of the problems he faces.[2] As a consequence of this process of *politicization* of private, cultural and other spheres of life, the number of people exposed to political stimuli increases while, furthermore, the significance of political conflicts becomes more evident. From this it follows that the level of political interest among the populace is a function of the degree of government intervention in society. When about one-third up to one-half of the national product is linked to the public sector, you do not need strong arguments to be interested in politics.[3] The seemingly universal phenomenon of rising political interest in advanced industrial societies referred to by Dalton and others, can be seen as a consequence of the process of politicization. Before we turn to the test of this proposition, both an operationalization of the concept political interest and a description of the developments of this type of interest in several countries have to be considered.

POLITICAL INTEREST AND POLITICAL DISCUSSION

Measuring political interest as a sense of curiosity about what is going on in the public sphere, is a rather complicated matter. In many studies the traditional measure to register the degree of *subjective political interest* is a variant of the straightforward question: 'How interested would you say you are in politics? Very interested, somewhat interested, or not at all interested?' This practice will not be followed here. The Eurobarometer surveys do not contain direct measures for involvement like the traditional one for subjective political interest. Consequently, sophisticated discussions on the ins and outs of this type of questions and the many faces of the concept political interest are irrelevant here.[4]

From the beginning of the Eurobarometer series in the early 1970s, a specific measure of political interest has been included in each survey in every country.[5] This measure does not register some abstract and noncommittal notion of curiosity about politics, but it refers to a direct utterance of that attitude. The exact question wording is: 'When you get together with your friends, would you say that you discuss political matters frequently, occasionally, or never?'[6] This question can be accepted as an indicator of political interest for several reasons. First, the behaviour referred to requires at least some minimal level of involvement in politics. Second, mentioning contacts with friends suggests an informal context where topics are raised according to the particular concerns of the participants. Direct violations of interests or serious conflicts are not excluded but clearly not meant with this phrase. Third, the unambiguous third alternative that you never discuss politics with friends definitely identifies each respondent with no curiosity at all about public affairs. In other words: even in case the motives for selecting a positive response are unclear or ambivalent, the negative response depicts people as not interested in a straightforward way. Therefore, I will use this question as an indicator of political interest and concentrate on the responses to the third alternative.

Figure 11.1 shows the developments in the relative number of people stating that they never discuss politics when they get together with friends in several European countries in the last fifteen years. The upper part of this figure depicts the results for the four larger countries: France, Germany, Italy, and Britain. The lower part shows the developments in the four smaller countries: Belgium, the Netherlands, Denmark, and Ireland. Time series data for this set of countries start in 1973 and continue from 1975 up to 1987 with regular intervals of half a year.[7]

Before we turn to a discussion of the developments visualized in Figure 11.1, let us first have a look at the distinct levels of political interest in these countries. The level of interest is more or less in the same range for France, Italy, Britain, and Ireland. For this quartet, the relative number of people never talking about politics is between 30 and 45 per cent of the population. The Dutch (after 1976) and the Danes appear to be somewhat more involved, while a huge majority of the Germans frequently or occasionally runs into political discussions. Belgium occupies the extreme position at the other side: in this country about half of the population does not show a sign of political interest as far as discussions with friends are concerned. The trends in Figure 11.1 reveal a somewhat different categorization of the eight countries, and the strong statements about rising levels of interest appear to be too simplistic for the last fifteen years. Broadly speaking, we see a decrease of the relative number of people never talking about politics in Germany, Belgium, Denmark and the Netherlands. In the Anglo-Saxon countries, the fluctuations do not show a consistent trend in the recent past. However, the most striking results are obtained for France, and especially for Italy. In these two countries we see an *increase* in the number of people never talking about politics with friends. These patterns of

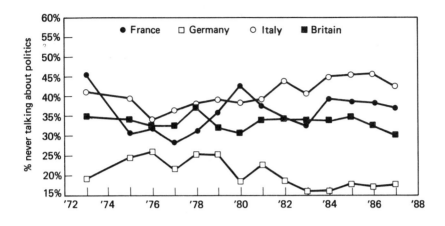

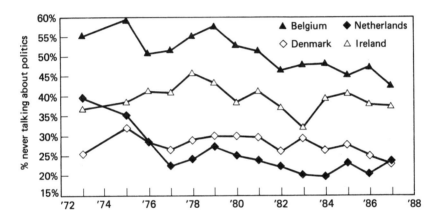

SOURCE: Eurobarometers
FIGURE 11.1: *Political discussion*

declining levels of interest in the recent past are clearly contrary to the observation that rising levels of involvement are some universal phenomenon in advanced industrial societies.

EMPIRICAL RESULTS

The empirical validity of the politicization thesis can be assessed by confronting the survey results presented in the previous section with information on the position of government in society. The total receipts of government as a percentage of the gross domestic product (GDP) is an indicator of the position of government in the economic and social sectors of society.[8] These figures show clear differences between the countries. In the early 1970s current receipts of government as a percentage of GDP was already up to 42 per cent in the Netherlands and Denmark, but about 30 per cent in Italy. Within a time span of less than twenty years the relative receipts of government rose to almost 60 per cent in Denmark and to almost 40 per cent in Italy. Only after the severe economic recession of the early 1980s became evident, did governments try to cut their spending and to reduce (the growth of) their share of the national product. These attempts eventually resulted in a slight reversal of the postwar trend toward ever-expanding government receipts.

Both the average percentages of people never discussing politics with their friends and the average percentages for current receipts of government are shown in Table 11.1. These results can be interpreted in two ways. On the one hand, we see that even a sympathetic critic cannot disregard the fact that there is no trace of a linear relationship between these two data sets. However, the derivation of a linear function might be asking too much from the simple theoretical perspective outlined above, and the appropriate test could be the search for a monotonic function only. So, on the other hand we see that there exist a more or less monotonic relationship between the level of political interest and the position of government in society. Apart from Germany, Belgium, and Britain, each country differs only one position in each column with the rankings (Kendall's Tau=.64). Germany ranks first on interest but third on government impact; the corresponding figures for Belgium and Britain are eighth and fifth, and fourth and sixth respectively. The overall picture, then, is rather disappointing. It cannot be denied that there is some covariation between the level of political interest and the position of government in society, but it is equally clear that there are some obvious violations of even the simple hypothesis of a monotonic relationship.

An evaluation of a test concerning the possible link between a rise in the share of government and the changes in the level of political interest presents a less ambiguous picture. The first column of Table 11.2 shows the differences between 1972 and 1987 in the receipts of government as a percentage of GDP. The largest increase is observed in Denmark (12.1 per cent), while Germany brings up the rear (4.9 per cent). Irrespective of these distinctions in the actual growth rates, it is clear that the position of government has been strengthened between 1972 and 1987 in each and every country considered here. But, as we already saw in the previous section, there is no corresponding pattern of rising political interest in every single country. The results for Denmark, the Netherlands, Belgium, and Germany are in line with our expectation that rising government receipts go together with an increase in political interest. But even if we ignore the more or less stable levels of involvement in Britain and Ireland, we certainly cannot pass over in silence the results for France and Italy.

TABLE 11.1: *Politicization and political discussion 1972–87*

Country:	Government receipts*		Never discuss politics+		
	%	rank	%	rank	cases
Netherlands	51.0	(1)	25.1	(2)	27,857
Denmark	50.8	(2)	27.9	(3)	27,226
Germany	44.1	(3)	20.4	(1)	27,778
France	43.6	(4)	35.9	(5)	29,601
Belgium	42.0	(5)	50.9	(8)	27,153
Britain	40.2	(6)	33.9	(4)	29,428
Ireland	37.8	(7)	39.5	(6)	27,114
Italy	34.5	(8)	40.8	(7)	30,031

* Average current receipts of government as a percentage of GDP for the period 1972 through 1986 (for France 1972–85; for Ireland 1972–84). Calculations based on OECD (1988:184).
+ Average percentages for the period 1973 through 1987.

TABLE 11.2: *Developments in politicization and political discussion 1972–87*

Country:	Change in current receipts*		Trend in political interest+
	%	rank	
Denmark	12.1	(1)	minor increase
France	10.3	(2)	decrease
Belgium	9.3	(3)	increase
Ireland	8.8	(4)	no change
Netherlands	8.3	(5)	increase
Italy	8.0	(6)	decrease
Britain	5.2	(7)	no change
Germany	4.9	(8)	increase

* Difference between 1972 and 1986 of current receipts of government as a percentage of GDP (for France: 1972–85; for Ireland 1972–84). Calculations based on OECD (1988:184).
+ For the period 1973 through 1987; see Figure 11.1 above.

While the share of government in France grew with no less than 10 per cent of GDP, the level of interest in that country declined in the corresponding period! Furthermore, the Italians expanded their public sector with 8 per cent, but show a clear trend of decreasing political interest.

The results presented justify only one conclusion: the recent developments in government activities in society cannot be related to changes in the level of political interest in a straightforward way. Before we accept this refutation of the politicization thesis, a closer look at country specific differences in background factors related to political interest is required.

PREDICTORS OF POLITICAL INTEREST

The country specific differences in levels and changes in political interest presented in the previous section might be the result of structural, compositional factors. For instance, it is known that political involvement is correlated with the level of education, and so cross-national differences in political interest might be mainly a reflection of corresponding cross-national differences in education. Is it possible to rescue the politicization thesis by introducing these kind of compositional factors? A number of studies in the last few decades has disclosed three background factors as the most relevant predictors of political interest: education, age, and sex. As mentioned, a higher level of education comes along with a higher level of political interest. Aging and interest are positively correlated, but it should be noted that involvement decreases rapidly in the last phase of life. Finally, men always show more interest in public affairs than women do. Although the strength of these correlations is usually rather modest at best, these results have been confirmed by many studies in many countries.[9]

Besides these traditional background factors, I should like to introduce a predictor of political interest of a clearly different nature. In the continuing debate on the changing values of citizens in advanced industrial societies, the rise of Postmaterialist value orientations has been marked as a main determinant of changes in the level and modes of political involvement (cf. Inglehart, 1977). Cross-national differences in political interest can be seen as a consequence of differences in the process of value change. Evaluation of the politicization thesis, then, should not be restricted to the impact of education, age, and sex, but also focus on the effects of value change.

Due to the nature of the multi-level analysis of the relationship between the position of government in society and political interest, no simple statistical corrections can be used to control for possible background variables. Instead, I will trace the possible consequences of compositional effects by estimating the impact of the four factors mentioned on the level of political interest in each country. Table 11.3 shows the results of a multiple classification analysis with the frequency of discussion about political matters as the dependent variable. The relative impact of the level of education, age, sex, and value orientation is indicated by the beta coefficients.

Several conclusions can be based on the results presented in Table 11.3. First, it appears that the signs of the beta coefficients are all in the predicted direction, i.e. higher education, aging, male sex, and Postmaterialism are related to relatively high frequencies of political discussions in each country. Second, the structural relationships between the four background factors and the dependent variable are more or less the same. With a few outlyers (sex in the Netherlands) the beta coefficients for each variable are in the same range in distinct countries. However, none of

TABLE 11.3: *Predictors of political discussion (multiple classification analysis)*

Country:	Beta coefficients: edu.	age	sex	values	adj.R^2	cases
Italy	.24	.12	.25	.17	.18	30,031
France	.27	.11	.12	.19	.14	29,601
Belgium	.24	.08	.14	.15	.13	27,153
Germany	.14	.09	.20	.15	.11	27,778
Denmark	.18	.11	.15	.17	.11	27,266
Ireland	.19	.15	.22	.09	.11	27,114
Netherlands	.21	.13	.04	.15	.09	27,857
Britain	.19	.14	.15	.10	.08	29,428

these coefficients reveals a substantial impact of the independent variables on the discussion frequency. Third, the total fit of the model is very disappointing. The (adjusted) indicator for the total variance explained is highest in Italy (.18) and lowest in Britain (.08).

Although these levels of the various indicators are not unusual for cross-national survey analyses, it cannot be ignored that education, age, sex, and value orientation explain only a rather insignificant proportion of the variance in the frequency of discussions about political matters. From this it follows that very substantial compositional differences in education, sex, age, and value orientation are required to induce cross-national differences in political interest. No such compositional differences exist in Western Europe in the last decades that we can use to count for the dozens of percentages that distinguish, say, Belgium from the Netherlands as the proportion of people never talking about politics is considered (see Figure 11.1). Therefore, the politicization thesis cannot be rescued by introducing the modest compositional differences between countries in terms of education, age, sex, and value orientation.

INTEREST AND OPINION CLIMATE

The results presented in the previous sections are rather disappointing from an empirical point of view. No convincing explanation of cross-national and longitudinal differences in political interest survives the simple confrontation with the available data. The relevance of the concept political interest for research and debates on the developments in advanced industrial societies, however, remains undisputed.

It has been observed that representative democratic government favors of the demands and needs of the more involved part of the citizenry (cf. Converse and Pierce, 1987: 766). Although the relationship between political orientations on the one hand and actual government policies on the other is hard to determine, it is rather easy to demonstrate the consequences of diverting levels of political interest for the opinion climate. After all, the beliefs and ideas of those people frequently participating in political discussions will stamp the opinion climate much more than people who never or occasionally talk about politics. The consequences of this process can be illustrated by looking, once again, at the impact of Postmaterialist value orientations.

The category of people with Postmaterialist value orientations makes up only a minority of the population of advanced industrial societies. Only rarely do we see that the proportion of Postmaterialists approaches 30 per cent of the population; much more usual are proportions of 10 per cent or 15 per cent. Materialists, on the other hand, are two or three times as numerous as their counterparts in most countries. Since Postmaterialists are much more willing to enter a discussion with friends about political matters, it is likely that Postmaterialistic ideas are more frequently encountered in political discussions than can be expected on the basis of the proportion of Postmaterialists among the population. In other words: the opinion climate shows a bias towards the ideas of Postmaterialists as a passionate minority.

The results presented in Table 11.4 indicate that the relative impact of Postmaterialists on the opinion climate is rather spectacular. The entries of this table are the quotients of the numbers of Postmaterialists and Materialists among distinct subgroups defined according to their frequency of political discussion. For instance, we find that the number of Postmaterialists equals .70 times the number of Materialists in the Netherlands; while there are 1.63 as many Postmaterialists as Materialists among Dutch people frequently talking about politics. These simple computations make it clear that Postmaterialists dominate political discussions in the Netherlands, Germany, Denmark, France, and Belgium. In each of these countries, the number of Postmaterialists among the regular discussants is larger than the number of Materialists. In Britain, Italy, and Ireland, the Postmaterialists do not exceed the Materialists, but their share in the discussions is certainly much higher than can be expected on the basis of their proportion of the total population.

As a passionate minority, Postmaterialists will encounter political discussions much more frequently than people with other value orientations do. It can be expected that they use these conversations to express their Postmaterialist points of view. By looking only at the distribution of value orientations among the population, the impact of Postmaterialism will be seriously underestimated. In most countries, the Postmaterialist minority will not only make up for their numerical arrears by entering political discussions frequently; they will even outnumber the Materialists and dominate conversations about political matters. An adequate and realistic depiction of an opinion climate, then, has to rely heavily on the use of some measure of political involvement.

TABLE 11.4: *Ratio of Postmaterialists and Materialists*

Country:	Total sample	Discussion frequency: never	frequently
Netherlands	.70	.24	1.63
Germany	.49	.13	1.29
Denmark	.40	.10	1.35
Britain	.38	.23	.38
France	.36	.10	1.40
Belgium	.32	.14	1.17
Italy	.19	.06	.72
Ireland	.16	.11	.34

Note: table entries are the quotients of the number of Postmaterialists and the number of Materialists.

IN CONCLUSION

This chapter is addressed to the frequently observed phenomenon of rising political interest in advanced industrial societies. Contrary to widely-held beliefs, the available data do not confirm the idea of rising political interest in each and every country in the last twenty years or so. Notable exceptions are France and Italy where political interest seems to have decreased instead of increased. Neither the cross-national differences in the level of political interest nor the distinct patterns of change in political interest could be explained with the politicization thesis. According to this line of reasoning, political involvement should be a function of the position of government in society. Broadly speaking, the data indicate that the level of political interest is indeed positively related to the current receipts of government as a percentage of the national product. Nevertheless, the conclusion cannot be avoided that the politicization thesis lacks empirical validity if we look at the developments in the last two decades. Heiden-heimer et al., and Webber and Wildavski studied the rise of welfare states and government intervention in advanced industrial societies. From their analyses it becomes clear that there are huge cross-national differences in the way government intervention is organized and social security provided. How, and to what extent government intervention and regulation is desired and required remain matters of dispute. The answers to these questions differ among countries and the available evidence suggests that beside economic development, differences in *political culture* in particular count for differences in sizes and growth rates of governments (Heiden-heimer et al., 1983: Chapter 10; Webber and Wildavski, 1986: Chapter 10). Furthermore, Bennett's research on the development of political apathy in the USA leads to the conclusion that 'political interest seems to be influenced more by political factors than by demographic attributes' (Bennett,

1986: 121). A renewed attention for aspects of the political culture might eventually result in an explanation of cross-national differences in the relative position of governments as well as in an explanation of cross-national differences in political interest. Instead of presuming that the level of political interest is a function of government intervention in society, both factors should be incorporated in a more sophisticated model of political change than the simple variants tested and refuted in this article.

NOTES

I wish to thank Ron Inglehart for performing the computer analyses presented in this chapter on his data set of Eurobarometer studies.

1. See, for an excellent overview of the literature in this field, C. Webber and A. Wildavski, 'A Cultural Theory of Governmental Growth and (Un)balanced Budgets', in Webber and Wildavski (1986: 560ff).
2. Notice that it has been demonstrated that aggregate economic circumstances shape political orientations. This finding contradicts the myth that personal economic conditions are a major determinant of political preferences (sociotropic versus pocketbook voting; see Kinder and Mebane, 1983).
3. This relationship between government intervention and political interest can be explained in presuming that growing government spending is a consequence instead of a cause of increasing political interest. Since the actual analysis is concerned with interest as a dependent variable, I will not pay attention to this line of reasoning here.
4. See, for the concept subjective political interest and the several meanings of the term interest, Van Deth (1989). A concise overview of the distinct aspects of the concepts interest and involvement is presented by Gabriel (1986: 178ff).
5. This specific measure is part of a set of other questions 'that should provide a reasonably good indication of how likely an individual is to play an active role in his or her country's political life' (Inglehart, 1977: 310).
6. This question has been used in electoral research for a long time. Berelson et al. refer to it as a 'behavioral manifestation of interest' (1954: 29). See Berelson et al. (1954: 29–31; 103–7) for early empirical results obtained with this measure. Verba and Nie use this instrument to register 'freedom of political communication' (1963: 115). In this article, I prefer Berelson's interpretation.
7. For the analyses presented here, each set of two waves of the Eurobarometers obtained every year are combined to get a single indicator for that specific year.
8. Current receipts of government consists mainly of direct and indirect taxes, and social security contributions paid by employers and employees.
9. See, for a concise overview of this literature, Van Deth (1989), and the empirical results presented by Bennett (1986: Chapter 5).

REFERENCES

Almond, G. A., and S. Verba (1963) *The Civic Culture; Political Attitudes and Democracy in Five Nations* (Princeton, NJ: Princeton University Press).

Bennett, S. Earl (1986) *Apathy in America 1960–1984; Causes and Consequences of Citizen Political Indifference* (New York: Transnational Publishers).

Berelson, B. R., P. F. Lazarsfeld, W. N. McPhee (1954) *Voting; A study of Opinion Formation in a Presidential Campaign* (Chicago: University of Chicago Press).

Campbell, A., Ph.E. Converse, W. E. Miller, D. E. Stokes (1960) *The American Voter* (New York: Wiley).

Converse, P. E., and R. Pierce (1986) *Political Representation in France* (Cambridge and London: Belknap).

Dalton, R. J. (1988) *Citizen Politics in Western Democracies; Public Opinion and Political Parties in the United States, Great Britain, West Germany, and France* (Chatham, NJ: Chatham House).

Gabriel, O. W. (1986) *Politische Kultur, Postmaterialismus und Materialismus in der Bundesrepublik Deutschland* (Opladen: Westdeutscher Verlag).

Heidenheimer, A. J., H. Heclo, and C. T. Adams (1983) *Comparative Public Policy; The Politics of Social Choice in Europe and America* (New York: St Martin's Press).

Inglehart, R. (1977) *The Silent Revolution; Changing Values and Political Styles Among Western Publics* (Princeton, NJ: Princeton University Press).

Kaase, M., and A. Marsh (1979) 'Political Action: A Theoretical Perspective', in Barnes, S. H., M. Kaase, et al. *Political Action; Mass Participation in Five Western Democracies*, (Beverly Hills, Ca. and London: Sage).

Kinder, D. R., and W. R. Mebane, Jr., (1983) 'Politics and Economics in Everyday Life', in K. R. Monroe (ed) *The Political Process and Economic Change* (New York: Agathon).

Neuman, W. Russell (1986) *The Paradox of Mass Politics; Knowledge and Opinion in the American Electorate* (Cambridge, Mass.: Harvard University Press).

OECD, Organization for Economic Co-operation and Development (1988) *Economic Outlook 43* (Paris: OECD).

Van Deth, J. W. (1989) 'Political Interest', in M. Kent Jennings, J. W. van Deth, et al. *Continuities in Political Action; a Longitudinal Study of Political Orientations in Three Western Democracies* (Berlin, New York: De Gruyter and Aldine).

Webber, C., and A. Wildavski (1986) *A History of Taxation and Expenditure in the Western World* (New York: Simon and Schuster).

12 The Dynamics of Party System Change

Russell J. Dalton, University of California at Irvine

In the past decade the dominant theme of comparative electoral research has changed from explaining the stability of partisan alignments to explaining the dynamics of partisan change. Citizens have presented new demands and new challenges to the established parties, and the evidence of substantial partisan change is now obvious (Dalton et al., 1984; Daalder and Mair, 1983). Party systems are more fractionalized; there has been a breakup of many established parties and a growing number of new parties. Fluctuations in voting results also increased. Voting in most European democracies is now characterized by higher levels of partisan volatility at the aggregate and individual levels (Crewe and Denver, 1985). In several nations, popular attachments to political parties generally weakened and discussions of the crisis of party systems became commonplace.

There is no simple explanation for these changes: indeed, the magnitude of the changes probably results from a convergence of several factors including the long-term social transformation of postwar Europe; the shorter-term effects of OPEC price increases and resulting economic instability; the rising importance of environmentalism and other quality-of-life issues; the increased assertiveness of citizen interest lobbies and citizen action groups; the growing political sophistication of Western publics; and other factors. In a single election, even in a single nation, it is nearly impossible to disentangle the various threads of electoral change to determine the major forces that are transforming Western party systems.

Despite this complexity, comparative political analyses identify two aspects of electoral politics that are broadly affecting most Western party systems. First, there appears to be a weakening of the social cleavages that have historically structured these party systems. Affluence, social mobility, and changes in the composition of the labor force have eroded the class basis of voting behaviour. Longitudinal data from almost every Western democracy point to a decrease in class-voting differences over the past several decades (Dalton, 1988, chap. 8; Lipset, 1981; Inglehart, 1984). The religious cleavage has similarly weakened as the result of a general secularization trend in Western societies. Increasing geographic mobility and diversity in life-styles has attenuated the importance of regional differences and community-based patterns of party support.[2] In short, the social cleavages that once provided the framework for party competition in most West European party systems are experiencing a general decay.

As old social cleavages fade, traditional voting behavior theory directs us to look for rising new social divisions as the underlying cause of this disruption of old alignment patterns. One thesis holds that we are witnessing a permanent restructuring of political alignments as Western European nations develop the characteristics of advanced industrial societies. Prominent amongst this literature is Ronald Inglehart's research (1977, 1984, 1989), which maintains that Western publics are developing greater interest in postmaterial goals such as environmental protection, citizen participation, and social equality. Inglehart argues that the conflict between traditional material values and new postmaterial values is a major source of the recent volatility in Western party systems. Most empirical analyses suggest that this New Politics value conflict is rising in importance as a basis of electoral politics (Baker et al., 1981; Dalton 1986, 1988; Inglehart, 1989).

The decline of the class cleavage and the rise of the New Politics cleavage represent only two parts of the process of electoral change, but they are two central elements that are apparently affecting most Western party systems. Moreover, there is a natural contrast between these two dimensions of cleavage: one is a traditional, institutionalized basis of political competition, the other is a new, challenging dimension of cleavage; one represents basic economic conflicts, the other signifies the rise of non-economic concerns; one represents traditional social-group structured political alignment, the other typifies the more fluid issue-group alignments of contemporary politics (Dalton et al., 1984, chap. 15; Knutsen, 1987).

This research focuses on this natural dichotomy to explore the dynamics of electoral change in contemporary party systems. We rely on the Eurobarometer studies for most of our empirical evidence, because their cross-temporal and cross-national richness provides an invaluable resource for exploring the dynamics of electoral change affecting Europe and other Western industrial democracies.

A MODEL OF ELECTORAL CHANGE

Given the historical and institutional continuity of democratic party systems, a fundamental change in partisan alignments is likely to be an evolutionary process (Dalton et al., 1984, chap. 15). The development of a new political cleavage in a highly mobilized system is presumably much more difficult to achieve because partisan lines are already drawn and there are fewer untapped bases of electoral support that might be mobilized by new party appeals. The established parties are also reluctant to project a fundamental change in policy image, particularly if the new issues cut across the parties' traditional political commitments. Furthermore, the shift from social-group cleavages to issue-group cleavages means that new political cleavages are more difficult to institutionalize (or 'freeze') via group identifications, thereby contributing to the fluidity of voting patterns. As a result, the abrupt shifts in social-group voting patterns (critical realignments) that marked the earlier histories of Western democracies provides a poor model for contemporary partisan politics.

Our view of contemporary electoral politics leads to a more evolutionary model of partisan change based upon a three-step process. As societal conditions change, the first step in this process involves a shift in the issue interests and value priorities of elites and the mass public. There is extensive evidence that the issue agenda of advanced industrial societies is already changing (Inglehart, 1977, 1989; Baker et al., 1981; Dalton, 1988). Concerns with non-economic and quality of life issues (such as environmental protection, citizen participation, social equality) are *added* to the traditional economic interests underlying the class cleavage.

The second stage in this evolutionary process occurs when new issue interests are generalized into broader political orientations. Although most citizens lack a sophisticated belief system, some reference structure is used in evaluating political stimuli. For example, politics is often discussed in terms of left/right positions, even though many individuals may not fully understand the ideological roots of these terms (Klingemann, 1979). Left/right orientations are often treated as a summary measure of the issues which concern the individual, as well as public perceptions of the lines of political conflict in a society. When citizens reorient their left/right framework to reflect their new values and issue interests, a potential new base of political cleavage is established. A change in the political belief system represented by left/right orientations involves a more fundamental transformation of mass politics than a simple change in issue interests, because it affects how citizens evaluate politics and orient themselves to the political process.

The third stage in the realigning process involves the transformation of broad political orientations into new partisan attachments. In addition to the sources of institutional inertia cited above, there are several other reasons to expect that changes in partisan attitudes will lag behind changes in political orientations. At the individual level, partisan behaviour is often determined by an enduring sense of party identification. Party attachments which carry the weight of family tradition are highly resistant to change, even if issue beliefs are no longer compatible with partisanship. In contrast, although left/right attitudes are also relatively enduring, the specific meaning of these orientations is partially drawn from the salient issues of the day. Thus, left/right attitudes are a 'leading' indicator of mass political change, while partisanship is a 'lagging' indicator (Beck, 1982; Inglehart, 1984). As the content of political orientations shifts away from traditional

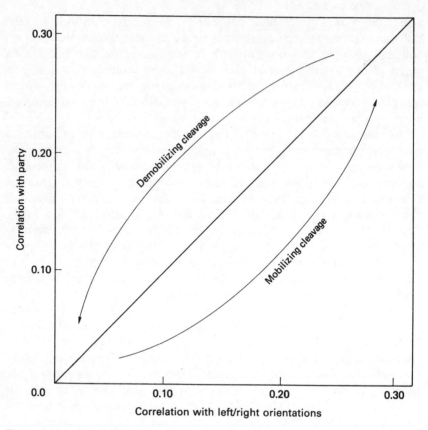

FIGURE 12.1: *Hypothetical models of the realigning process*

socio-economic matters toward postmaterial values, these trends should begin to influence party choice. If these new political orientations endure, the established parties will find it necessary to respond to the new political issues or new political parties will form to represent these voters.

This simple model of the realigning process suggests different patterns of change for the rising and falling forces of electoral politics (Figure 12.1). The horizontal axis in the figure represents the correlation between a dimension of political cleavage and left/right orientations; the vertical axis represents the correlation between a cleavage dimension and party preference. One pattern involves the *demobilization* of traditional social cleavages. Empirical research finds that traditional groups cues, such as social class, are becoming less important as a basis of political orientations. Our model of the realigning process suggests that the declining impact of social class will be tracked above the diagonal in the figure. That is, over time the correlation between social class and left/right orientations should decay more rapidly than the relationship between class and party preference.

As traditional cleavages wane, this increases the potential for new political cleavage, such as the New Politics dimension, to emerge as a basis for political competition. These new issue orientations should first influence general political orientations, represented by a strengthening relationship between New Politics value priorities and left/right beliefs. As these new issues become more central to voters' political orientations, these beliefs will also influence voting behaviour. Either the established parties will respond to the public's changing political orientations or new parties will emerge to represent these views. Thus, new cleavages will follow the *mobilization* curve in the lower part of Figure 12.1, with a stronger relationship between the new cleavage and left/right orientations than with vote choice.

This plotting of mobilization curves undoubtedly oversimplifies the actual historical pattern that any nation will follow. Indeed, in earlier research we spelled out the variety of institutional and individual factors that might hasten or retard the pace of electoral change in a nation (Dalton et al., 1984, Chapter 15). Progress along one trend line might be reversed at the next election, as new issues temporarily rise on the political agenda or party elites change the alternatives offered to the voters. Moreover, in any party system a variety of ascending and descending cleavages are intermixed, possibly confounding the simple model we present. For instance, the social forces that have generally weakened traditional social cleavages have sometimes led to a remobilization of regional differences. Still, this theory of the realigning process provides a parsimonious model of the long-term patterns of electoral change that might be expected in Western party systems.

A WEST GERMAN TEST

It is possible to illustrate the dynamic aspects of the realigning process with data from the Federal Republic of Germany (Dalton, 1986). The expectations of the general model seem to fit the mobilization of the New Politics cleavage in West Germany extremely well. Popular interest in New Politics issues such as environmental protection and citizen participation clearly increased over the past decade. Despite growing public concern for these matters, however, the established parties avoided taking clear stands on many of these same issues (Dalton, 1984, 1986). The battles over environmental quality, nuclear energy, and disarmament were fought within the parties or outside of the established parties, not between partisan camps. But in recent elections the party system responded to these new political demands, in large part because the newly-formed Green party forced these issues onto the electoral agenda. By tracking the degree of ideological and partisan polarization across a series of West German Federal elections, we

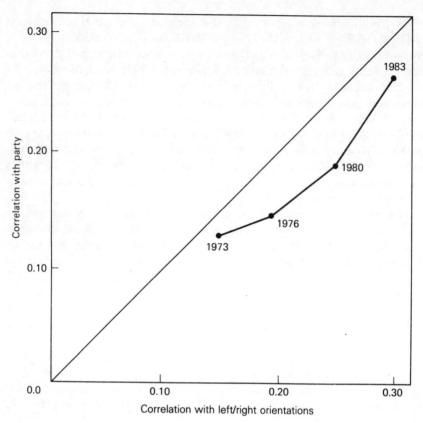

SOURCE: 1973 European Community Study: Eurobarometers 6, 7, 14, 15, 18, and 19.
Note: Table entries are the correlations of postmaterial values with Left/Right attitudes and party preferences at each election period. Cramer's V correlations are used.
FIGURE 12.2: *Value priorities and ideological partisan polarization*

can determine whether incorporation of these new issue interests into electoral politics conforms to our theory of the realigning process.

Figure 12.2 traces the realigning process over the past four elections for which the necessary survey data are available from the Eurobarometers. The location of each election in the figure is determined by the correlation of the New Politics dimension with left/right orientations and party preference.[3] Our expectation is that elections should follow a mobilizing trend below the diagonal in the figure, indicating that New Politics values are influencing left/right attitudes more strongly than partisan preferences. The growing salience of New Politics issues should also increase the relationship between values and voting preference, but at a slower pace.

The time line in Figure 12.2 conforms to our expectation. In 1973, values had a modest impact on left/right attitudes (Cramer's V=.15) and party preferences (V=.13). Since ideological polarization was stronger than partisan polarization, this election is located below the diagonal line. The relationship between values and left/right attitudes then strengthens steadily in subsequent elections, but partisan change clearly lags behind ideological change. Consequently, the gap between the correlation of values with left/right attitudes and party preferences widens in 1976, and then again in 1980. This was a period when the established parties failed to provide clear electoral options in terms of New Politics issues. The working-class orientation of the Social Democrats clashed with many postmaterial goals; the Schmidt government vigorously supported nuclear energy, shied away from strict environmental protection standards, and lacked a reformist zeal. The CDU/CSU voiced some concern about the 'New Social Question', but the party also failed to provide a clear choice of New Politics issues. In 1983, the Greens finally offered a viable electoral outlet for the changing ideological orientations of the public. If the realigning process was blocked by the established parties, a new partisan outlet was necessary. Figure 11.2 indicates that the correlation between values and left/right orientations strengthens substantially in 1983 – this time accompanied by a sharp increase in the relationship between values and partisanship. In sum, this process of electoral change closely follows the mobilization pattern we have described.

CROSS-NATIONAL EVIDENCE

A single nation does not provide an adequate test of our theory, especially since the West German experience is admittedly unique; mobilization on the New Politics dimension was unusually rapid and uniform.[4] Yet over a longer time period we expect that partisan change in other advanced industrial democracies would generally follow a similar course.

Even the exceptionally rich data resources of the Eurobarometer surveys do not provide the necessary data to fully test this developmental model for other European democracies because of the limited time frame over which the necessary survey questions are available. However, it is possible to test this model indirectly through cross-national comparisons. Democratic party systems are presumably at different stages in the processes of class demobilization and the mobilization of the New Politics cleavage, because of variations in popular concern with these cleavages, institutional constraints, strategic party choices, and other factors that vary across nations (and time). If there is a developmental pattern to the realigning process, then the longitudinal trend found for West German elections should also be apparent in cross-national comparisons of voter polarization along the class and New Politics cleavages. As a demobilizing cleavage, the social

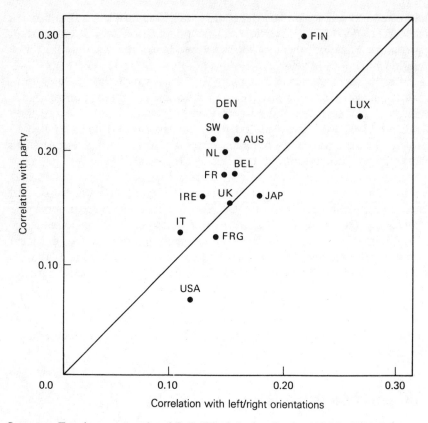

SOURCE: Eurobarometers 6 and 7; Political Action Study; 1976 JABISS Japanese Election Study. Table entries are the Cramer's V correlations of social class with left/right orientations and party preference.

FIGURE 12.3: *Class alignments in left/right orientations and party preference*

class of voters should generally be more strongly related to their partisan preferences than to left/right identities. Conversely, a mobilizing cleavage, such as the New Politics, should be more strongly correlated with left/right preferences than with party support.

We have assembled data from fourteen advanced industrial democracies to test our theories about the dynamics of partisan change.[5] The data are drawn from the mid-1970s to increase the number of nations by combining several data sets together. In addition, this timing enables us to study the beginnings of the mobilization process for the New Politics cleavage, while also tapping significant variations in polarization along the class cleavage. Within each nation four correlations (Cramer's V) were computed. Social class and the postmaterial values index were correlated with party prefer-ence and Left/Right self-identifications.[6]

Figure 12.3 presents the pattern of class alignment in our set of nations. On the whole, there is a strong relationship between national positions on both dimensions (r=.78). For example, when class is an important source of left/right beliefs – as in Finland and Luxembourg – class is also strongly related to party choice. Conversely, social class is only weakly related to both ideology and partisanship in the United States.

The expected pattern of class demobilization is shown by the location of nations relative to the diagonal line (the point where social class has an equal impact on left/right attitudes and partisanship). Ten of the fourteen nations lie on or above the diagonal line. For instance, social class is most strongly related to vote in Finland and Denmark – systems with socialist parties deeply entrenched in the working-class milieu. In these two nations, however, class cues are much *less* important in determining the left/right orientations of the public. This is clear evidence of the imbalance between partisan and ideological change. The ideological demobilization of the class cleavage has progressed further than partisan demobilization.

Figure 12.4 presents a contrasting pattern of postmaterial values becoming aligned with left/right orientations and partisan preferences. When value priorities influence the ideological beliefs of an electorate, they also have a strong impact on party choice (r=.84). Figure 12.4 further indicates that value priorities affect the left/right identities of voters more strongly than their party preferences; eleven out of fourteen nations are located at or below the diagonal in the figure. Although these differences are not large, they are consistent. For instance, postmaterial values have a substantial impact on the left/right orientations of West Germans in the mid-1970s, but as we have seen, these values were not as strongly related to partisan preferences. This pattern supports the use of the mobilization model to describe the process of electoral change on the New Politics cleavage.

PREDICTING PARTY POLARIZATION

The above data provide a snapshot of two dynamic processes at work – the demobilization of the class cleavage and mobilization along the New Politics cleavage. Longitudinal data show that class polarization is gradually declining in most Western democracies just as polarization along the New Politics dimension is increasing (Dalton, 1988; Inglehart, 1989).

In another study of electoral change, Oddbjørn Knutsen (1987) points out that cross-national variation in these sources of party cleavage is an unexplained aspect of the realigning process. At present, nations vary considerably in the extent of partisan polarization along class and values cleavages. In some nations (the United States, West Germany, Ireland, Italy, and Japan) class cues are only weakly tied to party choice. In other cases (Denmark, France, and the Netherlands) postmaterial values exert a strong impact on partisanship. To some extent, these national patterns reflect the unique political and historical conditions of each nation. In

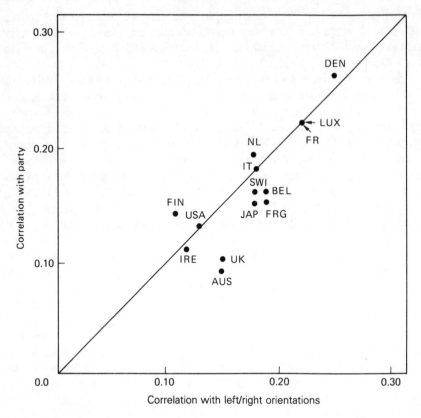

SOURCE: Eurobarometers 6 and 7; Political Action Study; 1976 JABISS Japanese election study. Table entries are the Cramer's V correlations of postmaterial values with left/right orientations and party preference.

FIGURE 12.4: *New Politics values alignments in left/right orientations and party preference.*

addition, institutional and political factors systematically influence the process of class demobilization and values mobilization. By examining the factors affecting these patterns of party polarization, we can begin to test past theories of the dynamics of party system change. In short, what explains why the class cleavage is still strongly related to party preference in some nations, while other party systems are more polarized along the New Politics dimension?

One set of factors that might affect the degree of partisan polarization along the class or New Politics cleavages is the social characteristics of a nation. Party polarization along the New Politics dimension ultimately is based on the changing social conditions which initially gave rise to postmaterial values. As societies develop the characteristics of an advanced industrial society (affluence, higher education, etc.), new demands are placed on the political parties. The impact of the New Politics cleavage on partisan preferences might therefore be strongest where the conditions of advanced industrialism are best met. Similarly, national social characteristics might affect the strength of party polarization along the class cleavage. On the positive side, the strength of the working class milieu – as measured by union density – might reinforce party polarization along the class dimension. On the negative side, the forces of advanced industrialism might attenuate the partisan impact of the class cleavage as they increase polarization along the New Politics cleavage.

The responsiveness of party systems to old and new cleavages should also be related to an intervening set of institutional variables which mediate the process of partisan change (Dalton et al., 1984, chap. 15; Hauss and Rayside, 1978). For example, the openness of an electoral system should affect its ability to represent diverse political demands. An open competitive system facilitates the formation of new parties to represent new issue conflicts and requires existing parties to remain responsive to their clientele. Electoral laws are a major factor determining the openness of a system. For example, proportional representation systems are generally more open than 'winner take all' systems. In the Netherlands, only 0.67 per cent of the vote is needed to gain representation in parliament, while an absolute majority in a district is normally required in American elections. Consequently, a PR system probably increases party polarization on both the class and New Politics dimensions: postmaterial values might more easily gain party representation in a PR system, and class interests might be better able to retain party representation.

The characteristics of the electoral arena also potentially influences the process of partisan change. A federal system or a system with strong local government provides a greater variety of political arenas and opportunities for representation (Dahl, 1966). A political movement may win subnational elections where its strength is concentrated, and these bases can provide the infrastructure for further party action. This has certainly been the case with the West German Greens. Conversely, unitary systems might limit the partisan impact of a new cleavage dimension by setting a higher threshold for political representation, such as the experience of the British Green party.

The size of electoral districts might also affect the realigning process (Katz, 1980, pp. 30–31). In systems with small-sized districts, the candidates may be more responsive to the interests of the constituency – whether they reflect class or value concerns. Conversely, in large districts the role of specific issue interests might be deflated because of the broader range of competing groups. Another distinction separates presidential and parliamentary systems. A presidential system tends to aggregate political interests to form a majority coalition, and therefore might discourage the representation of specific interests. In sum, federal systems, nations with small electoral districts, and non-presidential (parliamentary) systems should display higher levels of partisan polarization along both old and new political cleavages by increasing the potential outlets for group representation.

Another possible intervening variable is the balance between party and candidate voting (Katz, 1980, pp. 31–2). When straight party voting is required, there are fewer opportunities for experimentation and the representation of new issue interests within each party. Conversely, a candidate-oriented system encourages candidates to search out new issue interests while still drawing on the institutional resources of the party. Recent American presidential primaries provide ideal examples of this process. In addition, a number of PR systems offer a mix of party and candidate voting (e.g., *panache*). Candidate-oriented systems should facilitate partisan change, spurring mobilization along the New Politics cleavage and demobilization of the class cleavage.

A third set of intervening variables involve the characteristics of each nation's party system (see, e.g., Sartori, 1976). Issue interests are often diluted in systems based on large catch-all parties. In these systems, parties normally converge to consensual positions and avoid new issues, such as those advocated by Postmaterialists. In contrast, in multi-party systems the parties are more likely to focus on maintaining a distinct clientele, rather than broadening their political base. This provides more opportunities for the representation of new issue interests, either by one of the established parties or by the formation of New Politics parties. Thus, a fragmented party system and one with a large number of parties probably facilitates the representation of new value concerns, while allowing class-based interests to retain their already-established party links.

A host of other factors might influence the pace of partisan change; most importantly, the actions and strategic decisions of the established parties and the leadership of the New Politics movement (Dalton et al., 1984, chap. 15; Hauss and Rayside, 1978). These characteristics generally apply to specific actors within a political system, however. We will concentrate on the broader characteristics that define the political system for all actors and therefore might explain cross-national differences in party polarization along both the class and New Politics dimensions.

The data from our comparative analyses provide a unique opportunity to test these theories of partisan change. We have measures of the extent of voter polarization along both the values and class dimensions for fourteen nations, and can identify the institutional and political factors which enable citizens to translate their value priorities into party choices, or hasten the decline of class-based partisanship.

To test our theorizing, the strength of party polarization on the class cleavage and values cleavage in each nation was correlated with the nation's social and political characteristics (Table 12.1).[7] The first panel in

TABLE 12.1: *Correlates of party polarization on the class and New Politics dimension*

	Class	New Politics
Social Characteristics		
GNP per capita, 1975[1]	.18	.34
College enrollments[2]	−.33	−.19
Size of new middle class[3]	−.34	−.15
Postmaterial values[4]	.13	.02
Union density[1]	.60*	−.08
Electoral System		
PR system	.72*	.43*
Federal system	.34	.37*
Constituency size	−.73*	−.17
Presidential system	.09	−.37*
Candidate voting	.34	.42*
Party System		
Vote fractionalization, 1975[1]	.63*	.62*
Legislative fractionalization, 1975[1]	.74*	.63*
Number of parties	.46*	.61*

SOURCES: (1) Taylor and Jodice (1983), (2) UN Statistical Yearbook, (3) International Labor Organization Yearbook of Labor Statistics, (4) Inglehart (1979); other data compiled by author. Table entries are Pearson correlation coefficients, coefficients marked by an asterisk are significant at .10 level.

Table 12.1 displays the relationship between party polarization and various societal traits. On the whole, the characteristics identified with an advanced industrial society (affluence, college enrolments, the size of the new middle class, and the proportion of Postmaterialists) are related to the higher levels of party polarization along both cleavage dimensions, but none of these relationships are statistically significant. For example, the affluence of a nation (measured by GNP) is only weakly correlated with the level of class polarization (r=.18) and values polarization (r=.34). The one significant relationship in this set of variables is between the level of union density and the class cleavage; the class cleavage is strongest in nations where the working-class movement is most extensively mobilized (r=.60).

The strength of party polarization is more dependent on characteristics of the electoral system. Party polarization on both cleavage dimensions is greater in electoral systems based on proportional representation. For example, the average values/party correlation is .18 in the eight nations with a pure PR system, and only .11 in the two nations with a 'first-past-the-post' system. Similarly, party polarization on both dimensions is generally stronger in federal systems and those with some element of candidate voting. Larger constituencies also seem to weaken party polarization, especially for the class cleavage (r=-.73). In short, aspects of the electoral system that encourage political diversity seem to facilitate both the mobilization of a new cleavage such as the New Politics, as well as enable old cleavages, such as class-based voting, to endure.

The strongest factors affecting the level of party polarization are the characteristics of the party system. The fractionalization of the party system appears to be a crucial intervening variable in the process of partisan change. Proportional representation, federalism and a parliamentary system are all strongly correlated with party fractionalization, even though these electoral characteristics are virtually independent of one another. The third panel of Table 11.1 indicates that several different aspects of party fractionalization – vote fractionalization, legislative fractionalization, or the number of significant parties – are strongly related to party polarization on both the values and class dimensions. In fragmented party systems, Postmaterialists are more likely to find a party responsive to their interests and give disproportionate support to this party. This pattern may explain why partisan change tends to produce dramatic, critical realignments in two-party systems, where the pressures for change build until a political crisis occurs; while fractionalized party systems gradually adapt to changing political demands (Wolinetz, 1978). Similarly, diverse class interests can establish and maintain close party ties more easily in a fragmented party system. Party fractionalization thus emerges as the strongest correlate of partisan polarization on both dimensions; it facilitates the mobilization of the New Politics cleavage at the same time it discourages the process of class demobilization.

CONCLUSION

Modern democracies are in an unusual historical position. The industrial class structure is changing as European states become post-industrial societies. Many citizens are now preoccupied with new non-economic concerns, and it is even difficult to evaluate contemporary economic issues in simple class terms. The Marxist struggle between capitalists and a subservient working class bears very little resemblance to present-day social conditions. The industrial class structure is so fragmented and class positions are so removed from many contemporary political issues, that social class is becoming less relevant in determining political opinions. Conversely, more and more often, political conflicts are pitting the materialist goals of industrialism against the postmaterial goals of the New Politics. The political relevance of postmaterial values consequently is increasing.

The ebb and flow of these two political cleavages offers an extraordinary opportunity to study the process of electoral change. An important step in the realigning process is a transformation in the basic political orientations of Western publics: in our analyses measured by left/right self-placement. Social class is becoming less important as a predictor of left/right orientations as Postmaterialist values are becoming more important. National survey data from Western Europe and the United States indicates that left/right identities are now almost equally dependent on class cues and postmaterialist values (Inglehart, 1984; Knutsen, 1987). Moreover, these changing perceptions of politics are tied to on-going social trends which should increase the importance of the value cleavage. For example, among pre-World War II generations, class cues are strongly correlated with left/right beliefs; among the postwar generation values are more important than class position (Inglehart, 1979; Dalton, 1986, 1988).

Our model of the realigning process implies that the changing political orientations of Western publics are affecting voting patterns, but with lagged effects. The rigidity and inertia of party systems inevitably retards the pace of electoral change. But the adherents of New Politics issues continue to exert pressure on existing party alignments. Our analyses find that characteristics of the electoral system and party system play a crucial role in determining the pace of partisan mobilization along the New Politics dimension and demobilization of the traditional class cleavage. Indeed, substantial partisan change has already occurred in the past decade, and indirectly our findings suggest that the New Politics cleavage played a disproportionate role in stimulating electoral change.[8] If present trends continue, however, class demobilization and mobilization along the New Politics dimension will continue to contribute to a restructuring of contemporary party systems.

NOTES

1. This article is derived from earlier collaborative research with Scott Flanagan and Paul Beck. I would like to acknowledge my substantial debt to them for many of the ideas and analyses presented here.
2. Belgium and Britain might be exceptions to this general trend, because regional differences remained a significant aspect of party competition, but the conclusion holds for most other European states.
3. The New Politics dimension was measured by Inglehart's four-item material/postmaterial values index. Left/Right orientation is tapped by the ten-point self-placement scale. Cramer's V correlations were used because of the nominal level nature of the party variable and because this coefficient adjusts for the various number of categories on the variables being compared. Missing data (don't know and no answer) responses were included in the calculation of these correlations.
4. Even in the West German case, for instance, it is not possible to examine the

Eurobarometer

demobilization of the class cleavage, because the sharpest drops in class voting occurred before the time period covered by the necessary questions in the European Community surveys.
5. Analyses from Eurobarometers 6 and 7 (ICPSR 7511 and 7612) were merged to provide information for nine nations: France, Belgium, the Netherlands, West Germany, Italy, Luxembourg, Denmark, Great Britain, and Ireland. The Political Action survey (ICPSR 7777) furnished data for four additional nations: the United States, Austria, Switzerland, and Finland. Data from Japan are from the 1976 Japanese election study conducted; these data were kindly made available by Scott Flanagan.
6. Social class was measured by the occupation of the head of the household, which was collapsed into the following categories: (1) old middle class, (2) new middle class, (3) working class, (4) farmers, and (5) other.
7. The dependent variables in these analyses are the values/party and class/party correlations (Cramer's V) presented in Figures 12.3 and 12.4. The national scores on both dimensions are only weakly related (r=.25, n=14).
8. An index of party volatility developed by Pederson (1979) is more strongly related to value polarization (r=.80) than to class polarization (r=.52). Part of these relationships may be due to the strong correlation between volatility and party fractionalization (r=.63). When we control for this possible spurious influence, the partial correlation is .78 for the New Politics dimension and .14 for the class cleavage.

Baker, Kendall et al. (1981) *Germany Transformed* (Cambridge, Mass.: Harvard University Press).
Beck, Paul (1982) 'Realignment begins', *American Politics Quarterly* 10: 421–37.
Crewe, Ivor and D. T. Denver (eds) (1985) *Change in Western Democracies* (New York: St Martin's Press).
Daalder, Hans and Peter Mair (eds) (1983) *Western European Party Systems* (Beverly Hills: Sage Publications).
Dahl, Robert (1966) *Political Oppositions in Western Democracies* (New Haven, Conn.: Yale University Press).
Dalton, Russell (1984) 'The German party system between two ages', in R. Dalton et al. (eds) *Electoral Change in Advanced Industrial Democracies* (Princeton, NJ: Princeton University Press).
Dalton, Russell (1986) 'Wertwandel oder Wertwende?', in H. Klingemann and M. Kaase, eds *Wahlen und politischer Prozess* (Opladen: Westdeutscher Verlag).
Dalton, Russell (1988) *Citizen Politics in Western Democracies* (Chatham, NJ: Chatham House Publishers).
Dalton, Russell et al. (eds) (1984) *Electoral Change in Advanced Industrial Democracies* (Princeton, NJ: Princeton University Press).
Dunleavy, Patrick and Christopher Husbands (1985) *British Democracy at the Crossroads* (London: Allen and Unwin).
Epstein, Leon (1980) *Political Parties in Western Democracies* (New Brunswick, NJ: Transaction Books).
Hauss, Charles and David Rayside (1978) 'The development of new parties in Western democracies since 1945', in Louis Maisel and Joseph Cooper (eds)

Political Parties: Development and Decay (Beverly Hills, Ca.: Sage Publications).

Inglehart, Ronald (1977) *The Silent Revolution* (Princeton, NJ: Princeton University Press).

Inglehart, Ronald (1979) 'Value priorities and socio-economic change', in Samuel Barnes, Max Kaase, et al. (eds) *Political Action* (Beverly Hills: Sage Publications).

Inglehart, Ronald (1984) 'The changing structure of political cleavages in Western society', in R. Dalton et al. *Electoral Change in Advanced Industrial Democracies* (Princeton, NJ: Princeton University Press).

Katz, Richard (1980) *A Theory of Parties and Electoral Systems* (Baltimore: Johns Hopkins University Press).

Klingemann, Hans (1979) 'Measuring ideological conceptualizations', in Samuel Barnes, Max Kaase, et al. (eds) *Political Action* (Beverly Hills: Sage Publications).

Knutsen, Oddbjorn (1987) 'The impact of structural and ideological party cleavages in West European democracies', *British Journal of Political Science* 18: 323–52.

Lijphart, Arend (1981) 'Political parties: Ideologies and programs', in David Butler et al. (eds) *Democracy at the Polls* (Washington, DC: American Enterprise Institute).

Lipset, Seymour (1981) 'Revolt against the masses', in Per Torsvik (ed.) *Mobilization, Center-Periphery Structures, and Nation-Building* (Bergen: Universitetsforaget).

Pedersen, Mogens (1979) 'The dynamics of European party systems', *European Journal of Political Research* 7: 1–26.

Sartori, Giovanni (1976) *Parties and Party Systems* (Cambridge: Cambridge University Press).

Taylor, Charles and Peter Jodice (1983) *World Handbook III* (New Haven, Conn.: Yale University Press).

Wolinetz, Steven (1978) 'Continuity and change in Western European party systems', *Comparative Political Studies*, vol. 12, no. 1.

13 On the Electoral Persistence of Parties of the Right

Samuel H. Barnes, University of Michigan

INTRODUCTION

A puzzle in the political behavior of European mass publics is that successive cohorts of young people enter the electorate with higher levels of support for the left than those preceeding them, yet the overall electoral strength of parties of the right remains relatively constant through time. Electoral behavior can be volatile, and support for the right over any particular time span is likely to be increasing in some countries and stable or decreasing in others. Yet, given the leftist orientations of the young, generational replacement of the electorate implies an inevitable decline in support for parties of the right. Why has this not taken place? The reasons are undoubtedly various and complex. We will examine several explanations for which the Eurobarometers provide an excellent source of data.

One possibility is that the leftist orientations of the young may simply reflect the historical period in which they are socialized. It is not that youth as such are leftist; rather, possessing less resistance to trends of the moment, youth simply reflect most vividly the fads of the era. Thus while the present period may be one of overall leftist dominance, older cohorts may still carry with them the effects of growing up in more conservative times. This explanation for the leftist orientations of the young emphasizes the enduring effects of the period of youthful socialization, period effects that ripen into generational differences reflecting the diverse experiences of age cohorts.

A second possibility is that people move to the right as they pass through the life cycle. Time itself is the major influence. People become conservative as they age. The conventional wisdom and considerable research show that the elderly are indeed often conservative and the young progressive. But, as noted, research also demonstrates the importance of the era of socialization; older people may support the right because it was strong when they were young, not because they have changed as they age. Nevertheless, the strong relationship in Western Europe between age and support for parties of the right provides some face validity to the life cycle explanation.

233

A third reason for a recurring relationship between age and partisanship might be labeled the 'policy space' explanation: support for the right is a function of the division of the parties on the issues of the day. The very meaning of 'left' and 'right' in politics changes through time, and the eternal search for votes in the electoral game assures strong tendencies toward electoral equilibrium in established party systems.[1] Electoral competition forces parties to position themselves on economic and other issues and to adapt through time or wither as the electorate and the issues change. From this perspective, the nature of the right may change, but a right political alternative will always exist.[2]

These above explanations are not mutually exclusive. All may contribute to the persistence of support for the right. Periods of leftist attraction for the young may be followed by periods of the appeal of the right. The effects of the 1920s and 1930s on American politics have only recently faded, and the attractiveness of Ronald Reagan and Margaret Thatcher may leave a lasting imprint on the age distribution of support for the Republican and Conservative parties. Individuals may move to the right as they settle down, acquire jobs, property, and responsibilities. Political issues, personalities, and conditions certainly make a difference in support for particular parties. The 'policy space' explanation can coexist easily with others. Moreover, there are undoubtedly other possible influences not considered here.

The Eurobarometers provide an impressive data base for a new look at the puzzle. While no single study can be definitive, the present data base is excellent for a fresh assessment of generational, life cycle, and policy space influences. The analysis uses the surveys for the period 1975 through 1987. It combines the two yearly surveys, except that the 1987 observations are based on a single survey. It focuses on the countries for which data are available for the entire period, that is, Belgium, Denmark, France, Germany, Great Britain, Ireland, Italy, Luxembourg, and the Netherlands. All of the analyses presented below were carried out on both the entire set of countries and on each of the individual countries. To conserve space, only the results for Europe as a whole are presented in their entirety, though important country differences are noted.

GENERATIONS, THE LIFE CYCLE, AND SUPPORT FOR PARTIES OF THE RIGHT

Results of parliamentary elections in the nine countries included in this study demonstrate no overall trends in support for right parties in elections held during the 1975–87 period.[3] In France, the Netherlands, and Germany, votes for the right increased between the first and last elections of the period. In Belgium, Denmark, Ireland, and Italy they declined sub-

TABLE 13.1: *Support for right party by birth cohort and year of survey* (entry is % of birth cohort preferring right party in that year)

Survey Year	>1955	1946– 55	Birth Cohort 1936– 45	1926– 35	1916– 25	1906– 15	1894– 05	Total
1975	36	34	46	47	50	52	56	46
1976	35	36	42	46	49	55	53	45
1977	38	35	42	48	47	52	59	45
1978	31	37	43	44	50	51	55	43
1979	35	35	43	47	51	51	54	44
1980	29	33	40	42	46	46	52	40
1981	28	33	41	41	41	43	49	38
1982	34	34	46	44	51	51	57	42
1983	37	39	47	43	50	54	59	44
1984	34	38	44	45	47	51	65	42
1985	33	36	45	51	47	51	43	42
1986	33	35	45	43	48	55	50	42
1987	32	36	44	44	51	53	49	41
Total	33	35	44	45	48	51	55	43

stantially; in Luxembourg and Britain they declined slightly.[4] Italy is the only country in which three elections were held *and* in which there is a monotonic trend throughout the period. In all the other countries, electoral support for the right fluctuates from election to election without any clear trend – at least in this period of thirteen years.

The Eurobarometer data show clearly that each birth cohort provides less support for parties of the right than the one preceeding it.[5] Table 13.1 presents, for all countries combined, the percentage of each cohort that expressed support for one of the parties of the right.[6] The table also exhibits the logic of the analysis that follows: Each variable was coded for each cohort for each year for which data are available. There are thirteen years and seven cohorts for most of the variables (left-right self placement was not asked in 1975), so the analyses are based on ninety-one data points that reflect aggregated individual responses. They do not constitute a panel. Table 13.1 shows that mean support for right parties for each cohort progresses monotonically with age. Not surprisingly, half the total change takes place in the first two cohorts, that is, before the age of thirty-six.

The table also shows that variation by year of survey is much smaller than that by birth cohort. There is a decline from 1975 through 1979 and a rise starting in 1982, with 1980 and 1981 being the years of lowest support for right parties. Our claim that policy factors are important is strengthened by this pattern, for there were elections in Germany in 1980 and in Belgium, Denmark, France, Ireland, and the Netherlands in 1981, and in all six of these elections the right received its lowest vote percentage of any election in that country during the thirteen-year period studied. The survey data on party preference track the electoral returns. The yearly progressions exhibit remarkable regularity. Only ten of the ninety-one cells violate perfect monotonicity.

Table 13.1 makes visually clear the strength of the contribution to support for right parties of birth cohort compared with passage through the life cycle (survey year). A regression makes it possible to compare the two with greater precision and also provides a method for controlling for period effects. The basic model is simple. The dependent variable is the mean percentage of a birth cohort that supports right parties in a particular year. The independent variables are birth cohort and year of survey.

The first analysis regresses the birth cohort variable on support for right parties. Cohort alone explains more than a quarter of the variance in right support in the combined national samples:[7]

$$B = 3.464, SE = .199. \text{ Adj. r sq.} = .269.$$

The year of survey variable, on the other hand, has an insignificant impact when regressed on the percentage of a cohort supporting right parties:

$$B = -.145, SE = .125; \text{ adj. r sq.} = .0004.$$

The next stage of the analysis is to look at the possible impact of period effects. An initial strategy is to treat each birth cohort and each survey year as a dummy variable. The regressions reported above treated both as linear variables; they suggested that cohorts had a strong linear influence while survey year had none during the time period considered, whatever the long-term importance of passage through the life cycle.

By entering each cohort and each survey year as a dummy variable in all possible combinations of the two sets we can see whether particular birth cohorts or survey years are significant. The results for Europe as a whole are easy to interpret: six of the birth cohorts are significant at the 0.0001 level; the 1915–26 cohort only reaches the 0.07 level. Of the survey years, only 1981, the year with five national elections that were low points for the right, is significant at the 0.03 level. No other survey year reaches a significance level greater than 0.12. Moreover, without attaching undue significance to the portion of variance explained, it seems important that no combination of linear and dummy variables improves the adjusted r square of the linear birth cohort variable by more than 0.005! This latter variable, which is essentially a surrogate for age, is by itself the most important predictor of support for right parties. Treating these cohorts as generations socialized in different periods, and thus abandoning the as-

TABLE 13.2: *Variance in support for right explained by birth cohort and year of survey as linear and dummy variables* (entry is adjusted r square)

Country	Birth Cohort		Survey Year		Both
	Linear	Dummy	Linear	Dummy	(Dummies)
Belgium	.38	.36	.06	.02	.45
Denmark	.29	.29	.01	.12	.47
France	.53	.52	.13	.20	.83
Germany	.52	.52	.01	.00	.60
Great Britain	.08	.08	.13	.45	.58
Ireland	.14	.12	.03	.11	.26
Italy	.64	.70	.01	.09	.71
Luxembourg	.34	.34	.01	.21	.57
The Netherlands	.46	.58	.01	.02	.70

sumption of linearity, that is, emphasizing each cohort individually in the dummy variable analysis, does not increase understanding.

Elections are among the most important and the most obvious period effects, as they both politicize the electorate and contribute to the substance of the positions taken. Electoral campaigns are country-specific and, of course, take place at different times in different countries. Analyses of Europe as a whole are likely to mask their impact. For that reason it is useful to present the results for the individual countries as well. In addition, the presentation shows the wide variation in country patterns as well as the greater significance of birth cohort and survey year in the individual countries than in the data for Europe as a whole (see Table 13.2).

The importance of birth cohort varies greatly across countries. Generational differences are larger in France, Germany, Italy, and the Netherlands than in the other countries; they are smaller in Britain, Denmark, and Ireland. Only in the Netherlands is there much difference between birth cohort treated as a linear variable in the regression and as several dummy variables, suggesting that the massive electoral shifts in that country affect different cohorts in a non-linear fashion.

The importance of survey year also varies from country to country, with differences especially impressive for Great Britain, France, and Luxembourg. Thus years coded as dummy variables explain 45 per cent of the variance in support for parties of the right in Britain, presumably because of the volatility of British electoral preferences during this period. In France, the dummy variables of birth cohort and survey year explain an astounding 83 per cent of the variance in support for the right. The two dummy variables also explain a large portion of the variance in support for the right in Italy (71 per cent) and the Netherlands (70 per cent). In all countries except Britain, birth cohort, or generation, is much more important than life cycle in explaining support for right parties during the period studied. Only in France and Britain, both with adjusted r squares of .13, does survey year treated as a linear variable reveal a movement to the right through the life cycle.

Caution is in order in interpreting these results. Life-cycle effects may appear greater over a longer time span. The resurgence of the left was substantial in several countries during the middle years of our analysis period. Such period effects could mask, or even indicate a temporary reversal of, dominant trends. Over a lifetime, even a slight trend can have a large impact. Philip Converse (1976), in examining a related puzzle, labeled the discussion, 'On Finding the Very Small'. Thirteen years is a substantial period, but it is only one-quarter of the average voting life of those who live out their three score and ten. The absence of life-cycle effects in the present analysis does not mean that they would not exist over a longer time span, or even over a different time span.

The role of the changing composition of the electorate over time requires an extended comment. Conventional wisdom suggests that women and those with higher income, education, and religiosity are more likely to prefer parties of the right. Religiosity is especially relevant because Christian Democratic parties are important in Western Europe, and they are coded as right in the Eurobarometers. Gender is closely related to right preference because women are more religious – there are generally no gender differences in support for the right when church attendance is controlled. Women also live longer, so their greater support for the right combined with differential survival rates exaggerate the relationship between age and right support. However, gender and other aspects of aging relating to composition effects acquire great importance mainly past the age of sixty-five and even seventy-five (see Percheron, 1988, 1985).

The present analysis investigated the impact of income, education, and gender on support for the right. Religiosity could not be included because information on subjective religiosity and church attendance was obtained only on a sporadic basis in the Eurobarometers. Gender differences are of modest importance in Europe as a whole; they are significant in Italy, where the gender difference in religiosity enters. They do not reach an important level of significance in the general analysis.

The role of income and education cannot be evaluated in this analysis due to the impossibility of interpreting the results of individual-level data aggregated in the present manner. We created variables based on the percentage of a cohort-survey year with income above the country mean and on the percentage of a cohort-survey year who left school at the age of sixteen or before. Both these variables are highly correlated with birth cohort. The young are better educated and report higher incomes. For Europe as a whole, the product moment correlation between birth cohort and percentage above the mean on income is −0.77, and between the former and percentage completing their formal education by the age of sixteen is 0.83. For seven of the nine countries, the latter correlation is 0.92 or above. Hence further analysis would be meaningless.

But even if it were possible, it would be uninterpretable because of the ecological fallacy: that the older cohorts are more poorly educated and more supportive of the right is clear, but aggregated data do not tell us *which* of the old support parties of the right. It is not necessarily the poorly-educated old who endorse the right. The same logic applies to the interpretation of the other two variables. But it does not matter, for these three variables add nothing to the explanatory power of the models presented. Including them increases the adjusted explained variance only 0.003! The obvious conclusion is that, among the aggregated variables considered, only birth cohort has a substantial influence on support for parties of the right.

The influence of income and education merits investigation, but requires an analysis strategy different from that undertaken here.

THE CHANGING LEFT-RIGHT POLICY SPACE

The above examination of generation, period, and life-cycle effects on support for parties of the right suggests a dismal future for these parties. Each birth cohort is less rightist than that before it, and, at least over the period considered, there is no evidence of life cycle changes improving the prospects for the right. Yet electoral returns demonstrate no clear trend away from the right in Europe as a whole, hence the puzzle that inspired this analysis. We now turn to an alternative explanation of the puzzle.

Issues, personalities, electoral campaigns, value changes, and countless other particular matters influence the nature of political competition in a country. Demographic trends operate against the backdrop of these other matters and undoubtedly both influence them and are influenced by them. There is no simple way to operationalize these influences across nine countries and thirteen years. However, a promising summary measure has been widely used by analysts of public opinion as a surrogate for general political orientations or 'tendencies'. This is left-right self-placement, in which respondents are asked to place themselves on a scale that runs from one to ten.[8]

Numerous interpretations exist as to what these numbers actually represent. Left and right (or liberal and conservative, which are more often used in the United States) are habitually viewed as referring to a policy space, with the specific content varying according to the political concerns of the country. For example, the scale may tap the level of redistributive tax policies or public intervention in the economy desired. In many European countries it is especially sensitive to religious or, especially, clerical-anticlerical orientations. Ronald Inglehart and Jacques-René

TABLE 13.3: *Left/right self-placement (tendency)* (total sample entries are means; standard deviation in parentheses)

Birth Cohort	Total Sample	A Right Party Supporters	Difference
<1955	4.9 (2.1)	6.6 (1.7)	1.7
1946–55	5.0 (2.1)	6.7 (1.7)	1.7
1936–45	5.4 (2.1)	6.7 (1.7)	1.3
1926–35	5.5 (2.1)	6.8 (1.7)	1.3
1916–25	5.6 (2.2)	6.9 (1.7)	1.3
1906–15	5.7 (2.2)	7.0 (1.7)	1.3
1894–05	6.0 (2.3)	7.3 (1.7)	1.3

Survey Year	Total Sample	B Right Party Supporters	Difference
1976	5.4 (2.2)	7.0 (1.7)	1.6
1977	5.4 (2.2)	7.0 (1.7)	1.6
1978	5.3 (2.2)	6.7 (1.7)	1.4
1979	5.3 (2.1)	6.7 (1.7)	1.4
1980	5.3 (2.0)	6.7 (1.6)	1.4
1981	5.3 (2.1)	6.8 (1.7)	1.5
1982	5.3 (2.1)	6.8 (1.7)	1.5
1983	5.3 (2.1)	6.8 (1.7)	1.5
1984	5.2 (2.1)	6.8 (1.7)	1.6
1985	5.3 (2.1)	6.9 (1.7)	1.6
1986	5.3 (2.1)	6.9 (1.7)	1.6
1987	5.2 (2.1)	6.8 (1.7)	1.6
Total	5.3 (2.1)	6.8 (1.7)	1.5

Rabier (1986) argue that the meaning of left and right is shifting from an old politics of material concerns to a Postmaterialist new politics. For present purposes, it is sufficient to assume that left and right refer to substantive policy positions that vary both spatially and temporally, that is, the content differs from country to country and also may shift over time. The temporal shift is the principal focus of the present analysis.

It will be no surprise that each birth cohort places itself more to the left on the scale than the one preceding it, paralleling the shift away from supporting parties of the right. Table 13.3 (A) presents the mean cohort differences for Europe as a whole in the first column and for supporters of right parties in the second. The latter means make the principal point of this analysis quite strongly: the shift to the left affects supporters of the right as well as others. The monotonicity of both trends is impressive. The third column documents the differences between the overall means and those for supporters of right parties. They are constant among the five older cohorts and increase among the two youngest. Whether this reflects increasing polarization between the right and the rest of the political spectrum or merely the exaggeration of the young cannot be determined from these data.

The results by year, presented in Table 13.3 (B), show the expected period effects due, presumably, to the leftist trends of 1979–80. Supporters of right parties shifted even more sharply to the left in those years, giving rise to the smallest differences between the two groups. But right-party supporters shifted back toward the right more quickly than did the sample as a whole, resulting in increasing differences in later years. Most important, however, is the fact that the differences remain relatively constant over the thirteen-year period, and that supporters of right parties participate in trends of particular periods just as they reflect the differences in various birth cohorts.

Thus the spatial positions of the right change, and one source of the recurring appeal of the right is its flexibility. Recall that we are dealing with mean positions, with half the sample falling on either side. The standard deviations are large enough to ensure considerable overlap of the two groups. Undoubtedly a substantial portion of the overall samples is located spatially at positions held by many supporters of right parties. This large shared space provides right (and centre) parties considerable room for electoral manoeuvre. It also means that the right should be able to continue to attract supporters even as the electorate moves to the left, as the substantive issues presumably reflected by the left-right measure seem to lead to changes in the spatial location of supporters of right as well as other parties.

This transformation of the right may be easier in some countries than in others. The country differences in left-right self-location by birth cohort are particularly striking. Table 13.4 shows the spread between the youngest and oldest birth cohorts for both the total samples and the supporters of right parties. Some countries, such as France, Italy, and Denmark, exhibit great polarization, with the oldest birth cohort of the general sample being more than a full point more leftist than the youngest of the rightist cohort. In the two former countries, the economic component of left and right is probably dwarfed by the clerical-anticlerical component, as the conventional wisdom would suggest.

The Danish results were unanticipated. Table 12.4 shows the small difference between the youngest and oldest birth cohorts in that country (though it should be noted that there is some variation in the middle cohorts). Moreover, the Danish right supporters have moved steadily to the right over the twelve years covered (left-right was not asked in 1975), so that there is a large gap between the range of the total sample and that of the right (table not shown).

Other countries, such as Ireland, show an extensive overlap between the

TABLE 13.4: *Country differences in left/right self-locations, by total sample and supporters of right (entry is range of means for the youngest and oldest cohorts)*

	Total Sample	Right Supporters
Belgium	5.5–6.4	6.6–7.6
Denmark	5.1–6.1	7.2–7.4
France	4.7–5.8	6.9–7.2
Germany	5.2–6.3	6.6–7.4
Great Britain	5.3–6.3	6.6–7.9
Luxembourg	5.2–6.2	6.2–7.0
The Netherlands	5.1–6.0	6.8–7.6
Ireland	5.7–6.8	6.2–7.2
Italy	4.3–5.2	6.3–6.4
Total	4.9–6.0	6.6–7.3

two sets of means, reflecting the strong personalism and low salience of ideology and party differences on policy in the politics of that country. Other countries show gaps in between those just discussed. Thus in most of the countries there seems to be little to prevent the right from eventually attracting many supporters of the current centre and left. But the task may be more difficult in those countries that exhibit extensive polarization.

SUMMARY

The left orientations of the young are apparent in the above analysis of birth cohorts and support for parties of the right. Each cohort is less supportive of the right than the one preceding it. Yet there is no evidence of a secular trend away from the right in European electoral returns. Nor is there evidence of conversion through the life cycle: each cohort contains about the same percentage of supporters of the right at the end of the thirteen year period covered by the analyses as at the beginning. That is our puzzle.

The above analyses also demonstrate that each birth cohort is more leftist in left-right self-placement than the one preceding it, and this is true of the supporters of right parties as well. This finding points to one way in which right parties continue to be electorally competitive: they move left with the electorate. Assuming that movement on mean left-right positionings reflects movement on underlying policy orientations as well, electoral politics pushes parties in the direction taken by mass publics. In the present era as reflected in the Eurobarometers, that movement is to the left. As the mean positions of supporters of parties of the right shift to the left as well, these parties continue to occupy a densely populated policy space. Thus their ability to attract voters is not weakened by the leftward drift resulting from population replacement. This drift does cause individuals to shift through time from left to right in policy space: they remain stable in world view, but what was a left position in youth becomes a right position as people age and the policy space changes in content.

NOTES

1. The complexities of different types of party and electoral systems suggest caution on this point. Some parties in some systems place electoral success low on their list of priorities, but it seems reasonable to claim that a rightist political space exists in all electoral systems and that some party or parties seek to occupy it.
2. Samuel Huntington (1957) has argued that conservatism *as an ideology* is situational and positional, rather than a set of unchanging policy preferences. It is essentially the defense of the status quo against threats of change, and thus will differ depending on the nature of the status quo and the changes threatened. This view is compatible with the argument made here about the changing policy positions of right parties.
3. The analysis relies on the coding of parties as left, right, or center adopted by the principal investigators (Ronald Inglehart, Jacques-René Rabier, and Helene Riffault). See the codebook for a listing of the parties.
4. Electoral results were obtained from Mackie and Rose (1982) for the earlier years and from the *European Journal of Political Research* for the later ones.
5. The birth cohorts are taken from the cumulative file of the European Communities Studies, as updated by Ronald Inglehart. I appreciate his sharing this file with me. The birth dates of the cohorts are 1956–65, 1946–55, 1936–45, 1926–35, 1916–25, 1906–15, 1894–1905.
6. The question about partisan preference asked in all countries except Italy was 'If there were a general election tomorrow, which party would you support?' In Italy it was 'Do you feel closer to any one of the parties on the following list than to all the others? If yes: Which one?'
7. The data are weighted to provide a sample of the European Community. For details see the codebook.
8. The Eurobarometers present the respondent with a card with ten numbered boxes, and he or she is asked, 'In political matters, people talk of "The Left" and "The Right". How would you place your views on this scale'?

REFERENCES

Converse, Philip (1976) *The Dynamics of Party Support* (Beverly Hills, Ca: Sage).
Huntington, Samuel (1957) 'Conservatism as an Ideology'. *American Political Science Review*, 51: 454–73.
Inglehart, Ronald, and Jacques-René Rabier (1986) 'Political Realignment in Advanced Industrial Society'. *Government and Opposition*, 21: 456–79.
Mackie, Thomas T., and Richard Rose (1982) *The International Almanac of Electoral History*, 2nd ed. (New York: Facts on File).

Percheron, Annick (1985) 'Age, cycle de vie, generation, periode et comportement electoral'. In Daniel Gaxie (ed.) *L'explication du vote* (Paris: Presses de la FNSP) pp. 228–62.

Percheron, Annick (1988) 'Vieillesse et politique'. *Gerontologie et societe*, 44: 6–16.

14 The Use of Eurobarometer Data in a Study of Electoral Change

Mark N. Franklin, University of Houston, and Thomas T. Mackie, University of Strathclyde

INTRODUCTION

This is a report of the initial findings from a comparative study of electoral change in Western countries which has been investigating the links between social divisions and party choice, and the manner in which these links have changed since the 1960s. Complete findings will be reported in Franklin, Mackie, Valen et al (1991, forthcoming).

Post-war party systems, which as recently as the late 1960s were characterized as 'frozen', have everywhere seen developments that were quite unexpected. Until the late 1960s, stability was regarded as a central characteristic of both party systems and individual voting behavior. Except for countries subject to a change of regime in the aftermath of World War II, support for political parties in Western countries was remarkably stable. Rose and Urwin's study (1970: 295) of nineteen Western nations demonstrated that 'the electoral strength of most parties [since 1945] had changed very little from election to election, from decade to decade, or within the lifespan of a generation'. More recently, however, many countries have seen important changes in the nature of their party systems, and in all countries voters have shown increasing unpredictability in their choice between parties, often to the extent of voting for parties that are new to the political scene. Precisely when these developments started is not clear, but in many countries it has become evident that the period of the Vietnam War was critical (Franklin, 1985; Nie, Verba and Petrocik, 1981). Because of the visibility of the Paris 'events' of May 1968, this year is often taken as the turning point. For instance Beer (1983) and Tarschys (1977) have pointed to the significance of 1968 in stimulating the growth of support for the 'New Populism' in Britain and the 'New Left' in Scandinavia.

These developments put into question some of the major theoretical underpinnings of traditional explanations of voting choice. For if the classical theorists who explained the origins of party systems were correct in supposing that social cleavages played the central role in mediating the influence of historical developments, then changes in party systems should be based on changes in social structure. Our primary question was to what extent this linkage could actually be observed in an era of rapid political changes; and, if such a linkage is now visible, why the electoral consequences of social and economic changes since World War II were so long delayed.

Political cleavages are usually regarded as reflecting broadly-based and long-standing social and economic divisions within society. Beginning with Marx and Weber's contradictory accounts of the character of class conflict, contemporary scholars have emphasized the central importance of other divisions such as religious and ethnic differences. Most relevant to our current concerns is the seminal work by Lipset and Rokkan (1967: 1–64) on cleavage structures and the emergence of party systems. These two authors described cleavage structures as resulting from complex historical processes, triggered by the national revolution and the industrial revolution. They distinguished between four basic sets of cleavages: (1) subject versus dominant culture, (2) church(es) versus state, (3) primary versus secondary economy, and (4) workers versus employers. However, their model is not deterministic. Political conflicts may differ substantially from one nation to the next, especially with respect to ethnic and religious matters, since not all social-structural differences become politicized (Schattschneider, 1960; Sartori, 1969; Przeworski and Sprague, 1986).

In this way, the establishment of national cleavage structures was assumed to have been completed soon after the First World War (Lipset and Rokkan, 1967); and when Rose (1974) edited his masterly work describing the relationship between social structure and party choice, it was taken for granted that the picture being presented was one which would not soon be changed. Indeed, the very stability of party systems in periods of rapid social and economic change was seen as a confirmation of Lipset and Rokkan's argument. Ironically, even by the time Rose's book appeared, the picture was already changing in many countries. In Belgium, Switzerland, Canada and Britain new electoral support was given to parties based upon linguistic and ethnic cleavages long thought to have been depoliticized. In other countries new parties championed different causes that cut across existing party lines: constitutional reform for Dutch Democrats 66, traditional morality for new Christian Democratic parties in Denmark, Finland and Sweden, tax reductions for Glistrup's Progress Party in Denmark, and civil liberties for the Italian Radicals. In all countries a set of environmental issues were placed upon the political agenda, often by ecological or 'green' parties new to the political scene; and in most countries (whether or not new parties were involved) voter loyalties to established parties declined sharply so that no party could take the level of its vote for granted.

The first question that arose when we confronted these phenomena is whether they reflected changes in the social structure which earlier scholars saw as the foundation of party conflict. During the period since 1945 the world has seen technological, social and economic changes of a magnitude unparalleled since the industrial revolution. Consequential changes in occupational composition will clearly have affected political cleavages. Thus the decline of the manual working class will have reduced the core support for socialist parties. Similarly, in countries with agrarian parties, the decline in rural population will have weakened their support. On the other hand, the behavior of the growing new middle class may be less predictable than that of traditional class groups.

If social cleavages were the only long-term determinant of voting choice, then changes in social structure (changes in the distribution of social characteristics) would totally explain secular changes in the electoral fortunes of political parties. (Of course individual election outcomes might well deviate from this long term trend for idiosyncratic reasons.) In other words, the ability to predict the voting behavior of individuals on the basis of their social and other characteristics is also the ability to predict change at the societal level on the basis of changes in the distribution of these characteristics. On the other hand, to the extent that voting choice has other causes, these will also need to be considered as possible sources of secular change.

THE ROLE OF EUROBAROMETERS IN THE PROJECT

The very existence of this study would not have been possible without the existence of the Eurobarometer series of surveys. This series provided us with a set of comparable questions asked simultaneously in a large number of countries over a considerable period of time. For many of these countries, the Eurobarometer series are simply the only source of suitable data. However, there are other countries (outside the European Community) with lengthy series of appropriate surveys, and we wished to include in our study as many of these as possible. The additional countries were chosen on the basis of the availability of a series of surveys extending over a long enough period to capture the extent of recent change, and with large enough samples to do justice to each country's social diversity. In addition to countries of the European Community, the study includes Australia, Canada, New Zealand, Norway, Sweden and the United States. In the context of a book about usage of Eurobarometer data, we should perhaps point out that the inclusion of non-Eurobarometer countries created considerable problems of comparability which would not have existed had we limited our project to EC countries.

RESEARCH DESIGN

All comparative research (whether between different countries or between different periods) involves a fundamental dilemma. Unless concepts are standardized, comparison rests upon shifting sands; but to the extent that standardization is actually achieved, it will reduce the number of countries and concepts over which comparisons can be made. In this study we adopted a unique procedure in order to maximize both comparability and coverage. A core analysis was conducted in identical terms for every country, focussing upon variables that were generally available. For some countries, additional analyses were introduced which add extra variables that were widely but not universally available. Finally, every country study was rounded off with an analysis of variables important to an understanding of party choice within that country, but which are either not germane to the study of other countries or not available in identical terms elsewhere. So the analysis conducted for each country has the structure of an inverted pyramid, whose apex consists of variables analysed in identical terms within each chapter, and whose base consists of additional variables particular to specific countries in one way or another.

Contributors were asked to use for their analyses three national surveys, linked wherever possible to general elections. They were to be chosen so as to span as long a period as possible, though without moving too far before the 'events' of 1968.

THE DEPENDENT VARIABLE: LEFT VOTING

In order to be able to apportion the causes of changes in political alignment, we need to know how much change of this kind has occurred. Given that each of the countries studied has different numbers of political parties with different primary characteristics, we first of all had to establish a common measure of political support at the start of our period that would be comparable across countries. The measure chosen was support for left parties. Such parties have declined in electoral strength almost everywhere, and thus provide a common point of reference in evaluating what electoral change in different countries has in common. The use of this measure clearly limits the extent to which change can be identified, since particular countries have seen extensive changes not captured in this measure. On the other hand, many changes that might appear country-specific (for example, the rise of a party with ecological concerns) will have been reflected in our common measure to the extent that votes are taken from left parties. Conversely, important changes within the block of left parties (or within any block of parties outside the left) will have been completely overlooked in the comparative analysis.

Identifying the party (or parties) of the left in each country proved to be quite straightforward. However, it should be born in mind that the political complexion of left parties is by no means the same in all countries. At one extreme, the dominant component of the left block is Communist (generally with a strong minority socialist presence). In other countries, the dominant component is social democratic (sometimes with a minority Communist presence). In Canada and the United States, the left is dominated by parties which elsewhere would be considered liberal rather than socialist. For some purposes such diversity would make comparative analysis impossible, but our principal focus lies not so much in the ideological complexion of particular parties as in their relative positions within the spectrum of political choice available to voters in each country.

THE INDEPENDENT VARIABLES: SOCIAL CHARACTERISTICS AND POLITICAL ATTITUDES

Placing particular voters on one side or other of a social cleavage is not totally straightforward, and earlier researchers have employed different indicators of particular cleavage locations. In this study we start from the pioneering identification of salient political cleavages by Lipset and Rokkan (see above). The dominant culture cleavage can be reflected in language, religion or regional identity; and where salient we have measures of each of these characteristics. The church versus state cleavage is not only viewed in terms of religiosity (measured by frequency of church attendance). The primary versus secondary economy is identified by distinguishing between urban and rural residence. The workers versus employers cleavage is seen in terms of occupational class (working versus middle or blue-collar versus white-collar).

Most of these variables have been operationalised in virtually identical terms for all the countries included in this study. Two exceptions (language and ethnicity) pose no problems of comparability since, in countries where they are not measured, virtually all voters have the same characteristics with the consequence that no effects from language or ethnicity would have been found. So we were able to include these variables in the core analyses for countries where they are measured. Another variable (religious denomination) is missing from studies of voting behavior in five of our countries because it was not thought to be sufficiently important. For the purpose of the present discussion this is assumed to have no importance in countries where scholars did not think it necessary to measure it. Figure 13.1 places these variables within the pyramid structure of comparability across countries that was referred to earlier.

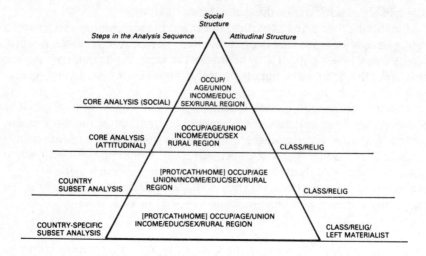

FIGURE 14.1 *The pyramid arrangement of the comparative analyses*

Items within the pyramid are independent variables. In each analysis the dependent variable is votes cast for the left party or parties. Country subset analyses with
variables in square brackets are only available for Australia, Canada, Denmark,
France, Great Britain, Greece, Italy, the Netherlands, Norway, Sweden, USA and
W. Germany.

PROJECTING THE CONSEQUENCES OF SOCIAL CHANGE

In order to decide how much electoral change is due to changing social
structure we had to be able to estimate the left vote from the aggregate
proportions of voters in each social group. Having done this for our first
election in each country, changes in the size of each group at subsequent
elections would determine the extent of the resulting changes in left voting
that were to be expected at those elections. A regression analysis of the
effects of social structure on party choice provides appropriate estimates,
since the regression equation for the first election specifies the connection
between social characteristics and left vote at that time. To the extent to
which this connection is a stable one, we are then able to predict the left
vote in subsequent elections on the basis of the social characteristics of the
electorate at those later points in time. Any differences between predicted
and actual outcomes at such subsequent elections would have to be
explained on grounds other than those of changing social structure. A full
description of the analysis procedures employed can be found in Franklin,
Mackie, Valen et al., (1991).

TABLE 14.1: *Timing of changes in electoral impact of social structure, by country and extent of initial effects**

	No decline	1960s–1970s	1970s–1980s
Canada	(L)		
U.S.A.	(L)		
France	(L)		
Germany	(M)		
Australia		M	
Britain		M	
New Zealand		M	
Sweden		H	
Ireland			M
Belgium			H
Denmark			H
Italy			H
Netherlands			H
Norway			H
Austria			

* Greece, Portugal and Spain not included because of lack of early data.

FINDINGS

The picture painted by the separate country studies is in central respects the same in most countries: the effects of social structure have generally declined in such a way as to lead to convergence. Countries where social structure had a dominant influence on party choice have seen a large decline in this influence. Countries where social structure was less important in the first place have generally seen a maintenance of this more modest impact.

The timing of these changes is not the same in all countries. As shown in Table 14.1, some countries saw a decline early in our time period, some later and some (parenthesised), although they may have seen changes outside our time-span, show no movement in our data. In this table, countries are differentiated both by the timing of the decline (across the chart) and also by the extent of impact when first observed, designated by 'L' for low (10 per cent or less of variance in left voting explained by social structure), 'M' for medium (11 to 20 per cent) and 'H' for high (over 20 per cent). It is immediately obvious that countries for which the decline occurred in different decades also show evidence of different degrees of cleavage politics at the earliest stage. Countries which saw their major decline between the 1970s and 1980s are also those with the strongest initial impact of social structure. Countries where the effects of social structure were already in decline a decade earlier are also generally those where cleavage politics appear to have been less important when we first observe them. More than one reason can be adduced for this finding, but it is clear that we are talking about a developmental process that started later in some countries than in others. Reasons why some countries should have declined earlier that others are a major concern of the study (Franklin, Mackie, Valen, 1991). The fact that certain countries show no decline in Table 14.1 tells us much about the general process we are observing, but we do not have space here to pursue this.

USING SOCIAL CHANGE TO EXPLAIN CHANGES IN LEFT VOTING

A strong implication of earlier scholarship was that any decline in left voting would be explicable very largely on the basis of changes in social structure, and this indeed seems to be the case in many countries. However, in the majority of countries, actual electoral change reflects only poorly the evolution of social cleavages. This appears to be due to the fact that in different countries the effects of social structure have declined to different levels. Where social structure no longer conditions partisanship to any appreciable extent, we would not expect it to condition developments in left voting. On the contrary, in those countries where the decline of social structuring has progressed far enough, we would precisely expect left voting to reflect other influences or to be random in nature. From this perspective it comes as no surprise to discover that those countries where social structure still largely determines partisanship are also the countries where compositional changes in the traditional cleavage structure still largely determine the extent of left voting. On the other hand, those countries where social structure has become largely irrelevant to party choice are also those whose compositional changes are no longer central, as shown in Table 14.2.

Some surprises in this table deserve comment. It has not been customary to group together within a single category countries where the left has done surprisingly well in recent years (Australia, New Zealand, France, Denmark) and those where it has done particularly badly (Britain, Canada, Ireland). The point is that where social structure does not condition voting choice to any great extent, new developments of any other kind can as easily benefit the left as harm it.

The position of the United States, among countries where social cleavages strongly determine partisanship, is at first sight extraordinary. In fact its presence in this category is not even marginal. In the 1970s, 16 per cent of variance in Democratic voting could already be explained by social

TABLE 14.2: *Effects of social structure on left voting*

		Deviations from projected left voting*	
		Low	High
Extent of Variance Explained**	Low		Ireland Denmark France Britain Australia New Zealand Canada
	High	Belgium Norway Netherlands Sweden Germany U.S.A.	

* Low 0–14%, High 15% + at last time point. No country shows variance explained between 11 and 15 per cent.
** Low 0–6%, High 6% + at last time point

structure (mainly race and region), and by 1984 this had risen to 19 per cent. Parenthetically we might add that it seems to us that the United States is actually in the vanguard of a new development, traces of which can also be seen in other countries, in which regional differentiation of voting preferences are rising to mirror within a nation with an integrative party system some of the effects which elsewhere have shown themselves in a rise of nationalist parties.

Another seeming anomaly occurs within the group of countries that show high deviations from expected left voting. This group is largely Anglo-Saxon, but Table 14.2 shows the Anglo-Saxon countries being joined by two continental European countries, France and Denmark. Again, the location of these countries in Table 14.2 derives from the data, and again neither of them are marginal cases. In both instances we are talking about under 9 per cent of variance explained in the contemporary period (in the case of Denmark this follows a staggering decline in the impact of social structure, from an ability to explain 28 per cent of the variance in left voting during the early 1970s). Denmark is the only country where left parties did better than expected without actually winning a parliamentary majority, but in Denmark this has been achieved to a large degree by a dramatic increase in the fractionalization of the left vote in that country. With many more parties catering to the client group, it is perhaps not surprising that the proportion of left voters should have been largely maintained, and Denmark should not be confused with other countries where the left has done well by espousing policies which elsewhere have been the hallmarks of successful right parties: a topic that will be of considerable importance in the book that is now being written.

These surprises are actually very reassuring. They serve to confirm that Table 14.2 does not simply reflect cultural peculiarities but, on the contrary, tells us important things about the impact of social cleavages on electoral politics in different countries. In the light of this table it seems clear that some recent developments in individual countries that seemed surprising to observers (particularly in France, Australia and New Zealand) would probably not have occurred in the presence of more politically salient social cleavages which constrain the rate of change in party support to the relatively more glacial rate of change in social structure.

This finding provides one possible answer to the question of why changes in party support did not follow more closely upon the heels of the changes in social structure that have occurred since World War II. It may be that there were indeed changes in left voting consequential upon changes in employment and other social characteristics, but that these changes were so relatively modest as to have been masked by short-term swings in political fortunes at particular elections. Perhaps it was only when the decline had gone so far as to liberate voters from the constraints of cleavage politics that rapid electoral change became possible.

CONCLUSIONS

The study whose initial findings are reported here is broad-ranging, and is intended to illuminate many questions central to the understanding of electoral change. Of those presented here, the most important is certainly the implication that the changes we observe in particular countries are part of a common developmental process, masked only by the fact that some countries have reached a more advanced stage in this process than others. Single country studies, however illuminating, could not tell us this.

The availability of comparable cross-national studies over a lengthy time-period, in the shape of the Eurobarometer series, enables scholars to escape from the straitjacket of ethnocentrism. We believe that our study will provide good evidence of the utility of such a series. In addition to the concerns summarized in this essay, it uses Eurobarometer and other data to investigate the way in which generational replacement has contributed to electoral change, and the extent to which issue concerns have replaced social cleavages as influences on voting choice. It is able to arrive a general theory that explains these developments.

Of course, answers always generate further questions, and our findings are no exception. However, we believe that they will turn out to have fundamentally changed the research agenda in electoral studies by ensuring future research questions will have to be phrased in comparative terms. This means that Eurobarometer studies will become an ever more important resource for scholarly investigations of electoral choice.

REFERENCES

Beer, S. (1983) *Britain Against Itself* (London: Faber).
Franklin, M. (1985) *The Decline of Class Voting in Britain: Changes in the Basis of Electoral Choice, 1964–1983* (Oxford: Oxford University Press).
Franklin, M., T. Mackie and H. Valen, *et al.*, (1991) *Electoral Change: Responses to Changing Social and Attitudinal Structures in Sixteen Countries* (Cambridge: Cambridge University Press).
Lipset, S. and S. Rokkan (1967) *Party Systems and Voter Alignments* (New York: Free Press).
Nie, N., S. Verba and J. Petrocik (1981) *The Changing American Voter* (2nd ed.) (Cambridge, Mass.: Harvard University Press).
Prezeworski, A. and J. Sprague (1986) *Paper Stones: A History of Electoral Socialism* (Chicago: University of Chicago Press).
Rose, R. (ed.) (1974) *Electoral Behavior: A Comparative Handbook* (New York: Free Press).
Schattsneider, E. (1960) *The Semi-Sovereign People* (New York: Hold Rinehart and Winston).
Tarschys, D. (1977) 'The Changing Basis of Radical Socialism in Scandinavia' in K. Cerny, (ed.) *Scandinavia at the Polls: Recent Political Trends in Denmark, Norway and Sweden* (Washington, D.C.: American Enterprise Institute).

15 The Role of the Eurobarometer in the Study of European Elections and the Development of Comparative Electoral Research[1]

Cees van der Eijk, University of Amsterdam, and Hermann Schmitt, University of Mannheim

The lasting significance of the Eurobarometer, created by Jacques-René Rabier, for empirical social research and the politics of European integration can hardly be overestimated. Its most distinguished features are its cross-national comparative nature and its longitudinal character. Either of these two characteristics by itself would already make it a very important project. After all, both national longitudinal surveys and cross-national transversal studies are usually deemed to be invaluable, and neither of these two kinds of studies exist in abundance. The possibility of conjoint cross-national and longitudinal comparison, however, renders the Eurobarometer into a truly unique enterprise, the scientific and applied potential of which will be difficult to exhaust.

In addition to providing data for secondary analysis, the Eurobarometer inspires the development of empirical social science also in a quite different manner. Its very existence, its evident success and the wise policy of its directors which permits separately funded projects to hook up to the common Eurobarometer questionnaire and to share its contents, all allow and encourage social scientists to envisage and design research projects which would otherwise have been dismissed outright as not feasible.

In this essay we will report on one such project which, although funded separately from Eurobarometer, could probably not have been conceived, let alone executed without it. The project in question, the **European Elections Study 1989**, can not only serve as one example from many which owe their existence to the existence of Eurobarometer, but also as one which in its design capitalizes on the possibility of simultaneous cross-national and longitudinal comparison.

THE EUROPEAN ELECTIONS STUDY 1989 – ITS PLACE AMIDST OTHER RESEARCH

The European Elections Study 1989 is a study of behavior, motivations, relevant attitudes and perceptions of the electorates of the member states of the European Community in the European election of 1989. It consists of a series of questions which have been added to the regular questionnaires of Eurobarometers 30 (November 1988), 31 (April 1989) and 31A (June 1989). The motivations for designing and conducting a European Elections Study can be understood from different points of view, two of which will be addressed here. First, a European Elections Study can be looked at from the perspective of studying European elections and their place in the process of European integration. Second, and complementarily, it can be viewed from the perspective of comparative electoral research.

The Perspective of European Integration

Protagonists of European integration have always showed a particular interest in the direct elections of the European Parliament. When these elections took place for the first time, in 1979, those who lamented the slow pace of development of the European Community, hoped that a directly-elected Parliament would provide a powerful stimulus to further integration. Unlike the other institutions of the Community, the Parliament would have its own popular mandate and would exemplify by its very existence the desire of the populations of the member states for a unified Europe. Some of these expectations reflected a certain degree of naivety with respect to the immediate political consequences of these elections. The actual turnout disappointed not only those who hoped that the election would be a boost to further integration, but also startled more detached observers. It was widely speculated that abstentions reflected to some extent indifference or even opposition to the idea of European integration. In addition to this, most of the campaigns for the Euro-elections contained very little from which a 'popular mandate' for further integration could be deduced. In most countries the competition between parties for votes was dominated by general, mostly national, political concerns. The few exceptions to this general rule offered little solace from a pro-integration perspective: in Denmark particularly and to a lesser degree in Great Britain, party choice appeared to reflect a sizeable amount of anti-EC sentiment. These experiences of 1979, reinforced by similar ones in 1984, raised a number of questions concerning both turnout and party choice of European voters, to which an answer was needed in order to evaluate properly the implications of direct election results on the process of Communal integration. The most important of these questions are specified below.

To what extent does low turnout reflect a widespread unfamiliarity with, indeed the invisibility of, the European Parliament? Or is it rather the feeling that this Parliament, or possibly the entire Community, is irrelevant to one's concerns, which is responsible for poor turnout figures? Are those abstaining from the European ballots critical about, or even hostile towards European integration in general and the European Parliament in particular? Or could it be that the inability or unwillingness of national parties to represent the EC concerns of European voters is the real cause of deficient electoral participation? Moreover, to which extent can the voters' choices between parties competing in European elections be interpreted as support for or opposition against the process of European integration? Does party choice of electors reflect different EC policy preferences, or is it caused mainly by general and domestic reasons?

Quite obviously, different answers to these questions would suggest different conclusions concerning the process of European integration. For most, if not all of these questions, survey data are necessary in order to answer them. No wonder, then, that the instrument *par excellence* to provide such data, the Eurobarometer, has been utilized in various ways to this avail. Questions concerning electoral participation have since 1979 been included in the Eurobarometers directly previous to, and directly following the European elections of 1979 and 1984. Questions relating to affective and evaluative orientations vis-a-vis European integration, the European Community, and its various institutions and policies have been included frequently in Eurobarometer surveys and constitute an important part of the 'trend' questions which are included in each one.

Still, in spite of the wealth of material which has been collected, a number of important *lacunae* remain. These originate partly from the fact that certain questions were never included (i.e. intended party choice, or recalled party choice in the European elections), and partly from the fact that the regular Eurobarometer surveys take place too far before (March), and too late after (November) the moment at which the European elections actually take place (June) to allow certain questions to be reliably asked with respect to these elections.

The Perspective of Comparative Electoral Research

The study of elections and individual voters' behavior can be counted among the most developed areas of empirical political science. In virtually all Western democracies it has become customary to field large-scale surveys in election periods, aimed at uncovering the forces that shape voters' behavior, and thereby election results. A number of valuable attempts have been made to utilize national election studies from various countries for cross-national comparisons.[2] The volumes which resulted from these efforts exhibit on the one hand the strong common strands in design and conceptualization in the various election studies, yet on the other hand reveal painfully the incomparabilities between them. National election studies are indeed strongly national in character. This is so partly by necessity, reflecting the differences between political systems and cultures. It is also partly a matter of economy: it is often not deemed sufficiently worthwhile to include questions in a survey which would establish comparability with other countries, but which have little explanatory value in the case at hand. Such incomparabilities will continue to exist in design, inclusion of questions, manner of operationalization, question format, codings etc. because great value is – justifiedly – attached to generating longitudinal comparison within the national series of election studies.

Whatever the causes may be, the national peculiarities and resulting incomparabilities of election studies in various Western countries have repeatedly curtailed the scope and plagued the execution of efforts to arrive at a comparative and more general understanding of the electoral process and its place in the operation of democratic political systems. The situation is somewhat of a paradox: while the field of electoral research is among the oldest, and certainly most developed areas of empirical social research, it has not generated the kind of large-scale cross-national survey projects which have been so successful in the development of other areas of comparative mass political behavior.[3] Neither the various surveys conducted at the occasion of previous European elections, nor the Eurobarometers themselves, fill this void. The former have focussed in particular on media effects,[4] or on various kinds of elites and party candidates standing for European election,[5] while the coverage of topics by the latter was too limited and ad hoc in this respect.

THE INCEPTION OF THE EUROPEAN ELECTIONS STUDY 1989

As has been indicated above, a cross-national European election study would gratify various kinds of researchers: those primarily interested in European integration, and those primarily interested in comparative electoral studies (not to mention those who combine both interests). In April 1987, in the corridors of the Joint Sessions of Workshops of the ECPR which were hosted by the University of Amsterdam, first contacts took place between scholars from both strands of primary interests for the purpose of designing and organizing a cross-national European elections study, to be conducted in 1989. After this start subsequent meetings were held in Mannheim in May and October 1987, during which a project group actually constituted itself and agreed upon a programme of activities.

The group was composed of six people: Roland Cayrol, Mark Franklin, Manfred Kuechler, Renato Mannheimer, Hermann Schmitt and Cees van der Eijk. Although various reasons prevented him from being a member of the group, Karlheinz Reif has to be regarded as its prime initiator and continuing supporter.

Various kinds of expertise were represented in the group. All members were intimately acquainted with the political systems of a number of EC member states. Some had already been active in previous research regarding European elections: the communications study and the middle-level party elites surveys at the occasion of the 1979 election, the comparative and national analyses of electoral behavior in 1979 and 1984, and the like. Some were versed in running large-scale surveys and designing questionnaires. Some had specialized in survey research methodology and the intricacies of comparative research. Some had been investigating European integration from various perspectives for a long time. All in all, various kinds of theoretical, empirical, methodological and organizational competence were present, and they were distributed sufficiently evenly to ensure the existence of a knowledgeable forum for serious discussion and evaluation of suggestions and proposals, yet sufficiently diverse to allow everyone the pleasure and occasional exhilaration of gaining new knowledge and insight from such discussions.

During two crucial meetings in Mannheim, the group hammered out the design of the European Elections Study, drew up a strategy for securing funding, made a division of labour for preparatory work and set itself up in an organized fashion. In terms of organization two things were of great importance: first, the fact that the University of Mannheim opened up a special position, to be occupied by Hermann Schmitt, to serve as a communication and coordination centre for the group; second, that the members of the group could communicate very frequently and intensively in spite of their lack of funds to travel to joint meetings, by using the electronic mail services of EARN/Bitnet. Without this new technology of communication, the project could not have succeeded.

Securing funds to realize as much as possible of the ambitious plans which originally existed turned out to be a major and enduring task. In the end the necessary funds were secured from various sources. The largest chunk, covering the costs of the questions to be asked in June 1989, was supplied by the British Social and Economic Research Council. The remainder was brought together by selling prospectively reports of analyses of the (yet to be collected) data to interested media and other institutions throughout Europe. All in all, not everything could be realized that was originally part of the design of the proposed study. Some shifts had to be made as to when (i.e. in which of the three scheduled surveys) certain questions could be included. Some questions could not be replicated, as originally desired, and some could not eventually be included at all. Still, the major part of the original plan could be carried out.

THE EUROPEAN ELECTIONS STUDY 1989 – DESIGN AND CONTENTS

At the start of the project a number of goals were formulated which largely determined the form it was to take. First of all, the project should result in the collection of survey data, as that was deemed to be the only useful source of data to study the behavior of voters and to interpret the determinants of the election results to come. Second, it was decided that the study was to be a cross-national comparative one, and that it had to cover all member states of the European Community. Third, the study was to be one of national electorates, not of specific groups or elites. Fourth, a longitudinal aspect was considered to be highly desirable, in order to study possible processes of cognitive, attitudinal and behavioral mobilization. A panel design was not considered to be necessary, however, partly because the emphasis was to be less on the dynamics of individual choice and more on that of groups and categories of voters and on patterns of association.

It was evident from the start that the financial and organizational investments to achieve these goals would be terrifying, and that the time to secure the necessary funds was short. Consequently, a study from scratch was not feasible, and 'piggy-backing' on other projects was the only way to achieve the objectives mentioned above. The obvious candidate for this was the Eurobarometer, and if it had not existed and potentially been available as a 'locomotive', none of the members of the group would have been willing to venture into a 'mission impossible'. The fact that the Eurobarometer did exist as an organization and research infrastructure reduced the magnitude of the problems to be overcome to just large, but not necessarily insurmountable. It was a logical decision that the project had to be hooked up to the Eurobarometer. By doing so, all four preliminary goals mentioned above could be fulfilled.

The information which was deemed necessary for a satisfactory comparative voter study of the European elections can be described in terms of the following clusters of variables.

Dependent Variable

In terms of the dependent variable, voters' behavior in the European elections, it was considered unsatisfactory to ask only for electoral participation and party choice in June 1989. Previous research and theorizing suggested convincingly that electoral behavior in European elections is to a large extent determined by national factors.[6] Consequently, intended national electoral behavior was to be probed, too. Furthermore, drawing on theories on voter behavior and party competition developed in the context of the Dutch national election studies, it was decided that in addition to asking for the party a respondent had eventually voted for, it would be desirable to assess the electoral attractiveness of other parties as well, for both European and national elections.[7]

Independent Variables

Explanatory or independent variables fall into five categories. First, variables which have to do with voters' social situation, and in particular their location within the cleavage structure of each country: social structural characteristics. These are necessary for explaining behavior in terms of sociological and cleavage theories, and for controlling their wide-ranging effects on attitudes, perceptions, experiences and behavior while probing various explanations of voter behavior. To deal with the pervasive problems of (in)comparability which traditionally plague researchers working with these characteristics, it was decided to draw on the conclusions relating to social structural variables that were reached in the design and analyses of the comparative electoral change project directed by Franklin, Mackie and Valen.[8] To a large extent the relevant information could be obtained from 'standard' Eurobarometer questions: only a few items of this nature had to be added to the questionnaires.

A second block of independent variables deals with substantive issue concerns. Obviously, to the extent that issues play a role in voters' decision-making, they may arise from different contexts. At the least, the following kinds of issues have to be distinguished: (1) Community issues (extending membership, common agricultural policy, payments to and subsidies received from EC, etc.), (2) supra-national issues: issues pertaining to all member states but are not, or only partly related to the EC (defense, unemployment, etc.), and (3) country-specific issues (the most salient of these having been determined, country by country, by the members of the group as well as by country-specialists invited to contribute to the research by country-specific advice and data-analysis). While it would be desirable to tap absolute and relative saliency as well as perceptions of party competence for each one of such issues, it was at the same time imperative to keep the amount of questionnaire space for this block within reasonable limits. The solution chosen was to construct a list of twelve issues covering all of the sorts mentioned, and to have respondents rate the importance of each, then indicate the most important three from the entire list, and finally to indicate which party would be best able to solve these three most important problems. In order to capture possible changes in these respects, it was also decided to replicate part of this entire set of questions at least once.

The third block of variables which might be used to explain electoral behavior can be termed European orientations, which deal with the European Community, its institutions, the idea of European integration, etc. As far as affective aspects of such orientations are concerned, many of the indicators can be used which are regularly included in the Eurobarometer questionnaires. In addition to these, it was deemed important also to tap cognitive aspects of such orientations. This resulted in a series of items dealing with perceived importance of various European and national institutions.

A fourth block of explanatory variables deals with specific perceptions of the political parties from which a choice has to be made in European and national elections. One set of such perceptions deals with parties' stands vis-a-vis Europe. The second deals with perceptions of parties' location on a left-right scale. Other questions would tap respondents' own location or preference on both kinds of dimensions. The combination of these two kinds of information allows the comparative analysis of party-choice from perspectives of rational or purposeful behavior.

Media Exposure and Information

A final block of questions covers media exposure and information. These questions are of importance for two different, though related, research projects. One is the European Elections Study, for which this information is part of the equation which possibly explains electoral participation and party choice. The other is a project devoted to studying communication in the electoral process.[9] This information is of even more central importance to the goals of that project, and the most relevant expertise for designing these questions existed in the communications study group. Therefore, the contents of the questions on media which were to be appended to the normal Eurobarometer, were designed by the communications study group, which emphasized replicating a number of questions from the 1979 Communications Study.

Although it was originally planned to include a number of items to tap possible candidate influences on party choice in the European elections, these had to be dropped when available funds turned out to be insufficient to cover all questions originally planned. Other victims of not entirely reaching the desired funding-target were replications across the three waves of surveys. For a number of blocks of questions inclusion in all three waves was planned, but could only be realized in just two, or in a few cases even in a single wave.

The absence of party identification in the listing of concepts and variables above is not accidental, nor is its absence in the planned questionnaire of the European Voters Study. The standard Eurobarometer questionnaire contains a question which approaches the concept of party identification by asking for the party attachment of the respondents. Moreover, the battery of questions in which the electoral attractiveness of all parties is to be rated (refer to the description of the dependent variable, above) seemed to offer sufficient possibilities, particularly in combination with other available information from the questionnaire, to measure the relevant aspects of voter-party relations.

RESULTS OF THE STUDY: A PRELIMINARY REVIEW

Notwithstanding the impossibility of listing the ultimate results of the project, the results of (preliminary) analyses which have been conducted so far can be summarized, so that it is at least possible to acquire a taste of what is yet to come. In this section we will briefly review a number of conclusions reached so far.

Turnout and Approval for the EC

As has been indicated above, one of the major questions concerning turnout is to which degree electoral participation is tied to approval for the EC and its institutions. Analyses on the occasion of previous European elections have not been totally conclusive in this respect. Sometimes the result seemed to indicate that turnout was strongly related to approval of the European Community; sometimes such correlations were very weak. The interpretation of such findings was complicated by the absence of sufficient and sufficiently comparable data for the various member states, and by the fact that some analysts looked at the association in question in a raw form, while others first applied statistical controls for variation in other variables. The European Voter Study allows longitudinal and cross-national comparisons at the same time, and allows the inclusion in the analysis of relevant other variables such as a voter's level of political interest, political knowledge, party attachment, and background vari-ables.[10] Looking at the data of the first wave (i.e. Eurobarometer 30, November 1988), a sizeable correlation between EC-approval and (in-tended) electoral participation emerges after controlling for numerous other possibly confounding variables (r=.22 on an amalgamated file, containing the samples of all member-states, and weighted so as to reflect the numerical size of the various electorates). This result underscores a number of previous findings, which suggested that not-voting is to a considerable extent a function of opposition to, or at best indifference to the EC.

When looking at the results of the third wave (Eurobarometer 31A, June

1989), however, the picture changes drastically, and in quite an interpretable fashion. The association of turnout with 'EC-approval' declines to at most a mere borderline-significant value, a similar drop strikes the associations which existed between turnout on the one hand and information on the EC, and perceived saliency of the European parliament on the other. At the same time, the effect on reporting having voted of (national) party attachment and habitual voting increases. These results support previous analyses which showed little or no relation between individual turnout and EC-orientations. The advantage, however, which the present study offers, is that the seeming disparity of previous results can be interpreted and that a number of general conclusions can be drawn:

(1) all EC-related orientations are significantly related to intending to vote, reported half a year in advance, and hardly any of them is still related to reporting having voted immediately after the election. The obvious difference is in the stimulus which the question involves: intending to vote when the election is still to take place is not equivalent to actually having voted. The first is apparently much more an attitude and much less a behavior intention than previously thought.[11] This interpretation is strengthened by the fact that, while EC-related orientations become weaker, 'normal' correlates of individual turnout become stronger, which concurs with numerous results of national election studies. This pattern of changes in relationships holds for all countries.

(2) determinants of turnout have to be assessed on the basis of reported behavior and not on the basis of intended behavior.[12] In previous research, results based on report of actual behavior tended to show at most weak effects of EC-related orientations on turnout, a finding which is reinforced by the results from the European Voter Study.

(3) substantively most important: the effect of EC-related orientations on actual individual turnout is virtually negligible.

Issues and Euro-voting

How important are EC-related issues in voters' minds, and to what extent do they influence party choice? As described in the section on the design of the European Voter Study, the data contain a large section in which not only saliency of issues is assessed, but also the perceived competence of parties in dealing with these issues. The set of twelve issues was divided in three sections: supra-national issues (unemployment, environment, arms-limitations, stable prices), Community issues (political unification, agricultural surpluses, single market in 1992, and possible Turkish membership), and four high-saliency national issues. When asked which of these twelve problems are the most important, EC-issues rank among the lowest in all countries.[13] A large part of this set of questions was included twice: in the second wave (Eurobarometer 31, April 1989) and in the third wave (Eurobarometer 31A, June 1989). It is important that between these two points in time, the period that the campaigns for the European elections took place, no systematic difference in the saliency of EC-issues occurred. It seems that the campaigns were largely irrelevant to the place of EC-issues on the public agenda.

It turns out that large segments of the electorates, between one-third and one-half in the various countries, are unable to indicate which party is best able to handle the problem which they rank as the most important. This finding is not altered when a distinction is made between countries where national elections were concurrent or closely located to European elections, and other countries. This makes it unlikely that it can be accounted for by the European election providing too little stimulation to become acquainted with parties' performance and stands. Although this finding has little specific relevance for interpreting the results of the European elections, it is of distinct interest from the more general point of view of comparative electoral research.

Not surprisingly, to the extent that voters are able to indicate a party as 'most competent', their choice most often matches this perception. To which extent this match reflects just affective ties with parties, or, alternatively, issue-based choice, has to be ascertained in further analyses.

European and National Party Choice

The experience of the 1979 and 1984 European elections has contributed to the interpretation of European elections as second-order national elections.[14] From this, it may be expected that, if people turn out to vote, their European party choice will in many cases be determined by the same considerations which shape their national party choice. Although relatively small in number, those who report a different party choice for European and national electoral contests are particularly interesting. At least two different interpretations present themselves for these differences in party choice.

First of all, it may be that these people attempt to express arena-specific concerns in their vote, i.e. national concerns in national elections and European concerns in European ones. It turns out, however, that this group cannot be distinguished from other voters on the basis of European orientations (approval, information, perception of saliency). This leads to the suggestion that the similarity of party choice in European and national contexts may not so much arise from lack of interest or knowledge or preferences respecting Europe, but from the national party systems failing to provide voters with a choice in European elections that is relevant to their European concerns. The relevancy of this suggestion is difficult to gauge empirically. In terms of 'pro-' and 'anti-Europeanness' we can look at peoples' perceptions of parties' positions. This information in itself is not entirely unequivocal. In virtually all systems, the range of perceived party positions in this respect is restricted, reflecting limited possibilities to choose among parties on these grounds. On the other hand, however, voters do perceive differences between these parties which are often of sufficient magnitude to offer some choice or co-determination of choice by this aspect of European concerns. At this moment the currently available evidence seems to point at the absence of European considerations in party choice in European elections,[15] but a final verdict has to wait for further and more conclusive evidence.

The second interpretation for differences between party choice in European and national elections does not focus on European, but on national political concerns instead. From theories of second-order elections it can be deduced that people base their choice in second-order elections on the same kinds of national considerations which they employ in national first-order elections, but that the relative weight of these considerations will be different.[16] In at least a number of cases this second interpretation has been corroborated;[17] how much of the differences between European and (intended) national party choice can be explained by this phenomenon in various systems still has to be assessed.

Media Usage During the Campaign

The part of the third wave (Eurobarometer 31A) questionnaire which deals with exposure to political communication during the campaign allows not only comparisons between countries, but also between 1989 and 1979, when a Europe-wide survey was conducted in which the same items were included.[18] A first series of analyses shows not only that self-reported interest in the European election campaign is invariably low in 1989, but that it is considerably lower than in 1979.[19] Both phenomena, low interest and diminished interest compared to 1979, are reflected in the degree of exposure to each of a series of ten different channels of political communication. In addition to these common findings, the responses and their associations with background variables also hint at differences in communication cultures between the various member states of the Community. To which extent these cultural differences are related to differences in voters' electoral behavior remains a topic for further analysis.

Importance of Elected Institutions

The questionnaires of the first and third waves of the European Elections Study 1989 (Eurobarometer 30 and Eurobarometer 31A) contain a series of questions dealing with the perceived importance of political institutions at various levels of government, including that of the European Community. One of the reasons for including these questions was to assess to which extent a 'perceived irrelevance' interpretation of not-voting would hold water. Were this to be the case, one would expect in terms of aggregate statistics that the rank-order of actual turnout figures for different sorts of elected institutions would be identical to the rank-order of perceived relevance of the assemblies in question. Furthermore, on the individual level one would expect perceptions of relevance of the European Parliament to be correlated with voting or not-voting in June 1989. In addition to this, these perception questions can be used to construct typologies of voters, in which the various types differ in terms of which institutions they do or do not deem to be relevant.

From the data of the European Elections Study 1989, a moderate zero-order relationship emerges in all countries between intended electoral participation and the degree in which one perceives the European Parliament to be important. In most countries the zero-order correlation with actual turnout is considerably weaker. Although this is in accordance with prior expectations, a test of the irrelevancy-hypothesis to explain not turning out requires a causal model in which the confounding effects of other variables are eliminated. Doing so reveals that the causal impact of the perceived importance of the European Parliament on individual turnout varies considerably across countries, from a moderate to a non-significant value.[20]

Further analysis of the responses to the set of questions on perceived (ir)relevance of elected institutions shows that they form a strong cumulative scale, or, in other words, that they tap a single, unidimensional latent attitude. Obviously, this latent dimension cannot refer to just the European Parliament and its (in)significance *per se*, as little as it can refer merely to the local, regional or national parliaments. Rather, the common aspect in the responses refers to the feeling that elected assemblies are or are not important. In other words, people may differ in how important they consider the European Parliament to be, but these differences are mirrored in their perceptions of how important other kinds of parliaments are. The order of the items in the scale (i.e. the differences between the degree in which a sample rates various institutions as important) obviously does not reflect a characteristic of individual voters, but the largely common perception that some institutions are more important than others, with the European Parliament figuring as the least important one.[21]

These results can be seen as one example of a more frequent phenomenon, namely that responses to survey questions purported to measure attitudes, orientations and perceptions with respect to 'Europe' are actually manifestations of more general orientations towards politics, which also include national and sub-national realms.

The Effects of Party Attachment

The level of electoral mobilization has not only been lower for entire electorates in European elections compared to first-order national elections, but also for the subgroup of adherents or sympathizers of political parties. It has been suggested by second-order elections theory that large parties would have more difficulties to 'get out the vote' in European elections than smaller ones. And also that parties in national government, irrespective of their size, would systematically face greater problems in mobilizing their 'core' first-order election support. These expectations, drawn from analyses of aggregate European elections results, have been tested for the first time on the basis of relevant individual-level data from the third wave of the European Elections Study. Variation in the capability of political parties to mobilize their adherents is first of all explained by the presence or absence of (first-order) national elections which take place simultaneously with European elections, and by the presence or absence of compulsory voting. After this factor has been taken into account, it has been found that parties in government do not, as could have been expected on the basis of earlier research, perform worse in mobilizing their adherents and sympathizers: they even did somewhat better than other parties in the 1989 European elections. And large parties were not found to be disadvantaged in getting their adherents and sympathizers to the European ballots – they did equally well or even better than their smaller competitors.

Large parties can be shown, however, to suffer from a different kind of relative disadvantage in European as compared to national elections: they profit in European elections to a much smaller degree than in national elections from the 'pull' exerted by their sheer size. At the same time, the adherents and sympathizers of large parties appear to be more vulnerable in European elections than those of smaller parties to mobilizing appeals of competing parties.[22]

These results demonstrate that a number of expectations which were drawn from aggregate European elections results do not apply when appropriate individual level data are used. As a result, earlier theorizing on the differences between first-order and second-order elections needs to be reconsidered.

Summing up

The various topics of which results have been summarized above constitute only a part of the numerous analyses which are under way on the basis of the data of the European Elections Study. An ambitious programme of analyses and publications has been drawn up in which attention will be paid to, amongst others, the sources and background of EC-related attitudes, the structure of party competition in European and national elections, the ideological components of the various countries' political cultures, comparisons of the impact of party attachments, and characterizations of the electorates of two relatively new (but hopefully not comparable) phenomena in Europe, the 'green vote' and the 'brown vote'. All together, it is indisputable that the efforts invested in the European Elections Study 1989 will generate a considerable return.

CONCLUDING REMARKS

Getting everything together to make the European Elections Study come true has been a formidable task which has dominated the agenda of the members of the project group for a considerable period. Still, in their opinion, it has definitely been worth the effort, as is amply illustrated by the summaries above of analyses which have already been concluded and which are under way. It should not be forgotten, however, that without the existence of the Eurobarometer, the European Elections Study 1989 could not have been conceived, let alone executed. This thought is a sobering one, and may serve as a reminder of our enormous indebtedness to Jacques-René Rabier who could not, as we could, build on the existence of a truly European infrastructure of survey research, but who had to construct it instead.

NOTES

1. The project reported in this article is, as will be evident from the text, a collective enterprise by a group in which the two authors take part. Therefore, to the extent that this project and this report deserve praise, it should be accredited to the other members of the group (mentioned in the text) as well, while any errors of omission or commission are entirely ours. In the description in this chapter of the design and contents of the European Elections Study, we have made use of parts of an extensive study description which was drawn up by the entire group for the purpose of fundraising.
2. Refer to, amongst others, Rose (1974), Budge, Crewe and Farlie (1976), Dalton, Flanagan and Beck (1984), Crewe and Denver (1985), and Franklin, Mackie and Valen (1991, forthcoming).
3. Among the most important cross-national studies in other fields of mass political behavior which have greatly contributed to the theoretical and empirical development of those areas are, Almond and Verba (1963), Verba et. al. (1978), Barnes, Kaase et. al. (1979), Inglehart (1977).
4. Refer to Blumler (1983).
5. Refer to, amongst others, the 'middle level elite project' (Reif et. al., 1980) and the Members of European Parliament Study (Inglehart et. al., 1980).
6. Refer to, amongst others, Reif and Schmitt (1980), Reif (1984b, 1985a).

7. Refer to Van der Eijk and Niemöller (1984), Van der Eijk, Niemöller and Tillie (1986).
8. Refer to Franklin, Mackie and Valen (1991, forthcoming).
9. This project follows up on earlier studies in this area, particularly during the 1979 European election, and which were reported in Blumler (1983).
10. The following is based upon the analyses conducted by Schmitt and Mann-heimer, reported in the special issue of the *European Journal of Political Research* (1991).
11. With respect to the differences between attitudes and behavior intentions, refer to, amongst others, Ajzen and Fishbein (1980), Fishbein and Ajzen (1975) and Liska (1984). For applications in electoral research, refer also to Granberg and Holmberg (1988).
12. It has to be stressed, however, that the report of actual behavior must follow the act itself relatively soon, as recall of behavior acquires an increasingly attitudinal (rather than reporting) character with an increasing time-span between act and report.
13. These and the other findings reported in this section have been taken from Kuechler's analyses of issues in the European Voters Study, reported in his contribution in the special issue of the *European Journal of Political Research* (1991).
14. Refer to n. 6.
15. The results in this section summarize findings of two papers presented at the Joint Sessions of Workshops of the ECPR in Paris, 1989: Mark Franklin, 'Euro-voting in European elections', and Cees van der Eijk and Erik Oppen-huis, 'Parties' attitudes toward the European Community'.
16. Refer to n. 6.
17. Refer to Van der Eijk and Oppenhuis (1990).
18. Refer to Blumler (1983).
19. This summary is based on analyses to be reported by Cayrol in the special issue of the *European Journal of Political Research* (1991).
20. Refer to n. 10.
21. This is a little surprising in view of the fact that the European Parliament is the only one of the institutions addressed, the election of which does not have any direct consequences for any government or executive body. Results of these analyses have been reported for the Netherlands in detail by Van der Eijk and Oppenhuis (1990). The cross-national analyses will be reported separately.
22. The results summarized in this section have been reported by Schmitt (1990).

REFERENCES

Ajzen, I. and M. Fishbein (1980) *Understanding attitudes and predicting social behavior* (Englewood Cliffs, N.J.: Prentice-Hall).
Almond, G. and S. Verba (1963) *The civic culture. Political attitudes and democracy in five nations* (Princeton, N.J.: Princeton University Press).
Barnes, A., M. Kaase et. al. (1979) *Political action: mass participation in five western democracies* (Beverly Hills, Ca: Sage).
Blumler, D. (ed.) (1983) *Communicating to voters. Television in the first European Parliamentary Elections* (London: Sage).

Budge, I., I. Crewe and D. Farlie (eds) (1976) *Party identification and beyond: representation of voting and party competition* (New York: Wiley).
Crewe, I. and D. Denver (eds) (1985) *Electoral change in western democracies: patterns and sources of electoral volatility* (London: Croom Helm).
Dalton, R. J., S. C. Flanagan and P. A. Beck (eds) (1984) *Electoral change in advanced industrial democracies: realignment or dealignment?* (Princeton, N.J.: Princeton University Press).
Eijk, C. van der (1984a) 'Dutch voters and the European elections of 1979', in: K. Reif (ed.), *European elections 1979/1981 and 1984* (Berlin: Quorum) pp. 55–61.
Eijk, C. van der (1984b) 'The Netherlands', *Electoral Studies* (special issue on the European elections of 1984) 3, 302–05.
Eijk, C. van der (1989) 'The Netherlands', *Electoral Studies* (special issue on the European elections of 1989) 8, pp. 305–12.
Eijk, C. van der and B. Niemöller (1983) *Electoral change in the Netherlands. Empirical results and methods of measurement* (Amsterdam: CT-press).
Eijk, C. van der and B. Niemöller (1984) 'Het potentiële electoraat van de Nederlandse politieke partijen', *Beleid en Maatschappij*, 11, 192–204.
Eijk, C. van der and B. Niemöller (1985) 'Voter behavior in the European elections. Suggestions to investigate the effect of "European" factors', paper, presented at Joint Sessions of ECPR, Barcelona.
Eijk, C. van der, B. Niemöller and J. Tillie (1986) 'The two faces of "future vote": voter utility and party potential', paper, presented at Joint Sessions of Workshops, ECPR Göteborg.
Eijk, C. van der and E. Oppenhuis (1990) 'Turnout and second-order effects in the European elections of June 1989. Evidence from the Netherlands', *Acta Politica*, 25, 67–94.
Fishbein, M. and I. Ajzen (1975) *Belief, attitude, intention and behavior: an introduction to theory and research* (Reading, Mass.: Addison-Wesley).
Franklin, M., T. Mackie and H. Valen (eds.) (1991, forthcoming) *Electoral Change: responses to evolving social and attitudinal structures in seventeen democracies* (Cambridge: Cambridge University Press).
Granberg, D. and S. Holmberg (1988) *The political system matters. Social psychology and voting behavior in Sweden and the United States* (Cambridge: Cambridge University Press).
Inglehart, R. (1977) *The silent revolution* (Princeton, NJ: Princeton University Press).
Inglehart, R., J-R. Rabier, I. Gordon and C. L. Sorensen (1980) 'Broader powers to the European parliament? The attitudes of candidates', *European Journal for Political Research* 8, 113–32.
Liska, A. (1984) 'A critical examination of the causal structure of the Fishbein/Ajzen attitude-behavior model', *Social Psychology Quarterly* 47, 61–74.
Mokken, R. J. (1971) *A theory and procedure of scale analysis* (The Hague: Mouton).
Niemöller, B. and W. H. van Schuur (1983) 'Stochastic models for unidimensional scaling: Mokken and Rasch', in D. MacKay, N. Schofield and P. Whiteley (eds), *Data analysis and the social sciences* (London: Frances Pinter) pp. 120–70.
Reif, K. (ed.) (1984a) *European Elections 1979/81 and 1984* (Berlin: Quorum).
Reif, K. (1984b) 'National Electoral Cycles and European elections 1979 and 1984', *Electoral Studies* 5, 289–96.
Reif, K. (1985a) 'Ten second-order national elections', in K. Reif (ed.), (1985b), pp. 1–36.
Reif, K. (1985b) *Ten European Elections: Campaigns and results of the 1979/1981*

first direct election to the European Parliament (Aldershot: Gower).

Reif, K., R. Cayrol and O. Niedermayer (1980) 'National political parties' middle level elites and European integration', *European Journal of Political research*, 8, pp. 91–112.

Reif, K. and H. Schmitt (1980) 'Nine second order elections', *European Journal of Political Research* 8, 3–44.

Rose, R. (ed.) (1974) *Electoral behavior. A comparative handbook* (New York: Free Press).

Schmitt, H. (1990) 'Party attachment and party choice in the European election of June 1989', *International Journal of Public Opinion Research*, 1990.

Verba, S., N. H. Nie and J. Kim (1978) *Participation and political equality. A seven nation comparison* (Cambridge: Cambridge University Press).

16 The Dynamics of Mass Political Support in Western Europe: Methodological Problems and Preliminary Findings

Manfred Kuechler, Hunter College (City University of New York)

INTRODUCTION

Following the Vietnam War and the student movement of the sixties the question of mass support for the political system received much attention both in Europe and elsewhere (e.g. Crozier, Huntington, and Watanuki, 1975). Depending on one's political preferences, a shift from representational democracy to large scale citizen involvement in politics ('grass root democracy' or '*Basisdemokratie*') was anticipated with joy and hope or fear and reluctance. Conservatives asked whether politics would still be benign; liberals proclaimed a silent revolution, the dawn of a Postmaterialist age in which old cleavages would become obsolete and party politics would be restructured along a 'new politics – old politics' dimension (e.g. Inglehart, 1977, Dalton et al., 1984).

Today, the 'crisis of democracy' rhetoric has by and large subsided. The revolutionary fervor of the New Left seem like faint memories from a past long gone. The students of the eighties are well integrated, the youth of today much more moderate than their counterparts a decade or so ago. Incremental social change – reflected in both public opinion and institutional arrangements – rather than marked disruption of the established social and political order seems to be the trade mark of the eighties. Consequently, conservatives have gained new confidence in the vitality and adaptability of Western democracies. And in fact, there is precious little evidence that the public in any of the Western European countries is ready for radical change by way of revolutionary action.[1]

So why address the issue of mass support for the political system? There are no imminent threats to the political system of the Western European democracies. But most of these countries face serious economic and social problems, a possibly widening gap between the promises of the capitalist welfare state and the actual output. Unemployment is the prime example. Compared to the mid-seventies, today unemployment is on a higher level throughout Western Europe; stagnating now in some countries, rising in others (see Figure 16.1(1)–16.1(8)). A lasting solution to unemployment is not in sight. In addition, incompatibilities between economic growth and protection of natural resources have become increasingly apparent.

The structural problems of advanced industrialized countries extend beyond traditional economic and new environmental concerns. The rise of new social movements (see e.g. Dalton and Kuechler, 1990) and related movement parties testifies to the existence of a more fundamental dissatisfaction with prevailing norms and values, a '*Sinnkrise*' (a search for meaning in life) of sorts. The number of core activists of these movements is small. It would be foolish to assume that all those expressing sympathy towards new social movements in public opinion polls share the fundamental concerns of alternative movement activists.[2] Yet the very limited success of movement parties in most Western European countries (most notably in France and Great Britain) may not sufficiently reflect the extent of latent discontent with the existing social and political order.

The established political order faces a challenge to which it must respond effectively. It remains to be seen whether Western European democracies will be able to meet the challenges lying ahead. Thus far it appears that the odds are in favor of gradual change and adaption, producing long-term stability, but much will depend on the public's continued support for the political system. It is useful, then, to examine past patterns and current trends of mass support in order to assess the future of the established political system.

A comparative analysis of this sort is faced with three sets of related problems. First, there is the measurement problem. 'Mass political support' is a general theoretical idea that does not lend itself easily to conceptual specification and subsequent operationalization. Second, there is the problem of data availability. Given the ambiguity of the concept, no single indicator is likely to be generally accepted as a valid measure. However, variation over time can meaningfully be assessed even if a given indicator is flawed: we need to base our empirical analysis on a fairly long time series, derived from repeated cross-sectional surveys. Finally, there is the problem of cross-national validity and indicator equivalence.

In this short paper I will take a pragmatic approach, using Eurobarometer data covering the period from 1976 to 1988, in an attempt to gauge their potential as the basis for a more comprehensive study of mass support for given political systems. Departing from conventional procedures, I will first briefly introduce the data, and then discuss the conceptual and methodological problems involved. In other words, rather than operationalize a theoretically defined concept, I will start with an *available* empirical indicator and assess its conceptual meaning. I will then discuss some preliminary findings.

DATA

Though there has been a vast amount of theoretical speculation about mass support for the political system, empirical data reflecting individual dispositions related to the problem are hard to find. To my knowledge, the Eurobarometer surveys are the sole source for survey data based on identical question wording over time[3] and covering a large, theoretically meaningful collectivity of countries – the members of the European Community.[4] The Eurobarometers contain a series of 'trend' questions that are repeated in every, or nearly every survey. Two of these relate to mass support for the political system:

1. 'On the whole, are you very satisfied, fairly satisfied, not very satisfied, or not at all satisfied with the way democracy works (in your country)?'
2. 'On this card [show card] are three basic kinds of attitudes vis-a-vis the society we live in. Please choose the one which best describes your own opinion.
    1. The entire way our society is organized must be radically changed by revolutionary action.
    2. Our society must be gradually improved by reforms.
    3. Our present society must be valiantly defended against all subversive forces.'

In my opinion, the second indicator is fundamentally flawed. While response choices 1 and 2 as well as 1 and 3 are mutually exclusive, choices 2 and 3 are complementary in nature, addressing two different dimensions. One dimension could be called the 'mode of social change' (reform vs revolution), the second dimension may be labeled 'mode of system preservation' (valiant vs laissez faire). Hence, this Eurobarometer trend question is 'double-barrelled', to use the technical jargon of survey research. These data allow us to assess the extent of support for the revolutionary option only. Here, the results are not particularly interesting; there is limited support for this option, rarely exceeding 10 per cent in any country at any time.[5] In keeping with national stereotypes, the French and Italian publics generally score highest, and the Danish and German publics lowest (falling between 1 and 4 per cent of the respondents in each country). I will restrict my attention to the first indicator.

The first indicator was included in identical form in all Eurobarometer surveys since the fall of 1976 (EB 6) with the exception of the spring surveys in 1980 and 1981 (EB 13 and EB 15). This creates a time series of twenty-two data points spanning a period of almost twelve years (up to the spring of 1988 – Eurobarometer 29).

CONCEPTUAL AND MEASUREMENT PROBLEMS

Practical restrictions have governed my choice of a single indicator. To move beyond mindless number-crunching, it is necessary to reflect on the concept that may be measured by this indicator. Given the wide recognition Easton's work (1965, 1975) has received, his concept of 'diffuse' and 'specific' support seems to be a logical point of departure for this discussion.

In his more recent article Easton (1975) deals extensively with criticism that questions the value of the specific/diffuse dichotomy. In particular, Easton rejects the notion that the two forms of support are so intimately linked that it is next to impossible to measure both forms independently. He cites Dennis' work (1966) as a 'most direct application of the concept of diffuse support' (Easton, 1975: 444). However, Dennis' survey items hardly fit Easton's fundamental definition of diffuse support as restated below:

> The briefest way of describing the primary meaning of diffuse support is to say that it refers to evaluations of what an object is or represents – to general meaning it has for a person – *not of what it does*. It consists of a *reservoir of favorable attitudes* or good will that helps members to accept or tolerate outputs to which they are opposed or the effects of which they see as damaging to their wants.[6]

Clearly, diffuse support is perceived as a long-term affective predisposition (very much like the concept of party identification). Diffuse support – as defined above – will not measure short-term reactions to the performance of the system (as opposed to that of the current incumbent.[7] But will 'specific support'? No, since 'it is only indirectly relevant, if at all, to the input of support for the regime or the political community' (Easton, 1975: 437). Easton's definitions are plagued with an asymmetry that fails to recognize an important form of support. Specific and diffuse support are distinguished by cognitions and assessments (including those based on little factual knowledge of the persons in charge) versus emotions and affections. While diffuse support can be displayed towards either political authorities or the regime (Easton, 1975: 447), the notion of specific support is more restricted in regard to its possible object. Easton's typology can be summarized in a four-fold table:

Obviously, the Eurobarometer indicator does not fit into Easton's

TABLE 16.1: *Types of support according to Easton*

Object Form	Incumbent	System
cognitive/ evaluative	Specific	??
emotional/ affective	Diffuse	Diffuse

conceptual frame. It is directed at the system, but it invites an evaluative assessment rather than a purely emotional response. Thus, it measures neither diffuse nor specific support in the Eastonian sense, but a form of support not recognized or inadequately conceptualized by Easton.

I feel that the concept of 'diffuse support' is useful, but that its definition is unduly restrictive. The separation of cognitions and evaluations from emotions and affections makes sense analytically, but does not reflect the empirical organization of information in the respondent's mind. This is to say, that in empirical reality emotions and affections are always intricately interwoven with cognitions and evaluations. Emotions and affections bias cognitions and evaluations (either positively or negatively), but these in turn affect emotions, and they can rarely be disentangled empirically. There are some exceptions, but these can be found in inter*personal* relationships rather than in person-symbol relationships. For example, a mother's love for her child may be totally unaffected by any sort of cognition, even cognition not biased or selectively reinterpreted in the first place. But interpersonal relationships of this sort are not common. The rising divorce rate illustrates the instability of affections in confrontation with the hard facts of life. In general, I will refer to any relationship in which affections are not significantly altered by (unbiased) cognitions as 'bondage'.

The question then is whether it is plausible to assume that the relationship between the individual citizen and the political system is predominantly of the bondage type. If so, Easton's definition should be followed closely in designing an adequate empirical indicator. If not, diffuse support should be reconceptualized by including an evaluative component. Yet, the relationship between citizen and political system is difficult to assess empirically. In addition, historical and national variations have to be taken into account.

Extreme patriotism may appear as an indication of a bondage-type relationship. But analytically the object here is the (national) political community rather than the political system. At times, people may be ready to die for their country, but are they ready to die for their 'political system', the 'regime' – unless they do not separate the two? Empirically, a lack of separation seems to be the rule rather than the exception in Western democracies.[8] Patriotism indicates a bondage-type relationship between citizen and political system only when system and community are confounded.

However, even if we consider patriotism as a valid indicator of the citizen-regime relationship, how frequent is this type of relationship? Here, cultural and historical differences across nations become important. Given the recent past, the relative absence of patriotic manifestations in German public life[9] does not necessarily indicate a lack of support for the regime (or the community), but may be an indication of political sophistication.[10] In contrast, patriotism in Germany is still the trademark of those who have not learnt this political lesson. Given Germany's history there does not seem to be a safe dividing-line between patriotism and (national) chauvinism. Rather than indicating diffuse support for the democratic system, patriotism would evidence a lack of such support. The case of Germany may be atypical. However, I contend that as far as a general trend is concerned, the days of bondage-type patriotism are past, for all of Europe. Emotions and affections toward symbolic objects – like the 'political system' – are affected by cognitions and evaluations, and vice versa.

Easton also distinguishes between two aspects of diffuse support: trust and legitimacy. There are several problems with the trust dimension – one addressed by Easton himself (1975: 450).[11] The objects of trust are not restricted; politicians, institutions, the regime at large are all eligible objects of trust. However, as Citrin (1974: 974) has convincingly argued, 'many people readily combine intense patriotic sentiments with cynicism about politicians'.[12] This argument can be extended: A cynical (or more appropriately, realistic) assessment of politics and politicians might guarantee stability as much as blind trust. There is additional empirical evidence that 'political cynicism' (or more precisely; a cynical assessment of politicians as a group) is not significantly related to other system support indicators. Muller et al. (1982) demonstrate that the 'trust in government' index bears no relationship to measures of antisystem behavior in samples from urban areas in the United States (New York), Mexico, and Costa Rica. Data from West Germany show no relation of (generic, not person/ party specific) cynicism items to system support or ideological position (Kuechler, 1982: 52). This clearly suggests that we should exclude 'cynicism toward politicians' in constructing a measure for diffuse support.

In sum, I conclude that diffuse support should be understood as actor- and issue-unspecific support for the political system, largely grounded in emotions and affections which serve to selectively perceive and interpret cognitive elements, but which are reciprocally affected by middle range evaluative assessments. Diffuse support reflects a sort of emotionally-biased running tally the citizen keeps on the performance of the system.

Notwithstanding the problems of single indicator measurement in general, the Eurobarometer question about political satisfaction seems to be a reasonable indicator for the concept of 'diffuse' support so defined. And certainly, the choice of this indicator is easily defendable for practical reasons.[13]

INDICATOR EQUIVALENCE ACROSS NATIONS

While the Eurobarometer question is a reasonable indicator for 'diffuse' system support overall, it is quite conceivable that the question wording does not constitute the same stimulus in all participating nations.[14] To illustrate this point: Any evaluation involves a comparison of the targeted object with alternatives (which are sometimes only implicit). The final assessment is contingent upon this choice of alternatives. In general, respondents may compare the current system at work with an idealized version of how democracy should work. And there may be national differences in the prevailing idealized image of 'democracy'. In addition, the comparison of the actual form with the idealized version may be supplemented or even replaced by looking at more concrete alternatives. In particular, German respondents may compare the Western form of democracy with the other democracy in the German Democratic Republic. Or they may compare it with the Nazi regime of the recent past. Though literally the same question, a different national context can change the meaning of the question in important details.

Looking beyond verbally-expressed support to the ultimate problem of stability of the political system, the relationship between attitudes (as measured in public opinion surveys) and behavior and behavioral intentions is likely to be contingent upon the (national) political culture. It would be shortsighted to consider the Eurobarometer indicator (or most other indicators) as a cross-nationally valid measure of the absolute level of system support. A comparison of national marginal distributions is not meaningful. For example, in Italy fewer respondents express satisfaction with the way democracy works than in any other Western European country. However, this does not necessarily indicate that the political system in Italy is much less stable than in the other countries.[15]

Elsewhere (Kuechler, 1987) I have discussed a number of methodological principles for the analysis of cross-national survey data. These include the principle that as a first stage, data for each nation should be analyzed separately to establish contingency patterns – eventually utilizing data from other sources such as census data, economic indicators, etc. and taking systemic characteristics into account. Cross-national comparisons should be made in a second stage on the level of contingency patterns. These comparisons may utilize statistical techniques, but are likely to include non-quantitative reasoning.

TABLE 16.2: *Level of satisfaction with democracy over time (1976–88)*

Country	Mean	Range	Minimum	Maximum	Lin. Trend*
F	44.4	18.1	35.3	53.4	.44 (.09)
B	47.8	23.9	33.8	57.7	.17 (.01)
NL	58.9	19.4	49.5	68.9	−.54 (.14)
D	73.3	15.3	64.8	80.1	−.59 (.19)
I	21.9	18.2	12.1	30.3	1.06 (.58)
DK	67.2	19.2	55.4	74.6	.86 (.38)
EIR	52.8	28.6	42.4	71.0	−1.42 (.41)
GB	56.5	15.8	48.6	64.4	.02 (.00)

* First entry is the unstandardized regression coefficient, the second figure is the coefficient of determination using standard OLS estimation.

   I will follow this principle in the data analysis presented below. However, given the space limitations, I will focus on one particular pattern found in an earlier analysis of the West German case (Kuechler, 1986)[16]: an apparent relationship between the state of the economy (as reflected in two major economic indicators, the unemployment rate and the change in the consumer price index, or 'inflation rate') and the level of satisfaction with democracy. As in the German case, a number of mitigating factors must be considered, through a detailed qualitative analysis of the political arena in each country over time. This paper then provides an outline of research yet to be completed rather than a fully completed analysis.

SOME PRELIMINARY FINDINGS

Table 16.2 provides simple summary statistics for the support indicator separately for each nation. These statistics lead to the following observations: First, the mean level of satisfaction with democracy varies greatly, between a low of 21.9 per cent for Italy and a high of 73.3 per cent for West Germany. As noted above, this difference in overall level may not have any deeper meaning at all. Yet, it reemphasizes the view that the level of the indicator must be assessed in the context of the national political culture.

   Second, there is no substantial lasting change in any nation, with the possible exception of Ireland. There are no strong linear trends. In most cases a simple regression line[17] does not fit the data well. Consequently the sign of the regression coefficient – reflecting the direction of a steady upward or downward trend – is mostly an artifact of method. Judged by the coefficient of determination, sufficient fit (lasting linear trend) is achieved for Italy, Denmark, and Ireland only. For Italy we note an upward linear trend of one percentage point per year, for Denmark we find a similar

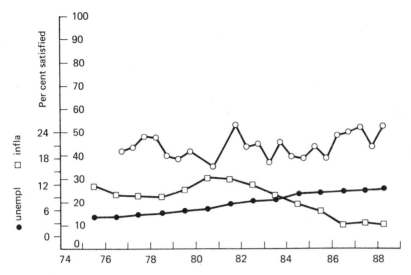

SOURCE: Eurobarometer surveys; OECD Economic Outlook
FIGURE 16.1(1): *Satisfaction with democracy – France*

upward trend of about .9 percentage points per year. A closer inspection of the Irish time series (see Figure 16.1(7) indicates that a downward trend between 1978 and 1983 was followed by a phase of consolidation in the last five years. Thus, the summary statistics for Ireland in Table 16.2 are misleading inasmuch as an earlier downward trend has come to a halt.

A more detailed inspection of the remaining five national time series (see Figures 16.1(1)–16.1(4), 16.1(8) shows several downward phases in mass support for the political system, but no general lasting erosion over time.[18] Except in Great Britain, these downward phases do not follow any short-term cyclical pattern such as the electoral cycle. The seemingly plausible hypotheses that satisfaction with democracy rises and falls with the amount of attention paid to the voter (reaching a peak in electoral campaigns) is not supported by the data – either in general or in Great Britain, where satisfaction with democracy reached a temporary maximum shortly before the 1983 and the 1987 elections, but declined sharply before the 1979 elections.[19]

The 'cycle of attention' hypothesis seems incompatible with the data. Let us examine possible linkages between the state of the economy and mass support for the political system. My earlier analysis of the German case (Kuechler, 1986) showed that the decline of mass support was largely synchronous with a simultaneous rise of both unemployment and inflation. In addition, a qualitative analysis of the political arena at the time indicated a lack of strong and decisive political leadership in general. This lack of leadership was evidenced by internal struggles within the governing

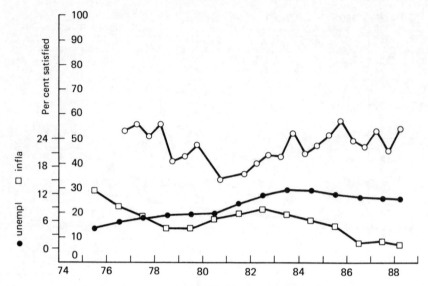

SOURCE: Eurobarometer surveys; OECD Economic Outlook
FIGURE 16.1(2): *Satisfaction with democracy – Belgium*

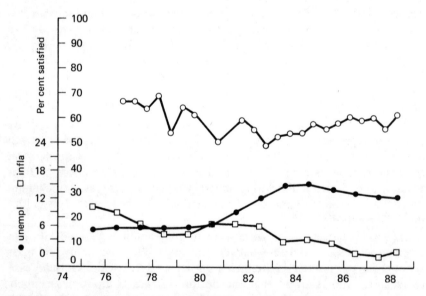

SOURCE: Eurobarometer surveys; OECD Economic Outlook
FIGURE 16.1(3): *Satisfaction with democracy – The Netherlands*

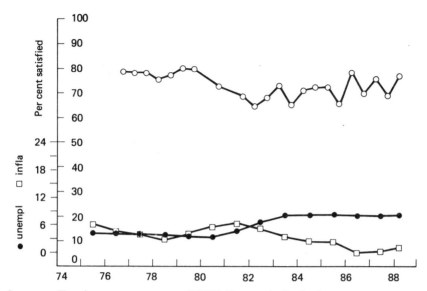

SOURCE: Eurobarometer surveys; OECD Economic Outlook
FIGURE 16.1(4): *Satisfaction with democracy – W. Germany*

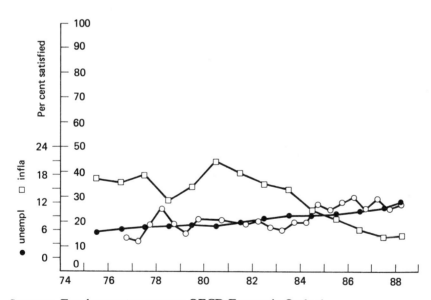

SOURCE: Eurobarometer surveys; OECD Economic Outlook
FIGURE 16.1(5): *Satisfaction with democracy – Italy*

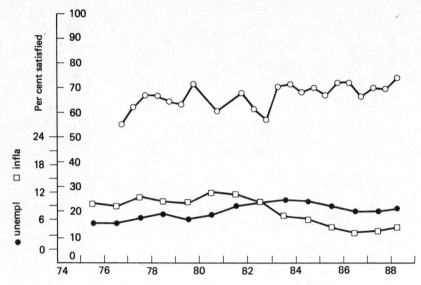

SOURCE: Eurobarometer surveys; OECD Economic Outlook
FIGURE 16.1(6): *Satisfaction with democracy – Denmark*

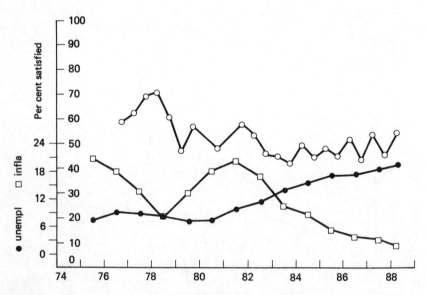

SOURCE: Eurobarometer surveys; OECD Economic Outlook
FIGURE 16.1(7): *Satisfaction with democracy – Ireland*

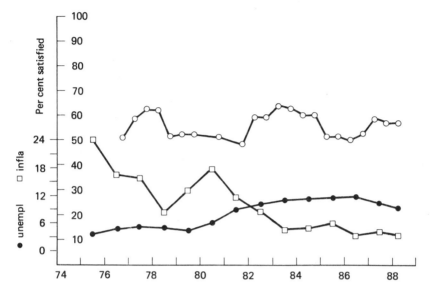

SOURCE: Eurobarometer surveys; OECD Economic Outlook

FIGURE 16.1(8): *Satisfaction with democracy – Great Britain (excluding Northern Ireland)*

coalition (of Social Democrats and Liberals) and also within the major coalition party. There, a popular chancellor (Schmidt) was rapidly losing the support of the party's rank-and-file. Furthermore, a series of spectacular terrorist attacks (including the assassination of prominent figures in public life) apparently evoked fear of chaos and disorder in the public. These components are almost impossible to assess in quantitative terms. An assessment of this sort requires a careful reconstruction of the 'political climate' relative to the specific national political culture. In contrast, the link between the state of the economy and the level of mass support can be assessed much more easily. Let us turn to these results.

A wealth of economic indicators are available, but most of them have no clear meaning to the general public. Consequently my analysis is restricted to two indicators, the unemployment rate and the inflation rate.[20] Both indicators are frequently reported in the mass media and both relate directly to the life of the average citizen. It is reasonable to assume that the public at large (and not just those with strong political interest) is aware of related information.[21] This is a necessary (but not sufficient) condition to establish a causal link between the state of the economy (one important output of the political system) and the level of mass support for the system. Yearly values for both indicators[22] are displayed, together with the current level of mass support, in figures 16.1(7) to 16.1(8).[23]

Examining possible links between the state of the economy and the level

TABLE 16.3: *Downward trends in satisfaction with democracy and in the economy*

| Country | | Satisfaction with Democracy | | | Economy | | |
		Period	(Fit)*	Decline†	Period	Unemployment	Inflation
F		F77–F80	(.77)	–13.6 –4.2	78–80	+1.0	+4.5
B		S78–F80	(.59)	–22.3 –6.6	78–82	+4.6	+4.2
NL		S78–F80	(.42)	–18.2 –5.1	78–81	+3.7	+2.6
D		S79–S82	(.98)	–15.3 –5.2	79–81	+1.3	+2.2
I		none		n/a		none	
DK		none		n/a		none	
EIR		S78–F83	(.53)	–28.6 –3.2	79–81	+2.8	+7.1
GB	a)	S78–F81	(.55)	–13.8 –2.7	none		
	b)	S83–S86	(.90)	–13.8 –5.2	83–85	+0.4	+1.5

* Fit is the coefficient of determination of a OLS regression line fitted for the period.
† First figure is the difference between empirical figures at beginning and end of the period; second figure is the unstandardized regression coefficient.

of satisfaction, down phases are summarized in Table 16.3. Economic down phases are defined by simultaneous continuous increase in both indicators over a period of at least two years. Down phases in mass support are defined as periods of at least two and half years (five time points) with a drop of at least 10 percentage points which can adequately be described by a straight regression line.[24] Overall, we find a good deal of support for a link between the state of the economy and the level of mass support. First, for the two countries with a continuous linear upward trend in satisfaction with democracy (Italy and Denmark) there are no periods of economic downturn. Second, all but one period of decline in satisfaction with democracy shows at least partial overlap with a phase of economic decline. The one deviating case is the first down phase in Great Britain.[25]

However, the association between level of support and state of the economy is far from perfect. In Belgium the support curve reaches its turning point well before the end of the economic down phase, whereas in Ireland the slide in mass support continues well beyond the point where the economy takes a turn for the better.

CONCLUSION

Clearly, the state of the economy does not fully determine the level of mass support. Indeed, it would be naive to expect a simple causal link of this form. First of all, the objective state of the economy does not necessarily correspond with the public's perception.[26] The public might be unduly optimistic at times and overly pessimistic at others. This observation leads back to the argument developed earlier: The dynamics of mass support

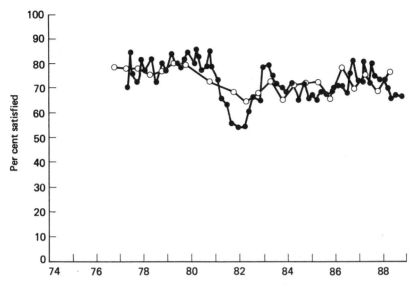

SOURCE: Eurobarometer surveys; Politbarometer Surveys
FIGURE 16.2: *Satisfaction with democracy – W. Germany*

must be interpreted in context with major political events. To do this in a more than impressionistic manner, systematic content analyses of mass media are needed to reconstruct the shifting political climate.[27]

In addition, there are some limitations of the Eurobarometer survey data, on which the determination of decline phases rests in the first place. These limitations include the relatively long time span between consecutive surveys, and the variable questionnaire context in which the 'support' question is asked. Such a sequence effect (like sampling error) may lead to substantial bias at times, possibly grossly distorting the overall flow of the mass support curve. Typically, there is little hard evidence that such phenomena are at work. However, in the case of Germany we can compare the Eurobarometer series with a similar series based on the Politbarometer surveys.[28] The question used in the German series is worded slightly different, but I contend that the two question are largely equivalent.[29] For the most part the two series render fairly similar results; they are well within the margin of sampling error. However, the decline phase is both much shorter and much more intense in the Politbarometer series. Here we observe a loss of 31 percentage points over fourteen months compared to a decline of 15 points over thirty months in the Eurobarometer data (see Figure 16.2). The rapid decline in the Politbarometer series is well supported by eight separate data points. Unfortunately, there does not seem to be an easy explanation for the discrepancy between the two series at this crucial time. The very fact of this discrepancy, however, indicates the need to increase the frequency with which the Eurobarometer surveys are conducted. As a quarterly survey the Eurobarometer would become an even more valuable instrument in monitoring the dynamics of public opinion in Western Europe.

NOTES

1. To avoid awkward language I will use the term 'Western European' throughout this chapter to denote the core members of the European Community (excluding Spain, Portugal, and Greece which joined the EC more recently). Also the term 'Great Britain' is used to refer to the commonwealth of England, Scotland, and Wales, excluding Northern Ireland given its special status. Finally, Luxembourg is not included in the empirical analysis due to the small sample size.
2. In my view (see Dalton and Kuechler, 1990, for a detailed exposition) the peace movement, the environmental movement, and the anti-nuclear movement are basically various transmutations (organizational forms) of one alternative movement characterized by a specific ideological bond.
3. Question wording remained constant starting with Eurobarometer 6 conducted in the fall of 1976. In this chapter I will exclude earlier data (European Community Survey 1973 as well as Eurobarometer 3 and 5) using (slightly) different question formats.
4. Restricting the attention to one particular country there are additional sources, most notably the Politbarometer series in Germany.
5. It should also be recognized that the supposedly radical outlook may be restricted to the verbal sphere. It should be seen as an outlet for more virulent dissatisfaction rather than as a definitive indication of corresponding behavioral intentions.
6. My emphasis; the second part is a self-citation from his earlier book (Easton, 1965: 273). Unfortunately, nowhere in Easton's writings is one precise definition given. Instead this basic description is continuously amended and modified in the course of the argument. However, since a full exegesis of Easton's writings is beyond the scope of this paper (and beyond my personal interest) I will use this definition for future reference.
7. Muller and Jukam (1977) have emphasized the incumbent vs. system affect distinction circumventing the pitfalls of 'diffuse support'.
8. In contrast, major segments of the population in most authoritarian systems (e.g. Nazi Germany or Pinochet's Chile) will make a clear distinction between community and regime. As a matter of fact, the very prevalence of such an empirical distinction indicates a lack of legitimacy.
9. The United States provide the most striking contrast with the ever-present singing of the national anthem (e.g. at the opening of any sporting event), the flying of colours by private citizens on a variety of occasions, pledges of allegiance in schools, etc.
10. I consider the recent trends to reinstall a sense of national pride and of national identity in the German public as at best an unfortunate regression. These efforts may also be seen as a deliberate attempt to diffuse the public's aware-

ness of the growing problems of an advanced welfare state, like the difficulties of continually providing the material welfare the citizenry has come to expect.

11. This objection dealt with the (minor) problem whether a particular trust/ cynicism scale (used by Citrin and Elkins in a British study) was really measuring attitudes towards (generalized) politicians or whether – due to instrumentation problems – real office holders (incumbents) were inadvertently the object of measurement.

12. This was in reply to Miller's (1974) analysis. Miller used political cynicism items as 'an indicator of the quality of American life' (1974: 971) and related several recent political issues to cynicism scores. His study was not directly focused on system or 'diffuse' support though.

13. It should be noted, however, that more sophisticated measures have been developed. With their Political Support-Alienation (PSA) scale Muller et al. (1982) have suggested an eight-item 'summated ratings' scale that in their judgment measures 'diffuse political support'. Some of these items tap the cognitive/evaluative dimension in addition to feelings of trust and legitimacy quite compatible with my conceptual argument here. Beyond face validity and satisfying internal reliability coefficients the PSA scale can claim criterion-related validity – its fairly high correlation with a measure of aggressive political participation. Unfortunately, this scale has been used in a few isolated studies only.

14. At this point, I assume that proper methodological procedures (including blind back translation) were followed in the translation of the English question into other languages. I take for granted that the national versions of this questions are all *literally* equivalent.

15. Likewise, the short life-span of Italian governments – averaging less than twelve months in the postwar period – does not indicate a fundamental instability, rather stability Italian-style. As a matter of fact, most of the newly formed governments do not reflect any significant change in the coalition structure.

16. This analysis utilized the much denser series of Politbarometer surveys and a somewhat differently-worded, but functionally very similar indicator.

17. OLS regression is used for solely descriptive purposes. Thus the ever-present problems in the regression analysis of time-related data (e.g. autocorrelation) can safely be ignored.

18. This could be documented in quantitative terms by fitting separate regression lines for two or three periods. However, given the small number of data points the coefficient of determination is likely to change drastically on the one hand, but becomes even more strongly affected by outliers on the other. At times, a visual inspection is more revealing and more reliable than supposedly objective statistics, mechanically computed.

19. Given the variable length of British election cycles and the brevity of election campaigns, the theoretical argument is anyhow less plausible in the British case. Empirically though, it is the strongest case to be found.

20. Data are taken from *OECD Economic Outlook* no. 43 (June 1988), Tables R18 (p. 87) and R11 (p. 180) – 1975 through 1987; Tables 16/17 (p. 3) and Table 22 (p. 49) for 1988. Unemployment rates are based on 'commonly-used' definitions, which are slightly different from the standardized rates bases on ILO/OECD guidelines. Inflation rates reflect the percentage change in the consumer price index from the previous year.

21. This is not to say that a majority of the population has precise knowledge of the indicators' exact meaning and of their current levels. It is quite likely that

many, if not most people store pertinent information in qualitative (e.g. 'high') or evaluative (e.g. 'too high', 'better') form only.

22. Alternatively, monthly figures could be used. However, very little is known about the way information of this sort is processed. It is plausible to assume that this information is actively processed (perceived) with some time lag. In addition, it may require additional time before information of this kind (stored in the individual's memory) actually has an effect on other assessments (such as the satisfaction with democracy). Economists are likely to try to determine these lags by extensive trial and error computer runs maximizing suitable correlations. However, it seems hardly possible to time both survey responses and availability of economic indicator precisely enough to warrant such exercises.

23. In these figures the horizontal axis represents calendar time. The economic indicator are plotted at mid-year (except for 1988 where they are plotted at the end of the first quarter) as an approximation of the precise point in time at which this information becomes effective. Survey data are plotted at x.25 and x.75 with x as the year of the survey.

24. These definitions are certainly somewhat arbitrary. It seems necessary, however, to guard against sampling fluctuations and require both a minimum of time points and a lower limit for decline. The fit of a regression line is considered as adequate if the coefficient of determination exceeds .35.

25. This is borderline case anyhow, because most of the decline occurs between two consecutive time points which hardly establishes a general trend.

26. In the German analysis (Kuechler, 1986), however, no major discrepancies between the economic indicators and citizens' perception of the present and future economic situation in general emerged. Unlike the Eurobarometer the German Politbarometer series regularly includes economic perception items leading to another survey-based time series.

27. It is conceivable to restrict this media analysis to the main evening news of the major television channels in each country. Even this, however, poses tremendous problems of data collection, processing, and analysis, clearly surpassing the capacities of any individual researcher.

28. The monthly Politbarometer surveys are sponsored by ZDF, one of the two major (state-operated) television networks in West Germany and conducted by the Forschungsgruppe Wahlen (Wolfgang Gibowski, Manfred Berger and Dieter Roth) in Mannheim, West Germany. The data are available for secondary analysis through the Central Archive for Empirical Social Research at the University of Cologne, West Germany.

29. A literal translation of the German question would be: 'In general, what would you say about the democracy in the Federal Republic of Germany, i.e. about our political parties and about our political system at large? Are you very satisfied, more satisfied that not, more unsatisfied that not, or very unsatisfied?' Starting with February 1988 the reference to 'our political parties' is omitted.

REFERENCES

Citrin, Jack (1974) 'Comment: The Political Relevance of Trust in Government', *American Political Science Review* 68, 973–88.
Crozier, Michel J., Samuel P. Huntington and Joji Watanuki (1975) *Crisis of Democracy* (New York: New York University Press).

Dalton, Russell J., Scott C. Flanagan, and Paul Allen Beck (eds) (1984) *Electoral Change in Advanced Industrial Democracies: Realignment or Dealignment?* (Princeton, NJ: Princeton University Press).

Dalton, Russell J. and Manfred Kuechler (eds) (1990) *Challenging the Political Order: New social and political movements in Western democracies* (London: Polity Press).

Dennis, Jack (1966) 'Support for the Party System by the Mass Public', *American Political Science Review* 60, 600–15.

Easton, David (1965) *A Systems Analysis of Political Life* (Chicago: The University of Chicago Press).

Easton, David (1975) 'A Re-Assessment of the Concept of Political Support', *Journal of Political Science* 5, 435–7.

Inglehart, Ronald (1977) *The Silent Revolution: Changing Values and Political Styles Among Western Publics* (Princeton, NJ: Princeton University Press).

Kuechler, Manfred (1982) 'Staats-, Parteien- oder Politikverdrossenheit?' in *Bürger und Parteien*, ed. by Joachim Raschke. (Opladen, West Germany: Westdeutscher Verlag).

Kuechler, Manfred (1986) 'A Trend Analysis of System Support in West Germany, 1976–1986', paper presented at the 1986 Southern Political Science Association Meetings, Atlanta, Ga.

Kuechler, Manfred (1987) 'The Utility of Surveys for Cross-National Research', *Social Science Research* 16, 229–44.

Miller, Arthur (1974) 'Political Issues and Trust in Government: 1964–1970', *American Political Science Review* 68, 951–72.

Muller, Edward N. and Thomas O. Jukam (1977) 'On the Meaning of Political Support', *American Political Science Review* 71, 1561–95.

Muller, Edward N., Thomas O. Jukam, and Mitchell A. Seligson (1982) 'Diffuse Political Support and Antisystem Political Behavior: A Comparative Analysis', *American Journal of Political Science* 26, 240–64.

17 Materialists and Postmaterialists: different Viewpoints or different Worlds?

Richard S. Katz,
The Johns Hopkins University

Among the many fruitful lines of research to have grown out of the Eurobarometer surveys, perhaps none have had so far reaching an impact as those based on Inglehart's distinction between Materialist and Postmaterialist values (Inglehart, 1977). In general terms, this research has developed along at least two major lines. On the one hand, a standardized and easily reproduced technique has been developed based on expressed 'goal priorities' which allows the population to be divided, albeit somewhat crudely, between Materialists and Postmaterialists, with an additional intermediate category, and this classification has been shown to correlate with a variety of attitudinal and behavioral variables (Barnes et al., 1979). In particular, the advent of Postmaterialism has been widely interpreted as a major cause of the rise of 'New Politics' parties and political action groups, as well as for the apparent increase in 'New Politics' modes of direct political action. Pursuing this line of inquiry, the Eurobarometer series itself has allowed the tracing of trends in the distribution of Materialists and Postmaterialists over time, especially allowing the testing of hypotheses about life-cycle versus generational change, and has provided the principal empirical basis for projections of likely patterns for the future (Abramson and Inglehart, 1979; Inglehart and Rabier, 1986).

On the other hand, research has been concerned with the structure of policy preferences and other attitudes. Based on the use of factor analysis, Inglehart, for example, has posited the existence of two underlying value dimensions, one corresponding to traditional, Materialist, left-right questions such as nationalization of industry, redistribution of wealth, and government management of the economy, and the other reflecting the New Politics, Postmaterialist issues such as control of pollution, development of nuclear power, and women's freedom of choice in abortion (Inglehart, 1984). Although some disputes exist about the correct number and exact identity of the latent dimensions (e.g., Dalton, 1985), this approach has been used to locate parties (operationally identified with the average

295

positions of elite respondents) and their supporters in one or another multidimensional issue space, especially relying on data from surveys of candidates to and members of the European parliament that were designed specifically to mesh with Eurobarometer surveys (Inglehart, 1984). Other analyses have used the same data to assess the representativeness of European parties (Dalton, 1985; Bardi, 1987).

These two lines of research intersect most directly in Inglehart's finding that the pattern of correlations between placement on a self-defined left-right scale and scores on his two issue dimensions is different for Materialists and Postmaterialists. This he interprets as indicating that the primary focus of the terms 'left' and 'right' differs for the two groups of respondents. In this he is undoubtedly correct, but the potential implications of the finding stretch far beyond this. Since factors are extracted only on the basis of the correlations among the observed indicators and identified only on the basis of their correlations with those indicators, the finding that left-right correlates differently with the two factors for Materialists and Postmaterialists raises the question of whether the patterns of correlations among the observed variables may also vary between the two groups, or, what is logically equivalent, whether the underlying factors/dimensions themselves may be different.

The object of this essay is to examine precisely that question. Do Materialists and Postmaterialists share a common opinion structure underlying the particular issue preferences voiced in the interviews – that is, not to ask whether they have the same distributions of opinions, which they clearly do not, but instead to ask whether they respond as if they saw the same interconnections among issues – or do they respond as if they see things as fitting together differently? In the former case although we might say that Materialists and Postmaterialists approach the political world from different viewpoints, it would nonetheless be the same world they both see. In the latter case, however, the differences would be far more profound, since the implication would be that Materialists and Postmaterialists do not share a common frame of reference. In this case we might indeed reasonably describe them, at least for political purposes, as inhabiting different worlds.

THE PROBLEM

The exploratory factor analysis of responses from the entire set of survey respondents, and the usual interpretation of the results as revealing the underlying dimensions which structure the public's attitudes or opinions, is actually based on a tacit, and often unrecognized, assumption: that although respondents may differ in their placement along the underlying dimensions, and although respondents' answers to individual questions may be the result of item specific and respondent specific idiosyncrasies,

TABLE 17.1: *Variable means and rotated principal components factor analysis for artificially-generated data*

Variable	Variable Means		Factor Loadings	
	Set M	*Set P*	F_1	F_2
V1	−.03	−.01	.99	−.01
V2	−.10	.17	.93	.35
V3	−.31	.63	.05	.99
V4	−.08	.11	.95	.24
V5	−.21	.34	.32	.94

the structure of the relationships among the items is the same for all respondents. As with linear regression (of which factor analysis may be seen to be a special variant), the technique provides the best possible fit of model to data and can tell us whether the model fits the data significantly better than the null model of no systematic relationship, but it cannot by itself tell us whether the model estimated was the best or most appropriate model that might have been chosen. Also as with linear regression, if the model is seriously misspecified (in this case if the assumption of a single structure of relationships among the variables is false), the results may be quite misleading.

The nature of the problem may best be elaborated by means of a simplified example and artificially constructed 'data'. Consider the 'results' displayed in Table 17.1. The essential features of two-dimensional factor analyses based on Eurobarometer issue opinion data are maintained, although in exaggerated form: some variables load highly on each of the two factors, while others apparently represent responses based on a combination of effects; there are two subgroups of unequal size (not coincidentally identified as 'M' and 'P'), with one group (the P's) showing markedly skewed scores on one of the dimensions. The standard interpretation of these results would be that there are two underlying factors, F_1 and F_2, for all respondents, such that the value of variable j for each respondent (iM) or (iP) (e.g, $V_{(iM)j}$) may be expressed by the equation:

$$V_{(iM)j} = \alpha_{1j}F_{(iM)1} + \alpha_{2j}F_{(iM)2} + e_{(iM)j}$$

where $e_{(iM)j}$ includes both measurement error and the unique (i.e., uncorrelated with the other variables) component of V_j (and, of course, similarly for $V_{(iP)j}$). In fact the 'data' from which these results were derived were constructed by using a random number generator to provide values for the F's and e's. Set P was constructed by drawing a random sample of the full data in a way that over sampled those cases with high values of F_2, while the remaining cases were assigned to set M. Thus in this case, the standard interpretation is exactly correct.

The problem is that virtually identical results for a full set of data could have been, and for this illustration were, constructed from two quite different models. For these models, sets P and M were specified in advance. Identifying the model just discussed as Model I, in Model II the values of all five variables were influenced only by F_1 for cases in set M and only by F_2 for cases in set P:

$$V_{(iM)j} = \beta_{1j} F_{(iM)1} + e_{(iM)j} + c_{jM}$$
$$V_{(iP)j} = \beta_{2j} F_{(iP)2} + e_{(iP)j} + c_{jP}$$

where the c's are constants added to the equations to reproduce the separation of variable means between sets M and P introduced in Model I by the biased sampling procedure and the other terms are defined as before. Each of the β's is greater than the corresponding to the same variable in Model I, and the variance of the α's was made greater in Model II than in Model I, thus keeping the overall proportions of the variances of the V's accounted for by the F's, as well as the overall correlations among the V's, nearly identical to that in Model I.

Finally in Model III, values of all the variables in both sets of cases are determined by two factors, but for two of the variables the functions are different:

$$V_{(iM)j} = \tau_{1Mj} F_{(iM)1} + \tau_{2Mj} F_{(iM)2} + e_{(iM)j}$$
$$V_{(iP)j} = \tau_{1Pj} F_{(iP)1} + \tau_{2Pj} F_{(iP)2} + e_{(iP)j}$$

but with $\tau_{1Pj} \neq \tau_{1Mj}$ for j = 4 and 5, and similarly for τ_{2Pj} and τ_{2Mj}.

As the expressions have been used here, the hypothetical respondents in sets M and P in Model I have different viewpoints while those in Models II and III inhabit different worlds. The problem, to repeat, is that performing a simple factor analysis on data generated by each of these very different models yields virtually the same results, and thus leaves the analyst unable to distinguish among them.

METHOD

The solution to the problem as manifested in this artificial example is to factor-analyse the two sets separately. As Table 17.2 shows, not only are the results very different for the three models, but moreover each reflects its genesis quite directly. Adapted to the real problem of attitude structures among Materialists and Postmaterialists, this calls for the separate factor analysis of these two sets of respondents in order that one may ask whether the factor structures are the same, and if they are not, then how they differ.

TABLE 17.2: *Factor analyses for three models constructed with artificial data, sets M and P analyzed separately*

Variable	Model I Set M		Set P		Model II Set M		Set P		Model III Set M		Set P	
	F_1	F_2	F_1	F_2	F_1	F_2	F_1	F_2	F_1	F_2	F_1	F_2
V1	.99	.01	.99	−.01	.97	.01	.03	.22	.99	.02	.99	−.08
V2	.94	.33	.93	.35	.97	.01	−.04	.74	.91	.38	.95	.30
V3	.03	.99	.04	.99	.05	−.03	.02	.95	.05	.99	.04	.99
V4	.96	.22	.96	.22	.96	.02	.08	.60	.97	.08	.66	.74
V5	.34	.92	.31	.94	.40	−.00	−.06	.95	.22	.97	.92	.35

In fact, one knows in advance that the factor structures will not be identical, and further that a better fit to the data will be obtained by analysing Materialists and Postmaterialists separately, if only because twice as many parameters are estimated in the separate as in the combined analysis. To address the question of whether the improved fit is better than would be expected on this basis alone, the problem can be reformulated as the contrast between alternative measurement models (with the observed variables taken as indicators of the latent concepts/factors) using the LISREL program (Hayduk, 1988). This allows use of confirmatory factor-analysis techniques in order to assess the adequacy of models in which various constraints are imposed on the two measurement models (i.e., that they are identical in some or all respects or that some correlations are fixed at 0). By making systematic comparisons of alternative models, one can not only tell whether the two groups ought to be analysed separately, but also can begin to identify the sources of their differences.

LISREL operates on the basis of maximum likelihood estimation. Within this framework, the test of whether the less constrained of two hierarchical models fits the data significantly better than the more constrained model is a X^2 test performed on the difference of the likelihood X^2's. As with all X^2 tests, this one is sensitive to the number of cases as well as to the strength of the relationships being tested, and so, although the N's are not extraordinarily large here, given that only the pure Materialists and Postmaterialists have been considered, the results must be interpreted with appropriate caution.

The data analysed here are the thirteen policy preference questions from Eurobarometer 11 which have figured prominently in much of the research cited above.[1] The data were weighted using the European weight variable to give a representative sample of the European Community as a whole. The basic input to the LISREL program was two correlation matrices, one for those coded as Materialists and the other for those coded as Post-materialists, each based on listwise deletion of missing data. In anticipation of subsequent analyses (not reported here) left-right self-placement was included in the correlation matrices, and hence cases for which this variable was coded as missing are also deleted. Overall, the Materialist and Postmaterialist correlation matrices are based on 1550 and 641 weighted cases respectively.

The initial strategy of analysis is to make paired comparisons between stacked LISREL models, comparing a model in which parameters are constrained to be equal for Materialist and Postmaterialist subsets and a model in which the same parameters are free to differ. In setting up these comparisons, two sets (matrices) of parameters are considered. The first is (in the language of LISREL) the Lambda X (LX) matrix which contains the correlations between the observed variables and the latent concepts or factors, and is thus equivalent to the matrix of factor loadings in a normal factor analysis. (It should be noted, however, that the maximum likelihood technique of LISREL does not produce the same correlations/loadings as a principal components or principal factors analysis.) The LX matrices can be constrained in either or both of two ways: the matrices for the two sets can be constrained to be equal and/or specific elements of the matrices can be fixed at 0. The latter type of constraint corresponds to confirmatory factor analysis in single group situations. The second set of parameters is the Phi (PH) matrix, which is a symmetric matrix with 1's on the diagonal containing the correlations among the factors. Again, it can be constrained to be equal across sets. Additionally, the off-diagonal elements may be fixed at 0, corresponding to orthogonal factors, or allowed to vary (oblique factors).

ANALYSIS

As a point of departure, Table 17.3 presents the results of the maximum likelihood exploratory analysis most like the factor analyses usually reported. The differences, aside from the method of estimation, are that this analysis allowed for oblique factors (the off-diagonal elements of PH unconstrained) and was based only on the Materialists and Postmaterialists, omitting those in the intermediate category. Although LISREL requires that the number of factors be specified in advance, the number of factors here was determined, as in conventional factor analyses, by taking the number of principal components with eigenvalues greater than 1.

Examination of the estimated LX matrix suggests a relatively straightforward and conventional interpretation of the factors. As indicated by the labels in the table, the first factor corresponds to the traditional economic left-right dimension, being indicated most strongly by the public ownership and government management variables, and somewhat less strongly by the variables concerning employee representation on the boards of businesses, public control of multinationals, and redistribution of income. The second factor concerns physical security, and is indicated by opinions regarding

TABLE 17.3: *Exploratory maximum likelihood factor analysis, Materialists and Postmaterialists only*

| | Factor Loadings (LX) | | | |
	L/R	Security	New Pol.	Aid
More control over multinationals	0.343	−0.002	0.320	0.028
Develop nuclear energy	−0.115	0.407	0.000	−0.077
Reduce income inequality	0.279	−0.020	0.393	0.096
More severe antiterrorist measures	−0.117	0.505	0.252	−0.048
More public ownership of industry	0.545	−0.050	0.056	0.105
More gov't management of economy	0.540	0.097	0.095	0.208
Stronger defense effort	−0.045	0.406	−0.096	−0.063
Women able to choose abortion	0.041	−0.250	0.339	−0.179
Equal representation of employees	0.350	−0.133	0.371	0.033
More aid to 3rd World countries	0.029	−0.096	0.107	0.628
Stronger antipollution measures	−0.084	0.047	0.466	0.176
Protect freedom of expression	0.082	−0.129	0.422	0.170
More aid to poor regions of Europe	−0.012	−0.063	0.185	0.683

| | Correlations Among Factors (PH) | | | |
	L/R	Security	New Pol.	Aid
L/R	1.000			
Security	−0.059	1.000		
New Pol.	0.074	−0.002	1.000	
Aid	0.003	−0.025	0.063	1.000

SOURCE: Eurobarometer 11

the punishment of terrorists, expansion of nuclear power generation, and military defense. The third factor may perhaps best be identified as 'New Politics', although its content is somewhat mixed. On one hand, it is most strongly indicated by opinions regarding pollution and free expression, issues which are intimately related to the operational definition of Post-materialism itself, but on the other hand it is also strongly related to opinions about income redistribution, employee representation, control of multinationals, and freedom of choice regarding abortion. The fourth dimension overwhelmingly reflects attitudes about aid to the less fortunate, whether in the Third World or in the less developed regions of Europe. Finally, as the PH matrix indicates, although the factors were not constrained to be orthogonal, as they are portrayed here they are very nearly so, the strongest correlation between two factors being only .074, corresponding to an angle of over 85 degress.

In this analysis, $PH_m = PH_{pm}$ and $LX_m = LX_{pm}$. An overall answer to the question of whether Materialists and Postmaterialists display the same underlying structure of opinions can be obtained by testing this model against one in which the PH and LX matrices are free to vary across the two sets. For the analysis in which the models are constrained to be equal,

X^2 is 448.07 with df=98; for the unconstrained model it is 276.28 with df=40. The difference (X^2=171.79, df=58) is highly significant, and allows us to conclude that undifferentiated analysis of data in which Materialists and Postmaterialists are combined does, in fact, represent a significant misrepresentation of the underlying factor structures of the two groups of respondents.

Both of these analyses correspond to oblique factor models. Perhaps the difference between the Materialists and Postmaterialists stems from the relationships among the factors, rather than from the nature of the factors themselves. This possibility was explored by comparing models in which first the PH matrices were constrained to be equal across groups while the LX matrices were estimated separately, and then in which the LX matrices were equated while the PH matrices were free, to the fully unconstrained model. The X^2 statistics from, these analyses (along with the result of the constrained model reported in Table 17.3) are shown in the first two columns of Table 17.4. Although the fit of model to data is significantly better when the PH matrices are estimated separately than when they are not (cell II compared to cell IV), the greatest improvement comes when the LX matrices are freed (cell III compared to cell IV); thus, although there is evidence that the factors do not relate to one another in the same way across subsets, this is by no means the whole story. Finally, for the sake of completeness, the last column of Table 17.4 shows the result of taking this analysis one step farther and constraining the factors to be orthogonal. So long as the LX matrices are full (i.e., no elements are constrained to be 0), there must be no further degradation of fit from this additional constraint. (This is equivalent to saying that the explained variance from a factor analysis is invariant under rotation.)

RESULTS

Table 17.5 presents the results of the parallel factor analyses of Materialists and Postmaterialists (corresponding to cell I of Table 17.4). Although there are obvious similarities to the overall analysis of Table 17.3, there are also clear differences both between each of these analyses and the overall analysis and between the two analyses in Table 17.5 itself. (The factors in this table, and in Table 17.6, are identified only by number both for reasons of space and because their substantive interpretations remains highly speculative and provisional.)

Rather than attempting a direct interpretation of these factor analyses, they were used as the starting point for further separate analysis of the two groups. In each subset, those elements of the full LX matrix in Table 17.5 which were under .100 were constrained to be 0 (as, indeed, they would normally be interpreted in a presentation of factor loadings with those

TABLE 17.4: X^2 *tests of alternative measurement models*

Factors (LX)		Correlations Among the Factors (PH)		
		Unconstrained Across Groups	Equal Across Groups	Orthogonal
Unconstrained	X^2	276.28	276.28	276.28
	df	40	46	52
		[I]	[III]	[V]
Equal	X^2	407.68	448.07	448.07
	df	92	98	104
		[II]	[IV]	[VI]

TABLE 17.5: *Separate unconstrained factor analyses for Materialists and Postmaterialists*

	Materialists				Postmaterialists			
	I	II	III	IV	I	II	III	IV
Multinationals	0.409	−0.029	0.333	0.016	0.122	0.080	0.340	0.027
Nuclear energy	−0.095	0.318	−0.007	−0.112	−0.087	0.565	−0.027	−0.021
Income inequal	0.279	−0.040	0.367	0.135	0.281	0.012	0.423	−0.011
Terrorism	−0.123	0.541	0.311	0.013	−0.023	0.515	0.099	−0.181
Public owners	0.529	−0.057	0.043	0.098	0.694	−0.072	0.033	0.076
Govt. econ. m.	0.598	0.101	0.119	0.229	0.277	−0.038	0.138	0.022
Defense	−0.016	0.350	−0.080	−0.100	−0.034	0.476	−0.190	0.024
Abortion	−0.053	−0.278	0.374	−0.208	0.276	−0.166	0.216	−0.074
Employee rep.	0.344	−0.196	0.400	0.005	0.374	−0.049	0.286	0.059
3rd World aid	0.042	−0.112	0.122	0.593	0.065	−0.005	0.032	0.845
Pollution	−0.101	0.114	0.473	0.186	−0.025	−0.027	0.513	0.152
Free express.	0.048	−0.181	0.383	0.196	0.139	−0.021	0.488	0.111
Regional aid	−0.010	−0.098	0.178	0.731	0.009	0.048	0.182	0.500

Correlations Among Factors

	I	II	III	IV	I	II	III	IV
I	1.000				1.000			
II	−.080	1.000			−.046	1.000		
III	.061	−.008	1.000		.105	−.010	1.000	
IV	.012	−.044	.062	1.000	.013	−.017	.052	1.000

$X^2=217.63$ $X^2=58.65$
df=20   df=20

under .100 – or even .200 – omitted). In addition, those variables that most clearly defined each of the four factors (factor I: public ownership; factor II: nuclear energy, terrorism, and defense; factor III: free expression; factor IV: Third World aid and regional aid) were constrained to correlate only with the relevant factor. These constraints then were gradually relaxed until the improvement in the X^2 statistic was no longer significant.

TABLE 17.6: *Separate constrained factor analyses for Materialists and Postmaterialists*

	Materialists				Post materialists			
	I	II	III	IV	I	II	III	IV
Multinationals	0.462		0.353	–0.202			0.362	
Nuclear energy		0.419				0.571		
Income inequal	0.331		0.310		0.155		0.495	–0.102
Terrorism		0.584	0.366			0.539	0.201	–0.230
Public owners	0.550				0.844			
Govt. econ. m.	0.630	0.152		0.182	0.237		0.151	
Defense		0.447					0.468	–0.111
Abortion		–0.173	0.551	–0.482	0.192	–0.168	0.250	–0.127
Employee rep.	0.428		0.465	–0.234	0.266		0.348	
3rd World aid				0.638				0.716
Pollution		0.307	0.626				0.420	0.126
Free express.	0.112		0.453				0.573	
Regional aid				0.760				0.615

Correlations Among Factors

	I	II	III	IV	I	II	III	IV
I	1.000				1.000			
II	–.288	1.000			–.220	1.000		
III	.158	–.445	1.000		.277	–.146	1.000	
IV	.234	–.410	.654	1.000	.168	–.021	.338	1.000

$$X^2 = 243.09 \qquad\qquad X^2 = 76.70$$
$$df = 47 \qquad\qquad\quad df = 48$$

The results of this procedure are reported in Table 17.6. As comparison between the final X^2 statistics in Table 17.6 and those of Table 17.5 shows, there is no significant loss in ability to account for the overall pattern of correlations among the original indicators, although each of these analyses has roughly half the cells of the LX matrix fixed at 0.

Looking at Table 17.6, the interpretation of factor II is straightforward. In both cases, this factor still appears to address concerns about physical security. For the three core variables defining the factor, there is little difference between the two groups. For both groups, freedom of choice in abortion is negatively related to the physical security factor. Somewhat surprisingly, the Materialists appear to see control of pollution to be significantly related to the physical security factor, while Postmaterialists do not. Materialists also appear to see government management of the economy as contributing to physical security. Although further research would clearly be necessary, one might speculate that this reflects the greater economic vulnerability of those social groups that contain dispro-portionate numbers of Materialists.

Factor IV is similarly easy to interpret; it again primarily addresses questions of aid. The correlations of variables other than the two aid questions with this factor suggest, however, a subtle difference. Although the evidence is extremely slim, one might speculate that for the Postmaterialists, this is a more political factor (as indicated by its negative correlation with the question about penalties for terrorism), while for the Materialists, it is more a 'people' factor (indicated by the strong negative correlation with abortion). This difference may also be reflected in the fact that the closer-to-home question of intra-European aid correlates more highly for the Materialists while the question of Third-World aid correlates more highly for the Postmaterialists.

Much larger differences between the two groups are evident when one turns to factor I. For the Materialists, it remains the classic left-right dimension, with just a tinge of 'freedom of speech' added in; control of multinationals, income redistribution, public ownership of industry, government management of the economy, and employee representation all correlate highly. For the Postmaterialists, however, the factor is overwhelmingly dominated by only one of these variables, public ownership, while control of multinationals is not significantly related at all. One possible explanation of this difference lies in the use of the word 'public' in one question and the word 'government' in the other. If Postmaterialists separate the conventional left-right dimension into two separate concerns, one aspect of leftness being 'economic democracy' in the sense of popular or *public* control over the economy and the other being hostility to 'concentration of power' including *government* power, then the conclusion would be that for the Postmaterialists, factor I represents only the economic democracy sense of left-right. Control of multinationals, on the other hand, would be primarily a question of controlling concentration of economic power, and thus would load on a different factor.

If this argument is correct, it then suggests that different interpretations of factor III are required in the two groups as well. As before, the 'usual' interpretation of this factor as 'New Politics' fits the Materialists fairly well, although in part this only underlines that 'New Politics' is a label attached to a rather amorphous collection of issues. For the Postmaterialists, however, one is led to speculate that this represents the 'concentration of power' aspect of left-right. In this case, one would be assuming that for Postmaterialists concern with income inequality refers less to giving to the poor, the traditional concern of the left, and more with leveling down the top of the income/wealth/power distributions; that pollution control summons up images of large corporate and irresponsible polluters; that abortion and free expression are seen as specific examples of centralized power telling people what to do or say.

A direct consequence of constraining many of the entries in the LX matrices to be 0 is to force the correlations among the factors to increase. This effect, however, is markedly stronger for the Materialists than for the Postmaterialists, indicating that the factors, as defined here, are far more independent of one another for the latter. For the Materialists, while the left-right factor is relatively independent, the other three factors are significantly intercorrelated, in particular the third and fourth factors sharing a common variance of over 42 per cent. This suggests that, although at least four dimensions are required to adequately account for the Materialists' covariance matrix, they have not yet been adequately disentangled. Whether this is because at least one more dimension is necessary or because the stimuli (questions) themselves elicit responses based on multiple concerns must remain a subject for future research.

Finally, returning to the original question of whether Materialists and Postmaterialists share a common opinion structure, we can use the parameters reported in Table 17.6 to assess the fit of the model estimated for one group to the data of the other. In each case, the result is to more than triple the X^2 statistic, with a correspondingly radical decrease in other indicators of goodness of fit. Thus with this method as well one is led to conclude that Materialists and Postmaterialists do indeed see different worlds.

CONCLUSION

It is appropriate that this first step down this line of investigation conclude with the traditional call for further research, and several avenues of development immediately present themselves. First, the measurement model itself needs to be refined. Although it is clear that the parallel analysis of Materialists and Postmaterialists is superior to analysing the two groups together, neither of the individual group models presented here is fully adequate on its own. On one hand, other sets of stimuli need to be considered if one is to have a firmer sense of the structure of underlying values and attitudes that produces responses to particular questions. On the other hand, problems of measurement errors, and especially correlations among measurement errors, need to be addressed as possible confounding influences in derivation and interpretation of factor analyses.

In the terminology of LISREL, this essay has been concerned with moving from exogenous indicators to exogenous concepts. A second avenue for future research is to move from exogenous to endogenous concepts, or in common language, from causes to effects. What behavioural difference does a person's score on whatever factors are derived make? Not only is the ability to answer this question the ultimate test of whether the whole procedure was worthwhile, but the answers should shed additional light on the substantive nature of the exogenous factors themselves. Third, the respondents in the intermediate category need to be considered, both because they are the most numerous group and even more to further illuminate the differences between the two categories at the extremes.

Fortunately, the data required to pursue much of this research agenda is already available in the rich series of Eurobarometer surveys. Here, as with many other lines of research, the Eurobarometer data not only allow the preliminary formulation and testing of hypotheses, but their refinement and confirmation over time and space with data that are truly comparable. For this rare opportunity, the scholarly community should be extremely grateful.

NOTES

1. The Eurobarometer data were collected under the direction of Jacques-René Rabier and Ronald Inglehart and were provided by the Interuniversity Consortium for Political and Social Research. Neither the Consortium, nor the original investigators, bear any responsibility for the analyses of interpretations presented here.

REFERENCES

Abramson, Paul and Ronald Inglehart (1986) 'Generational replacement and value change in six West European societies', *American Journal of Political Science* 30: 1–25.

Bardi, Luciano (1987) 'Representation in the European parliament', Ph.D. dissertation, The Johns Hopkins University.

Barnes, Samuel, Max Kaase, et al. (1979) *Political Action* (Beverly Hills, Ca: Sage).

Dalton, Russell (1985) 'Political parties and political representation', *Comparative Political Studies* 18: 267–85.

Hayduk, Leslie A. (1988) *Structural Equation Modeling with LISREL* (Baltimore: Johns Hopkins University Press).

Inglehart, Ronald (1977) *The Silent Revolution* (Princeton, NJ: Princeton University Press).

Inglehart, Ronald (1984) 'Changing cleavage alignments in Western democracies', in R. Dalton, S. Flanagan, and P. Beck (eds) *Electoral Change in Advanced Industrial Democracies* (Princeton, NJ: Princeton University Press).

Inglehart, Ronald, and Jacques-René Rabier (1986) 'Political realignment in advanced industrial society'. *Government and Opposition* 21: 456–79.

18 Post-modernity, Postmaterialism and Political Theory

Klaus von Beyme, University of Heidelberg

In the social sciences theories of post-modernity mainly play the role of super theories with holistic explanatory powers. They are new sets of ideas, conceived to supersede all-embracing general theories and general notions of the logic of systems. Therefore it seems to be adequate that theories of post-modernity develop in a manner different from the development of older global theories. The notion of a broad systematic concept of reality was once used for the deduction of smaller partial theories. Theories of post-modernity, however, typically are eclectic compilations of previous ideas and lifestyles, such as pop art, ecological protest, libertarian alternatives. There is hardly an element of the theory of post-modernity which has not already had some earlier thought invested in it, or has not already been lived through by subcultures.

French theory, especially, has reached a level of abstraction which disproves the common assumption that post-modernity is a popular fashion or fad. Its new elitism is to some degree just as offensive as the elitism of classical modernity, its enemy. Outside France this has occasionally led to allergic reactions, which even imitated the stale jokes of some post-modern treatises (Laermann, 1986).

A good part of the debate in the German social sciences did not take note of this fad. Only occasionally was there a conscious reception of some theoretical elements, as in the writings of Albrecht Wellmer. In general, it is surprising how strongly authors from Habermas to Luhman agree to ignore theories of post-modernity. Political theory, which is typically a short-range theory, may be excused for its ignorance. The insights of the debate on post-modernity which could be used for empirical theories are few. Nevertheless post-modernity as a reformulation of hidden common-sense assumptions, influences political theory so strongly – even without explicit references in this theory – that it does not seem to be a wasted effort to throw some light more systematically on theoretical approaches of post-modernity. Like all composites with a 'post' the expression 'post-modernity' has the disadvantage that one cannot start the discussion of this concept from zero, but one has to evaluate one's argument in relation to an antecedent, in our case: modernity. We will begin by looking into the meaning of modernity and post-modernity in art. Then we will go on to discuss the meaning of an extended notion of modernity in the theory of science as it is debated in philosophy. Only in the third part of our analysis we will concentrate on those elements of the theory of post-modernity which are directly relevant for political theory.

POST-MODERNITY – A PARADIGM OF ART?

The fact that the notion of post-modernity has its origin in art gave the term a certain bias. If it was true that post-modernity was only possible 'where a basic pluralism of languages, models, and modes of actions is practiced not only in different *oeuvres*, but in one and the same *oeuvre*' (Welsch, 1987, p. 16), then it would hardly be possible to find any kind of post-modernity in science. In science there are limits to the technique of collages. Umberto Eco's abilities as a writer are presumably more apt to create a broad interest in medieval history than learned treatises. But even the most successful authors with respect to the popularization of medieval history, from Borst to Tuchman, have kept their distance to many techniques of post-modernity in art and have opted instead for the upholding of scientific standards.

There was, apart from this, a long-standing scientific tradition to identify post-modernity with its presentation in the arts pages of the newspapers and to play it down as a fashion of art production which has no significance for scientific work. This suspicion found additional proof in the aestheticism of many philosophers of post-modernity, especially the francophone ones. Was it not true that under the guise of the slogan that the aim must be to break up the 'totalitarianism of rationality' and the 'terrorism of scientism' scientific methods and logical rules were very often ignored altogether? The disappearance of the boundaries between art and science could best be demonstrated by an analysis of Feyerabend's contribution. Helmut Spinner has tried to explain Feyerabend's overstated criticism of rationalism and science by a hidden preference for dadaism. In 1920 George Grosz and John Heartfield called Oskar Kokoschka an academic 'scoundrel of art' because of his defense of bourgeois art. In a parallel manner Feyerabend characterized the heads of the Popper school as the 'scoundrels of knowledge' of our times (Spinner 1980, p. 45). So far Feyerabend has always commented very arrogantly on Spinner's empathetic approaches. Will he again reply: 'But Helmut, baby, don't get so annoyed. What on earth do you want?' (Feyerabend 1979, p. 90, n. 70) or will he finally feel understood when he is characterized as an artist? Perhaps. But a parallel interpretation of most of the French structuralists would more than not insult their philosophical honour. However, what can be gained by an understanding of post-modernity in the spirit of art? The daily experiences on which the development of theories is based say nothing about the validity of insights. Is not there the danger, too, that a transfer of art concepts to science will create more problems in the field of politics than it can solve?

The problems start with the terms modernity and post-modernity when they are meant to stand for different eras. Where post-modernity is interpreted as being nothing more than the completion of the principles of modernity, as in the writings of Marquard and Welsch, the characteristics of both eras become intertwined. A clear notion of modernity as an era can at best be found in architecture. In this sphere for decades the predominance of functionalism was so obvious, especially in the years of reconstruction in Europe after the war, that one can clearly mark off the beginning and the end of this predominance, namely roughly 1955 and 1975. Only in this respect one can follow Habermas' characterization of modernity as a 'style which was the only valid one and was also shaping day-to-day life, a phenomenon not found since the days of classicism' (Habermas, 1985, p. 15). In painting the boundaries are already no longer clearly drawn. That is, if one does not identify modernity with one dominant style, like abstract expressionism, which has been given such a solid shape that it became possible to treat it as a kind of object which could have been stolen, as was said to have happened in 1947 when 'modernity' was stolen and was brought from Paris to New York (Guilbaut 1983). Where no aesthetic crime was reconstructed, a quasi-teleological development of modern art is assumed. The transfer is no longer caused by theft, but through emigration from Paris via Berlin and Moscow to New York (Huyssen/Scherpe, 1986, p. 22). Less narrow descriptions of the success story of modern art have already recognized for a long time that the abstract principle was less dominant in art itself than in the sphere of distribution of art, as it is represented by galleries and museums. Dada and surrealism had declared the bankruptcy of rationalism and the bourgeois art dominated by it, long before this new iconoclasm again became the fashion in the new pop art. Important art collectors have time and again found it difficult to chose between different varieties of modernity. Peggy Guggenheim is reported to have one said: 'I have worn an earring by Tanguy and one by Calder to show my impartiality in the confrontation of surrealism and abstract art' (*The Peggy Guggenheim Collection* n. d., p. 3).

After the Second World War surrealism was declared dead. But new forms of the 'old disgust' (Tristan Tzara) were prepared to keep on holding up the banner of protest against rationalism in art. Where modern art seemed to be subdued in a totalitarian manner to the pressure of a single formalistic truth, the essence of being an artist was described as being something profane, and art as an object was more and more seen as a secular phenomenon (Gottlieb, 1978, p. 345ff). By the time of the student rebellions these ideas became current among the general public. All schools of modernity left their esoteric circles and transformed themselves into elements of mass culture. The fight against 'concrete fascism' in architecture started its ideological battle even before Feyerabend declared war on the 'ratio fascists' (Von Beyme 1987, p. 91f). The unity of art and production, which was once proclaimed by the *Werkbund* with the best progressive intentions, namely to fight the falseness of decorative art in Imperial Germany, had disastrous consequences, which no-one had foreseen, or wanted. Post-modernity has, however, made explicit the danger that social and political questions can be raised on an aesthetic level, and that the social sciences neglect them. It should not be denied that the interpretation of post-modernity in the spirit of art provides important insights. But in this kind of 'understanding' the danger is inherent that because of sympathy for their genesis questions about the validity of such ideas for science are not given sufficient thought. Many get carried away with intellectual pleasure, which is even felt by those criticized, when Feyerabend presents his all-embracing polemics, as those concerned have admitted with a bad conscience (Naess, 1980, p. 184).

There are new dangers inherent in a dogmatic non-dogma. The credo. *popular instead of modern*, which Charles Jencks has proclaimed for architecture has not stopped him from keeping a vigilant eye on those who, in addition to himself, claim for their person the honorary title 'post-modern'. Lyotard was robbed of this title. Efforts to institutionalize a kind of ranking in importance with regard to post-modernity have made it easy for critics like Habermas to classify all adherents of post modernity as neohistoricists and neoconservatives. Social scientists should be warned by the quarrel post-modernity has triggered off in architecture. Although there are clear criteria for styles, there is no unanimity with regard to the question whether post-modernity is a new style or only a gap-filling architecture after the end of reconstruction. There is an easy way out. One can declare functionalism a non-style, as an error and a 'step out of architecture'. In this argument only post-modernity can reclaim for itself the category of a 'style', because it has advocated the 'reconquest of the architectural dimension' (Fischer et. al., 1987, p. 13). Seen from outside, post-modernity looks less epoch-making, and in its importance more like mannerism, a style which developed during the timespan between renaissance and baroque. Research in this field has explained why mannerism did not develop into a unitary style, like renaissance or baroque, and kept the traits of a 'manner' through the paradox, the *discordia concors*, the combination of irreconcilable contrasts (Hauser, 1964, p. 13). There are obvious parallels with post-modernity. But there is little comfort in these parallels for the champions of traditional classical order. Mannerism was not followed by a new classicism but by baroque.

Just as this is the case for mannerism, one will have to give up efforts to construe clearly-delimited time phases of post-modernity. The only glue for the diverging phenomena is the post-modernity of common life styles. The simultaneous presence of phenomena with different historical implications seems to be a basic characteristic trait of post-modernity (Welsch, 1987, p. 4). The systematic question of the social scientist remains unanswered, however, when this kind of explanation based on the diversity of common life styles is given, namely: why have life-styles, in which elites of all spheres of society participate on an equal footing, such a different importance for the spheres of science, art and politics? Does it make any sense to transform notions of architectural and literary history into phases of the history of political thought? The existing examples for such efforts are not very encouraging. Very often modernity and post-modernity have been understood as a sequence of eras, almost in the manner Wœlfflin described the change from renaissance to baroque. A closer look at the phenomenon makes us aware of the problems of this analogy. Is post-modernity really a kind of new baroque? The baroque period is the object of the secret longing of quite a number of the champions of post-modernity. At the end of one of his books Charles Jencks confessed his longing for a baroque which united all art 'in order to achieve a rhetorical whole' (Jencks, 1980, postscription). Such confessions cause immediate counterreactions in the camp of post-modernity. So, even the prophet of post-modernity in architecture does not take seriously the pluralist credo and looks for a new whole! Lyotard was quick to point out this weak spot in this theory of *differend* (unresolvable conflict) (Lyotard, 1983, lin 12/24).

The baroque period gives us a fairly good insight into parallels of art and politics. A characteristic of this period too is the incompatibility of its elements. The search for unity, which is a driving force in the baroque period, brings out an exaggerated will to possess power, which was discovered by Carl J. Friedrich in phenomena as diverse as Hobbes and the baroque palace architecture (Friedrich, 1954, p. 56ff). Is this unity not more 'rhetorical' than real, as was even assumed by Jencks? Is it possible to interpret the whole epoch from the point of view of Thomas Hobbes' anthropology? It is obvious that this would mean singling out the baroque of the royal courts, to overestimate the Italian model and to ignore the Dutch variety. Was not there also the quiet genre-painting, which provides little evidence for the will to possess power, and is more a kind of indicator of a retreat into the niches of bourgeois society? Friedrich did not answer any of these questions. The history of political thought did not follow him in his expeditions to the sphere of art. It is true that the epithet 'baroque' is often found in the history of thought, but it remains ornamental. In the literature on Hobbes it is reduced to a question of style. Meinecke compared the theoretical constructions of Botero's Jesuitical machiavellianism with a 'richly decorated Jesuitical church' (Meinecke, 1963, p. 78). But all this remained an arabesque.

With regard to post-modernity, parallels between art and political theory are even more problematic. Post-modern iconoclasm intended to question the status of art as an 'institution' – a huge difference from the baroque period, in which art as institution was given additional weight. Politics and the state are much less suitable for quasi-anarchist tendencies which further their decomposition, than is architecture. States are not rebuilt every ten years, as – if necessary – public buildings can be.

MODERNITY AND POST-MODERNITY IN THE DEBATE OF THE THEORY OF SCIENCE

The interest of social scientists in the debate in the arts on post-modernity is only a marginal one, which is occasionally aroused on the level of reporting in the arts pages of newspapers. Only the philosophical discussion in the theory of science provided access for the social sciences to the debate on post-modernity. This second history of the reception of the concept is connected with new problems. It may be daring to point out analogies between art and social theory, but it is possible to refer to a common framework for periodization: modern art starts with Manet and Cézanne, modern social science theory exists as a genuine concept since the contributions of Durkheim, Max Weber and Pareto. In the sphere of art nobody would trace back modernity to the renaissance and then criticize *in toto* this 'project of a modernizing effort'. This is, however, exactly what philosophy tries to do. The 'project of a modernizing effort' is the accused party in the dock. Only a few early acquittals are known for Pascal and Nietzsche, Kierkegaard and later Heidegger. Some parts of the writings of Kant and Wittgenstein can hope for acts of grace, because they can be used for post-modern reasoning. The most important of the accused ones is Hegel and, for political reasons, Marx. Where a plea of 'not guilty' is entered, as Hennis does for Max Weber, the observers are quick to point out the Nietzschean logic of the argument. The philosophical analysis of details from a non-partisan distance has, however, great difficulties with this method of collecting evidence. It was possible to prove strong similarities between Hegel, who was prematurely found guilty and Heidegger, who was prematurely whitewashed, especially with regard to the evaluation of modernity (Kolb 1988, p. 201ff). These difficulties were overcome in the traditional manner by stressing the differences between the writings of the philosopher in question during his youth and in old age. Literary science has provided a clever example of how to do this: the Joyce of *Ulysses* was described as the embodiment of modernity, while the author of *Finnegan's Wake* was given the label 'post-modern'.

The global attack against modernity as a whole was facilitated by the construction of great *meta stories*. Lyotard changed their classification with every book he wrote. For once we find the differentiation between the idealistic meta story, which believes in a teleological development of the spirit; the enlightenment meta story, which hopes for the emancipation of mankind, and the historical meta story, which chases the hermeneutic of meaning. Later typologies present this trinity in blunter form: emancipation, satisfaction of spiritual needs and capitalism (Lyotard, 1984, p. 9ff). This last differentiation reminds us of Voltaire's verdict against Montesquieu's three types of government, which were logically not on the same level of abstraction. Voltaire said, this sounds like a note in a church register: 'male-female-illegitimate'. Whoever can be put in one of the three negative categories is also put on trial. 'Late Hegelianism', especially late left-wing Hegelianism, is arousing suspicion. Those who remain true to the old ideals of enlightenment are immediately found guilty of advocating 'total enlightenment' and are arrested as 'project managers of modernity' (Koslowski, 1986, p. 4f.). With his support for classical modernity Habermas has suffered this fate. And he wins little respect for the fact that in his defence of life styles against the system he opposes many aspects which are also disliked by the intellectual heads of post-modernity. Whoever among them wants to save Habermas' reputation, because he has hidden feelings of sympathy for him, has to excuse him: 'Habermas must have committed an error', at least with regard to his equation of post modernity and neo-conservatism (Huyssen/Scherpe, 1986, p. 29). Lyotard, however, sees little hope for Habermas. In his view he remains 'crypto-totalitarian': 'He changes the heterogeneity of language plays by the use of force', when he aims at consensus in an authority-free discourse (Lyotard, 1979, p. 8). Habermas has untypically ignored these attacks. Perhaps this is the only way to prevent the quarrel from ending like ancient tragedies: the heroes die behind the scene and the stage slowly empties.

Social scientists will tend to leave labelling to scientific retrospective, which has a greater distance from today's battle noises. Defining boundaries for post-modernity hardly seems to be possible. But what can be called 'modernity' from the point of view of social science theory can be defined about as clearly as in art; and this means it is a shorter period than most post-modern philosophers assume. Even Lyotard himself once gave a useful differentiation of modern theory. He saw modernity represented in two models, which either comprise society as a whole or see society as a dichotomic conflict. The positions of Parsons and Marx respectively represent these extremes (Lyotard, 1979, p. 25). This dichotomy is by no means novel: the suspicion of advocating ontology has been raised against both models for a long time. The first model has an ontological approach towards what unites societies; the second one, towards all that separates them. The critical theory which formulated this reproach had stronger preferences for the conflict model. Today it is accused of propagating a hidden integration model because of a deeply-felt longing for harmony.

No matter how bitter the confrontation between these two tendencies was, which clashed in the dispute on positivism, one has to stress as an antithesis to the equal status post-modernity gives to Marxism and systems theory, that even if some formal similarity cannot be denied, both approaches do not have the same degree of modernity. Neither the notion of integration nor the notion of conflict are, in addition, connected with the respective model from the start. Marxism in power has shown extreme integrative capabilities. Systems theory was able to develop very dynamic varieties, from Etzioni's concept of an 'active society' to Karl Deutsch's cybernetics (von Beyme, 1987, 6th ed., p. 172ff).

There are three special traits which differentiate modern theories from the more pre-modern/historical ones: (1) The differentiation between evolution and history; (2) The importance of comparisons; (3) The assumption that parts of society exist in their own right without a theoretical imperialism, which gives preference to one part of societies over all the others.

The Differentiation between Evolution and History

Modern theories in the narrow sense of the word differentiate between evolution and history. It is premature for post-modern criticism to put systems theories and holistic Marxism on an equal footing. It overlooks the fact that its criticism of Hegel and Marx reaches the open ears of the guardians of the holy grail of modern science theory, for Popper's characterization of Hegel and Marx as false prophets was meant no less seriously than Lyotard's. In contrast to the renegades of the French left, who left behind the abstractions of structural Marxism Althusser had provided as a guiding thought, Popper at last exempted Marx's radical moralism from the global suspicion of totalitarianism (Popper, 1970, p. 347). Important parts of Marxism, especially in the less sophisticated variety going back to Engels, Kautsky, Lenin, and Stalin, who reduced critical thinking to 'histomat', could not do without a teleological philosophy of history, including a laical hope for salvation. Max Weber and Durkheim were the first to give up such varieties of a determinist interpretation of evolution, which had dominated the debate of the nineteenth century under the influence of Comte and Spencer. This is true, no matter how many efforts are made to find even in Max Weber's writings the traits of neo-evolutionism. He was certainly primarily a sceptic with regard to evolution theories. Functionalist theories, too, which still keep the notion of evolution, have more modern than pre-modern characteristics. They clearly make a difference between evolution and history. Causality is reduced to contingent causality (Schluchter, 1979, p. 3); a sequence is only discernible in retrospect; prognosis on future developments of sequences are not possible. The sequences seen in retrospective are not evaluated, as in pre-modern theories with relation to the realization of certain ideas or to the compatibility with causalities which are postulated as being of a certain necessity, but in regard to the ability of societies to adapt themselves to change and to survive (Luhmann, 1975). It is therefore necessary to stand up against the sweeping attacks of post-modernity against supposedly modern theories in general, which have widely different modern contents.

The Importance of Comparisons

This lack of differentiation in their analysis results from the fact that advocates of the theory of post-modernity are indifferent with regard to *comparisons*. The incompatibility of language games formed Lyotard's opinion that the comparison of theories is in the last instance at best a useless mind-teaser. Theories of post-modernity reproduce in this way the pre-modern inability to compare. The old evolutionist schools, too, showed in spite of occasional *aperçus* on other cultures, a fundamental ignorance of them: Hegel's remarks on America are an obvious example. Max Weber was the first author to compare cultures systematically. His ability to differentiate by making comparisons was an even more remarkable effort than the stringent logic of his questions which, indeed, were central to the heuristic stage of his science. The search for the stringent logic of Weber's argument, started again by Hennis, has recently hindered the appreciation of the method of difference in Weber's writings.

Where evolution pushed the development into a certain direction there was no need for systematic comparisons. It was sufficient to overemphasize the elements of those societies which represented the future, be it Prussia for Hegel or a several-times-relocated future proletarian state for Marx, and to present the elements of social decline in other countries as aphorisms. Durkheim was the first author who saw in the comparison not just 'one method', but 'sociology itself' (Durkheim, 1950, p. 137). The comparison of the similar, although John Stuart Mill had stressed the necessity of applying the method of difference in addition to the method of concordance, was later developed by some functionalists into the method of functional equivalents. In a comparative perspective, apparently dissimilar phenomena displayed 'similarities'. These were not similarities of substance, but equivalent functions for the survival and the development of systems. Pre-modern and post-modern theoretical approaches, however, frequently agree in their low esteem for the comparative method in the social sciences.

Acceptance of the Existence of Parts of Society in their Own Right

The acceptance of the existence of parts of society in their own right, without making a systematic effort to find normative reasons why one sphere of society should dominate all others, is important for modern theories. It is certainly true that this rule has frequently been ignored. But most of the really modern theories only foretell in a more or less plausible manner the danger of colonization of one sphere by the other. They do not start by reducing the development of all spheres, which they characterize as super-structure, to the logic of the development of one and misinterpret the autonomy of the process of rationalization in different spheres. There is empirical evidence that where one sphere actually begins to colonize another (for example in phases of political mobilization) we generally find arguments against this process on the theoretical level. It is not by accident that the normativists of the Freiburg school of thought joined hands with the Cologne-Mannheim school of neo-positivism, when it came to fend-ing-off the political challenge of the student movement, although they basically had little in common. When the outside pressure had subsided they again marched separately. Normativists of many shades of opinions have developed a bias towards the political as long as it does not come uncontrolled from below. In the case of grassroot movements the separ-ation of *oikos* from *polis* is evoked. When, however, after the movement has died down, the state is too lax with regard to its attitude towards the formation of subcultures and autonomous circles, the primacy of the political in normative theory is revived in many varieties.

Normativists have kept fairly aloof, not only from the complexity of the detailed differentiation of modern societies, but also from the way its separate spheres are interconnected. A mere social differentiation into parts does not make a modern society. Differentiation as such also existed in ancient India or China, as we learnt from Max Weber. But the degree of intermix between different structural components in modern institutions and the interpenetration of different social spheres with the intention of control from both sides is unique to modern societies. These observations must have their place in any theory which deserves the name 'modern' (Münch, 1984, p. 22f.).

In the meantime the two meta theories, which for quite a while kept elements of pre-modern theories, namely normativism and neo-Aristotelian-ism, on the one hand and the critical Frankfurt school on the other, have gone different ways. Habermas and Offe have time and again produced other varieties of theoretical models for the differentiation and interdepen-dencies of autonomous spheres of societies. They have to some degree moved toward functionalist thinking without repudiating the idea of the wholeness of society. The normativists have generally not wanted to get involved in theoretical work on empirical details. Small wonder that they are profoundly impressed by the general negation of modernity, which was formulated most clearly by Nietzsche in the nineteenth century. The post-modern revolt against thinking in fields of a system theoretical super matrix therefore led (not by chance) to a renaissance for Nietzsche's thought. These days Nietzsche's slogan, 'God is dead', only fundamentally challenges a few schools of thought, in contrast to its effects in the nineteenth century. Post-modernity, with a few exceptions, like Robert Spaemann's position, does not believe that it is possible to return to pre-modern ethic ideals. But it recognizes the same enemy Nietzsche saw in his new clothes. The place of the *priest as ruler* has been taken by the *ruling technocrat*. God remains dead for most of the post-modern philosophers. The more important problem is, as was once said by the Italian Vattimo, 'to find out whether we are able to live without neuroses in a world in which "God is dead"' (Vattimo, 1985).

The consequences of the Nietzsche renaissance for the social sciences at first seemed to be negligible: it is hardly possible to base social theories on Nietzsche's writings. So it was not by accident that Nietzsche's contribution was brought into the debate via the history of thought. This was at first the case above all in Latin countries. They used to be proud of their Cartesian tradition of philosophical thinking, but this tradition which provided very few answers for important contemporary problems.

In Germany, wherever a frontal attack on modern theory in politics seemed to be impossible, this attack was launched on the level of the history of ideas. Max Weber was picked as an appropriate object for criticism. For decades there had come the message (via America) that he was the true father of modernity in the social sciences. Weber's achievements, his elaboration of different spheres of life and their inherent logic of action, were now given a second-rate status. Although post-modern critics pour scorn on the method of reconstruction of the central topics of an *oeuvre* because it polishes the 'dim glamour of functionalism', they themselves have chosen this approach to filter out 'the real topic' and the 'genuine research interest' as represented in cryptic remarks or asides in Max Weber's writings. New varieties of the 'jargon of genuineness', not influenced at all by Heidegger's thought, were heard from the Freiburg school. In fact all this fell on open ears. No 'orthodox Weberian' denies that there is little discrepancy between the writings and the person of Max Weber. When Wilhelm Hennis writes that 'Weber saw what was dear to his heart', he defends himself with the archaic language he uses against the suspicion to have followed a fashion of post-modernity. Nevertheless, it remains remarkable that he, as a daring challenger of fashions in theoretical thought, quite enjoys following the contemporary mood. Certainly without reading much of the *'frankolatrie'*, he rediscovers enough of Nietzsche's footprints in Weber's writings to be able to snatch the latter from functionalist modernity (Hennis, 1987, p. 57). The citations chosen to prove this hypothesis are more than far-fetched. But even those authors who criticize this interpretation of Max Weber as being a mere construction will understand why Hennis is so impatient with Weber's functionalist epigones, who have taken possession of the ideas of a differentiation of society into parts and the intermix of social spheres with an enthusiasm for classification of Linnean dimensions. But does all this justify a fundamental misreading of the contributions of the intellectual heads of modernity in a way which eliminates the boundaries of modernity and which results in a pre-modern practical philosophy, which has little to do with Weber except for the 'holy rage', which is so characteristic of the easy polemic of not spectacularly creative temperaments? A closer look at arguments of this kind will show that this effort is not post-modern. Post-modern theory would prefer to find inconsistencies in Max Weber's writings. In contrast to the doubts Hennis had, the theory of post-modernity can not only live with inconsistencies: it also sees them as an enrichment. Post-modern thinking does not feel the need for the interpretative synthesis of hidden unity when it comes to finding a political thinker acceptable.

Even if Hennis' effort was to convince a majority of Weber experts, what would be gained if one knew Weber's true research interest and his motivation in the heuristic stage of the conceptualization of his research? The genesis of an *oeuvre* is never identical with the importance it gains in the history of thought. Not even revocations help posterity. Lévy-Bruhl is still cited as the one who formulated the theory of primitive mentality, although he revoked it in *Carnets*. Weber did not revoke anything, but he will remain important for a theory of modernity and of occidental rationalism, no matter what he himself thought was his central research interest.

This detour to the subject of the reception of Weber was necessary to show that the debate on post-modernity takes diverging directions, depending on one's attitude towards classical modernity. In this in fact lies a parallel with the debate on abstract art. Habermas in his exchange with modernity has increasingly enriched his once fairly idealistic-looking theory of evolution and has prepared it for empirical theory construction. The liberation and ecological wing of post-modernity has therefore emotionally given up on him: 'he is regarded as only a kind of technocratic social democrat with a bad conscience with regard to the life style problem'. Hennis' pre-modern interpretation of theory has also not excused Habermas' proximity to the position of orthodox Weberians. According to Hennis, Habermas 'simply turned upside down' Weber's primary research interest by the reconstruction of Weber's theory he presents in his *Theorie des kommunikativen Handelns* (Habermas, 1981, p. 234; Hennis, 1987, p. 11, n. 18). In spite of such idiosyncratic patterns of interpretation, Hennis has worked out one of Max Weber's traits, which was seen, too, by those theoretical heads interested in the differentiation of society in partial social systems. Diverging partial rationalities were bound together by Max Weber in his notion of an ethic of responsibility for the political leadership (Offe, 1986, p. 152). Maybe Weber is not the first choice for a practical philosophy, which sees the solution of the problem of the modern fragmentation of society into spheres of action with their own logic in a greater stress on the predominance of the political sphere. But true post-modern theoreticians have occasionally stressed the superior status of a state, free from the mythology of many aspects of the theory of social systems. Koslowski, for example, basing this opinion on a different argument, shares with Hennis a stress on the political (Koslowski, 1986, p. 177). Hardly anybody goes so far as to claim for Max Weber the role of a forefather of a genuine political science and to snatch him from sociology. The whole debate on the autonomy of the political is not an exclusively German affair. Crick in England, and Sartori in Italy, have in a similar way defended politics and have fought against the colonization of political science by political sociology. A long time before post-modernity had been invented there had been a debate in political theory on the status of the history of ideas (von Beyme, 1988). Scientists are inclined to separate strictly modern political theory from the history of ideas. Modernity, like modernity in art, is no older than a hundred years, but this does not stop followers of scientism from occasionally citing Tocqueville, Montesquieu or Machiavelli as if they were contemporaries.

A theory of modernity in the social sciences has to insist on no longer giving politics the role of a 'monarch of science', and it has to stress that the theory of differentiation into parts has to be accepted. The task of political scientists in this debate is to fight against a superficial bridging of boundaries between separate differentiated notions, and also to oppose a mixture of economic categories and rational choices of strategies for action in the political field, as well as the post-modern aestheticism, which dominates the diagnosis of our contemporary condition. From the political point of view such an attitude is in the meantime no longer regarded with suspicion. This defense of modernity is more than a 'fuss about standards', (Hennis, 1987, p. 57) and on the other hand is no longer under the suspicion of radicalism. The defense of modernity has today aspects of conservatism. Habermas, too, has to live with this reproach.

THE CONTRIBUTION OF THE THEORY OF POST MODERNITY TO POLITICAL THEORY

Only after the front lines of a controversy which involves many disciplines have been clearly marked out, does it become possible to filter out those elements of post-modern thought which are immediately relevant for the formation of political theories. In this process one has to be careful not to limit the choice of elements prematurely by treating post-modernity as a synonym for neo-conservatism, as Habermas does. It should not be forgotten that the new traditionalism, which openly or in a hidden manner uses post-modern patterns of arguments, re-interprets social questions as questions of style, and by doing so shelters these questions from the political discussion (Habermas, 1985, p. 26). But the opponents of post-modernity are not the only champions of enlightment. Lyotard, who is ignored by Habermas despite the latter's immensely broad knowledge of the literature, would be justified in claiming components of enlightment for his post-modern thinking. Habermas would have to excommunicate some members of the younger generation of the Frankfurt school from the community in discourse, if it was true that the reception of post-modern theories was synonymous with neo-conservatism. Albrecht Wellmer has chosen a middle position between Lyotard and Habermas with regard to the presentation of arguments connecting structures of micro-level life-styles and the system (Wellmer, 1985, p. 107). This fruitless controversy has its origins, above all, in the attitude of the Frankfurt school toward the Green party. The younger generation (for example Claus Offe) has dealt with Green and Alternative movements with rather strong though some-what hesitant sympathies. Habermas remained suspicious. He saw an unholy alliance of ideas of anti-modernity with a whiff of pre-modernity in the following of the Greens and the Alternatives (Habermas, 1981, p. 464). This quarrel about their correct classification is still not finished. Without an appropriate historical distance it can be assumed that this will remain one of the rare cases which are fully characterized by Lyotard's notion of '*differend*' (unresolvable conflict). For this conflict there is no interme-diation and it is not a situation which would allow a resolution by a court decision or a political majority.

For those on the left of Habermas, post-modernity and neo-conservatism are synonyms for the u-turn a good part of the left-wing intellectuals have made. Not everybody, however, who has turned his back on Marxism, is automatically a conservative. In France we find the most abstract versions of a structuralist Marxism. It is not by chance that the post-modern counterreaction was strongest there. The power of the intel-lectuals has become a mystique in many countries. But in the classic country for post-modernity, the United States, this philosophy prospered more on the base of a traditional anti-intellectualism. In France the change to a post-modern position was much more frequently a conversion. Numer-ous intellectuals revoked their former ideas and started to question funda-mentally the role of the intellectual as responsible for the great meta stories. It was exactly this idea – that by a voluntarist act of willpower one could eliminate the intellectual as a central figure – that showed, however, that this initiative came from relatively pre-modern intellectuals, who are fairly blind to the social function of the intelligentsia. Still, the tombstones for the intellectuals provided some building bricks for an adequate contem-porary political theory. It was above all three elements of theory which influenced the social sciences: (1) the fight against technocracy; (2) the radicalization of pluralism; (3) a sceptical attitude toward majorities and the demand for an improved status for minorities.

The Fight against Technocracy

In contrast to some approaches of *posthistoire*, from Gehlen to Baudrillard, there is no praise or angry acceptance of the inevitable *rule of technology* by the theory of post-modernity. The information revolution in society has brought into the open a new form of technocracy. Post-modernity provides resistance against the danger of total social control which is caused by this development. The obsession of francophone theoreticians with a technocratic uniformity of the language sometimes sounds on a more intellectual level like the battle cries against the predominance of '*franglais*' and the advance of Anglo-Saxon computer language. Insights can pass the new channels of technology, according to Lyotard, only when it is possible to translate them into *information bits* (Lyotard, 1973, p. 13). This not only gives technocrats in general, but also the anglophone ones, an advantage. A uniform code language as a medium for communication would, however, affect above all the ability of the English language to differentiate, and in the medium-term it would create roughly comparable conditions for all languages. It would just be the less widely understood languages, like French, which cannot hope to defend their regional or sectoral predominance, that would lose from the victory of a more uniform and standardized English.

Lyotard's theory of post-modernity shares some of the characteristics of enlightenment, because his scenarios do not lead to resignation. Active counter-movements, opposing the language of technology, are possible:

> It [technology] can also help those groups which discuss meta prescriptions by giving them the kind of information they usually lack for an informed decision. The best strategy to use information in this alternative way is in principle a very easy one, namely open access to the computer memories and data banks for the public (Lyotard, 1979, p. 50).

For the time being this hope still sounds overoptimistic. Only the 'hackers' have so far justified this trust in the positive effects of computers for the defense of pluralism. Their unsystematic and far from fundamentally hostile activities, however, are an incentive for the technocratic establishment to erect additional hurdles against common access to the means of information. Though there may be overoptimistic hopes invested in post-modernity, it has no nostalgic premodern elements, like the ones which impressed Marcuse so much when he idealized life in pre-industrial societies: 'In lyrics and in prose of this pre-technical culture we find the rhythm of human beings, who walk about, sit in coaches, and who have

Eurobarometer

time and the inclination to reflect, to watch things, to feel and to tell stories' (Marcuse, 1967, p. 79). The main achievement of post-modernity is the proof it provides that this pleasure in life can be revived by making use of modern technologies. Chances for alternatives exist: against what Lyotard calls 'economic discourse' which he rejects, it is possible to preserve 'the accident, the feat, the wonder, the expectation of an emotional community' in reality and not only as a *non sequitur* in the form of a reported happening in the arts pages. Lyotard sees possibilities for an 'extreme escalation of conflicts' (Lyotard, 1983, lin. 252). These thoughts can also be found in more concrete scenarios of the social sciences which do not find their justification in references to post-modern philosophy. In Ulrich Beck's *Risikogesellschaft* similar solutions of the dilemma of modernity are described without reference to Lyotard. Industrial society and modernity are moving apart, as in art the 'avantgarde' and modernity are doing likewise. The separation into halves can, however, be overcome, since it has become obvious that the general alternatives, like capitalism and socialism, which dominated the classical modern debate, are no longer valid (Beck, 1986, p. 361ff).

The Radicalization of Pluralism

Theories of pluralism, stemming from the theory of post-modernity, at first sight do not seem to be new, especially for political scientists (Kremendahl, 1977). They are at the centre of every democratic theory of politics. But the broadening of the idea of pluralism in the theory of post-modernity acquires a new quality. 'Incompatibility' becomes constitutive of the new pluralism, whereas old pluralism insisted on a minimal consensus, at least with regard to procedures. The rationality of a conflict is no longer predominantly formed after the model of science, as in the old pluralism developed by political theory in the writings of authors from the days of Bentley to Truman or Fraenkel. The competition of different rationalities of art, religion, myths, life styles complicates the discourse of new pluralism. Even for a sociologist like Beck, scientific and social rationality have grown apart, but in contrast to the opinion of some post-modern philosophers there remains at least a relationship between them (Beck, 1986). Their differentiation increasingly causes problems. The evaluation of the consequences of new technologies, for example, has to concentrate more and more on the social acceptability of these new technologies, and the given expectations of the citizens are by no means overwhelmingly based on scientific sources. The unorthodox/orthodox thinking of critical rationalism still thought that it was necessary to unmask the demand for a *double truth* as an obscure strategy for fending off criticism. It insisted on the one 'critical' truth (Albert, 1968, p. 105). Even the notions of truth and rationality have become pluralized in the theory of post-modernity. Feyerabend's provocation of 1975, his slogan 'anything goes', has broken the mould of critical rationalism (Feyerabend, 1976, p. 45). Critical rationalists, who were not ready to burn the house down, as Feyerabend had done, reacted in an adequate manner with self-criticism, but remained true to their basic convictions, like Helmut Spinner, who opted for a broader concept of pluralism (Spinner, 1980, p. 38). This was more than an extension of the interior pluralism of science, which tended to prematurely reduce the competition among concepts to those it had previously defined as being scientific. Now a *double rationality* was accepted, which was already assumed to exist in Max Weber's writings. (Its discovery could have saved Hennis from a great number of exaggerations.) A difference is made between a *basic rationality* which allows an orientation on the level of principles and rules and a *situational rationality*, which is defined by the occasion and what is opportune. Most of the empirically-found mixtures of rationality lie between these two extremes, but seldom in the middle. Rationality is in itself already plural and multi-dimensional (Spinner, 1986, p. 933f.). Influences of the theory of art are obvious, where for a long time the extremes of rationality and expressivity, observation and consciousness were juxtaposed. The non-theoretical experiences, which are closer to the abilities of seeing things and expressing oneself, keep on leading counter-attacks against the colonization of art by theoretical rationality (Kamper, 1986, p. 72). Allowing for a time-lag, we can observe a similar development in social theories.

Is it possible for political theory to follow this broadening of pluralism in the debate on post-modernity? Its notion of pluralism was relatively similar to the one of classical modernity. This is especially true for the 'democracy in permanent self-defense' of the Federal Republic, which is inclined to limit pluralism by exclusion of the extremes. Small wonder that critical rationalism here became a kind of official state doctrine for quite a while (Lührs, et al. 1978). To free the constitution of a democracy in permanent self-defense from narrow-mindedness is already difficult enough, as long as there is no general consensus on the existing order, and as long as terrorism at the extreme ends of the political spectrum still raises fears. The theory of many truths and the concept of a double rationality, however, can hardly form the base for a democratic theory. The clever difference made between conflict (*differend*) and legal conflict (*litige*) is not very helpful for the sphere of politics. Especially in the Federal Republic, politics itself finds a safety valve in the possibility of *taking political conflict to court* as a reaction to being confronted with a pluralism of growing contradictions. The concept of a judicial system without loopholes does not allow a political question in the final instance – doctrine in the name of which the Supreme Court, as in the United States, can claim not to be responsible for those political questions which it does not accept as legal ones.

But politics cannot do without court procedures. They may not solve conflicts in most cases, but they at least close them down. Court procedures are guarantees that the political struggle for a majority does not develop into an unresolvable conflict in the meaning Lyotard has given this expression. Political conflict, too, a third type which was neglected by Lyotard, works toward compromises. Court procedures very often result in both parties being discontented and the decision finds general criticism, though without any consequences. Political conflict aims at compromises, but the gains for the parties involved are not shared out equally. Very often a group which holds the majority profits more from a decision. The minority accepts the asymmetric compromise only temporarily, hoping that it itself one day will be in the majority. Therefore democratic pluralism has to avoid that any relevant group permanently remains in the minority position. Wherever this is unavoidable, because of structural reasons, as with regard to ethnic minorities, the conflict must be de-escalated by political veto powers, offers of participation or autonomous rights of decision-making with regard to a few questions. Politics cannot transfer incompatible point-of-views, as characterized by Lyotard, into the political arena. The result would be civil war, or the breakdown of the community into subcultures. Both developments have in most cases not been very helpful for weaker groups.

One point of criticism made by the theory of modernity against Habermas' model of rational discourse is that there is no discourse which is power neutral (Koslowski, 1986, p. 14). Without an acceptance of the rules of the game – an acceptance which Habermas defines as the condition *sine qua non* for discourse – any conflict will from the start be dominated by what the most powerful participant defines as right or wrong. Lyotard's slogan 'we want to play, leave us alone' would have as a result the predominance of the strongest group through the depoliticization of the rest of society. Polemical attacks against Habermas, who is accused of using brute force against language rules by defining rules of discourse, are not very convincing in the light of a comparison between Habermas' and Lyotard's ideas of a debating society (Lyotard, 1979, p. 8). Both models are based on rational self-determination, democratic decision-making and the solution of conflicts without the use of force (Wellmer, 1985). It is hardly fair to criticize Habermas for the fact that in public debate his model of a discourse is understood as a synonym for the procedures of a general meeting of university students.

The Validity of the Majority Principle in Doubt

The broadening of the notion of pluralism and the idea that traditions of thought are incompatible has lead to the logical conclusion that *the validity of the majority principle is in doubt*. Lyotard's enthusiasm for a '*patchwork of minorities*', as if he was describing a post-modern building erected according to the principles of decomposition architecture, sound neutral and unpolitical. But ideas of this kind cannot be reserved for subcultures, which flee into an aesthetic world, to escape from the logo-, techno- or phallocentrism, or whatever else may be a dominant principle which irks a special group.

Of all post-modern philosophers, only Robert Spaemann took up the challenge of the majority principle in the political sphere: 'Wherever a person's subjectiveness is under threat, everybody is free to help the affected person who has been stripped of the duty of being loyal. Every such person himself can now revoke his allegiance' (Spaemann, 1984, p. 252). The two cases Spaemann compared are hardly convincing in the light of today's majorities. He argues that the industrial use of nuclear power has the effect of freeing the citizen from his loyalty to the state in a similar way as the pogroms against the Jews. In his opinion it is true in both cases that the majority rule loses its binding power because it may lead to decisions which are irreversible. The idea of a 'patchwork of minorities' looks for a new majority – the majority of those affected over the generations is greater than the majority of those who decide today. In the past conservatives, like Conrad Ferdinand Meyer, liked to evoke the majority of the dead: 'We the dead, we the dead have bigger armies than you have in your countries and you have on your seas'. Today we are justified in making reference to the armies of the unborn whose life chances we are threatening. Although there are some plausible arguments, it remains unclear who should declare himself a defender of the unborn, and under what circumstances, especially if one takes into account that the prognosis of the future can never be more than mere speculation. The classical law of resistance of the monarchomanians, like the school of Salamanca, developed politically more differentiated rules for the mobilization of resistance. Civil disobedience used to be only one step away from the final escalation (the murder of the tyrant). Today for some eco-radicals civil disobedience already seems to be the first step in heating-up conflict. The American civil rights movement, which so many of the neo-resistance fighters use for the legitimization of their actions, has frequently been misinterpreted in this context. Martin Luther King never questioned positive law. His limited offenses against the law had as their unescapable consequence sanctions by the state, which he even welcomed as part of his strategy to develop the consciousness of those affected and to form new majorities. He never assumed that sanctions themselves were illegitimate. The division between legitimacy and legality, which is foreign to American tradition, has already caused more than enough mischief for the history of thought in Germany.

Post-modern philosophy refuses to obey the demands of systems, so it is not by chance that it has to proceed from an angle which differs from the great systematic theories of modernity. Post-modernity develops the relationship between elements of thought of different groups and traditions of thought.

Only for Lyotard's writings could one say there is a 'systematic' framework. It therefore seems to be an obvious thought to look for equivalents
of elements of the theory of post-modernity in the real world. One can do
this by testing the opinions of citizens and by quantifying value change.
This empirically-minded procedure hardly succeeds in formulating a general theory. Its underlying theoretically abstract concept is *Postmaterialism*, which was filtered out as a topic by the analysis of question items
(Inglehart, 1977, p. 40f.). Less empirically-minded procedures tend to
construct a *life style paradigm*, and to concentrate more on the change of
organizational patterns of society. Empirics, too, share the opinion that the
term 'new social movements' is no mystification. There are empirical
criteria which allow us to differentiate between new social movements and
the old social movements of classical modernity, which are mainly based on
the values of modern industrial society. For the adherents of the new social
movements some ideas of the debate on post-modernity have a prominent
status, but it would be wrong to classify every new social movement as a
post-modern one. Groups of the old social movements have jumped on the
bandwagon of the new ones; some of these are in their tendency *pre-
modern*, even if they support the Green party. Many of the new social
movements have a *new holistic approach*, which is incompatible with
post-modern theories in the narrow sense of the word. It would be just as
wrong to equate *post-modernity* and *Postmaterialism*, as is frequently done
in popular debate. Even less convincing is the characterization of Postmaterialism as an early stage of post-modernity, even though many elements
of post-modernity go beyond those values which are on the abstract level
designated as Postmaterialism in measuring value change. Some of the
questions used to measure Postmaterialism reflects the more abstract
elements of the theory of post-modernity, but it is identical with them.

Post-modernity is better characterized as the absolute negation of modernity, even if it sees itself as its completion. But in this case, too, it has to
overemphasize many criteria of modernity in a so far unknown manner.
Postmaterialism is at best the questioning of some of the 'modern' values of
an industrial society. With regard to social movements, experience has
shown time and again that by no means do we find uniform non-modern
attitudes amongst them, and therefore no homogeneous anti-modern
social environment either. The membership of *new social movements* show
in their actual behaviour, as can be measured by *objective indicators* of
organizational research, an even more contradictory pattern than the
search for *subjective indicators* with the help of interviews produces. The
support for postmaterial values is very often connected with a readiness to
form coalitions with the classic modern organizations such as parties or
unions. Time and again purists have been disappointed by the lack of
consistency in the behavior of Postmaterialists. This is one reason why the
new social movements, despite their potential for creating changes, have

brought about a less dramatic paradigmatic change than was originally assumed (von Beyme, 1988). If, against all these warnings, some sociologists still set out to find post-modernity in society, then their only hope are the elitist circles of the producers of culture. Empirical research which does not limit its interest to the study of some elites would therefore be well-advised to avoid biasing the term postmaterialism by not insisting on the inclusion of all elements of post-modernity. It can be assumed that strictly post-modern thought will never completely dominate society, but that it will remain contingent on the subsystem culture and science, because other autonomous spheres of the social system have developed their differing varieties of a greater inclination to compromise, namely the law, the economy and last but not least, politics. Traits of post-modernity could at best be shown with respect to the above-mentioned contradictions, which can be found in some Postmaterialist individuals or new social movements. But only the post-modernity of the art pages would be inclined to identify itself with a 'praise of inconsistent behaviour'.

POST MODERNITY AND POSTMATERIALISM

Theories of post-modernity affect the construction of theories in social sciences in their function as holistic meta theories. The mood of post-modernity influences many spheres of the theoretical debate in the social sciences, even if there is no explicit reference to post-modern philosophy. The development of identity and autonomy of social subsystems, *autopoiesis*, has become today's fashion for many partial theories. The leading lights of abstract systems theory, like Niklas Luhman, have carefully moved away from the notion of the system and have moved into the direction of '*processes of life*' via bio-poiese (Lipp 1987). There is a hardly discernible narrowing of the distance between highly abstract theoretical constructions, no matter how noisy their conflict is. Lyotard's model of unresolvable conflict develops in this way even in the sphere of science, for which it was conceived, into a self-destroying prophecy. For quite a while it has become obvious that the major theories are moving closer together, like Marxism and systems theory, in efforts towards a policy-orientated partial analysis. The further development of highly abstract thought in the theory of post-modernity hides a process of *rapprochement*, which is taking place behind the verbal smokescreen of increasingly autonomous language games, and which softens the model of unresolvable conflict.

There is no empirically-secure integrated theory of post-modernity which could be used as a recipe for the construction of political theories. Judging by the demand for the plurality and autonomy of theories post-modernity upholds, there will never be such a theory. Post-modern terms have their origin in the debate on art. There we have never seen a competition which led to the exclusion of varieties of pluralism in such a way as was the case for other sectors of society. The only exception in this respect is architecture, which now has to pay the bill of post-modernity for this development. Terms for periods in the history of art remain problematic, as can be shown for other eras, too (see pp. 310–14). But for art the notions of modernity and post-modernity are still more useful than the broader interpretation these notions find in the philosophical debate (see pp. 314–21).

Just as it is relatively easy to mark off the limits of classical modernity in art, so there are some criteria to be found for modernity in social science theory, by making a difference between evolution and history, by looking at the status of comparisons or by testing the assumption of autonomous spheres of society, without accepting an anti-theoretical imperialism with regard to one of these spheres. One should stand up against the downgrading of 'general theory' as such by the theory of post-modernity. It is necessary to realize the dangers inherent in a reduction of the complexity of societies by overexaggerated efforts to revive life styles. The unity of the social dimensions of life could perhaps be reconstructed under the banner of community or solidarity. The populist drive which would be necessary to achieve this bears in itself, however, more likely than not the threat that it may result in a new 'forced community' created by command from above (Offe, 1986, p. 152).

The contributions of post-modern theoretical approaches to political theory in the more narrow sense of the word (see pp. 321–9) are their discovery of new varieties of resistance against the rule of technology and the preparation for the needs of the electronic age. They include a useful broadening of the concept of pluralism, which, however, in its exaggerated rigidity provides no access for a democratic theory. Efforts concentrating on a new interpretation of the right to resistance lack thorough deliberations with regard to the implementation of derived strategies and are in their intentions incompatible with the rules of parliamentary democracy. In future one would need more stress on the theoretical possibility of sharing pressure among the different models of discourse: 'scientific and unresolvable conflict', 'court case' and 'political compromise'. It may be true that in science little damage is caused by *itio in partes* of incompatible positions. For the political system this model would be a catastrophe. The 'tombstone for the intellectual', which Lyotard demanded, still has to be built. In this tomb one should also bury the idea that Lyotard's model of conflict can be transferred from the sphere of science to the field of politics.

REFERENCES

Albert, Hans (1968) *Traktat uber kritische Vernunft* (Tübingen: Mohr).
Beck, Ulrich (1986) *Die Risikogesellschaft* (Frankfurt: Suhrkap).
von Beyme, Klaus (1987) *Der Wiederaufbau. Architektur und Städtebau in beiden deutschen Staaten* (München: Piper).
von Beyme, Klaus (1987) *Die politischen Theorien der Gegenwart* (München: Piper) 6th ed.
von Beyme, Klaus (1988) 'Die Rolle der Theoriegeschichte in der modernen Politikwissenschaft: Das Beispiel Amerikas' in Klaus von Beyme: *Der Vergleich in der Politikwissenschaft* (München: Piper) pp. 88–105.
von Beyme, Klaus (1988) 'Neue soziale Bewegungen und politische Parteien' in Klaus von Beyme: *Der Vergleich in der Politikwissenschaft* (München: Piper) pp. 247–68.
Durkheim, Emile (1950) *Les règles de la méthode sociologique* (Paris: PUF) 11th edition.
Feyerabend, Paul (1979) *Erkenntnis für freie Menschen* (Frankfurt: Suhrkamp).
Feyerabend, Paul (1976) *Wider den Methodenzwang* (Frankfurt: Suhrkamp).
Fischer, G. et al. (1987) *Abschied von der Postmoderne* (Braunschweig: Vieweg).
Friedrich, Carl J. (1954) *Das Zeitalter des Barocks. Kultur und Staaten Europas im 17. Jahrhundert* (Stuttgart: Kohlhammer).
Gottlieb, Carl A. (1976) *Modern Art* (New York: Dutton).
The Peggy Guggenheim Collection (Venedig, undated).
Guilbaut, Serge (1983) *How New York Stole the Idea of Modern Art. Abstract Expressionism, Freedom, and the Cold War* (Chicago: Chicago University Press).
Habermas, Jürgen (1985) 'Moderne und postmoderne Architektur', in Jürgen Habermas, *Die neue Unübersichtlichkeit* (Frankfurt: Suhrkamp) (11–29).
Habermas, Jürgen (1981) *Theorie des kommunikativen Handelns* (Frankfurt: Suhrkamp).
Habermas, Jürgen (1985) *Die Neue Unübersichtlichkeit* (Frankfurt: Suhrkamp).
Habermas, Jürgen (1981) 'Die Moderne – ein unvollendetes Projekt' in Jürgen Habermas, *Kleine politische Schriften I–IV* (Frankfurt: Suhrkamp).
Hauser, Arnold (1964) *Der Manierismus* (Munchen: Beck).
Hennis, Wilhelm (1987) *Max Webers Fragestellung* (Tubingen, Mohr).
Huyssen, Andreas and Klaus R. Scherpe (eds) (1986) *Postmoderne. Zeichen eines kulturellen Wandels* (Reinbek: Rowohlt).
Inglehart, Ronald (1977) *The Silent Revolution. Changing Values and Political Styles Among Western Publics* (Princeton, NJ: Princeton University Press).
Jencks, Charles (1977, 1980) *The Language of Postmodern Architecture* (London: Academy Editions) 3rd edition.
Kamper, Dietmars (1986) *Zur Soziologie der Imagination* (München: Hanser).
Kolb, David (1988) *Critique of Pure Modernity, Hegel, Heidegger and After* (Chicago: Chicago University Press).
Koslowski, Peter (1986) 'Die Baustellen der Moderne', in Peter Koslowski et al. (eds) *Moderne Postmoderne* (Weinheim: Acta Humaniora).
Koslowski, Peter (1986) 'Sein-lassen-können als Überwindung des Modernismus', in Peter Koslowski et al., op. cit. (173–84).
Koslowski, Peter (1986) 'Baustellen der Postmoderne', in Peter Koslowski et al., op. cit. (1–16).
Kremendahl, Hans (1977) *Pluralismustheorie in Deutschland* (Leverkusen: Heggen).

Laermann, Klaus (1986) 'Lecancan und Derridada. Über die Frankolatrie in den Kulturwissenschaften', *Kursbuch* 84, pp. 43–53.

Lipp, Wolfgang (1987) 'Autopoiesis biologisch, autopoiesis soziologisch. Wohin führt Luhmanns Paradigmawechsel?' *Kölner Zeitschrift für Soziologie und Sozialpsychologie*, vol. 39.

Luhmann, Niklas (1975) 'Evolution und Geschichte', in Niklas Luhmann (ed.) *Soziologische Aufklärung II* (Opladen: Westdeutscher Verlag).

Lührs, Georg et al. (ed.): (1978) *Theorie und Politik aus kritischrationaler Sicht* (Berlin: Dietz).

Lyotard, Jean-François (1983) *Le différend* (Paris: Editions de Minuit).

Lyotard, Jean-François (1984) *Tombeau de l'intellectuel* (Paris: Editions Galilee).

Lyotard, Jean-François (1979) *La condition postmoderne* (Paris: Editions de Minuit).

Marcuse, Herbert (1967) *Der eindimensionale Mensch* (Neuwied: Luchterhand).

Meinecke, Friedrich (1963) *Die Idee der Staatsräson in der neueren Geschichte* (Munchen: Oldenbourg) 3rd edition.

Münch, Richard (1984) *Die Struktur der Moderne* (Frankfurt: Suhrkamp).

Naess, Arne (1980) 'Paul Feyerabend – ein Held der Grünen?' in Hans-Peter Duerr (ed.) *Versuchungen. Aufsätze zur Philosophie Paul Feyerabends* (Frankfurt: Suhrkamp) vol. 1 pp. 185–199.

Offe, Claus (1986) 'Die Utopie der Null-Option. Modernität und Modernisierung als politische Gütekriterien', in Koslowski, op. cit. (143–72).

Popper, Karl R. (1970) *Falsche Propheten. Hegel, Marx und die Folgen* (Bern: Francke) 2nd edition.

Schluchter, Wolfgang (1979) *Die Entwicklung des okzidentalen Rationalismus* (Tübingen: Mohr).

Spaemann, Robert (1984) 'Technische Eingriffe in die Natur als Problem der politischen Ethik', in Bernd Guggenberger and Claus Offe (eds): *An den Grenzen der Mehrheitsdemokratie* (Opladen: Westdeutscher Verlag) (240–53).

Spinner, Hellmut F. (1989) 'Gegen Ohne Für Vernunft, Wissenschaft, Demokratie etc. Ein Versuch, Feyerabends Philosophie aus dem Geist der Kunst zu verstehen', in Hans-Peter Duerr (ed.): *Versuchungen. Aufsätze zur Philosphie Paul Feyerabends* (Frankfurt: Suhrkamp) vol. 1 (35–109).

Spinner, Helmut 'Max Weber, Carl Schmitt, Bert Brecht als Wegweiser zum ganzen Rationalismus der Doppelvernunft. Über die beiden äußersten Möglichkeiten sich in einer irrationalen Welt rational zu orientieren', *Merkur*, 1986 (923–35).

Vattimo, Gianni (1985) *Al di la soggetto* (Mailand: Feltrinelli). Interview with *Lotta continua*.

Wellmer, Albrecht (1985) *Zur Dialektik von Moderne und Postmoderne* (Frankfurt: Suhrkamp).

Welsch, Wolfgang (1987) *Unsere postmoderne Moderne* (Weinheim: VCH, Acta humaniora) 1987.

19 On the Real Withering-away of the State

Ghiţa Ionescu, Professor Emeritus,
University of Manchester

Among the questions posed by Eurobarometer to the Europeans interviewed, there is one which I consider most pertinent, and the answers which it received most relevant. This is the question asked regularly about whether people feel that society should be changed, and if so, whether the change must be brought about by reformist or revolutionary action. Interestingly enough, mass support for the revolutionary option has been eroding steadily, ever since this question was first asked in the 1970s.

I would like to submit two comments which are, I believe, directly relevant to this survey question and to the answers it gets. The first comment concerns the meaning of the concept of revolution. Although the word 'revolution' originally meant 'revolving' or turning round a circular itinerary to come back to the point from which it started, after the eighteenth century it changed into something quite contrary, into an irreversible qualitative jump effected by people in history from one kind of society to another, or in Marxist terms from the state-ridden society to the society liberated from the state, either by having it first smashed, and then, as society begins to function by itself, by 'withering away' in uselessness. The first point which I submit is that as first the French Revolution and then the Russian Revolution proved that they only had the effect of *reconstructing* and *imposing* a stronger state than that which they initially proposed to eliminate – so the meaning of 'revolution' becomes again what it initially meant: revolving around a given circuit, coming back after a circular journey to the point wherefrom it started, to the 'structure' and 'super-structure' which it failed to change.

The second point is that, as confirmed by the events of 1989–90, we see the state disappearing, both in the Eastern so-called Communist society, and in the Western so-called capitalist society. The industrial-technological revolution, and the information-revolution have linked the developed free society – roughly the list of countries grouped in the OECD – in one single network of linkages and mutual relations. Within it the tendency of erstwhile individual nation-states is to unite themselves into larger regional units, which, in turn, are inextricably bound into vast inter-, multi- and ultimately transnational organizations. Underneath these two trends of integration and cooperation the sovereignties of the nation-states, big and

333

small nation states, are increasingly pressurized by the common constraints
and requirements; and their welfare is now conditioned by the welfare of
the society as a whole. Nationally and transnationally the state is getting
more and more subordinated to the 'civil society'; and the 'nation-state' to
the iron laws of transnationalization. The nation-state is withering away in
the Western information society. But let us return to the concept of
revolution.

REVOLUTION

Hannah Arendt (1963:34–52) starts her enquiry *On Revolution* by drawing
attention to the contradictions in the concept itself, as also shown in the
investigations made by Karl Griewank (1955). The word 'revolution,' she
says,

> was originally an astronomical term which gained increasing importance
> in the natural sciences through Copernicus's *De revolutionibus orbium
> coelestium*. In this scientific usage, it retained its precise Latin meaning,
> designating the regular, lawfully revolving motion of the stars. It was
> known to be beyond the influence of man and hence irresistible, and was
> certainly characterized neither by newness nor by violence. On the
> contrary, the word clearly indicates a recurring, cyclical movement . . .
> If used for the affairs of man on earth, it could only signify that the few
> known forms of government revolve among mortals in eternal recur-
> rence and with the same irresistible force which makes the stars follow
> their preordained paths in the skies. Nothing could be further removed
> from the original word of 'revolution' than the idea of which all revol-
> utionary actors have been possessed and obsessed, namely that they are
> agents in a process which spells the definite end of the old order and
> brings about the birth of a new world.

J. H. Elliot (1969) also meditated, but on purely historical grounds, on
the origins of the expression 'revolution' in political language. Warning us
first of all that it would be foolish to:

> ignore the possibility that, in using a concept of revolution which is
> relatively recent in origin, we may unconsciously be introducing ana-
> chronisms, or focussing on certain problems which accord with our own
> preoccupations, at the expense of others which have been played down
> or overlooked [he then asks directly] How far can historians accustomed
> to look for *innovation* among revolutionaries, enter into the minds of
> men who themselves were obsessed by *renovation*, by the desire to

return to old customs and privileges, and to an old order of society?'
(italics in the text).

Professor Elliot then argues that to apply to 'many of the early modern
revolts the word "revolution" suggests the possibility of unconscious
distortions, which may itself give us some cause for unease.' He reminds us

> how slowly and with what uncertainty the idea of revolution was brought
> down from the heavens of Copernicus and applied with any precision in
> the mutations of states. Sedition, rebellion, *Aufstand*, mutation, revolt
> revoltment (John Knox) – these are the words most commonly employed
> in sixteenth century Europe. Gardiner's Puritan Revolution was Claren-
> don's Great Rebellion. Only towards the end of the eighteenth century,
> under the impact of events in America and France, did 'revolution'
> effectively establish itself in the European political vocabulary, and
> acquire those connotations by which we recognize it today.

In order to bring further clarity into the diachronic turbulence of the
concept of revolution, we ought to divide it, for the purpose of further
analysis, into three questions. The first question deals with the mutations
of the meaning of the concept of revolution, the way it has changed from its
meaning of restoration to a break or innovation. The second question is
what is actually meant by 'revolution' – the ultimate sense which the word
acquired in the nineteenth century and which it has kept more or less intact
until the middle of the twentieth? And the third is why and how since the
middle of the twentieth century has the concept begun to lose – first among
learned circles, but later in the general parlance of the Western developed
states – its nineteenth-century meaning, and has therefore gradually reverted to its previous meaning?

What Revolution is *Not*

The innovative and rectilinear meaning of 'revolution' superseded the
renovative and cyclical meaning in the language of politics and of political
theory much later than in philosophical language and even in general
language. Indeed, there was a long period in the seventeenth and eighteenth centuries when philosophers particularly concerned with political
problems, and above all Voltaire, spoke of 'revolutions' in all fields and
ways of life, while in political language they still spoke only of rebellions
and revolts. The title of Voltaire's *Essai sur les Revolutions des Moeurs et
sur l'histoire de l'esprit humain depuis le temps de Charlemagne jusqu'á nos
jours* is almost that of a manifesto proclaiming both a new kind of philosophy which he actually called philosophy of history, and a rationalistic

dedication to the idea of progress. Voltaire called revolutions the stages into which he divides the progress of human civilization. Rousseau too sometimes used the word revolution metaphorically as the 'instruments' of progress, although Rousseau was more reserved towards the idea of progress than Voltaire, since his own Utopianism originated more from the Golden Past and the state of nature than from the mirage of future civilizations.

At the time the prevalent meaning of revolution was that of change in all directions. Voltaire and his contemporaries saw and felt that a threshold had been passed in most human activities, that Europe, notably England and France, had entered abruptly upon a new way of life and a new understanding. There was a 'revolution of commerce,' a 'revolution of the sciences,' a foreseeable 'industrial revolution,' and a multitude of other revolutions in practically every direction.

This was why the purpose of the *Encyclopedie* was 'to enclose in the unity of a system the infinitely various branches of knowledge'. This was why Voltaire called above all for a '*révolution des esprits*', the revolution of human minds which alone could prepare mankind for the cosmic transformation which progress was bringing to mankind. And indeed historians of the French Revolution have now fully demonstrated how the '*révolution des esprits*', actively organized by what was going to be called the '*academies*' and the '*societes de pensee*' preceded and helped to prepare the political and social revolution which was to come in France.

But strangely, neither Voltaire – an incessant critic of the court and government of Louis XV – nor Montesquieu, Turgot or Rousseau, or indeed most theoreticians of the time associated the concept of revolution, of which they constantly spoke, with the political changes they were constantly advocating. What they asked for in political terms was 'regeneration'. On the contrary, as we have seen, the word 'revolution', especially in the case of the English Revolution, had fully preserved its neo-astronomical sense of return to the previous and normal order, of restoration.

Those who, like Griewank (1955), enquired into the semantic birth of the new concept found that it was Mirabeau who first spoke in 1789 of '*une grande révolution*' in a political sense. But he applied it to Prussia, which according to him as the most 'enlightened' of contemporary states, could generate 'the freedom of men and things' in the world. Soon, the expression '*la grande révolution*' or '*les grandes révolutions*' spread like a forest fire. The adjective '*grande*' thus affixed to revolution in the political sense gave it at once a different philosophical, moral and unilinear sense than it had had hitherto. But Camille Desmoulins still explained that such a happy great revolution would fulfill the 'regeneration' so long sought for. It was superior and completely different from rebellions, revolts and civil wars. Because it was '*grande*', it was presumed to link into a single and coherent movement the scientific, economic, social and political revolution.

The expression '*la grande révolution*' or 'revolution' became popular in a short time. A sense of somewhat mysterious expectation, in hope or in fear was attached to it. Hence the almost admonitory undertone in La Rochefoucauld de Liancourt's answer to the King, when the latter asked whether the fall of the Bastille was a 'revolt.' '*Non, Sire, c'est une révolution,*' in the sense of 'No, sir, it is much worse, it is a revolution, have you never heard the word before?'

This anecdote is treated even by Brunot (1928: 617–62) as the moment of the official birth of the expression, or indeed when it became a reality. He writes: 'Politicians, philosophers had caught sight of such an event and insisted that it might happen, but now it was becoming a reality. From the spheres of dreams and of speculation, revolution had now come to life.' And moreover, he also noticed how quickly the new word gave birth to other words hitherto unheard: *révolutionnaire* which prompted Condorcet in June 1793 to write an essay: 'Sur le sens du mot révolutionnaire,' *révolutionnairement* (which soon acquired the sense of promptly and effectively), and a new verb, *révolutionner*, which Babeuf also used in the opposite sense: *dérévolutionner* – as in modern language: 'to decelerate.' Moreover, once revolution had triumphantly acquired its new linguistic legitimacy, it legitimized other words hitherto banned. The most significant, as Brunot notes, was the word '*innovation.*' 'Innovation carried within it the idea of an offence against the established order', he says and therefore was banished from the official vocabulary until then. This was why an orator of the day whom he quotes explained with enthusiasm: 'Henceforwards an innovation is no longer a dangerous thing!' And, finally, it was with astonishing speed that the people during and after the French Revolution adopted almost unanimously the expression *ancien régime*, for a form of traditional government which had just been replaced, indeed was still being replaced. This, if anything, showed how much a revolution, by innovating, gives to contemporaries a vertiginous feeling of the acceleration of history, to use Daniel Halevy's expression.

The answer to the first question: whether 'revolution' acquired a second meaning, that of a rectilinear and irreversible change in the nineteenth century, opposed to that it had previously had of the rotation and cyclical movement of bodies in an orbit, is therefore in the affirmative.

Simultaneous Centralization of the State and of the 'Revolution'

The second question concerns the difference between the word revolution and the words with which other kinds of events were described before the end of the eighteenth century such as rebellion, revolt, jacquerie, *Aufstände*, riots, etc., as, for instance the peasants' war in Germany of 1525, the revolt of the Catalans (1640–52) which failed and that of Portugal (1646) which succeeded against Spain, the *'révolte paysanne'* of the Croquants in 1636, and of course the Fronde (1645–53) in France, the revolt of Naples against Spain (1647–8) and that of the Netherlands (1568–1648) or even the uprising of the Ukranian Kossacks against Poland in 1648.

The meaning of the concepts of 'rebellion' is that of a *local, popular uprising* against the relevant authority. Such local popular uprisings became more frequent towards the end of the Middle Ages. They were a growing feature in the history of the social life of Europe, and especially of that of Western Europe as the more developed countries became more centralized, with more visible national structures. Or, in other words, the more the burgeoning state was exacting from its miserable population taxes, duties and corvées, from the population, and the more the burghers (people living in towns) not to speak of the nobles, living in their castles, were beginning to enjoy quite different conditions of living from those of the poor of the countryside and faubourgs, the more frequent did the revolts and rebellions become. And the more centralized and bureaucratic these states became, the more discernable and unifying became the targets of the rebellion. As the movements grew in frequency, they were comparable, seen with hindsight, to the early scattered seisms, which will ultimately necessarily converge toward a single epicentre.

The process of the centralization of power by and under the state, so systematically interpreted, especially in France by the doctrine of the absolute monarchy as an attribute of kings by divine right, had a direct effect on the simultaneous centralization of the hitherto multiple revolts or rebellions. They could be, and were, now concentrated into one single, albeit protean, opposition against the easily located, indeed self-proclaimed, unique power in the realm and, what is more, by divine right. But the more unique it wanted its action to be, the more unified was to become the action against it. This interrelatedness between the then newly called *state*, and what was to be the newly-entitled *revolution* was historically first and best seen in the French Revolution, to which we should now turn for a short while.

The French Revolution exhibited four characteristics of discontinuity which make it unique in history, in the sense that neither the previous two great revolutions, the English and the American, nor the derivative Russian Revolution, cumulated all the four characteristics together into one single, historical event. But it also presented several elements, the most relevant of which was that of the continuation, acceleration and ultimate consolidation of the French nation-state, effected through and by the revolution itself.

The greatest achievement of *continuity* performed by the French revolution was the maintenance and consolidation of the nation-state during the 'Year One' of revolutionary government of the Jacobins. The absolute monarchy had deliberately set out to assist the progress of the central authorities of the one sovereign state, and the establishment of its absolute authority over the multiple suzerainities of the dying feudal society. In French history, philosophical logical arguments always seem to explain – sometimes with inevitable over-simplification – the social changes. The centralization of the state under absolute monarchy reached extremes of explicitness, best exemplified in Louis XIV's apocryphal exclamation *L'état c'est moi*. What Jacques Ellul (1962) emphatically calls 'the take-over of the nation by the State' consisted, from a political point of view in the replacement of the *états-généraux* (states-general) by the *Etat*, the plural or diffused having again thus been even grammatically absorbed by the singular and centralized. From an administrative point of view, it consisted of the unification of the administration of the towns which had emancipated themselves *de facto*, and partly *de jure* by their leadership in the modernization of science, trade and industry, and by their ownership of the financial and commercial capital, so badly needed by the state and by the new, proto-industrial society; from the religious point of view through the emancipation of the temporal power of the King and the state from Papal authority; and from the military point of view through the transformation of the *milice* into a national standing army, based on conscription; and from a financial point of view through the incessant escalation of fiscality imposed by the state and its growing bureaucracies: This was the principal cause of the increasingly frequent peasant and workers' revolts'.

But what was still and badly lacking in the French monarchical nation-state thus established was the new and ultimate legitimacy, i.e. the equation, so simply formulated in one sentence by Siéyés, of the French *nation* and its *state* with the *people* of France. It was this equation that the Revolution achieved through its constitutional proclamation of the 'sovereignty of the people' in place of that of the King. The French people were the *subjects* of the King: the state was dynastic, not national or popular. After the revolution, the subjects became citizens. Moreover, in severe political logic, the King was parricidally executed, thus not only making him disappear physically, but also defying and rejecting God whose representative on earth he and his forerunners had been. If the people is sovereign there can be no other sovereign in earth or in heaven. It was not *monarch* which was absolute. It is *sovereignty* which is absolute or nothing, whoever is invested with it.

Finally, the revolutionary wars, then and ever since, catalyzed the newly-fused nation-people and demonstrated better than anything else the need for centralized effort under the authority of the state. On 25 December 1793, Robespierre proclaimed the replacement 'for the duration of the war,' of *constitutional government* – the will of the people – by *revolutionary government* – the will of those who have taken over the power of the state. It was during 'Year One' of the Revolution that the new state mobilized, in all senses of the word, the resources of the nation and the valiant efforts of its people.

Then, again, because of the inexorable political logic, the French State thus perfected by the absolute revolution on the mould designed by the absolute monarchy reached its apogee in the absolute empire of Napoleon. Since then, having become again with one more imperial exception, a republic, the French state acquired, deservedly or not, the reputation of being the most centralistic of all constitutional-pluralistic states.

Obviously, those who expected the Revolution to result in a general liberation of mankind from all unnatural limitations saw the revival of the state and of its central power as a total betrayal of the ideals of the Revolution. Proudhon, Blanqui, Marx, Bakunin denounced the 'bourgeoisie' for having 'stolen' the revolution in its own socio-economic interest and for having reintroduced *the state* as the instrument of its socio-economic domination.

Their predecessor was Babeuf, the first anarchist to be killed by the Revolution pregnant with a new state (it is noteworthy that 120 years or so later the Russian anarchists were also the first victims of the new state terror introduced by the Russian revolution). Babeuf had proclaimed that 'the French Revolution is only the forerunner of a much bigger, much more solemn revolution which will be the final one', words echoed in the Communist anthem, the *Internationale*. Ever since, believers in revolution for the sake of revolution have anticipated the coming of the 'final' revolution with Messianic fervour. The new Messianic revolution was expected to succeed in destroying in one blow both the political centre: the state and the socio-economic centre: bourgeois capitalism or the capitalist bourgeoisie.

The two nineteenth-century schools of revolutionarism, the Communist and the anarchist, uneasy bed-fellows in the International, were in principle united in the purpose of overthrowing both these centres. But that was only on the surface. In reality, they profoundly differed on what would replace private ownership and the state after the revolution. No text can sum up this unbridgeable gulf between viewpoints and ultimate goals better than Bakunin's own declaration of 1868: 'I detest Communism because it is the negation of liberty . . . I am not a Communist because Communism concentrates and abridges all the powers of society into the state, because it necessarily ends in the centralization of property in the hands of the state, while I want the abolition of the state.'

The new revolution predicted by Babeuf took place in October 1917 in Russia. To the tragic disappointment of those who had expected that the state, any kind of state, would be 'smashed' by the revolution, because they had been promised the replacement of the state by a federation of territorial and professional communes, the state re-emerged in the guise of Lenin's dictatorship of the proletariat leading to the Commune (Soviet)-

state. As early as 1921 the American Anarchist, Alexander Berkmann, wrote in his diary: 'One by one the embers of hope have died out. Terror and despotism have crushed the life born in October. The Revolution is dead; its spirit cries in the underworld' (quoted in Joll, 1958: 27). So once more the dialogue had been reduced to the two interlocutors: the State and the Revolution, and once more the state had won.

Thus the answer to our second question can be reduced in the historical light of the 'great' revolutions as follows: revolution really amounts to the overthrow of an obsolescent nation-state, and its replacement by a new and stronger nation-state, in which 'nation' is constitutionally equated with 'people', the constitutional sovereign.

Simultaneous 'Withering Away' of the State and of the Revolution

The political deformation of the Russian Revolution was caused directly by Karl Marx's own confusions on the role of the state in general, and especially 'after the revolution'; and by Lenin's application in practice of Marx's confusion. For Marx that problem of the state had never been clear. Ever since his early *Critique of Hegel's Philosophy of Right* he failed to solve the problems of the state in the future civil society. When later he was forced by Proudhon to define his thoughts on the question of what political order would emerge from the revolution, he gave the notoriously confusing answer: 'The working class in the course of its development will substitute for the old civil society an association which will exclude classes and their antagonism, and there will be no more political power properly so-called, since political power is precisely the official expression of antagonism in civil society' (Marx, 1977: 215). This confusion was maintained thereafter by Marx, who whenever he could not avoid the question permanently shifted the ground between his theory of the autonomy of the state, his theory of the bourgeois state and his theory of the dictatorship of the proletariat – so much so that when poor Lenin came to think what kind of political organization would appear after the imminent Russian revolution, he was reduced to exclaiming in 1917 in the *Blue Notebook* which accompanied *The State and the Revolution* 'But further on Marx speaks of the 'future of *Communist* society! Thus even in Communist society, the State will exist! Is there not a contradiction in this?' (Ionescu, G., 'Lenin, the Commune and the State', *Government and Opposition*, vol. 5, no. 2, 1970)

Finally, a compromise was worked out by Lenin, according to which the 'dictatorship of the proletariat' created by the revolution would be a state, but a commune state (Soviet), which would effect the transition from the state organization to the commune (Soviet), by the 'withering away' of the state – a state to put an end to all states. In reality, the USSR has been for a long time the least 'witherable away' of all states in the world, so powerful, centralized and totally in control of society that only a structural break-down could change it.

Marx's prediction that the state would wither away was, to some extent at least, correct. But he was wrong in asserting that his withering away would only happen *after* the revolution. To the extent that such a withering-away is now taking place at all, it is happening as a result of the *evolution* of society, indeed worse still, for Marx, of the evolution of capitalist society, or to use Dahrendorf's expression, post-capitalist society. Moreover, the more the centres of power in the new, industrial, transnational, post-capitalist society are being multiplied and diffused, thus reducing the functions and powers of the sovereign state and of the central government to increasingly limited and 'dignified' ones, the less likely are revolutions, i.e. Great Revolutions, to recur. The revolution designed either to smash the state, or to dissolve it (Marx's equivocal alternatives) loses its *raison d'etre* when the state is dissolving itself by evolution, when it has become too transparent to be seized and smashed. And indeed, as we shall soon see, although the modern revolts in post-capitalist society spread worldwide, from the USA to Europe and to Japan, like the students' revolt of 1968, such movements are no longer directed against the state but against society.

There are two ways of looking at the withering-away of Great Revolutions. One is that of Tocqueville, who with his shrewd prophetic sense, as opposed to Marx's less refined one, boldly entitled Chapter XXI of the second volume of *De la démocratie en Amérique*, published in 1844, 'Why Great Revolutions will become rare'. The fact that Tocqueville had not then read Marx does not affect the strength of his implicit rejection of Marx's philosophy, including the prediction of world communist revolutions. Tocqueville's grounds for his reasoning were drawn from the syllogism which he derived from his observation on the nascent American society: According to this argument, if (first premiss) revolutions are the historical corrections of gross political and socio-economic inequalities in societies, then (second premiss) if these inequalities are constantly being reduced as revolutions take place in developed democracies, then (conclusion) there will no longer be any grounds for revolutions to take place.

Obviously Tocqueville's affirmation, made in 1844, has seemed for a century or so to be utopian. First of all, the great Russian revolution occurred in the meantime (but not in a democracy). And, second, it seemed utopian to extend whatever prediction he might make, based on his experience of American society, pragmatic, materialistic, and born in a rich continent and founded on an ideal democratic constitutional framework, to other continents, and notably to Europe, when he himself noted in that very same passage: 'In America, they have democratic ideas and passions; in Europe, we still have revolutionary ideas and passions'.

Besides, contemporary American society was notorious for its glaring inequalities, for the contrast between the few multi-billionnaires and the numerous unemployed, queuing up with their families before the soup-kitchens run by private charities. But Tocqueville's idea of inequality was not based on such inevitable extremes and on socio-economic criteria alone. His image of equality was the result of a combination of political democracy with a socio-economic majority of middle classes. The political and socio-economic *majority* of individuals economically dependent only on their work, and politically on their judgment, was Tocqueville's idea of equality. The democratic middle-class majority existed in early American society, and not only continues to exist there today but has spread, because of the inherent transnational character of industrial technological society, to Western Europe, Japan and many other parts of the world touched by this new economic Gulf Stream.

Even a super-power like the United States is on the one hand bound by the interdependence of its world-stretched relations, and, on the other, impotently witnesses the multinationalization of its capital. The USSR remained the only relic of a powerful state – but this is also why we witness now the desperate efforts of Mr Gorbachev to begin to decompress the USSR from the deadly embrace of the Stalinist structures.

It is here that the second way of looking at the withering-away of the state comes in – and this is the viewpoint of the modern anarchists. It is a perfectly proper viewpoint from which to examine the phenomenon of the contrary meanings of revolutions. The anarchists are the authentic, i.e. absolute and apocalyptic revolutionaries, those who want to smash all rules, rulers and ruling systems (*arkhos*), in order to set human beings free. For 150 years they have claimed that what ought to be smashed is 'the state' – echoed in principle by the Communists, but certainly not in practice, thus dramatically experiencing in practice Marx's theoretical bungles on this question too. But what do the anarchists do and think now when the state itself is dissolving under the impact of the formidable new transnational society?

In 1984 there took place in Venice a *Rencontre Internationale Anarchiste*. Its proceedings have seen been published in four volumes, the third of which deals with *L'etat et l'anarchie*, and the fourth with *La Revolution*. Most of the texts published there start from the dictum of Alain Touraine that 'the era of revolution is now drawing to its end'. Most of the authors try, with great intellectual honesty, even if more often than not in modern sociological jargon, to explain how this has happened. I shall therefore only quote from probably the best-written of them, Claude Orsoni (1985), 'La revolution en question':

> A revolutionary project can assemble a collective will around it only if, amidst the social movements of different, but always present, magnitudes there could be discerned the representatives of a collective aim to

fulfill, of a collective adversary to bring down . . . But modern society is in fact arranged in such a way as to present itself as too complex, too frail, and also too threatened (be it by the 'crisis' or by other enemies) to be able to offer any other possibility of radically redefining or re-constituting it. On the other hand, political power seems now much too shredded and decentralized to be regarded as an identifiable adversary to be defeated.

Recalling Foucault's pre-condition of a revolution, namely the existence of a 'massive binary divide' between 'them and us, the top and the bottom, the dominating and the dominated', Orsoni concludes, 'if such a social polarization is necessary . . . to produce a revolutionary process . . . then this becomes absolutely improbable'. The 'molecularization' of society and the 'remoteness and elusive (*insaisissable*) character of the state' put revolution out of the question. Moreover, 'the idea of revolution not only gives rise to indifference or incredulity, *but indeed to anxiety, even aversion*'. Orsoni further describes that aversion as 'the fear in particular that what would follow a revolutionary overthrow would be a *monopolization* of power by one or more individuals, or even by a whole class (who can hardly be entrusted with the overpowering mission to emancipate the human race)'. Nevertheless, in his conclusions Orsoni expresses his belief that the 'idea of a necessary rupture re-appears periodically' and that it could achieve practical results, but, and this is most significant, *even if at the price 'of renouncing the confused ideas of "the revolution"'*.

The cycle of the revolution seems to have come full circle in 150 years. Revolution, worshipped in 1789 and even in 1917, is now feared and regarded with aversion. The state is melting away, and the real centres of power are too remote and too diffuse to be directly attacked. The state is melting away, not in Marx's sense, but on the contrary, in the federalistic sense which goes from Kant to Mounet, to de Rougemont and to Jacques-René Rabier.

INTERDEPENDENCE AND THE STATE

One of the best-known and most popular definitions of interdependence is that it is the outcome of the new historical development whereby 'the nations of the world have become *mutually sensitive and vulnerable* through an interrelationship of socio-economic and technological issues' (Spanier, 1987: 17). Interdependence is therefore intrinsically a *trans-national* phenomenon – as against an *international* one, i.e., it is not caused by the relation of causality of actions and reactions of nation-states as in 'the old billiard ball model,' or in the policy of the balance of 'powers.' 'Interconnectedness is not interdependence', Keohane (1977: 9) reminded us. And Lijphart (1981: 223–51) rightly argues in a similar context, a paradigm under which the international actions are now taking place. Hence it was and is inappropriate and counter-productive to apply a national-international political judgment to political problems which require a transnational political judgment.

The Second World War was in itself a negative demonstration of interdependence, for no part of the world could avoid being involved in it. The whole world was at war as a result of the interdependence of communication and its chain of chain reactions. After the fall of fascism, interdependence seemed to come into its own and to assert its positive aspects. Internal interdependence manifested itself through the welfare society, deliberately misnamed 'the welfare state'. External interdependence manifested itself through the United Nations, GATT, the IMF and later the Marshall Plan with its transnational undertone. Still later the new economic regional units emerged, or as it is more fashionable to call them now, 'regimes'. The most important of these is the European Community, preceded as it was by the separate European Communities. On the other hand, there emerged also the specific transnational organizations of consultation and coordination, the most effective of which is the OECD, which groups all industrial democracies.

But this was not a sign of 'new idealism,' or even Utopianism as it is often described. It was only a belated awakening to the old realistic need, deliberately neglected, to open up the political judgment of national interest and its projection in international affairs, onto the transnational perspectives of interdependence. However, it was then said, even if the concept of national interest had been cut down to size in small and medium-size countries, it had reappeared with a vengeance in a new and formidable shape, that of the *super*-national interest of each of the two nuclear *super*-powers which for some decades were to divide the world into two ideological camps. For a whole generation we believed that super-national interests had replaced the concepts and methods of national interests, but at another level.

Yet, as the information revolution was progressing so rapidly, the super-powers themselves found that they could not resist the sway of accelerating interdependence. The super-national interests could no longer maintain the instruments of their respective 'hegemonies'. The dollar, on which both GATT and the IMF had depended until then, lost its unique position in 1968, dragging down with it many other institutions of financial, commercial and monetary exchanges of the free world. In part this was due to the fact that the costly Vietnam war, based on computerized utilitarianism, had been lost. Suddenly too, Japan, a small and defeated country but which had ridden out the information revolution particularly well, became a technological and financial giant, though not a political or military one. The European Community, and within it especially the Federal Republic of Germany, also became a troublesome technological and commercial rival of the Western super-power, who in the exercise lost its enthusiasm for the United States of Europe, though it maintained its interest in NATO. Besides, something called the 'multinationals', true instruments of interdependence, emancipated themselves from the direct control of states, creating their own markets, transnational organizations, and even currency, the Eurodollar. And though the 'multinationals' were in principle linked to one nation-state (mainly the USA), they often acted against the 'national interest' (the oil companies during the oil crisis, the American-owned Japanese electronic companies, etc.). The free world was becoming, on its own a single financial market, as was being repeatedly stated by the IMF, GATT and the OECD, in which the risk of *super-national myopia* of the US and of its domestic economy affected the whole world. American economists stress 'the need to rebuild international economic institutions so that they may be relevant in the world of the 21st century . . . Joint leadership will be necessary . . . Each [country] has a vital stake in the management of inter-dependence, because its welfare depends on other countries as never before' (Aho and Levinson, 1988–9: xxx.)

Here we arrive at the final point. The concept of 'national interest' was born almost at the same time as the concept of the nation-state, which had first to be legitimized by the utilitarian philosophy, and by the utilitarian political philosophy, and then became the functional logic of the politics of state-centrism in external affairs. But the nation-state is a *historical institution*, which had fully emerged by the eighteenth century. It was already showing signs of external and internal fatigue in the twentieth century. Its last desperate bids for supremacy were the totalitarian states.

So, what gradually appeared was the utilitarian functionalism, the logical reflex of which is 'What's in it for me?'; the nation state was becoming dysfunctional in the conceptual perspectives of transnationalism, of which the corresponding reflex question might well be for instance, 'how do I get into the boat without rocking it?' The politics of interdependence require a new transnational political judgment, which in turn needs to run in a different direction from the state-centric political judgment of today.

Once the new political judgment provides the policy-makers with the right optic and the right spirit and the right approach, they can chart to the best of their ability the course of their own state, or community of states, through the transnationally prescribed channels, and in accordance with the transnational traffic rules. The transnational world is inherently polycentric in the sense of multiple geopolitical units, or 'regimes' as well as in the sense of diversification of policy-makers, in which constitutional political institutions mix with socio-economic, non-constitutional institutions (multi-national companies, international associations, employers, trade unions, farmers as well as *ad hoc* groupings of international 'interests' exerting as much influence as the constitutional political institutions). A new technique of many-sided and heterogenous consultations and negotiations, helped on by telex, fax, and teleconferences, is already replacing the solemn formalities.

No doubt even in the politics of interdependence there will remain differences between superior and inferior agents, even powers. But interdependence will pressurize them all proportionately at their respective level (Singer, 1961); the superior powers, like the inferior powers will have first to consider *where* and *how* they can act without upsetting the applecart, provided they have the new know-how of consultation and negotiation.

And it is precisely the problem of how to acquire the new know-how, how to replace the state-centric political judgment with the transnational judgment which now comes to the fore. It is here that the old 'utopian' federalistic judgment proves now to be much more realistic than national 'real-politik' – and the 'utopian' European Community to provide a new and more solid basis for all its members states than they themselves could now provide separately for themselves.

REFERENCES

Aho and Levinson, 'The Economy after Reagan,' *Foreign Affairs*, vol. 67, no. 4, Winter, 1988–9.

Arendt, Hannah (1963) *On Revolution* (London).

Brunot, F. *Histoire de la langue francaise*, vol. 9. 'La revolution et l'Empire,' Paris, 1928, vol. 2, pp. 617–62.

Elliott, J. H. (1969) 'Revolution and Continuity in Early Modern Europe' in *Past and Present* 42, 35–6.

Ellul, Jacques (1962) *Histoire des institutions de l'époque franque à la révolution* (Paris) Fourth Part: 'La Monarchie absolue', Chapter 1 'Mainmise de l'etat sur la nation.'

Griewank, Karl (1955) *Der Neuzeitliche Revolutionsbegriff* (Weimar).

Joll, James (1958) *The Anarchists* (London).

Keohane, Robert O. (1977) *Power and Interdependence* (Cambridge, Mass.: Harvard University Press).

Lijphart, Arndt (1981) 'The new paradigm in international relations' in Richard L. Merritt and Bruce M. Russat, (eds) *From National Development to Global Community* (London).

Marx, Karl (1977) 'The Poverty of Philosophy' in D. McLellan, *Karl Marx: Selected Writings* (London).

Orsoni, Claude (1985–6) 'La Révolution en question' in *Un anarchisme contemporain* (Paris) four vols.

Singer, J. David (1961) 'The level of analysis problem in international relations' in Klaus Knorr and Sidney Verba (eds), *The International System: Theoretical Essays* (Princeton, NJ: Princeton University Press).

Spanier, John (1987) *Games Nations Play* (Washington, DC).

20 How Poverty is Perceived

Hélène Riffault, *Faits et Opinions*, Paris

The European Community of Europe, with its 320 million inhabitants, produces a fifth of the gross world product, which in turn supports nearly 5 billion people. Although Community countries vary widely in terms of per capita gross national income, jointly they form part of the family of rich, or relatively rich, nations. For this reason, poverty is associated in our minds primarily with Third World countries. We cannot, however, ignore the pockets of poverty in European countries.

Over the years, the Eurobarometer programme launched by the Commission of the European Communities has provided significant data on Europeans' attitudes to poverty (see the reports cited below in References). The data relate to four areas: (1) How Europeans assess their own situation and place themselves on a rich/poor scale; (2) How socio-economic disparities between regions are perceived; (3) How extreme poverty in European countries is perceived; (4) Attitudes to the Third World.

The surveys cover the last fifteen years and provide a modest contribution to the study of a major subject.

FEELING POOR

In 1976 the following question was put for the first time in all nine countries then included in the Community: 'Taking everything into account, at about what level is your family situated as far as standard of living is concerned? (You may answer by giving a figure between 1 and 7 – number 1 means a poor family and number 7 a rich family.)' The question was asked again in 1983, in the same nine countries, plus Greece. In the space of seven years, the percentage of Europeans regarding themselves as poor rose in all countries, reaching slightly more than 10 per cent of the Community's total adult population by the time of the second survey (see Table 20.1).

The correlation between the proportion regarding themselves as poor and per capita gross national income was, in 1983, 0.86 for point 1 and 0.91 for points 1 + 2, for the Community as a whole. Certain countries stand out however: feelings of poverty were significantly higher in France, the United Kingdom and Greece and lower in Ireland, Denmark and Luxembourg than the Community average. Non-economic factors undoubtedly also play a part in the way people position themselves on the scale. What is

349

TABLE 20.1: *Where respondents situate themselves on the rich/poor scale*
(points 1 and 2 on the 7-point scale)

	1976			1983		
	Point 1 %	Point 2 %	Total 1+2 %	Point 1 %	Point 2 %	Total 1+2 %
European Community	2.0	5.6	7.6	2.9	7.8	10.7
Italy	3.0	7.8	10.8	3.6	10.5	14.1
United Kingdom	2.5	6.8	9.3	4.1	7.4	11.5
France	1.6	6.0	7.6	3.1	8.5	11.6
Ireland	2.2	4.4	6.6	3.6	11.0	14.6
Belgium	1.0	4.0	5.0	1.8	7.1	8.9
Germany	1.1	3.3	4.4	1.0	4.9	5.9
Netherlands	1.2	3.2	4.4	2.1	7.2	9.3
Denmark	1.5	2.7	4.2	.7	4.1	4.8
Luxembourg	1.1	1.1	2.2	1.3	3.0	4.3
Greece	(not sampled in 1976)			8.0	12.7	20.7

involved here is a general subjective classification. Movement over the 1976–83 period shows the number of people regarding themselves as poor rising significantly in these years.

Without more recent data based on the same question, we cannot say how the impression of being poor has progressed in Europe in the last few years. However, a series of questions regularly asked by the International Gallup Institutes in Europe at the end of each year indicates that from 1983 to 1988 people in the Community sensed a steady improvement, year by year, in their countries' general economic condition and their own households' financial situation. However, we have no indication how the minority which considers itself poor has changed since 1983, when it represented about a tenth of the population. This indicator should be updated periodically. It should also be amplified by research on the extremely poor fraction of the population which tends to fall through the mesh of traditional opinion-poll sampling.

SOCIO-ECONOMIC DISPARITIES BETWEEN REGIONS

Both subjectively and objectively the question of poverty is bound up with the general regional situation. There is a far greater likelihood of a European actually being poor if he lives in Calabria than if he lives around Cologne or in Piedmont.

In 1980 the European Commission launched exploratory research to find out to what extent and in what areas the general public saw disparities between regions. This involved focusing each respondent's attention on a specific geographical area; it was decided to base this on the 'basic administrative unit' defined by Eurostat, which at the time distinguished 112 such units in the territory covered by the nine member countries. Each respondent was questioned in three main areas: does he consider that the region he lives in is holding its own, going down or making progress; does the region pay its way, help to support other regions or need support from outside; is the region better or worse off than others in various respects (pleasant way of life, opportunities for work, wage and income levels, go-ahead industry and agriculture, transport and communications, prospects for young people, socio-cultural facilities).

Seven types of region emerged from the analysis, ranging in overall descending order from that in which the feeling that the region was well off was strongest, down to that in which it was most commonly felt that the region was badly off. However, this overall order is not necessarily followed for each of the elements used in constructing the classification, as would be the case if the differences between types were only ones of degree; in other words, certain questions (e.g. as to the dynamism of agriculture) were of greater significance for certain types of region, while other types are better defined by their attitude to other questions, such as the impression of living in a region that is making progress or declining. The collective perception of a region's situation is often influenced by the way it is considered to have changed, for better or for worse, since some point in time, whether recent or more remote.

Of all the factors covered in the analysis the ones showing the highest degree of correlation with the final type pattern were opportunities for work, whether the region was in need of outside support and the feeling that the region is or is not in decline. At the time of the survey, in 1980, about a fifth of the European population lived in regions ranking lowest on the 1–7 scale. These included:

(1) Seven very poor regions (southern Italy, including Sicily and Sardinia, and north-western Ireland), with 7 per cent of the Community's population. The salient feature here is the overwhelming conviction that the region needs support from outside: the regions of this type show the gloomiest views in respect of all the indicators. These regions consist predominantly of rural communities and small towns; the proportion of self-employed (farmers, craftsmen, tradespeople) is high; the level of education is particularly low.

(2) Nineteen regions spread over six different countries which represent 15 per cent of the Community's population. It is here that people feel most strongly that their region is declining and where pessimism is most prevalent. Such regions include, in Belgium, Hainaut and Liege, in France, the North and Lorraine, in the United Kingdom, the North-West and Wales. The proportion of manual workers is higher than elsewhere.

This initial, region-based study shows that for a better understanding of poverty, the study of the regional environment will need to be combined with study of individual and family socio-demographic factors (particular attention being given to various subgroups such as the unemployed, the 'Fourth World', persons living in dire poverty within developed countries, and single-parent families).

AWARENESS OF THE VERY POOR

In our 1976 survey, slightly less than half the Community population were prepared to say that there were people in need living in their town, neighbourhood or village. This social phenomenon, the poverty of others, was for most a somewhat abstract concept: barely 10 per cent said they had had occasion to see for themselves the living conditions of the very poor.

Extreme poverty was seen then as primarily resulting from a deprived childhood; next, from lack of education, ill health, old age; after which came laziness, drink, chronic unemployment and too many children. A third of those interviewed regarded extreme poverty as something immutable ('they have almost no chance of escaping'). As for the causes, public opinion divided into three attitudes, held with virtually the same frequency: the first group took a fatalistic view ('it is inevitable in the modern world' or 'they have been unlucky'), the second blamed society ('there is much injustice in our society'), while the last group held the poor themselves responsible ('it is because of laziness and lack of willpower').

Curiously enough, the least rich did not feel any closer than others to the very poor. They were doubtless more likely than others to see cases of destitution with their own eyes, but tended to blame those concerned rather than to sympathize with them. It is in fact the better-educated, the better-off who in their replies most frequently put the blame on social injustice.

The most striking thing in this study, is that extreme poverty is something which most Europeans are not aware of, which perhaps they do not even wish to see. The 1990 European Values study will show whether the situation has changed in the meantime.

POVERTY IN THE THIRD WORLD

The bank of European opinion data on attitudes to poverty in the Third World has much more to offer: major surveys were carried out in 1983 and 1987 and, on certain questions, notably the importance the public attaches to aid to poor countries, we have a chronological series going back to 1973.

Undoubtedly, Europeans are alive to the acute problems facing the world's underprivileged countries: two out of three think that helping them is important or very important. This attitude has been well established in

Europe for some fifteen years. It was somewhat less strongly held in 1974–6, that is, when Europe began having economic difficulties, but since 1983 there has been a return to the original level.

Information seems to have improved considerably during this period. Europeans are now capable of distinguishing different situations in countries often lumped together as the 'Third World'. Three countries are associated by a very high percentage of public opinion with famine: Ethiopia (82 per cent), Bangladesh (62 per cent), and India (60 per cent). Three countries are associated with the idea of progress: China (55 per cent), Saudi Arabia (34 per cent), and Egypt (26 per cent). Brazil rates equally high among the countries where many people die of hunger (26 per cent) and among the countries that are making progress (27 per cent). These results may be regarded as an undeniable success for the work of the press and television in spreading information. Indeed, in 1987 three Europeans out of four said they had recently read something in the papers or heard something on the radio or television about the Third World.

Poverty in the Third World is attributed chiefly (in descending order of frequency) to the population growing too fast (89 per cent), to a small, rich minority exploiting the rest of the population (83 per cent), to political instability (78 per cent), and to a very unfavourable climate (71 per cent). A high proportion of Europeans also blame themselves: six out of ten people think that the fact that they were colonies held back the development of Third World countries and that they are exploited by developed countries. Reservations or blame were much less common: one European out of four thinks that Third World countries 'were happier when they were colonies' and that 'they do not really want to work'.

POTENTIAL WILLINGNESS TO HELP THE POOR

The overall impression that emerges from the studies reviewed here is that European opinion is more ready to recognize the tragic situation in certain Third World countries than the existence of deprivation among minorities in our own countries. One could go so far as to say that the situation in the Third World comes within the domain of public opinion, while the perception of extreme poverty at home is still a matter of private opinion.

This major distinction having been made, it can be said that there is a potential willingness to help the poor, wherever they may be. On questions of principle there was very wide consensus, over three Europeans out of four supporting ideas involving a reduction of inequality: 'trying to reduce the number both of very rich people and of very poor people', 'reducing the differences between regions of our country by helping the less-developed regions or those in most need', 'helping poor countries in Africa, South America, Asia, etc'.

As for personal involvement, nearly half the Europeans interviewed said that if requested they would be prepared to 'contribute some money' to help the underprivileged; the proportion of positive answers was almost the same when the question related to the needy at home and when it related to Third World countries. Naturally, it is easier for a respondent, with an interviewer in front of him, to answer yes than no to questions of this kind. It might be difficult to convert these good intentions into action, but the fact remains that the climate of opinion is receptive to actions of solidarity. But is this the only desirable goal? That those Europeans who enjoy the privilege of being born in a rather wealthy part of the planet be ready to ease their conscience by taking part in solidarity actions in favour of the poorest, this is a first step. Much more important would be to reach the point where the general public understand clearly the mechanisms of interdependence, if social progress is to be achieved.

REFERENCES

The Perception of Poverty in Europe: report on a public opinion survey carried out in the member countries of the European Community as part of the programme of pilot projects to combat poverty, March 1977 (V/171/77).
Europeans and their Regions: public perception of the socio-economic disparities: an exploratory study, December 1980 (XVI/29/81).
Europeans and Aid to Development: study for the European Consortium for Agricultural Development, May 1984.
Europeans and Development Aid in 1987: study for European Cooperation and Solidarity, Commission of the European Communities, Campaign North-South, Council of Europe, March 1988.

21 The Factual Data Obtained from Eurobarometer Surveys: how they Help in Describing the Member States

Jean-François Tchernia,
Faits et Opinions, Paris

Although the Eurobarometer surveys serve, first and foremost, to measure opinion across the Community, factual questions have always had a place in them. By factual questions we mean all those where the people interviewed are asked not to express judgement, opinion, preference or viewpoint, but rather to describe their situation (generally personal) or past or future actions. Indeed, these factual questions make up the larger part of the socio-demographic section in the questionnaires, giving us information on the respondent's age and occupation, the occupation of the head of household, household income, the number of people the household comprises, and so on. Generally these factual data are used for analysing people's answers to questions probing into their opinions, but quite often they can also serve a wider purpose in that they throw up hitherto unknown information. The object of this paper is to present some of these data and to show the interest there can be in using Eurobarometer surveys in this way to obtain a clearer picture of the people making up the Community.

The area covered by such factual questions is extensive. This paper concentrates on surveys that took in the whole Community including Spain and Portugal, in other words all the Eurobarometers since the autumn of 1985. The advantage of limiting our study in this way is that it enables the whole present-day Community of Twelve to be given comparable treatment. A further limitation stems from the fact that we have narrowed down the types of question selected for study. Reviewing all the factual questions, as defined above, we find that they fall into five categories, according to the type of information they yield.

The first type of question yields information concerning long-term personal characteristics of respondents – for instance, whether they are smokers or non-smokers, whether they are on the electoral register and what their occupation is. The term that seems to cover this type of question best is 'personal situation', which is wider than permanent characteristics in that it embraces the respondent's environment (social, family or other).

A second category of factual question relates to characteristics found with some degree of regularity (implicit or explicit) but not permanently present. One example is the number of cigarettes smoked:[1] naturally, in a question of this kind the reply given is for average consumption – the information sought being not so much the precise number of cigarettes but the overall frequency with which the respondent smokes. The chief difference between this and the previous type of question is that here the information solicited does not apply at every moment in the respondent's life, or even, necessarily, every day, unlike a general characteristic such as being a smoker or non-smoker. By and large these questions serve to bring out behavioural patterns.

The third class of question is distinguished by the fact that the information sought relates to something (actions, events, behaviour) in the past. This variety of question, frequently used in the Eurobarometer surveys, typically asks what recollection the respondent has of a particular news item or experience: 'Have you read anything in the papers, seen anything on television or heard anything about . . .?'. The obvious criticism often voiced in respect of these questions is that the reliability of the information obtained depends on how good the respondent's memory is – something which will vary from one person to another.

A fourth type of question that can still be ranged in the factual category explores future behavioural intentions. Here, for instance, the respondent is asked whether or not he is intending to vote in national elections or what energy savings he might be prepared to make.

The last category of questions that can be regarded as factual are those which establish the extent of the respondent's knowledge of a given subject. As an example, people might be asked to pick out the European flag among four flags shown. Although questions of this type do not probe the physical or social characteristics of those interviewed but rather the cognitive pattern, they may be considered factual in that their aim is not to obtain an opinion but to establish a fact – the level of knowledge in the general public concerning a given subject.

This paper covers only questions of the first category. The reason for this is that these are the ones that seem most likely to produce objective data that are not covered by official statistics and throw new light on people in Europe. The other types of question all have certain limitations: behavioural surveys presuppose regular sampling, and often those interviewed have to interpret the scale put before them; the questions regarding recollection of past events are subject to the distorting effects of memory;

the questions concerning intended behaviour, though useful for predictive purposes provide information which is necessarily unreliable; lastly, the questions that test people's knowledge give only a partial picture of the general level of awareness – a true description of the population cannot be obtained in this way.

The questions that are going to be analysed here relate to three main areas in the lives of those interviewed. In the order in which they are taken, these are living conditions, the family, and economic and social circumstances. The questions in full, with references, are given in the Appendix.

LIVING CONDITIONS

Three main aspects of living conditions have been investigated: housing, household appliances or facilities and personal luxuries. (Table 21.1 summarizes the answers to the various questions in these three areas.) The predominant pattern in housing seems to be that the typical European lives in a house rather than an apartment and is an owner rather than a tenant. These two characteristics define the way nearly two out of every three Europeans are housed (61 per cent occupy a house and 64 per cent are owners). This is the general pattern almost everywhere except in Italy, where more people seem to live in apartments than houses.

It should however be noted that this pattern occurs with a much higher frequency in some countries than in others. The countries where it is most prevalent are Ireland, Luxembourg, and the United Kingdom, while it is least common in Germany and Portugal. It is interesting to see that this geographical distribution does not tally with any of the traditional sharp distinctions between Catholic countries and Protestant, or North and South, or between more advanced and less developed economies.

There are two quite separate indicators relating to household facilities. The first covers heating and cooking (coal, oil, gas, electricity), where the form of energy used tells us something about the country's economic environment and the availability of different sources of energy for households. The second indicator relates to certain consumer durables. The question on heating offers a reminder of the extreme diversity of national economic situations. Although gas seems, on average, to be the commonest source of heating, the extent to which it is used varies greatly from one country to another: almost nine Dutchmen out of ten (88 per cent) use gas, but only by one Greek in twenty (4 per cent). The use of oil and electricity for heating purposes varies almost as much. On the other hand, coal has lost favour in almost all countries (roughly one person in ten says he uses it for heating), with the notable exception of Ireland, where it is used in nearly two homes out of three (61 per cent).

358

TABLE 21.1: *Living conditions*

	B %	DK %	G %	GR %	S %	F %	IRL %	I %	L %	NL %	P %	UK %	EC12 %
HOUSING													
Type of housing													
. House..................	81	64	51	60	62	62	82	45	80	78	59	80	61
. Apartment..............	15	29	46	40	36	26	2	52	14	16	28	8	32
. Council or municipal housing	1	1	1	–	2	10	14	1	1	3	6	10	5
Occupancy													
. Owner..................	61	68	50	74	78	61	79	70	78	49	56	72	64
. Tenant.................	36	29	48	26	22	37	19	28	17	48	37	26	34
Type of locality													
. Rural area.............	46	28	36	33	39	38	48	35	51	41	46	25	35
. Small town.............	34	34	29	24	37	39	21	35	45	34	27	49	37
. Large town.............	20	37	35	43	24	22	31	30	4	24	27	25	28
HOUSEHOLD FACILITIES													
Heating													
. Coal...................	12	7	12	9	11	6	61	4	4	–	7	12	9
. Oil....................	36	49	42	54	6	26	24	27	50	3	–	4	23
. Gas....................	38	12	39	4	26	31	7	55	38	88	15	75	45
. Electricity	8	13	13	11	40	26	7	5	12	6	52	19	18

	1	2	3	4	5	6	7	8	9	10	11	12	13
Cooking													
. Coal	1	–	4	1	3	1	7	–	3	–	3	1	2
. Oil	1	1	1	–	1	–	2	–	1	–	1	–	1
. Gas	60	18	20	34	84	88	46	97	48	84	82	61	66
. Electricity	37	83	77	63	10	11	46	5	59	15	14	44	33
Consumer durables													
. Car	76	75	74	55	58	87	70	84	90	70	42	73	74
. Motorcycle (125 cc or more)	5	2	7	7	8	5	3	15	6	5	22	7	9
. Central heating	65	76	79	39	13	70	57	53	85	78	8	73	60
. Washing machine	88	77	92	72	89	94	87	95	97	90	51	91	90
. Dishwasher	24	31	29	9	11	33	11	20	48	9	12	9	21
. Separate water-heater	63	18	54	71	68	62	44	48	73	77	59	57	58
. Refrigerator	95	97	99	97	95	99	98	98	98	96	88	97	97
. Deep-freeze	59	78	60	8	9	50	29	33	83	41	29	55	44
. Electric power tools	64	69	69	25	28	69	42	50	84	65	35	70	58
. Colour television	88	91	94	48	80	84	89	81	92	92	57	91	85
. Telephone	67	94	86	67	60	94	50	90	98	91	36	84	82
PERSONAL LUXURIES													
. Driving licence	66	70	61	31	40	71	48	62	68	60	27	59	58
. Smoking	39	45	32	43	40	35	36	33	33	44	27	35	35

The second indicator for household facilities relates to the possession of certain energy-consuming durables: one or more cars, motorcycle (125 cc or more), central heating, washing machine, dishwasher, separate electric or gas water-heater, refrigerator, deep-freeze, electric power tools, colour television set, and telephone. This list was first drawn up in 1982 for a survey on Europeans and energy problems, when it served to establish a scale for domestic energy consumption. But the insight it gives into the consumer durables which European households possess is also of interest, although this is not its primary purpose.

The commonest appliance is the refrigerator; almost every European household owns one. But even here differences exist from one country to another: refrigerators are found in only 88 per cent of homes in Portugal, against 99 per cent in Germany and France, and 98 per cent in Ireland, Italy and Luxembourg. Here the survey reveals not the precise number of appliances owned in each country, but the percentage difference in ownership from one country to another.[2]

With the less widespread items, wider divergences appear between the Twelve. In the case of central heating, for example, which is found in six European households out of ten, the figure varies from 8 per cent in Portugal to 85 per cent in Luxembourg. With deep-freezes (owned by an average of 44 per cent of Europeans) there is a similar spread, ranging from 8 per cent in Greece and 9 per cent in Spain to 83 per cent in Luxembourg and 78 per cent in Denmark.

By and large, there seems to be a broad correlation between the level of ownership of these goods and a country's level of development. However, variations in living standards cannot fully explain the differences uncovered, and we are bound to conclude that the relative frequency of one appliance or another in a country is indicative of a pattern in the way of life which reflects cultural influences rather than purely economic circumstances.

One example among many others that illustrates this is the deep-freeze. Although ownership of a deep-freeze does indeed reflect a certain standard of living, the fact remains that deep-freezes are much commoner in Portugal than in Greece or Spain, despite their higher level of economic development. Systematic pin-pointing and analysis of such phenomena would probably tell us a lot about different people's ways of life in Europe.[3]

The last aspect of living conditions on which the Eurobarometer surveys throw some objective light is personal luxuries, in other words things that are specific to the person interviewed – and not shared by the whole household, as in the previous examples – from which he or she derives satisfaction as an individual. Two of these have been considered: holding a driving licence and smoking.

Over half of all Europeans hold a driving licence. But there are conspicuous variations yet again: the proportion of licence holders ranges from 27 per cent in Portugal to 71 per cent in France. The correlation between living standards and car ownership here is undeniable, but it does not explain everything. For instance, it is perhaps significant that the French, who are not the richest nation in Europe, should be the leading driving license holders; has France not sometimes been called a motor-car culture?

Turning now to the last indicator of living conditions – smoking – we find that about one European in three is a smoker (35 per cent). Here national differences are much less marked and would seem to bear little relation to economic prosperity: the countries with the highest proportion of smokers are Denmark, the Netherlands and Greece, those with the lowest are Portugal and Germany, while the others are close to the European average. The important point here is that smoking is fairly evenly spread across the Community, as in the case of socio-demographic characteristics such as sex or age. In point of fact, variables of this kind appear to have more to do with individual personalities than with the national economic or cultural context.

THE FAMILY

The respondent's immediate everyday environment is often poorly mirrored in sample surveys. While it is true that serious studies of this type of variable normally use different methods, concentrating more on in-depth analysis of particular cases, it is well known that factors of this kind influence psycho-sociological patterns in general, and opinions in particular, and the Eurobarometer surveys have sometimes attempted to identify these. The findings presented here centre on the family, but the surveys have also looked at other areas, particularly the working environment. (Table 21.2 summarizes the findings on the family.)

Three main types of data on the family have been gathered since the autumn of 1985; composition of the household, family characteristics and the language spoken at home. Other related information, such as the number of persons in the household or the number of children under fifteen, appear in the survey findings but are not discussed here as they have already been covered in appropriate demographic studies. The purpose of the question on the composition of the household is to discover the number of single-parent families, i.e. families composed of a single adult and one or more children. The question is therefore worded to cover the full range of possible alternatives to the single-parent family, so that a reliable picture of the composition of European households can be obtained.

It was found that half the households surveyed were composed of a couple with children. This, then, seems to represent the predominant

TABLE 21.2: *The family*

	B %	DK %	G %	GR %	S %	F %	IRL %	I %	L %	NL %	P %	UK %	EC12 %
COMPOSITION OF HOUSEHOLD													
Couple with no children	18	35	20	17	16	24	14	15	15	24	15	30	21
Couple with one or more children	53	38	42	62	58	55	58	55	55	44	64	42	50
Single adult with no children	12	21	27	9	9	12	15	7	15	19	7	17	15
Single adult with one or more children	8	4	4	2	5	5	4	3	5	6	5	6	5
Others	4	–	6	2	10	4	8	20	5	6	9	5	8
FAMILY CHARACTERISTICS													
Includes regular smokers	35	51	32	23	27	26	19	24	36	26	30	30	28
Spouse in paid employment	38	43	29	37	28	46	26	33	37	36	39	41	36
LANGUAGE USED AT HOME													
The (or a) national language	99	95	96	100	97	98	99	99	96	97	100	97	98

family pattern in Europe, but the spread is uneven from country to country: almost two-thirds of Portuguese families follow this pattern (64 per cent), compared to barely one third of Danish families (38 per cent). This is a considerable discrepancy, somewhat reminiscent of the difference observed in housing: in both cases we find a dominant overall pattern, corresponding to what might be termed the ideal, but with a very uneven geographic distribution. However, the comparison is purely superficial as there is apparently little common ground between the variations in each of these variables.

The next commonest type of household after couples with children is the couple without children. One household in five (21 per cent) falls into this category, and here again there are significant differences between countries (the figure ranging from 35 per cent in Denmark to 14 per cent in Ireland). All in all, adding in households of single persons (i.e. those comprising just one adult and no children) over half of Danish households have no children, compared with about one in five in Italy and Portugal. These findings seem to tally with demographic observations concerning birth-rates in the community, but the Eurobarometer surveys give a more immediate picture of people's ways of life, going beyond the official census statistics.

Sometimes the Eurobarometer surveys can bring particular family characteristics to light. For example, it has been possible to establish whether there is a smoker in the family and whether the respondent's spouse is in paid employment.

Slightly more than one in four people (28 per cent) said that their families included one or more smokers, which seems to corroborate the figure for those who said they themselves smoked (35 per cent). However, although there is a close correlation between the two sets of figures, they do not tally absolutely. This indicates that the same habit is perceived in different ways. In Greece, for instance, closer analysis shows that it is chiefly the men who smoke, which explains the gap between those who say they smoke themselves (43 per cent) and those who have a smoker in the family (23 per cent): the only member of the respondent's family who is old enough to smoke is usually the spouse – in other words in one out of two cases a woman, who is unlikely to smoke. This finding suggests – or at least the theory can be advanced – that in Greece not only is smoking a male attribute, but it is also conditioned by social rather than family influences. Conversely, in Denmark the figures for self-confessed smokers and for those who say they have smokers in the family are very close and both well above the average, which suggests that here smoking belongs more to the private sphere and tends to involve several members of the household.

The other aspect of family life on which information was gathered was whether the respondent's spouse was in paid work. This was the case in slightly more than one in three households (36 per cent). In view of the overall percentage of Europeans gainfully employed (60 per cent) and the fact that seven out of ten are married, the proportion of working spouses, based solely on a calculation of probabilities, would be 42 per cent. The difference stems not from any imperfection in the sampling method, but simply from the fact that the proportion of those who are married and of those who are in paid employment is not the same for the two sexes. This analysis was possible only by obtaining direct information on whether a person's spouse was working, separately from the other two questions, and also because it was possible to analyze the results by sex. These two considerations make a strong case for collecting this kind of information in surveys such as the Eurobarometer polls.

The last aspect of family life that will be discussed here is the language used at home. This is almost always the official national language, but in some countries those who said they used a language other than the national language at home accounted for as many as one in twenty – by no means a negligible proportion. The chief interest of this information is that we now know that a substantial number of interviews, varying from one country to another, are conducted in a language which is not the one that the respondent uses at home (and with which he or she is probably most familiar).

Leaving aside its interest from the purely methodological point of view, the question gives only an imperfect picture of the languages used in European homes. Two factors should be noted which can lead to overestimates of the importance of the official language as compared with the languages actually used. Firstly, only nationals of the country where the survey is being conducted are interviewed, thus effectively excluding all foreign residents, who are generally more likely to use their mother tongue at home. Furthermore, those who do not have a good command of the language (or languages) of the country they live in, even if they have the nationality, will probably decline to be interviewed.

ECONOMIC AND SOCIAL LIFE

The Eurobarometer surveys cover two main aspects of economic and social life: people's occupation and their involvement in political and social life. The findings in these two areas are summarized in Table 21.3. Data on people's occupation are plentiful, as the subject is regularly covered in specific surveys (e.g. on women or young people) and also occupies a large place in the socio-demographic section of the Eurobarometer surveys. However, there is not room here to discuss all the questions in detail. Those that have been singled out have been chosen, once again, for the light they shed on the possibilities this type of question offers.

The first question simply asks whether respondents are in paid work, and if so, whether full-time or part-time. On average just under half the people surveyed (45 per cent) said they had paid work. But rather unexpectedly, national differences are again quite marked: among the Dutch, just over one in three (38 per cent) works, compared to more than half the Luxemburgers or Portuguese (56 and 55 per cent respectively). The figures for part-time work also show considerable differences, with three times as many part-time workers in the United Kingdom as in Portugal.

The factors generally put forward to explain these differences are linked with major sociological trends, such as the extent to which women go out to work or the length of time which young people spend at school or in higher education. At all events, the Eurobarometer surveys help to establish the actual facts and, by the same token, to confirm or refute the explanations advanced.

One item of socio-demographic information that has regularly been collected, ever since the Eurobarometer surveys first began, concerns people's occupation. Framing the questions in such a way as to elicit a concise, but accurate description is no easy matter. The difficulty becomes ever greater when the survey is international: in a way, the occupations actually pursued in a given country are a facet of its culture and do not lend themselves readily to categorization in general terms. For the last five years. European market research professionals, working together in ESOMAR,[4] have been trying to standardize this type of question, but so far have been unable to produce a satisfactory international definition of people's occupations.

The approach adopted in the Eurobarometer surveys is to ask people a double question, first regarding their general status (self-employed, employed, not employed) and then regarding their particular type of occupation within each of these categories (for instance, in the case of the self-employed: 'farmer', 'professional', or 'owner of a shop or company, craftsman, proprietor'). This approach has recently been refined through the addition of a few more categories of occupation, but the general structure and spirit of the question have been kept.

The answers to this question bring out certain fundamental trends in society in different parts of Europe, such as the importance of agriculture in Greece, Ireland and Portugal, or industrial labour in the United Kingdom. However, leaving aside these quite well-known trends, the Eurobarometer statistics show that the distribution of the various occupations is relatively constant throughout the Twelve.

Lastly, a rather original approach to occupational activities was tried out in the autumn 1988 Eurobarometer: the people interviewed were asked whether they belonged to one of the health or teaching professions.[5] Although the replies depend in part on the respondent's interpretation of the scope of these very general categories, such information would seem both valid and relevant. Those who framed the questions took the

TABLE 21.3: *Economic and social life*

	B %	DK %	G %	GR %	S %	F %	IRL %	I %	L %	NL %	P %	UK %	EC12 %
PAID WORK													
. Full time	43	41	35	39	31	40	36	39	50	28	51	37	37
. Part time	8	11	8	11	7	7	5	5	6	10	4	14	8
. Not in paid work	49	48	55	50	58	52	58	55	41	60	43	48	53
OCCUPATION													
. Farmer, fisherman	1	2	1	10	2	5	9	1	1	1	8	1	2
. Self-employed professional	1	1	1	6	1	1	1	2	2	1	–	1	1
. Owner of shop or company, craftsman, proprietor	7	3	5	7	4	3	5	9	3	2	7	4	5
. Employed professional	1	1	2	1	2	–	4	1	1	1	1	8	2
. General management	2	2	4	–	–	4	1	1	3	4	–	2	2
. Middle management	4	10	11	2	3	8	2	2	13	8	3	4	6
. Other office employee	10	9	3	9	4	5	3	12	9	8	9	9	7
. Non-office employee	8	7	5	1	4	9	5	6	3	9	9	5	6
. Supervisor	1	1	1	1	1	1	1	1	2	1	1	1	1
. Skilled manual worker	9	8	8	6	9	10	6	4	6	5	12	9	8
. Other manual worker	5	9	4	3	5	3	6	7	8	2	5	11	6
FIELD OF ACTIVITY													
. Health	5	12	6	4	6	9	4	4	7	13	5	10	7
. Education	10	12	5	5	6	10	5	10	6	9	5	9	8

NAME ON ELECTORAL REGISTER													
. At present address	95	98	97	72	83	85	89	96	97	90	90	86	90
. At another address	2	1	2	27	8	10	7	3	1	3	7	7	6
. Not registered or doesn't know whether registered	3	1	1	1	9	5	4	1	2	7	3	7	4
MEMBERSHIP OF ASSOCIATIONS													
. Belongs to at least one association	51	83	47	22	19	44	65	36	77	71	31	61	45
MEMBERSHIP OF CAMPAIGN MOVEMENTS OR AID ORGANIZATIONS													
. Nature protection	3	15	2	1	1	1	1	2	15	9	–	3	2
. Ecology movement	1	–	1	–	1	–	1	1	5	3	–	1	1
. Movement to stop the construction or use of nuclear power plants	–	1	1	–	1	–	1	1	2	1	–	1	1
. Anti-war or anti-nuclear weapon movement	1	1	1	1	1	–	1	1	2	1	–	1	1
. Association to help the Third World	8	10	6	3	4	5	7	5	10	10	1	12	7

precaution of indicating by examples what was meant by a health or teaching profession; furthermore, it seems reasonable to suppose that the categories in question are so embedded in everyday life that errors of judgement will be rare.

The answers to these two questions show several things. Firstly, it appears that the categories in question cover a fairly wide range, since on average one European in seven (15 per cent) claims to be employed in either one sector or the other. The second major finding is that while the size of these sectors varies from one country to another, the Community seems to form a fairly homogeneous whole in so far as occupations in these categories occupy a considerable place, whatever the country. In view of these results, it is to be hoped – speaking from the methodological standpoint – that this approach will come to be more widely used so as to provide a description of the whole population, rather than just of a seventh, and to reveal the relative size of the various sectors of activity.

There are two main sets of statistics obtained through the Eurobarometer surveys regarding people's active involvement in the life of the community. The first concerns the electoral register. In the Community as a whole, almost everyone interviewed said his name was on an electoral register, either at his present address or at another one. Only in Spain, the Netherlands, the United Kingdom and France did the proportion of people who said they were not registered come to more than 5 per cent. Besides telling us that the number of persons registered is very high,[6] the replies tell us two other important facts. The first is that on a fundamental political question like this, the similarity between all the countries of the Community is very strong. The second concerns people who are registered at an address other than their home address; the subject is only partially covered and evaluated here. This phenomenon seems very widespread in Greece, while in other countries it is virtually non-existent.

The second main statistic on participation in the life of the community concerns membership of associations or movements. Several questions of this kind have been asked in the Eurobarometer surveys, and only a summary is given here. It emerges that almost one European in two (45 per cent) belongs to some kind of association. The proportion, however, varies greatly from one country to another: it is highest in Denmark and Luxembourg, where the figure is nearly eight out of ten, and lowest in Greece and Spain, where only around two people in ten are involved.

To be more specific, people were asked whether they were members of certain associations and movements with very clear-cut profiles: nature conservation bodies, ecology movements, anti-nuclear power movements, pacifist movements, and associations for Third World aid. Of all these types of group, it is the last – those concerned with assistance for the Third World – which seem to enjoy the widest support, 7 per cent of those interviewed saying they belonged to an association of this kind. Membership

369

TABLE 21.4: *Table for indicating membership of organisations*

	Approve		Disapprove		Don't know	Is a member	Might join	Would not join	Don't know
	Strongly	Some-what	Some-what	Strongly					
The nature protection associations	1	2	3	4	5	6	7	8	0
The ecology movement	1	2	3	4	5	6	7	8	0
Movements concerned with stopping the construction or use of nuclear power plants	1	2	3	4	5	6	7	8	0
Anti-war and anti-nuclear weapons movements	1	2	3	4	5	6	7	8	0

(Eurobarometer 25 – Spring 1986)

of the other types of movement appears very low in comparison, representing only 1–2 per cent of the population sampled.

The national variations observed seem to agree with the general level of association membership in a given country. Thus it is hardly surprising to find that the Danes, Luxemburgers and Dutch are particularly likely to belong to nature conservation organizations, as these three nationalities seem to be the most inclined to join associations in general. Simply taking these few indications, it would seem that while institutionally-channelled participation in the life of the community (as evidenced by the electoral register replies) varies little from one part of Europe to another, more informal participation through membership of associations, movements or organizations is very much a matter of national mores.

What conclusions can we draw from this review of factual findings? The first is that the Eurobarometer sample surveys carried out across the Twelve are in a position to supply valid data provided the questions are carefully framed. The usefulness of this kind of question also emerges quite clearly. The questions make it possible to pinpoint fairly accurately the family, social, and even national environment of the people interviewed. This kind of information is in fact extremely valuable, since opinion polls often tend to concern themselves too closely with the individual, ignoring his surroundings.

Lastly, one major contribution made by such factual questions is towards a better understanding of the differences and similarities between countries. In certain cases, for instance, the broad homogeneity of the answers would seem to reflect the similarity of the environment in the Twelve. In other cases, however, the range of answers is such that they can hardly be ascribed to a single influence. It may reasonably be supposed that as the corpus of statistics of this kind builds up it will be possible in the future to distinguish what are the structural and what are the short-term external factors influencing national opinion.

NOTES

1. This is the actual question to people who had previously said that they smoked cigarettes (in Eurobarometer 29, Spring 1988). ' How many cigarettes do you smoke a day? less than 5; 5 to 9; 10 to 14; 15 to 19; 20 to 24; 25 to 29; 30 to 34; 35 to 39; 40 or more'.
2. The most underprivileged are poorly represented in opinion polls, which probably means that the level of ownership of consumer durables is overestimated. On the other hand, the gap between Portugal and the other countries in the case of refrigerators would seem to reflect a very real difference.
3. See Victor Scardigli, *L'Europe des modes de vie* (Editions du CNRS, Paris, 1987).

4. European Society for Opinion and Marketing Research.
5. A second question of the same type, concerning the rest of the family, is not discussed here as it gave much less direct information about the person interviewed.
6. These results are intended only as an initial general indication; to find out the exact situation in each country a more subtle approach would be required.

APPENDIX: QUESTIONS COVERED IN THIS PAPER

Housing

Type of Housing and Occupancy

557. Do you live in a house or an apartment? And for you and your family are you owners of where you live or do you rent it?

(1) Owners of the house
(2) Renters of the house
(3) Owners of an apartment
(4) Renters of an apartment
(5) Renters in council or municipal housing
(6) Other (rent a room, live as lodger, squatters, etc.)
(0) ?

(Eurobarometer 30 – Autumn 1988)

Size of Locality

558. Would you say you live in a:

(1) Rural area or village
(2) Small or middle size town
(3) Big town

(Eurobarometer 30 – Autumn 1988)

Household Facilities

Heating and Cooking

313/ Here is a list of different ways of home heating and cooking. Which do you use
314. for heating? Which for cooking?
    (SHOW CARD)

Way of . . .

313 *Heating*	314 *Cooking*	
1	1	Coal
2	2	Oil
3	3	Gas

4	4	Electricity
5	5	Other (SPECIFY)
		....
0	0	?

(Eurobarometer 28 – Autumn 1987)

Consumer Durables

317. Do you have any of the following appliances or vehicles at home? (READ OUT AND MARK ALL MENTIONED).

(1) A car or cars
(2) A motorbike (125 cc or more)
(3) Central heating
(4) A washing machine
(5) A dishwasher
(6) An independent electric or gas waterheater
(7) A refrigerator
(8) A deep-freeze separate from refrigerator
(9) Electric power tools
(X) A colour television
(Y) Telephone
(0) ?

(Eurobarometer 28 – Autumn 1987)

Personal Luxuries

Driving License

222. Do you hold a current license for car driving? IF YES, for how long have you had one?

(1) Less than 1 year
(2) 1 to 2 years
(3) 3 to 5 years
(4) 5 to 10 years
(5) 11 to 20 years
(6) 21 to 30 years
(7) More than 30 years
(8) Not holding a current driving licence (GO TO QUESTION 231)
(0) ?

(Eurobarometer 26 – Autumn 1986)

Smoking

155. Which of the following things applies to yourself? (MULTIPLE ANSWERS POSSIBLE 1 AND 2)

(1) You smoke cigarettes (including Roll-your-own)
(2) You smoke cigars or a pipe

(3) You used to smoke but you have stopped)
(4) You have never smoked   ) GO TO QUESTION 157/158
(0) ?

(Eurobarometer 30 – Autumn 1988)

Composition of Household

169. Can you tell me, looking at this card here (SHOW CARD AND READ IT AT THE SAME TIME), which of these items best describes the usual composition of your household?

(1) A couple with no children at home
(2) A couple with one or more children at home
(3) A single adult and no children at home
(4) A single adult with one or more children at home
(5) Other types
(0) ?

(Eurobarometer 28 – Autumn 1987)

Family Characteristics

Regular Smokers

222. Are there regular smokers among the people you usually find yourself in the company of? IF SO, has this happened at home, where you work, or elsewhere?

(1) At home
(2) At work
(3) Elsewhere
(4) Do not find oneself among regular smokers
(0) ?

(Eurobarometer 27 – Spring 1987)

Spouse in Paid Work

157. Are you married (or living as married)? IF YES, is your (husband) (wife) (partner) in paid employment?

(1) No (husband) (wife) (partner) GO TO 159
(2) Spouse in paid employment
(3) Spouse not in paid employment
(0) ?

(Eurobarometer 27 – Spring 1987)

Language Used at Home

150. What language do you use at home?

(1) Danish
(2) German
(3) French
(4) Italian
(5) Dutch
(6) English
(7) Spanish
(8) Portuguese
(9) Greek
(X) Other
(0) ?

(Eurobarometer 28 – Autumn 1987)

Paid work

159. Are you in paid employment? AND IF YES, do you work full-time (30 hours a week or more) or part time?

(1) Yes, full time
(2) Yes, part time
(3) Not in paid employment
(0) ?

(Eurobarometer 27 – Spring 1987)

Occupation

541/ What is your occupation? (WRITE IN AND CODE).
542.

Self-Employed

(01) Farmer
(02) Fisherman
(03) Professional (Lawyer, practitioner, accountant, etc . . .)
(04) Owners of shops or companies, craftsmen, proprietors

Employed

(05) Employed professional (employed lawyer, practitioner, accountant, etc . . .)
(06) General management
(07) Middle management
(08) Other office employees
(09) Non-office employees, not manual work (service sector, e.g. shop-assistants, etc . . .)
(10) Supervisors
(11) Skilled manual worker
(12) Other manual worker

Without Paid Work

(13) Retired

(14) Housewife, not otherwise employed
(15) Student
(16) Military service
(17) Temporarily not working, unemployed

(Eurobarometer 30 – Autumn 1988)

Field of Activity

157/ Do you yourself (or did you) belong to one of the health professions (doctors,
158. pharmacist, dentist, nurse, hospital services, medical or pharmaceutical research, etc.)? And do any of your immediate family (spouse, parents, child) belong to these health professions?

	157 Self	158 Immediate family
Yes	1	1
No	2	2

159/ Do you yourself (or did you) work in education (school, college or university
160. teacher or educational administration)? And do any of your immediate family (spouse, parents, child) belong to these professions?

	159 Self	160 Immediate family
Yes	1	1
No	2	2

(Eurobarometer 30 – Autumn 1988)

Electoral Register

111. Are you .... (British)? IF YES, do you know whether your name appears in the Electoral Register (the register of people entitled to vote at the next General Election), under your present address, at another address or does not appear at all?

(1) At present address
(2) At another address
(3) Don't know if registered
(4) Does not appear at all
(5) No answer
(0) Is not .... (British) (CLOSE THE INTERVIEW)

(Eurobarometer 30 – Autumn 1988)

Membership of Associations

146. Which, if any, of the following groups or associations do you belong to? (SHOW CARD, MULTIPLE ANSWERS POSSIBLE).

(1) Community or social action groups
(2) Churches or religious organizations

(3) Education or arts groups
(4) Trade unions or professional associations
(5) Political parties or groups
(6) Organizations concerned with human rights (in your country) and abroad
(7) Conservation of nature, environmentalist or animal welfare groups, ecologists
(8) Youth work (e.g. scouts, guides, youth clubs etc.)
(9) Consumer groups
(X) Sporting clubs or associations
(Y) Other groups or associations for a particular interest (e.g. stamp collecting, music, or such)
(0) Do not belong to any group or association

(Eurobarometer 28 – Autumn 1987)

Membership of Campaign Movements or Aid Organizations

253/ There are a number of groups and movements seeking the support of the
256. public. For each of the following movements, can you tell me . . .
  (a) Whether you approve (strongly or somewhat) or do you disapprove (somewhat, or strongly)?
  (b) Whether you are a member or might probably join or would certainly not join?

250/
252. Coming back to the Third World . . .

	Yes 250	No 251	? 252
• Are you aware of any actions in your town or area or where you work to help in some way a country or countries of the Third World?	1	1	1
• Have you been asked to give money for particular activities in the Third World, such as medical aid, building schools, wells, etc.?	2	2	2
• Have you been asked to give some of your time in taking an active part in campaign or activities to help the Third World?	3	3	3
• Are you a member of a group or association which does things to help the Third World?	4	4	4
• Would you be prepared to give some of your time to help in some activity for the Third World?*	5	5	5
• Would you be prepared to give money or to give more money than you do now to support some activity to help the Third World?	6	6	6

(Eurobarometer 28 – Autumn 1987)

* Only the fourth item in this list is discussed in this paper.

22 Values and the Challenging of Europe's Identity

Jan Kerkhofs, S.J., Katholieke Universiteit, Leuven

Europe, in our days, has known a number of founding fathers, and not only on the level of economic policy. Behind the Centre Europeen de la Culture we find Denis de Rougemont; behind the College of Europe, Hendrik Brugmans. Jacques-René Rabier will enter history not only as 'Mr Eurobarometer' but as much more, for his interest in Europe has never been limited to the study of evolving opinions with regard to the 'Europe-mindedness' of Europeans. He has been deeply concerned with the funda-mental cultural identity of Europe and the in-depth shifts in the collective conscience of its citizens. This was the major reason why, from the outset, he agreed to be one of the members of the small steering committee which, in 1978, launched the risky initiative of a major study on European Values and Value Systems known as the 'European Value Systems Study Group' (EVSSG).

THE DREAM OF A LONGITUDINAL STUDY OF EUROPE'S IDENTITY

Belonging to a culture is the core factor for growth towards everyone's own personal being. In times of rapid change people automatically look back, afraid of being cut off from their roots. Migrants, for example, feeling threatened by the values typical of the surrounding majority, try for several generations to maintain the social, cultural and religious traditions of their own group, attempting to defend themselves in subcultures, particularly in the melting pot of the modern megalopolis.

For non-Europeans, and more broadly for non-Westerners, Europe is not only a foreign but most probably a far more mysterious world than the Chinese or Indian cultures would appear to a European. Indeed, Euro-peans know that they were the ones who, from the late middle ages onward, discovered and conquered – often violently – other continents. They know that it was Europe which, in the nineteenth and twentieth

377

centuries, became the spearhead of scientific, technological and industrial progress. Subconsciously, Europeans consider it normal that their continent is or has been the birthplace of modernization, influencing similar developments in the non-Western world, a process summed up by François Perroux in the phrase '*l'Europe sans rivages*'.

At the same time, however, Europeans are afraid that it is their very acceleration of world history which is causing them to lose the driving force of their – increasingly limited – superiority. Statistics show that despite the formidable economic strength of the EEC there is a steady decrease in the number of young people in Europe. Economists and politicians are aware that in comparison with the last decade of the nineteenth century, Europe is no longer the only heavyweight. We Europeans are faced with the power of our grandchildren in the USA and shortly in Brazil. We have our hopes and fears with regard to our half-brother Russia. We know that next to Japan we shall find other mighty competitors in Asia, that region of swiftly awakening giants. And at home we are forced to co-exist with a minority culture which is still to some extent rooted in the same 'Abrahamic' soil, but one which challenges us in a way very different from the historical encounters in Poitiers, Granada or Vienna, when feudal lords, crusaders or commandoes of the Teutonic Order tried to defend Christendom. Islam, world-wide, will soon have more followers than Catholicism, and we shall find more Muslims present in traditionally Christian cultures than vice versa.

Within this context, Europeans try to reflect on their own identity in a very different way than they began to do in the seventeenth century, when Leibniz was struck by the *Lettres édifiantes* sent to Europe by the small group of Jesuit astronomers at the Court of the Emperor in Pekin, and which revealed the existence of a real humanism outside Europe.

Furthermore, Europeans realize that they themselves will have to cope with new values which are developing within their own communities, and that a synthesis of tradition and modernity will create many tensions within their own basic sub-systems such as the family, the education models, the organization of work and leisure. Aware of this mutation, a group of scholars decided to launch a survey of values under the umbrella of the EVSSG-Foundation in Amsterdam.[1]

This survey resulted in a series of European and national studies representative of some 240 million Europeans. The enquiry centred on the major value areas: work, leisure, the family and sexuality, politics, religion, morals. The nine countries in which the survey was carried out initially were: Great Britain, the Republic of Ireland (with Northern Ireland considered as a separate entity), the Federal Republic of Germany, Belgium, the Netherlands, France, Italy, and Spain (a total of 12 463 interviews altogether). The study was made possible through the cooperation of various foundations in addition to the European Cultural Foundation, and the EEC. A first analysis of the overall European results was prepared by Prof. J. Stoetzel and published under the title *Les valeurs du temps présent* (P.U.F., 1983). Spanish and Italian translations were published in 1984. A second analysis by S. Harding, *Contrasting Values in Western Europe* (Macmillan, London) appeared in 1986.

In the meantime, other European countries had carried out their own surveys using the same questionnaire: Finland, Sweden,[2] Norway, Iceland,[3] Malta and Hungary. The project aroused interest outside Europe, and similar surveys have been carried in the USA, Chile, Mexico, Argentina, South Africa, Japan, and Australia, several of them in close cooperation with the Gallup organization. Indeed, the questionnaire has even been tested in part of Russia. As a result, we had available data representative of approximately 700 million people.

Although the EVSSG focuses its research on Western and, where possible, Eastern Europe, the findings of the first round of research show that parallel trends exist on the other side of the Atlantic. North America has much in common with North-Western Europe,[4] just as, in many ways, Latin America reflects Latin Europe.[5] The Mediterranean *mare nostrum* has expanded into the Atlantic.

The EVSSG-Foundation has done a second survey for 1990. This survey covers the whole of Western Europe plus the Soviet Union, Poland and Hungary. North America, Australia, and some Asian and Latin American countries will repeat their enquiries. Thus, probably for the first time and on such a scale, what, culturally, we know as the Western world will be able to gain insight into basic trends in cultural identity. The Foundation aims to repeat these surveys in the course of the coming decades, and it hopes that the next generation of sociologists will also look into the scanner at regular intervals in order to detect changes in the collective conscience of the West.

Our dream is that not only those in a position of leadership in politics, industry, the trade unions, education, the Churches and cultural organizations will take our findings into account in their efforts to improve dialogue with the human reality but that people at the grass-root level will also gain a better understanding of themselves. Indeed, from the outset, the initiators of the survey thought not primarily of the happy few, the owners of select information as a means towards power, but rather about the men and women in the street who also have the right to know what is going on in the shaping of their identities within their communities, their nations and their continent.

In order to observe the dynamism of people's minds as closely as possible, the Foundation, as far as it is able, encourages more detailed research, enabling us to gain a more refined knowledge of differences. Polyphonic Europe remains a product of a long and varied history which has a deep influence on people's scales of values. Thus, for example, we intend to compare Hungary with Austria to discover how far four decades of different political regimes have, or have not, influenced a centuries-old common tradition. We shall also be able to compare Northern Italy with the Swiss Ticino; the German-speaking part of Switzerland with Bavaria; or the cantons of the Suisse Romande with France; or the Spanish and French Basque regions. We can gain information by studying differences and common factors in the five Scandinavian countries, or among the provinces of Spain. In Belgium, as is already being done in Switzerland, there will be in-depth studies of the different linguistic regions as laboratories of federalism. Is it still true that what Wallonia has in common with France and Flanders with the Netherlands is much less relevant than what they share in common? And what about Dutch and Belgian Limburg, divided in 1839 against the wishes of their respective leaders?

One aspect which would seem to be particularly important is a comparison of age cohorts through the years: what is changing and what is not? How far are values really lasting, and where are older generations influenced by the values of the younger ones, and where are the conflicting pressure groups in a process of change? The first survey revealed that the differences between the generations are much less important than most people usually think. It was also striking that gender has no significant influence on opinions with regard to values, but that religious practice is an important variable in explaining a broad range of attitudes. With decreasing Church-relatedness, will other, alternative systems of meaning emerge as influential or not? In any case, in the next century the files of the EVSGG may well prove a treasure for historians continuing the tradition of the great scholars of the school of *Les Annales* such as F. Braudel, J. le Goff, or J. Delumeau.

THE DREAM OF LONG-TERM, INTERCONTINENTAL VALUE STUDIES

Some years ago Hélène Carrère d'Encausse published an impressive picture of Russia's future in *L'Empire eclaté*: in the next century the Union of Soviet Socialist Republics will no longer be dominated by its European region and peoples but will face growing political and cultural pressure from its Asian majority. In the meantime, North America has been experiencing several peaceful – but all-pervasive – demographic invasions from the Latin South and from the peoples of the Pacific in the West. If the thaw in Eastern Europe holds, many Eastern Europeans will try to enter Western Europe, while some Westerners will move east.

There is, however, another trend which would seem to be far more important. Europe has already taken in more Asians and Africans than ever before, and even in Norway and Sweden we find thousands of

Vietnamese and Chileans. It is probable that many more Chinese will look to Europe as a second choice after the USA. Soon Europe will also have to face the consequences of its reversed age pyramid. Our old continent will need nurses from younger, probably Asian, countries. The whole process will result in a gigantic cross-fertilization not only of genetic codes but also of cultural and religious traditions. The year 1993 will see the beginning of the removal of many boundaries within the EEC, but the coming decade will also mark the beginning of a new phase in the removal of boundaries between the continents; and in the long term this could have a much deeper impact on universal history.

If the whole world is in a process of acceleration towards the so-called 'global village', peaceful coexistence is vital. This will only be possible through greater mutual understanding, tolerance and respect of differences. The presupposition is that the peoples discover that what they have in common is more fundamental than that which makes them distinct.

Comparative value studies may foster increased dialogue and reciprocal sympathy. This, however, implies the stimulation of intercultural research with the help of cultural sociologists and anthropologists. Simply applying a Western questionnaire to other cultural areas such as Japan, India, the Chinese world or the Muslim countries would be meaningless. We must hope that states, universities and foundations make greater investments in the comparative study of the ways in which peoples' cultural roots are expressed in their mentalities. Bridge-building between segments of the world's population among whom democracy and participation, freedom and tolerance, the role of women and emancipation, pluralism and harmony have meanings often very different from those currently prevailing in the West would seem to be becoming a primary task for common survival. In a world in which, through technology, business, tourism, sports and communication we are all entering into our neighbour's house, the use of one common language such as English could hide very profound misunderstandings. Value studies on a world scale may demonstrate where deep gulfs are in danger of polarising people, but they may also show where there are bridges, and provide a better picture of what we all share with our foreign brothers and sisters. Surely this could improve the long and painful march towards a dynamic harmony in which mutual enrichment will overcome reciprocal suspicion resulting from closed-mindedness. Let us hope that young people, through their training, and adults through our highly-developed, audio-visual, permanent education systems will increasingly enjoy the fruits of these studies and that they will cease looking at 'foreigners' with black-and-white prejudices, and that instead they will develop a mental hospitality and prepare for a common refining of what is really human.

An example may illustrate the importance of this approach. World-wide action to protect the environment, the wounding of which affects everyone across mountains, deserts and oceans, requires a common conviction. In as far as this is a universal opinion, politicians and businessmen will be forced to realise that what is needed is another approach to economic progress. On the threshold of the third millennium mankind has the technological tools to save the planet, if there is a world-wide conviction pressing for the right political decisions. The same is true of the world's health. Diseases such as AIDS can spread very rapidly and reach the farthest corners of the globe. If a sense of collective responsibility could extend into every village and every living room, we should have taken a great step forward.

What the great French paleontologist Teilhard de Chardin stressed remains true: either we grow together as many minds into a global spirit or we shall, precisely through our proximity, kill one another. Common markets without a common responsibility for that which, in mankind, is more precious than production and consumption, will sooner or later results in new and more terrible battlefields.

VALUES STUDIES: A DEFENCE AGAINST THE CLOSING OF THE EUROPEAN MIND?

American universities have recently been seriously challenged by Allan Bloom's *The Closing of the American Mind*. One of the positive side-effects of the European Value Studies could be to play the role of jester, as in a medieval court, by opening proud Europe's eyes to the darker side of all its glitter. Indeed, an only child – and this is the case for a growing number of children – will have to live without a brother or sister, an uncle or aunt. In some countries, one out of two children will have to go through the experience of integrating successive 'fathers' and 'mothers'. As a result, Christopher Lasch's *Culture of Narcissism* could invade Europe and foster the darker sides of individualism described in Gilles Lipovetsky's *L'ère du vide* or *L'empire de l'éphémère*. This only child will often be unable to accept the role of caring for grandparents, or the growing number of great-grandparents. He or she will look for cheap foreign labour, chiefly women from the non-Western world, to take up nursing roles in homes for the elderly or psychiatric hospitals. Values studies may provide a warning of the consequences of an egotistic society. They may reveal other needs in an anonymous society: the uprooting of many who suffer the negative influence of internationalised television programmes which bombard those who watch them with images of violence, sexual deviations and alienating dream paradises, emptying their human identity.

The Studies may also reveal healthy reactions in the collective mind: the willingness to promote the emancipation of women; the concern for all who suffer through new class divisions created by a dual economy; the preference for intermediate networks which foster self-help and subsidiarity as opposed to faceless power structures and depersonalised control by computerised systems. The EVSSG, in one of its major findings, has already shown that concern for the family is a widespread phenomenon. More detailed analyses may open Europe's mind to what is going on in the minds of young people, to their hopes and fears, to the dreams of a generation which will be responsible for shaping Europe's policy at the turn of the millennium. Value studies may help Europe to see where it is still closed to the needs of the 40 million poor people and of those who belong to the 'Fourth World'.

We can also hope that specialised studies will reveal where Europe's leaders are closing their minds to the wider world and its needs. Indeed, Europe is no longer a concentration of colonial power, nor is it the only centre of economic and financial decision-making. But it was in Europe that the concept of universal human rights originated, that organisations such as the Red Cross, Amnesty International, the peace movements and hundreds of non-governmental organisations for development work were born. Europe, which started two devastating world wars, is also the region where an awareness of moral leadership is becoming an aspect of national and continental politics. Value studies may support this awareness by revealing the high level of tolerance, anti-racism, willingness to foster intercultural exchange, and commitment to the protection of creation to be found in majority opinion. They may protect people from the poisoning influence of nationalistic and noisy minorities. They may help people to become aware of the humanising effects of a new dialogue between culture and technology in factories, townships, and educational systems, linking roots and creativity. In the context of the Erasmus and Jean Monnet programmes they may poll mentalities in the universities and sound out the presence or absence of a dialogue between 'the arts' and 'the sciences'.

As a result, they may save Europe from the closing of its mind. But this, however, will mean that first of all the social sciences will need to have their eyes open to the authentic elites in society and that they ensure that their voices are listened to in the marketplace of competing opinions, where all too often the silent majority is kept silent by leaders more concerned about immediate success rather than the real common good – mainly of future generations.

In selecting topics of importance for these Europeans and world citizens of tomorrow, value researchers may become 'prophets' for vast collectivities. J.-R. Rabier is one of them, when, for example, he selects the child, women, or the Fourth World as particularly important subjects of ethical concern in the collective consciousness. In a modern way, he echoes the voices of the great prophets of the Old Testament, proclaiming the rights of the weak and the poor.

384 *Eurobarometer*

NOTES

1. The Secretariat is located at the University of Tilburg, The Netherlands.
2. Petterson, Thorleif (1988) *Bakom dubbla las* (Stockholm).
3. Petursson, Petur (1988) 'The Relevance of Secularization in Iceland', in *Social Compass*, XXXV/1, 107–24.
4. This is developed in Halman, Loek et al. (1987) *Traditie, Secularisatie en Individualisering* (Tilburg: Tilburg University Press); and Ronald Inglehart, *Culture Shift in Advanced Industrial Society* (Princeton: Princeton University Press, 1990).
5. Carballo de Cilley, Marita (1987) *?Que pensamos los argentinos?* (Buenos Aires).

Bibliography of Jacques-René Rabier

(1945) 'La participation ouvrière au produit et à la gestion'. Collection des Groupes 'Travail', sous la direction de François Perroux. Domat Montchrestien, Paris.

(1945) 'Une politique de nationalisations', *Esprit*, 5, mai, 660–70.

(1948) 'Plan Monnet et Plan Marshall', *Esprit*, numéro spécial sur 'Le Plan Marshall et l'avenir de la France', n. 4, avril, pp. 575–97.

(1949) 'Qu'est-ce que l'incivisme?', *Esprit*, numéro spécial sur 'L'incivisme', 1, janvier, 5–14.

(1950) 'Une expérience de planification souple en régime démocratique: trois ans de réalisation du Plan Monnet', *Droit Social* XXXVI, 3–10.

(1951) (Signing Bernard Jarrier) 'L'économie de la guerre tiède', *Esprit* 4, avril, 636–45.

(1952) (Idem) 'La "croisade" pour la productivité', *Esprit*, 2, février, pp. 285–306.

(1952) (Idem): 'Le mystère des indices et l'offensive d'automne'. *Esprit*, 10, octobre, 549–55.

(1953) (Idem): 'L'Etat investi par les intérêts'. *Esprit*, numéro spécial sur 'Pouvoir politique et pouvoir économique', 6, juin, 878–902.

(1961) 'La construction de l'Europe et la recherche d'opinion', *International Congress of the World Association for Public Opinion Research*, Baden-Baden, September (with English translation).

(1964) 'Comment les peuples européens se voient et voient les autres', *Revue de Psychologie des Peuples*, 19ème année, 1, ler trimestre, 22–32.

(1965) 'L'intégration des Européens et l'intégration de l'Europe' (Brussels: Université Libre de Bruxelles, Institut d'Etudes Européennes).

(1966) 'L'opinion publique et l'Europe: essai d'inventaire des connaissances et des lacunes', Exposé fait à l'occasion de la XXXIème Semaine Sociale Universitaire, organisée par l'Institut de Sociologie de l'Université libre de Bruxelles. Publication en 1971.

(1967) 'The European idea and national public opinions'. *Government and Opposition*, special issue on 'The politics of European integration', 2, 3, April–July, 443–54.

(1967) 'La formazione di un'opinione pubblica europea'. *Tempi Moderni*, 30, 60–6.

(1968) 'Préjugés français et préjugés allemands'. *Revue de Psychologie des Peuples*, 23ème année, 2, 2ème trimestre, 186–202.

(1968) 'La presse imprimée franchit-elle les frontières?', *Revue du Marché Commun*, 117, novembre, 955–71.

(1969) 'Le Marché Commun et la diffusion du livre', *Revue du Marché Commun*, 121, mars, 119–33.

(1969) 'La psychologie sociale, la sociologie et la science politique devant l'intégration européenne', *Il Politico*, anno XXXIV, 4, 701–8.

(1972) Introduction au numéro spécial de la revue *Sondages*, Paris, sur 'L'opinion française et l'union de l'Europe, 1947–1972', 1–2, 5–8.

(1975) 'Différences et différenciations interrégionales dans les attitudes et comportements du public', in *Les régions transfrontalières de l'Europe*, Centre européen de la Culture, Genève, Bulletin XV, 1–2, 195–237.

(1975) 'L'étude des publics européens et l'intégration de l'Europe', in *Sondages et Opinion publique*. Université de Liège (Belgique), département de science politique, 101–8.

(1976) 'Les attitudes du public à l'égard de l'élection du Parlement européen au suffrage universel direct', in *Autour du Rapport Tindemans*, colloque d'Athènes, organisé par le Centre européen de la Culture, Genève, pp. 80–96.

(1977) (With Hélène Riffault), 'International Dimension in Social Research', Seminar on Social Research, ESOMAR, London, November–December, 245–62.

(1978) (With Ronald Inglehart), 'Economic Uncertainty and European Solidarity: Public Opinion Trends'. *The Annals of the American Academy of Political and Social Science*, 440, pp. 66–97.

(1979) 'Y a-t-il des pauvres parmi nous, en Europe?' *Projet*, 133, mars, pp. 342–52.

(1979) (With Ronald Ingelhart) 'Europe Elects a Parliament: Cognitive Mobilization and Pro-European Attitudes as Influences on Voter Turnout', *Government and Opposition*, special issue 'After the European Elections', 14, 4, Autumn, pp. 479–507.

(1979) 'L'opinion publique et l'élection européenne', in *Les partis politiques et les élections européennes*, sous la direction de Dusan Sidjanski, Dossier n.2 du Centre européen de la Culture, Genève, décembre, pp. 45–53.

(1980) (With Ronald Inglehart, Ian Gordon and Carsten Lehman Sorensen): 'Broader Powers for the European Parliament? The Attitudes of Candidates'. *European Journal of Political Research*, special issue on 'The First European Elections', 8, 1, March, 113–32.

(1980) 'Les études comparatives de l'opinion publique en Europe: expériences et perspectives'. Exposé devant l'Asociacion de Estudios de Mercado y Opinion. Madrid, 23 mai. Edité ultérieurement en espagnol.

(1980) (With Ronald Inglehart): 'Europe Elects a Parliament: Cognitive Mobilization and Pro-European Attitudes as Influences on Voter Turnout', reprinted in Leon Hurwitz (ed.) *Contemporary Perspectives on European Integration* (Westport, Conn: Greenwood Press) pp. 27–51.

(1984) (Avec Ronald Inglehart): 'La confiance entre les peuples: déterminants et conséquences'. *Revue française de science politique*, 34, 1, février, 5–47.

(1984) 'Les paradoxes d'un scrutin: les citoyens de dix pays élisent le Parlement européen'. *Revue d'Intégration européenne / Journal of European Integration*, 8, 1, Fall, 5–32.

(1984) (Avec Ronald Inglehart): 'Du bonheur . . . Les aspirations s'adaptent aux situations: analyse interculturelle de la qualité subjective de la vie', suivi de 'Sentiment personnel et norme culturelle'. *Futuribles*, 80, septembre, 29–57, et 81, octobre, pp. 3–29).

(1984) 'Les élections européennes de 1979 et 1984: les études par sondage de la participation électorale au moyen de l'Euro-Baromètre', in *European Elections 1979/81 and 1984*, (ed.) Karlheinz Reif (Berlin: Quorum Verlag).

(1985) 'Où sont donc les citoyens de l'Europe? Votants et abstentionnistes lors de l'élection de juin 1984'. Paper presented at the workshop 'The 1984 Direct Elections to the Euro-Parliament', *European Consortium for Political Research*, Barcelona (España), March. Partiellement publié dans *Economie et Humanisme*, 285, septembre-octobre, 12–16.

(1986) (With Ronald Inglehart): 'Political Realignment in Advanced Industrial Society'. *Government and Opposition*, 21, 4, Autumn, 456–79.

(1986) (With Ronald Inglehart): 'Aspirations Adapt to Situations – But Why Are the Belgians so Much Happier than the French, A Cross-Cultural Analysis of the

Subjective Quality of Life', in *Research on the Quality of Life*, (ed.) Frank M. Andrews (Ann Arbor (Mich.): Institute for Social Research) pp. 1–55.

(1986) Préface au numéro 4 de *Documentation européenne*, sur 'Les Européens vus par eux-mêmes: regards sur l'opinion publique des Européens de 1973 à 1986'. Luxembourg: Office des Publications officielles des Communautés européennes).

(1987) (With Ronald Inglehart and Karlheinz Reif): 'The Evolution of Public Attitudes Toward European Integration, 1970–1986'. *Revue d'integration européenne/Journal of European Integration*, special issue, on 'Socio-Political Integration in the European Communities: Contemporary Aspects', edited by Dusan Sidjanski and Ural Ayberk, X, 2–3, Winter/Spring, 135–55.

(1987) 'L'Europe et les Européens', in *Europe: Rêve – Aventure – Réalité*, (ed.) Henri Brugmans (Bruxelles: Elsevier) pp. 222–30. English edition: *Europe: Dream – Adventure – Reality*.

(1988) 'L'état de santé des Européens tel qu'ils le perçoivent', in *L'Europe et la Santé: hasard et/ou nécessité*, (ed.) Françoise Massart (Louvain-la-Neuve: Academia (collection Europerspectives)) pp. 169–84.

(1988) Short version of the previous paper in d'Houtaud A., Field M. and Guegen, R.: *Les Représentations de la Santé* (Paris: Les Editions de l'INSERM) pp. 249–64.

(1989) 'Les Européens et la prévention du cancer: une étude d'opinion publique'. *Solidarité Santé – Etudes statisques*. Ministère de la Santé, Paris, 1, janvier-février, pp. 39–60.

(1989) 'L'opinion publique et l'intégration de l'Europe dans les années '50', in *La Relance européenne et les Traités de Rome*, (ed.) Enrico Serra (Bruylandt (Bruxelles), Guiffrè (Milano), L.G.D.J. (Paris), Nomos Verlag (Baden-Baden)), pp. 561–84.

(1989) 'Jean Monnet ou la stratégie de la confiance', in *Témoignages à la mémoire de Jean Monnet*, (ed.) Henri Rieben (Lausanne (Suisse): Fondation Jean Monnet pour l'Europe) pp. 409–11.

(1989) 'L'utilisation comparative et diachronique des données d'enquêtes par sondage', in *Les enquêtes d'opinion et la recherche en sciences sociales: hommage à Jean Stoetzel*, (ed.) Daniel Derivry (Paris: Editions de l'Harmattan).

Index of Proper Names